D0793378

LB 1574.5 M37                                    [NLRC]
C. 1 LAB
CLUSTER APPROACH TO ELEMENTARY VOCABULARY

          M7/1385012

| DATE DUE | | |
|---|---|---|
| Three (3) week loans are subject to recall after one week | | |
| [SEP 2 4 1993] | | |
| MAR 1 9 1994 | | |
| MAR 2 6 1994 | | |
| APR - 2 1994 | | |
| APR - 9 1994 | | |
| MAR 1 1995 | | |
| MAR 3 0 1995 | | |
| | | |
| | | |
| | | |

APR 2 2 1992

Reading Aids Series

# A Cluster Approach to Elementary Vocabulary Instruction

**Robert J. Marzano**
Mid-Continent Regional Educational Laboratory
Aurora, Colorado

**Jana S. Marzano**
Englewood, Colorado

An **ira** Service Bulletin

International Reading Association
Newark, Delaware 19714

Curr
LB
1574.5
M37

# INTERNATIONAL READING ASSOCIATION

## OFFICERS
### 1987-1988

*President*   Phylliss J. Adams, University of Denver, Denver, Colorado

*Vice President*   Patricia S. Koppman, PSK Associates, San Diego, California

*Vice President Elect*   Dale D. Johnson, Instructional Research and Development
Institute, Boston, Massachusetts

*Executive Director*   Ronald W. Mitchell, International Reading Association,
Newark, Delaware

## DIRECTORS

*Term Expiring Spring 1988*
Margaret Pope Hartley, The Psychological Corporation,
North Little Rock, Arkansas
P. David Pearson, University of Illinois, Champaign, Illinois
Carol M. Santa, School District #5, Kalispell, Montana

*Term Expiring Spring 1989*
Marie C. DiBiasio, Rhode Island Department of Education,
Providence, Rhode Island
Hans U. Grundin, Language and Literacy Consultant, London, England
Nancy E. Seminoff, Winona State University, Winona, Minnesota

*Term Expiring Spring 1990*
Jerome C. Harste, Indiana University, Bloomington, Indiana
Jane M. Hornburger, Brooklyn College, CUNY, Brooklyn, New York
Merrillyn Brooks Kloefkorn, Jefferson County Public Schools, Golden,
Colorado

Copyright 1988 by the
International Reading Association, Inc.

**Library of Congress Cataloging in Publication Data**

Marzano, Robert J.
A cluster approach to elementary vocabulary instruction.

(Reading aids series)
Bibliography: p.
1. Vocabulary – Study and teaching (Elementary) – United
States. 2. Reading (Elementary) – United States.   I. Marzano,
Jana S.   II. Title.   III. Series.
LB1574.5.M37      1988           372.6           88-2923
ISBN 0-87207-232-0

Cover design by Boni Nash

# Contents

IRA DIRECTOR OF PUBLICATIONS   Jennifer A. Stevenson

IRA PUBLICATIONS COMMITTEE 1987-1988   James E. Flood, San Diego State University, *Chair* • James F. Baumann, Purdue University • Janet R. Binkley, IRA • Phyllis E. Brazee, University of Maine • Susan W. Brennan, IRA • Kent L. Brown Jr., *Highlights for Children* • Marie DiBiasio, Rhode Island Department of Education, Providence, Rhode Island • Dolores Durkin, University of Illinois • Claudia Gentile, Syracuse University • Philip Gough, University of Texas at Austin • Margaret K. Jensen, Madison Metropolitan School District, Madison, Wisconsin • John Micklos, Jr., IRA • Ronald W. Mitchell, IRA • Joy N. Monahan, Orange County Public Schools, Orlando, Florida • Allan R. Neilsen, Mount St. Vincent University • John J. Pikulski, University of Delaware • María Elena Rodríguez, IRA, Buenos Aires • Jennifer A. Stevenson, IRA • Anne C. Tarleton, Albuquerque Public Schools, Albuquerque, New Mexico

The International Reading Association attempts, through its publications, to provide a forum for a wide spectrum of opinions on reading. This policy permits divergent viewpoints without assuming the endorsement of the Association.

iv

# Foreword

*A Cluster Approach to Elementary Vocabulary Instruction* is a major work. Its contribution to vocabulary literature is invaluable. It is certain to become a useful resource for teachers, researchers, and authors and publishers of instructional materials.

Marzano and Marzano present an articulate discussion of two opposing positions in vocabulary acquisition: that vocabulary needs to be taught directly and that wide reading is the primary vehicle of vocabulary growth. They wisely take a middle position that both are important. The authors recognize that learners acquire thousands of new words through context. Context, however, is often insufficiently rich to enable learning words that may be important to understand a particular reading passage or content discipline or to expand general background knowledge. When context is not rich, vocabulary must be taught.

The authors argue for a categorical cluster approach to vocabulary instruction. Such an approach recognizes the power of schema theory and the elegance of learning words in association with semantically related words. They describe and exemplify such proven instructional strategies as semantic mapping (referred to as "attribute comparison"). Drawing on the work of other vocabulary researchers and scholars, Marzano and Marzano explain the strength of learning three types of meaning for each new word: conceptual/associational, contextual, and definitional.

Certainly the strongest feature of the book and the unique contribution it makes to scholarship and pedagogy is the development and presentation of semantically related categories of words. Using several sources, the authors selected 7,230 elementary school words and organized them into three levels of instructional clusters.

At the top are 61 superclusters (e.g., feelings and emotions). These superclusters contain words that are semantically related. At the middle level are 430 clusters that contain words with closer semantic ties (e.g., fear, anger, excitement, joy). Beneath the clusters are more than 1,500 miniclusters that list words with the strongest semantic ties (e.g., *startle*: scare, frighten, terrify). For each word, the authors have provided a recommended grade level, its part of speech, and a

description of whether it is a basic, fundamental building block word. Their procedures are well described; they are systematic, rigorous, and sensible.

The only shortcoming of the lists is acknowledged by the authors: "It is important to note that many of the words on the list are sex stereotyped because these lists are based on basals written before publishers began to reduce sex stereotyping in books for children."

The book contains four chapters that describe vocabulary theory, procedures for forming the clusters, instructional uses of the clusters, and additional vocabulary instruction. The book also contains three appendixes. Appendix A presents the words within their clusters; Appendix B is an alphabetized, referenced list of the words; and Appendix C defines commonly confused words such as *infer* and *imply*. Teachers, writers, and researchers will refer frequently to these appendixes.

Marzano and Marzano are to be congratulated for their scholarly contribution, and the International Reading Association is to be commended for this publication.

Dale D. Johnson
Instructional Research and Development Institute
Brookline, Massachusetts

# Preface

In recent years, teachers and researchers have become increasingly aware of the importance of vocabulary knowledge to reading and other academic areas. Yet there is also growing disagreement as to how much emphasis should be placed and how much time should be spent on direct vocabulary instruction. Research indicates direct vocabulary instruction does improve vocabulary knowledge for words taught directly, especially when certain practices and procedures are observed. However, no clear evidence indicates that vocabulary instruction transfers to words not taught directly. Students encounter so many words in their content area textbooks that direct instruction in all words is virtually impossible. Some theorists and researchers suggest the use of wide reading and language rich activities as the primary vocabulary development technique.

In this monograph we take a compromise position, asserting that use of wide reading and language rich activities should be a primary vocabulary development tool, but that direct vocabulary instruction can augment incidental vocabulary learning if structured in specific ways. We have developed a cluster approach to direct vocabulary instruction in which words are taught in semantically related groups. Such a structure provides for many diverse instructional activities, including teaching a word as a label for a known concept, providing an experiential base for new concepts, and relating new words encountered during reading to known concepts and categories.

To facilitate a categorical approach to instruction, we have organized 7,230 words found in elementary school textbooks into 61 instructional clusters, each containing two levels of subclusters. These are presented in the Appendixes. The four chapters preceding the Appendixes describe underlying theory and how the instructional clusters were developed and suggest ways to use the clusters for vocabulary instruction.

The clusters and accompanying strategies are tools to aid the elementary school teacher in the difficult task of fostering in students a deep and comprehensive vocabulary knowledge.

RJM

JSM

# Chapter 1

# A Theoretical Base
# for Vocabulary Instruction

The importance of vocabulary development to general academic achievement has been recognized for years. Anderson and Freebody (1981) report a strong relationship between vocabulary and academic performance. For example, the relationship between vocabulary knowledge and intelligence test performance is one of the most robust findings in the history of intelligence testing. Similarly, vocabulary knowledge has been found to predict reading comprehension in various countries and across age groups and content areas (Thorndike, 1973).

The importance of vocabulary is most easily understood if considered from a linguistic perspective. Condon (1968) explains that a word is a label for an internal reality. When you create a label, you also create a set of new perceptions. To illustrate, he talks about taking a course in astronomy. Before taking the course, you might look at the night sky and see only a sea of stars. After a few weeks of the course, you begin to see novas and galaxies. The creation of labels (words) is a tool we use to structure perceptions; new labels foster new perceptions. As Condon (p. 31) says, "when names are learned we see what we had not seen before, for we know what to look for."

Given Condon's explanation of the nature of words, we might conclude that a society's words represent its concepts. Indeed, the isomorphic relationship between concept knowledge and word knowledge is commonly accepted by most researchers and theorists. For example, Klausmeier and Sipple (1980, p. 78) define concept knowledge in terms of word knowledge, stating that a concept is the "socially accepted meaning of one or more words which express the concept." It is no wonder that vocabulary knowledge is so closely related to academic success. The number of words students know represents the concepts and information they know. Because of the close tie between vocabulary knowledge and concept knowledge, we will use the terms *word* and *concept* interchangeably in the remainder of this text.

## The Inequality of Vocabulary Knowledge

There is an obvious discrepancy among different age and socioeconomic groups relative to their vocabulary knowledge. In 1941, Smith (cited in Nagy & Herman, 1984) found that for students in grades four through twelve there was about a 6,000 word gap between students at the 25th and 50th percentiles on standardized tests. Using a more advanced method of calculating vocabulary size, Nagy and Herman (1984) estimated the difference to be anywhere between 4,500 and 5,400 words for low versus high achieving students. They also found this differential to be consistent between different socioeconomic strata. They estimated a 4,700 word difference in vocabulary knowledge between upper and lowerclass students. Similarly, they estimated that middleclass first graders know 50 percent more words than do lowerclass first graders.

These findings imply that vocabulary instruction should be a focal point of education for students lacking in general concept knowledge. After reviewing various programs designed for the educationally disadvantaged, Becker (1977) recommended intensive vocabulary training for students from environments where linguistic development is not strongly reinforced.

Recently, however, the notion of teaching vocabulary directly has drawn considerable criticism. Nagy and Anderson (1984) argued that the sheer number of words one would have to teach to prepare students for the concepts in content area textbooks casts serious doubt on the utility of direct vocabulary instruction. Some have taken Nagy and Anderson's comments to mean vocabulary should be fostered solely by wide reading and other general language building activities. Others have taken a position in favor of direct vocabulary instruction and have demonstrated its usefulness in a variety of situations (Beck, McKeown, & Omanson, 1987).

We prefer a compromise position, asserting that some vocabulary should be taught directly using varied instructional approaches and that some should be reinforced via wide reading and language development activities. A diverse theoretical base about word knowledge underlies the instructional approaches presented in this book.

## What Do You Know When You Know a Word?

As we have seen, words can be considered labels for concepts. That is, when you know a concept, you also know the label for it. At least two types of labels—phonological and orthographic—are important to vocabulary or concept knowledge. Research (Cohen, 1972; Slowiaczek, Nusbaum, & Pisoni, 1987) indicates the processing of these two types of labels is related. Once an individual learns the phonological label (the sound for the word) and the orthographic label (the letters for the word), the recognition of one label acts as a strong cue to the recognition of the other. This suggests that teaching the phonological and the orthographic labels for a word might be combined more often than they are. Rather than learning spelling and word recognition separately, students can be taught to

spell a word at the same time they learn to recognize it and associate meaning. In a review of research spanning twenty years, Templeton (1986) concluded that learning to spell a word is facilitated by explicit reference to the phonological label and the experiences associated with the word. Similarly Frost, Katz, and Bentin (1987) found that the ability to recall a phonological label is greatly affected by the orthographic salience of the word. Knowing both the phonological and orthographic labels for the word can be considered an important aspect of word knowledge from both cognitive and educational perspectives.

Of course, learning a new word is not just a matter of learning a label. Vocabulary knowledge implies a rich understanding of the word. Pearson (1985) contrasts those words for which students know the meaning (meaning vocabulary) with words students can recognize but to which they attach little meaning. Vacca (1986) makes the same distinction in his discussion of simple versus complex word knowledge. At the simple level, students know a word by definition; at the complex level, they associate experiences with the word. Vacca's complex level of word knowledge is similar to what Beck (1984) calls owning a word and what Pearson calls knowing a word in its fullest sense. As an example, being able to say *Duralumin is a strong, lightweight alloy of aluminum* is knowledge of the word at the simple level. Such knowledge does not indicate a pupil really knows what the word means. Nagy (1985) warns that it takes far more than this simple, superficial knowledge of words to make a difference in reading comprehension.

How can complex knowledge or a rich understanding of a word be characterized? The answer to this question lies in an understanding of how information is stored in long term memory. There are a number of theories about how to describe information storage. One common distinction is between episodic and semantic information. Episodic memory contains events that have occurred (Lindsay & Norman, 1977). If you recall your last birthday you probably replay that event in your mind as though it were a movie. Episodic memory is specific; it is about discrete instances in one's past.

Semantic memory is more general. It contains decontextualized information extracted from episodic memory. For example, you might store general information about birthdays in your semantic memory (e.g., they occur once a year, they are pleasant). Researchers once believed that knowledge about words begins as episodes and is transformed gradually to a more semantic representation. In other words, word knowledge initially is made up of specific events and then gradually transforms to general characteristics. However, Whittlesea (1987) has shown that even a fairly sophisticated knowledge of words can be primarily episodic. We associate specific events with words we know, even words that are abstract and fairly general in nature.

Another common distinction about the types of information in long term memory is that between linguistic and nonlinguistic information. Bower (1972) and Paivio (1969, 1971) assert that nonverbal imagery and verbal symbolic processes are the two major components of thinking. This has been referred to as the dual

3

coding theory. Images are more than just pictures in the mind. They include information stored as mental pictures with auditory, kinesthetic, tactile, and emotional elements. Thus, a mental image of a past event would include pictures of the event along with associated memories of smells, sounds, tastes, sensations, and emotions.

Information stored linguistically usually is realized as inner speech. Both Vygotsky (1978) and Piaget (1959) emphasized the importance of inner speech to human cognition. In fact, both asserted that human thought could be characterized primarily in terms of the linguistic representation of information. However, it is a misconception to think that linguistic thought is represented only as words , just as it is a misconception to think that mental images are only pictures in the mind. Linguistic thought probably is represented in its most basic form as highly abstract semantic units. In his explanation of the semiotic theory of language processing, Slobin (1979) asserts that humans code information linguistically into basic forms such as agents, objects, and relationships. We tend to separate our experience into persons, places, and things that act on or are acted on by other persons, places, or things. This occurs at a very deep, prelinguistic level that might be likened to a deep structure semantic level (Schlesinger, 1971). This is similar to the contention of case grammarians (e.g., Fillmore, 1968), who assert that all languages have a deep semantic regularity. The linguistic coding of information contains abstract symbolic representations of information commonly expressed as words. Relating the dual coding theory to word knowledge, we might conclude that information about a word is encoded as images and linguistic symbols. The imagery information can be expressed in a number of ways (e.g., mental pictures, sensations), as can the linguistic information (e.g., words, relationships between words, abstract symbols).

A third perspective of word knowledge is provided by the split brain research of Gazzaniga (Gazzaniga, 1985, Gazzaniga & LeDoux 1978) and others. Working with patients whose corpus callosums had been severed surgically, Gazzaniga was able to isolate fairly specific brain functions. He concluded that the mind stores information in a modular fashion.

> By modularity I mean that the brain is organized into relatively independent functioning units that work in parallel. The mind is not an indivisible whole operating in a single way to solve all problems...the vast and rich information impinging on our brains is broken into parts... (Gazzaniga, 1985, p. 4).

So strong are the modular components in determining human behavior that Gazzaniga characterizes the human mind as consisting of multiple but parallel selves. Sometimes a module or a self contains auditory, olfactory, tactile, visual, and other types of information. Sometimes it consists of only one type of information. Regardless of the composition of a module, it is usually mediated and integrated by language:

4

The behaviors that these separate systems emit are monitored by the one system we come to use more and more, namely the verbal natural language system (Gazzaniga & LeDoux, 1978, p. 150).

As it relates to word knowledge, Gazzaniga's theory implies that our knowledge of words can be encoded in many modular forms as combinations of different types of information.

A final view of word knowledge is offered by Underwood (1969), who lists nine cues associated with information stored in long term memory.

*Temporal.* Recalling when something occurred (remembering the school picnic was just before July 4).

*Spatial.* Recalling where objects are in relation to one another (remembering that you sat in front of a boy with blond hair in second grade).

*Frequency.* Recalling how frequently an event occurred (remembering that your teacher said "ah" every time she paused).

*Modality.* Recalling an event because it made a strong impression on you visually, auditorily, or tacitly (remembering an event because it was associated with a loud noise).

*Acoustic.* Recalling a word on the basis of its sound (remembering the word *oxymoron* because it sounds strange).

*Visual.* Recalling a mental image associated with information (remembering the term *bubble search* because it elicits a strong image).

*Affective.* Recalling information because of an associated emotion (remembering the day you were not picked to be a cheerleader because that made you sad).

*Context.* Recalling information because of the general context in which it appeared (remembering the classroom in which you learned the difference between *there* and *their*).

*Verbal.* Recalling information because of a word associated with it (remembering the events of the last Super Bowl when you hear the term *Super Sunday*).

Underwood's nine cues suggest that different types of experiences can be associated with words and those experiences create cues by which words can be retrieved and used.

## Changes in Word Knowledge

The fact that word knowledge can be either deep or superficial suggests that knowing a word involves a developmental process (Klausmeier, 1980, 1985; Tennyson & Cocchiarella, 1986).

According to Klausmeier, concept formation progresses through four levels: concrete, identity, classificatory, and formal. Attainment of a concept at the con-

crete level occurs when something is attended to one or more times, discriminated from other things, and remembered; then later it is attended to, discriminated, and recognized as the same thing. For example, a young child attends to a clock on a wall, discriminates it from other objects, represents it internally, then later retrieves the earlier representation of the clock and recognizes it as the same thing. At this point, the child knows the concept of that particular clock at the concrete level.

Attainment of a concept at the identity level occurs when an individual observes an item and recognizes it as the same one previously encountered in a different context. For example, the child who recognizes the clock after it is removed from one room and placed in another room has attained an identity level concept of that particular clock.

To learn a concept at the classificatory level, a person must already have learned at least two examples of the concept at the identity level. Attainment of the lowest classificatory level of a concept occurs when an individual regards at least two different examples of a concept as equivalent. For example, the child who treats the clock on the wall and the other one on the desk as equivalent has attained the concept of clock at a beginning classificatory level.

Finally, attainment of a concept at the formal level occurs when an individual can correctly identify examples of the concept, give its name, discriminate and name its defining or critical attributes, give a socially accepted definition, and indicate how examples differ from nonexamples.

For instructional purposes, Klausmeier breaks concept formation into three phases. The first phase fosters knowledge of concepts at the concrete and identity levels, the second at the beginning classificatory level, and the third at the mature classificatory and formal levels. The three instructional phases are summarized below.

Phase 1. Concrete and identity levels
1. Make available an item or a picture or other representation of it.
2. Give the item's name and help students associate the name with the item.
3. Immediately provide students with situations in which they must recognize the item (concept). Provide immediate feedback.
4. Make the item (concept) available later, and determine whether students recognize it.
5. Repeat the sequence as necessary.

Phase 2. Beginning classificatory level
1. Make available at least two different examples and one or two obvious nonexamples of the concept.
2. Help students associate the name of the concept with examples. (This differs from the second step of Phase 1 because in this case the student is required to provide the name for the concept.)
3. Help students identify and name the salient attributes of the concept.

4. Ask students to define the concept.
5. Arrange for students to recognize the concept in newly encountered examples. Also ask them to identify nonexamples of the concept.
6. Provide feedback.

Phase 3. Mature classificatory and formal levels
1. Prepare students by establishing an intention for them to become aware of related concepts.
2. Provide examples and nonexamples.
3. Help students identify examples and nonexamples by determining the attributes most commonly associated with the concept.
4. Have students name the concept and list its attributes.
5. Provide for complete understanding of the concept by having students define it.
6. Provide for use of the concept in oral and written language.
7. Provide feedback as to the accuracy of students' knowledge and use of the concept.

We can see from this model that the development of complete concept or word knowledge is a long and detailed process—one that teachers cannot expect to occur incidentally. In fact, Klausmeier says most students cannot attain concepts at the formal level unless they receive explicit instruction.

The work of developmental psychologists such as Carey (1978) and Case (1985) offers another view of changes in word knowledge. It appears that young children initially both undergeneralize and overgeneralize the meaning of newly learned words because they fail to understand important semantic features. Over time, children learn to make finer discriminations among word meanings. For example, children might learn the words *deep* and *shallow* as they apply to swimming pools and use them correctly when applying them to unfamiliar swimming pools. However, they may not see the similarity between how a swimming pool is deep and how holes and puddles are deep, or they may not know that *deep* can be applied to situations in which no water is involved.

One promising area of research in cognition is knowledge restructuring. According to Vosniadou and Brewer (1987), much of the learning that occurs in life cannot be characterized as a gradual linear process of adding new information to old knowledge. Rather, knowledge changes in different degrees and different ways. Piaget (1959) attempted to differentiate between two basic types of knowledge change with his notions of assimilation and accommodation. Simply stated, assimilation involves incorporating new knowledge; accommodation involves modifying prior knowledge. Rumelhart and Norman (1981) describe three types of learning: accretion, tuning, and restructuring. Accretion is change that occurs in existing knowledge structures (called schemata) through the gradual accumulation of factual information. Tuning involves changing schemata through generalizing their application, determining default values, and improving their

accuracy. Restructuring refers to changes in knowledge through the creation of new structures.

Vosniadou and Brewer (1987) emphasize restructuring in their discussion of learning, primarily because their studies indicate that some of the most important content related learning involves creation of new knowledge structures. They cite research in science education indicating that young children have gross misconceptions about basic scientific concepts. These are not gradually changed over time, but are replaced with more accurate concepts. To illustrate, young children believe the earth is shaped like a flat disc rather than a sphere. The flat earth notion cannot be changed adequately by accretion or tuning. Instead, a new structure modeling a spherical earth must be created.

Vosniadou and Brewer identify three instructional tools for restructuring: analogies and metaphors, physical models, and Socratic dialogue. Analogies and metaphors facilitate both the spontaneous restructuring of new knowledge and the explicit teaching of new structures. Scientists often construct analogies or metaphors to existing schemata when they try to understand anomalies in existing information. Vosniadou and Ortony (1983) found that both adults and children can use analogies and metaphors to transfer information from a familiar domain to help construct a new schema. For example, light can be understood as a particle and a wave.

Physical models often can do the work of analogies when easily identifiable analogies are not present. Physical models are particularly useful with concrete concepts in the physical sciences because students can construct a schema or representation for the concept by internalizing the physical model. For example, presenting students with a physical model of an atom can help them understand such concepts as *nucleus, neutron, proton,* and *electron.*

Finally, Socratic dialogue can be used to make students aware of inconsistencies in their knowledge of concepts. They can probe their concept knowledge to discover and correct misconceptions in their thinking.

In summary, learning a word fully can be a long term process, a process in which knowledge of the word changes and sometimes is drastically restructured or replaced by a new knowledge structure.

## Two Views on Direct Vocabulary Instruction

There have been a number of general reviews of research on vocabulary instruction. Among the most noteworthy are those by Anderson and Freebody (1981), Graves (1986), Mezynski (1983), and Stahl and Fairbanks (1986). According to these reviews, direct teaching of vocabulary almost always is successful in improving understanding of words taught specifically. Many of the most powerful techniques involve the different ways of knowing a word discussed in the previous section. For example, Pressley, Levin, and DeLaney (1982) report consistently powerful effects for mnemonically based vocabulary strategies. Un-

fortunately, many reviewers (e.g., Graves, 1986) consider mnemonically based techniques useful only for learning labels and not appropriate for increasing word knowledge per se. However, Belleza (1981) and Pressley, Levin, and McDaniel (1987) have shown that mnemonic techniques are not artificial, but tap into nonlinguistic ways of knowing (described in the theories of Paivio, Gazzaniga, and others) that almost always are part of word knowledge.

As powerful as direct vocabulary instruction appears to be, its transfer to reading comprehension is not strong. As Beck, Perfetti, and McKeown (1982, p. 507) have noted, "since virtually all such studies have succeeded in boosting vocabulary knowledge but few have demonstrated corresponding gains in comprehension, additional considerations are necessary." In a series of experiments, Beck, McKeown, and their colleagues (Beck, Perfetti, & McKeown, 1982; McKeown, 1985; McKeown et al., 1983, 1985) found that:

- Direct vocabulary instruction can increase the comprehension of texts containing the words taught.
- In order to affect comprehension, vocabulary instruction needs to be extensive (up to 20 minutes of instruction per word) and to include frequent encounters with the words (up to 24).
- Instruction in vocabulary should be multifaceted, including associating new words with a variety of contexts, creating contexts for words, contrasting words to discover relationships, and using the words outside of class.
- Instruction should include speed training to build automaticity in word recognition and lexical access.
- Instruction can be particularly fruitful when words are grouped in semantic categories and taught in relation to one another.

The Beck and McKeown studies suggest that direct vocabulary instruction could be a focal point of education if approached systematically and intensively. In a summary analysis of their research and that of others Beck, McKeown, and Omanson (1987) described direct approaches to vocabulary instruction that improve vocabulary knowledge. These approaches range from narrow exposures to new words (telling students the meaning of new words) to rich exposures to new words (having students identify personal experiences related to new words and relationships among new words) to extended rich activities (having students identify words in their outside reading and make varied connections with known words and experiences).

The studies by Beck and McKeown seem to support heavy classroom emphasis on direct vocabulary instruction. However, other research suggests that direct vocabulary instruction is of little value. Given the amount of time that must be devoted to vocabulary instruction and the large number of words students encounter in their reading, Nagy and Anderson (1984) question the utility of direct vocabulary instruction. We have seen that for students to learn words well enough to affect reading comprehension they must be exposed to the words many

times for extended periods of time. Nagy and Anderson estimate there are 88,500 different words in student reading materials for grades three through nine. The direct teaching of all 88,500 words would require students to learn about 12,600 words per year. Assuming that each word would require twenty minutes of instruction under Beck and McKeown's criteria, direct vocabulary instruction would require more than twenty-four hours of instruction per day.

From this, one might conclude that most vocabulary learning should be left to students' reading. This conclusion is supported by the research of Nagy and Herman and their colleagues, who demonstrated in a series of studies (Herman et al., 1987; Nagy, Anderson, & Herman, 1987; Nagy & Herman, 1984; Nagy, Herman, & Anderson, 1985a, 1985b) that students can and do learn new words from context and that the number of words learned from context is significantly greater than words learned from direct instruction. Specifically, students learn about one in twenty of the new words they encounter in their reading. Although this number might seem small, Nagy and Anderson estimate that if students spent twenty-five minutes a day reading at a rate of 200 words per minute for 200 days of the year, they would read a million words of text annually. Given this amount of reading, children would encounter 15,000 to 30,000 unfamiliar words and would learn between 750 and 1,500 of them. Thus, "A period of sustained silent reading could lead to substantial yearly gains in vocabulary, probably much larger than could be achieved by spending the same amount of time on instruction specifically devoted to vocabulary" (Nagy & Herman, 1987, p. 26).

Jenkins, Stein, and Wysocki (1984) add a note of caution to the notion that wide reading should be used as the primary method for vocabulary development. They found that incidental learning of vocabulary is not an automatic by-product of wide reading. Rather, students must be primed for the new words they will encounter to use context effectively to understand and learn new words. However, the supportive research on incidental learning from wide reading is clear and defensible from many perspectives (Drum & Konopak, 1987; Sternberg, 1987). Simply stated, wide reading greatly enhances vocabulary development.

In summary, the research on vocabulary instruction cited thus far shows that direct instruction increases knowledge of words taught directly. However, for instruction to transfer to reading, it must be relatively long in duration and foster a deep understanding of words. Even the most ambitious instructional program could not possibly cover all words students encounter in their reading. Consequently, wide reading and language development activities must play a dominant role in vocabulary instruction.

From the discussion above, there appear to be two diametrically opposed camps relative to vocabulary learning—those who assert that new words should be taught directly in an intense and rich fashion and those who assert that wide reading should be the vehicle for teaching new words. Actually, there is a relatively well articulated middle ground on which virtually all researchers and theorists agree. Those who say wide reading should be the primary vehicle for

vocabulary learning do not discount the need for or importance of direct vocabulary instruction. Nagy and Herman (1987, p. 33) state:

> We do not want to overstate our case and imply that classroom time should never be devoted to teaching the meaning of new words. But reports of new effective methods of vocabulary instruction seldom contain any warning about their limitation. We feel that methods of vocabulary instruction can be effectively developed and implemented only if their limitations as well as their strengths are understood.

Similarly, those who believe vocabulary should be taught directly do not say that students should receive direct instruction on all words. Nagy and Anderson's (1984) estimate that many of the 88,500 words in printed school English are so rare they may be encountered only once in an avid reader's lifetime and that students already know many of those words when they enter school. Using that estimate, Beck, McKeown, and Omanson (1987) conclude that there are only about 7,000 words that students do not know and that appear relatively frequently in reading materials. If less than half of these words were singled out for direct instruction and the rest left to incidental learning, the target words could be taught directly in most classrooms. This would require teaching about 400 words each year in grades three through nine—a task that is not impossible even assuming these words would be taught in a rich fashion.

In other words, a safe middle position appears to be that wide reading should be the primary vehicle for vocabulary learning, yet some selected words can be the focus of direct vocabulary instruction. It is this middle position we will develop in this book.

## Some Principles of Vocabulary Instruction

We believe current research and theory on vocabulary provide some rather clear guidelines and principles around which instruction can be planned.

- Wide reading and language rich activities should be the primary vehicles for vocabulary learning. Given the large number of words students encounter in written and oral language, general language development must be encouraged as one of the most important vocabulary development strategies.
- Direct vocabulary instruction should focus on words considered important to a given content area or to general background knowledge. Since effective direct vocabulary instruction requires a fair amount of time and complexity, teachers should select words for instruction that promise a high yield in student learning of general knowledge or of knowledge of a particular topic of instructional importance.
- Direct vocabulary instruction should include many ways of knowing a word and provide for the development of a complex level of word knowledge. Since word knowledge is stored in many forms (mental pictures, kinesthetic

associations, smells, tastes, semantic distinctions, linguistic references), direct vocabulary instruction should take advantage of many of these forms and not emphasize one to the exclusion of others.

- Direct vocabulary instruction should include a structure by which new words not taught directly can be learned readily. Again, given the large number of words students encounter and the limited utility of direct instruction, some structure must be developed to allow the benefits of direct vocabulary instruction to go beyond the words actually taught.

## References

Anderson, Richard, and Freebody, Peter. Vocabulary knowledge. In John T. Guthrie (Ed.), *Comprehension and teaching.* Newark, DE: International Reading Association, 1981.

Beck, Isabel. Developing comprehension: The impact of the directed reading lesson. In Richard C. Anderson, Jean Osborn, and Robert J. Tierney (Eds.), *Learning to read in American schools: Basal readers and content text.* Hillsdale, NJ: Erlbaum, 1984.

Beck, Isabel, McKeown, Margaret, and Omanson, Richard. The effects and uses of diverse vocabulary instructional techniques. In Margaret McKeown and Mary Curtis (Eds.), *The nature of vocabulary acquisition.* Hillsdale, NJ: Erlbaum, 1987.

Beck, Isabel, Perfetti, Charles, and McKeown, Margaret. Effects of long-term vocabulary instruction on lexical access and reading comprehension. *Journal of Educational Psychology, 1982, 74* (4), 506-521.

Becker, Wesley C. Teaching reading and language to the disadvantaged—what we have learned from field research. *Harvard Educational Review, 1977, 47,* 518-543.

Belleza, Frances. Mnemonic devices: Classification, characteristics and criteria. *Review of Educational Research, 1981, 51,* 247-275.

Bower, Gordon. Analysis of a mnemonic device. In Max Coltheart (Ed.), *Readings in cognitive psychology.* Toronto: Holt, Rinehart & Winston of Canada, 1972.

Carey, S. Semantic development: The state of the art. In E. Warner and L.R. Gleitman (Eds.), *Language acquisition: The state of the art.* Cambridge, England: Cambridge University Press, 1978.

Case, Robie. *Childhood development.* New York: Academic Press, 1985.

Cohen, Gillian. Some evidence for parallel comparisons in a letter recognition task. In Max Coltheart (Ed.), *Readings in cognitive psychology.* Toronto: Holt, Rinehart & Winston of Canada, 1972.

Condon, John C. *Semantics and communication.* New York: Macmillan, 1968.

Drum, Priscilla, and Konopak, Bonnie. Learning word meanings from written context. In Margaret McKeown and Mary Curtis (Eds.), *The nature of vocabulary acquisition.* Hillsdale, NJ: Erlbaum, 1987.

Fillmore, Charles, J. The case for case. In E. Beck and R.T. Harms (Eds.), *Universals in linguistic theory.* New York: Holt, Rinehart & Winston, 1968.

Frost, Ram, Katz, Leonard, and Bentin, Shlomo. Strategies for visual word recognition and orthographic depth: A multilingual comparison. *Journal of Experimental Psychology: Human Perception and Performance, 1987, 13* (1), 104-115.

Gazzaniga, Michael S. *The social brain.* New York: Basic Books, 1985.

Gazzaniga, Michael S., and LeDoux, Joseph E. *The integrated mind.* New York: Plenum Press, 1978.

Graves, Michael. Vocabulary learning and instruction. In Ernst Z. Rothkopf (Ed.), *Review of research in education,* volume 13. Washington : American Educational Research Association, 1986.

Herman, Patricia, Anderson, Richard, Pearson, P. David, and Nagy, William. Incidental acquisition of word meaning form expositions with varied texts. *Reading Research Quarterly,* 1987, *22,* 263-284.

Jenkins, Joseph, Stein, Marcy, and Wysocki, Katherine. Learning vocabulary through reading. *American Educational Research Journal,* 1984, *21* (4), 767-787.

Klausmeier, Herbert. *Education psychology.* New York: Harper & Row, 1985.

Klausmeier, Herbert. *Learning and teaching concepts: A strategy for testing applications of theory.* New York: Academic Press, 1980.

Klausmeier, Herbert J., and Sipple, Thomas S. *Learning and teaching concepts.* New York: Academic Press, 1980.

Lindsay, Peter H., and Norman, Donald A. *Human information processing.* New York: Academic Press, 1977.

McKeown, Margaret. The acquisition of word meaning from context by children of high and low ability. *Reading Research Quarterly,* 1985, *20,* 482-496.

McKeown, Margaret, Beck, Isabel, Omanson, Richard, and Perfetti, Charles. The effects of long-term vocabulary instruction on reading comprehension: A replication. *Journal of Reading Behavior,* 1983, *15* (1), 3-18.

McKeown, Margaret, Beck, Isabel, Omanson, Richard, and Pople, Martha. Some effects of the nature and frequency of vocabulary instruction on the knowledge and use of words. *Reading Research Quarterly,* 1985, *20,* 522-535.

Mezynski, Karen. Issues concerning the acquisition of knowledge: Effects of vocabulary training on reading comprehension. *Review of Educational Research,* 1983, *53* (2), 293-323.

Nagy, William E. *Vocabulary instruction: Implications of the new research.* Paper presented at the conference of the National Council of Teachers of English, Philadelphia, Pennsylvania, 1985.

Nagy, William, and Anderson, Richard. How many words are there in printed school English? *Reading Research Quarterly,* 1984, *19,* 303-330.

Nagy, William, Anderson, Richard, and Herman, Patricia. Learning words from context during normal reading. *American Educational Research Journal,* 1987, *24,* 237-270.

Nagy, William, and Herman, Patricia. Breadth and depth of vocabulary knowledge: Implications for acquisition and instruction. In Margaret McKeown and Mary Curtis (Eds.), *The nature of vocabulary acquisition.* Hillsdale, NJ: Erlbaum, 1987.

Nagy, William, and Herman, Patricia A. *Limitations of vocabulary instruction.* Champaign, IL: University of Illinois, Center for the Study of Reading, 1984.

Nagy, William, Herman, Patricia, and Anderson, Richard. Learning words from context. *Reading Research Quarterly,* 1985a, *20,* 233-253.

Nagy, William, Herman, Patricia, and Anderson, Richard. *Learning word meanings from context: How broadly generalizable?* Champaign, IL: University of Illinois, Center for the Study of Reading, 1985b.

Paivio, Allan. *Imagery and verbal processing.* New York: Holt, Rinehart & Winston, 1971.

Paivio, Allan. Mental imagery in associative learning and memory. *Psychological Review,* 1969, *76,* 241-263.

Pearson, P. David. Changing the face of reading comprehension instruction. *The Reading Teacher,* 1985, *38,* 724-728.

Piaget, Jean. *Language and thought of the child.* Cleveland, OH: World, 1959.

Pressley, Michael, Levin, Joel, and Delaney, Harold D. The mnemonic keyboard method. *Review of Educational Research,* 1982, *52* (1), 61-91.

Pressley, Michael, Levin, Joel, and McDaniel, Mark. Remembering versus inferring what a word means: Mnemonic and contextual approaches. In Margaret McKeown and Mary Curtis (Eds.), *The nature of vocabulary acquisition.* Hillsdale, NJ: Erlbaum, 1987.

Rumelhart, David E., and Norman, Donald A. Accretion, tuning and restructuring: Three modes of learning. In J.W. Cotton and R. Klatzky (Eds.), *Semantic factors in cognition.* Hillsdale, NJ: Erlbaum, 1981.

Schlesinger, M. The production of utterances and language acquisition. In Dan I. Slobin (Ed.), *The ontogenesis of grammar.* New York: Academic Press, 1971.

Slobin, Dan I. *Psycholinguistics.* Glenview, IL: Scott, Foresman, 1979.

Stowiaczek, Howard, Nusbaum, Howard, and Pisoni, David. Phonological priming in auditory word recognition. *Journal of Experimental Psychology: Learning, Memory and Cognition,* 1987, *13* (1), 64-75.

Stahl, Steven A., and Fairbanks, Marilyn M. The effects of vocabulary instruction: A model based meta-analysis. *Review of Educational Research,* 1986, *56* (1), 72-110.

Sternberg, Robert. Most vocabulary is learned from context. In Margaret McKeown and Mary Curtis (Eds.), *The nature of vocabulary acquisition.* Hillsdale, NJ: Erlbaum, 1987.

Templeton, Shane. Syntheses of the research on the learning and teaching of spelling. *Educational Leadership,* 1986, *43* (6), 73-78.

Tennyson, Robert D., and Cocchiarella, Martin J. An empirically based instructional design theory for teaching concepts. *Review of Educational Research,* 1986, *56* (1), 40-71.

Thorndike, Robert L. *Reading comprehension education in fifteen countries.* New York: Wiley, 1973.

Underwood, B.J. Attributes of memory. *Psychological Review,* 1969, *76,* 559-573.

Vacca, Richard T. *Content area reading.* Boston: Little, Brown, 1986.

Vosniadou, Stella, and Brewer, William F. Theories of knowledge restructuring on development. *Review of Educational Research,* 1987, *57* (1), 51-67.

Vosniadou, Stella, and Ortony, Andrew A. The influence of analogy in children's acquisition of new information from text: An exploratory study. In J. Niles (Ed.), *Searches for meaning in reading/language processing and instruction.* Rochester, NY: National Reading Conference, 1983.

Vygotsky, Lev S. *Mind in society.* Cambridge, MA: Harvard University Press, 1978.

Whittlesea, Bruce W. Preservation of specific experiences in the representation of general knowledge. *Journal of Experimental Psychology: Learning, Memory and Cognition,* 1987, *13* (1), 3-17.

# Chapter 2

# A Category Structure for Vocabulary Instruction

Of the four principles listed at the end of Chapter 1, the most important is the need for a structure that allows direct instruction to reach beyond words taught directly. Nagy and Anderson (1984) assert that any vocabulary instruction strategy can be justified only if it can demonstrate its transfer to words not taught. They add, "The challenge to those who would advocate spending available instructional time with individual words is to demonstrate that such instruction will give the child an advantage in dealing with the ocean of words not instructed" (p. 328).

We believe a categorical or cluster approach to vocabulary instruction can meet this challenge. Beck, McKeown, and their colleagues (Beck, Perfetti, & McKeown 1982; McKeown, 1985; McKeown et al., 1983) found that presenting words in semantically related categories is a highly flexible tool for vocabulary instruction. The technique provides students with a set of implicit clues as to what new words might mean. For example, imagine being given the following words and being told their meanings are alike in some way: *middle, mean, mode, centroid.* Even though you may not know the meaning of *mode* or *centroid*, your understanding of *middle* and *mean* would suggest that the unknown words have something to do with measuring the middle of things. Mervis (1980, p. 279) says categorization is a basic cognitive tool that allows us to make sense of the world: "By categorizing, a person is able to render the unfamiliar familiar, and because one is able to generalize about an object based on knowledge about its category, one is able to know more about the object than just what can be ascertained by looking at it."

Categorization is an excellent tool for rapid vocabulary expansion because of this transfer of characteristics from known to unknown words. Through categorization, students can form immediate associations for new words. Even though such links are weak initially, they provide students with a starting place for developing a deeper understanding of new words. Students do not have to use context

or definitions to discover where a new word fits into an existing knowledge base—the fit is implicit in the categorization process.

In this chapter, we describe a system of semantic clusters developed for vocabulary instruction in kindergarten through grade six.

## Instructional Clusters

The most difficult aspect of structuring vocabulary instruction using a category approach is developing the semantic categories. To make the process easier, we have organized into instructional clusters 7,230 words commonly found in elementary school texts. As the name implies, an instructional cluster is meant for instructional purposes and is not intended as a model of how the human mind might organize concepts semantically. The clusters presented here are an instructional aid developed to facilitate teaching vocabulary through categories.

We used the following process to develop the instructional clusters.

1. We selected about 7,000 words from *Basic Elementary Reading Vocabulary* (Harris & Jacobson, 1972), *The American Heritage Word Frequency Book* (Carroll, Davies, & Richman, 1971), and *Word Frequency of Spoken American English* (Dahl, 1979). It is important to note that many of the words on the list are sex-stereotyped because these lists are based on basals written before publishers began to reduce sex stereotyping in books for children.
2. The first author then categorized the words into semantically related groups.
3. Sixty elementary school teachers reviewed the clusters to identify any words that did not fit well in an instructional sense.
4. We reclassified all words identified by the teachers as not fitting.
5. We repeated steps 3 and 4 until the teachers identified as miscategorized fewer than 5 words in 1,000.

This process produced three levels of instructional clusters: superclusters, clusters, and miniclusters. The 61 superclusters (clusters of clusters) are the largest organizational groups; the 430 clusters are groups of words with closer semantic ties than superclusters; and the more than 1,500 miniclusters are groups of words with the strongest semantic ties.

To illustrate, consider supercluster 32, Shapes/Dimensions. It contains 8 clusters: Shapes (General Names), Circular or Curved Shapes, Rectangular or Square Shapes, Straightness/Crookedness, Sharpness/Bluntness, Dimension, Fullness/Emptiness, Inclination. The Sharpness/Bluntness cluster contains 3 miniclusters dealing with Length, Thickness, and Width.

All of the superclusters, clusters, and miniclusters are listed in Appendix A. They are ordered by size; the supercluster containing the most concepts is listed first. Figure 1 summarizes the superclusters.

Clusters within superclusters are identified by the number of the supercluster followed by a letter. For example, there are 24 clusters within supercluster 2, Types of Motion. The clusters within the supercluster are identified as 2a, 2b,

# Figure 1
## Superclusters Identified in Elementary Textbooks

| Superclusters | Number of Words in Supercluster |
|---|---|
| 1. Occupations | 364 |
| 2. Types of motion | 321 |
| 3. Size/quantity | 310 |
| 4. Animals | 289 |
| 5. Feelings/emotions | 282 |
| 6. Foods/meals (names for various food types and situations involving eating) | 263 |
| 7. Time (names for various points and periods of time and words indicating various time relationships between ideas) | 251 |
| 8. Machines/engines/tools | 244 |
| 9. Types of people (names for various types or categories of people that are not job related) | 237 |
| 10. Communication (names for various types of communications and actions involving communications) | 235 |
| 11. Transportation | 205 |
| 12. Mental actions/thinking | 193 |
| 13. Nonemotional traits (general, nonphysical traits of people) | 175 |
| 14. Location/direction | 172 |
| 15. Literature/writing | 171 |
| 16. Water/liquids (names for different types of liquids and bodies of water) | 164 |
| 17. Clothing | 161 |
| 18. Places where people live/dwell | 154 |
| 19. Noises/sounds | 143 |
| 20. Land/terrain (names for general categories of land or terrain) | 142 |
| 21. Dwellings/shelters (names for various types of dwellings/ places of business) | 141 |
| 22. Materials (names for materials used to make things) | 140 |
| 23. The human body | 128 |
| 24. Vegetation | 116 |
| 25. Groups (general names for groups and organizations) | 116 |
| 26. Value/correctness | 108 |
| 27. Similarity/dissimilarity (names indicating how similar or different things are and the sameness or difference between ideas) | 108 |
| 28. Money/finance | 102 |
| 29. Soil/metal/rock | 102 |
| 30. Rooms/furnishings/parts of dwellings | 97 |
| 31. Attitudinals (words indicating the speaker/writer's attitude about what is being said or written) | 96 |
| 32. Shapes/dimensions | 90 |
| 33. Destructive/helpful actions | 87 |
| 34. Sports/recreation | 80 |
| 35. Language (names for different aspects of written and oral language) | 80 |

## Figure 1
## Superclusters Identified in Elementary Textbooks (continued)

| Superclusters | Number of Words in Supercluster |
|---|:---:|
| 36. Ownership/possession | 68 |
| 37. Disease/health | 68 |
| 38. Light (names for light/darkness and things associated with them) | 68 |
| 39. Causality | 59 |
| 40. Weather | 55 |
| 41. Cleanliness/uncleanliness | 53 |
| 42. Popularity/knownness | 52 |
| 43. Physical traits of people | 51 |
| 44. Touching/grabbing actions | 50 |
| 45. Pronouns (personal, possessive, relative, interrogative, indefinite) | 50 |
| 46. Contractions | 49 |
| 47. Entertainment/the arts | 48 |
| 48. Actions involving the legs | 46 |
| 49. Mathematics (names for various branches of mathematics, operations, and quantities) | 46 |
| 50. Auxiliary/helping verbs (forms of *to be,* modals, primary and semiauxiliaries) | 46 |
| 51. Events (names for general and specific types of events) | 44 |
| 52. Temperature/fire | 40 |
| 53. Images/perceptions | 39 |
| 54. Life/survival | 38 |
| 55. Conformity/complexity | 34 |
| 56. Difficulty/danger | 30 |
| 57. Texture/durability | 30 |
| 58. Color | 29 |
| 59. Chemicals | 28 |
| 60. Facial expressions/actions | 21 |
| 61. Electricity/particles of matter | 21 |

and so on. Miniclusters are identified by numbers to the right of a decimal point after the supercluster number and cluster letter.

Figure 2 illustrates the coding procedure. It shows the Joining Actions cluster from supercluster 2, Types of Motion. It is the twenty-second cluster in supercluster 2, so it is designated 2v because *v* is the twenty-second letter of the alphabet. Figure 2 also contains two miniclusters—2v.1 and 2v.2. Note that each minicluster is introduced by an italicized header word. Header words are representative of the words within a minicluster; they are neither names for the minicluster nor the most general concepts in the minicluster.

## Figure 2
## Sample Cluster

Cluster name:   Joining Actions
Cluster number: 2v

| Minicluster | Grade Level | Part of Speech |
|---|---|---|
| **2v.1 Connection** | | |
| connection | 4 | N |
| bond | 5 | N, V |
| **2v.2 Join** | | |
| join | 3 | V |
| marry | 3 | V |
| wed | 3 | V |
| link | 4 | N, V |
| connect | 5 | V |
| unite | 5 | V |
| fuse | 6 | V |
| combine | 6 | V |
| adjoin | 6 | V |
| merge | 6 | V |

Finally, Appendix A contains some words or groups of words with no header word. For example, immediately following minicluster 2v.2 is the word *fusion* listed in the following way:

2v.2.1 _____
   fusion

Words coded in this fasion are closely related to the words in the preceding minicluster but their relationship is somehow different from that of the words within the minicluster. Many times such words are simply a different part of speech from the words within the minicluster. For example, *fusion* is a noun, whereas the words in minicluster 2.v are all verbs. Hence, words listed with no header word can be considered closely related to but in some meaningful way different from the words in the preceding minicluster.

## Special Features of the Clusters

To get the maximum benefit from the instructional clusters, it is useful to consider the information presented with the words in each cluster: grade level, part of speech, and basic word designations.

# Grade Level

After most words in Appendix A, we suggest a grade level at which the word might be introduced. We established the grade level designations by using the levels reported by Harris and Jacobson (1972), who obtained their grade level estimates by analyzing a number of elementary school reading series. For words not on the Harris and Jacobson list, we obtained initial grade level estimates by consulting the Thorndike and Lorge list (1943).

These initial grade level estimates were then reviewed by the sixty teachers participating in the project. We asked the teachers to change estimates they found inconsistent with their own teaching experiences. If more than 50 percent of the participating teachers suggested a grade level change for a word, we assigned a new grade level by calculating the grade level most commonly suggested by the teachers.

Some grade level designations in Appendix A are accompanied by an asterisk, indicating that the word does not appear frequently in student reading material, but when it does appear it is introduced at the grade level identified. We asked participating teachers if words should be considered of secondary importance within their designated grade levels. If more than 50 percent of the teachers felt a word was of secondary importance, it was listed with an asterisk.

Some words in Appendix A have no grade level designation. According to Harris and Jacobson, these words rarely appear in basal reading series, but they do appear in elementary content area textbooks. Again, these content specific words were reviewed by participating teachers, who identified words that should be given a grade level rather than content area designation.

For those words designated as content specific, the following codes are used in Appendix A:

SS    Social Studies
EN    English
MA    Math
SC    Science

Some words in Appendix A have the grade level designation 6+. The participating teachers felt sixth grade students can learn these words, but the words usually are taught at higher grade levels. Virtually all of these words were identified by teacher suggestion. That is, the teachers identified words that were not on the lists we consulted initially but that were, they believed, important to a particular supercluster, cluster, or minicluster.

Finally, a number of phrases—such as *in that* and *in the meantime*—appear in Appendix A. These were not assigned a grade level or subject matter designation because no grade level estimate could be obtained from the source lists, and the participating teachers did not feel they were able to estimate the grade level at which phrases should be introduced. These words are listed with a dash in place of the grade level designation.

In developing grade level designations, we relied heavily on the subjective judgments of participating elementary school teachers. Obviously, the validity of this process is dependent on the extent to which the experience of the participating teachers represents common instructional practice. Readers are cautioned to view grade level designations as suggestions about when words might be introduced to students.

## Part of Speech

For each word, we identify the part of speech in which the word is commonly used. Again, these designations are based on recommendations of participating teachers. The following codes are used to designate part of speech:

| | |
|---|---|
| N | Noun |
| V | Verb |
| A | Adjective |
| AV | Adverb |
| AV(+ly) | Adverb when suffix -ly is added |
| PRO | Pronoun |
| PREP | Preposition |
| INT | Interjection |
| DET | Determiner |
| AX | Auxiliary verb |
| RM | Relationship marker |

Some of these categories stray from the conventions of traditional grammar. In the system used here, nouns, adjectives, adverbs, pronouns, prepositions, and interjections are used in their traditional sense. Determiners are best described as special types of adjectives. Their primary function is to quantify the nouns they precede. They include such words as *a, an, the,* and *no* (when used before a noun, as in *We have no money.*).

Auxiliary verbs include *might, could,* and *would.* Their function is to signal the tense and mood of the verbs they accompany.

Relationship markers include *and, because,* and *however.* In traditional grammar, such words are commonly called coordinating conjunctions. We refer to them as relationship markers so phrases not traditionally classified as coordinating conjunctions (such as *in any case* and *regardless of*) can be included. The general function of relationship markers is to signal specific types of relationships between ideas.

## Basic Words

The final type of designation for words in Appendix A is the basic word designation. Inclusion as a basic word is signaled by a *b* immediately in front of a word. Basic words are fundamental in English; they are the building blocks of

other words. If students are taught the basic words, they can more easily learn derived and semantically related words.

Dupuy (1974) defined a basic word as a single word form that is not proper; is not classified by dictionaries as foreign, archaic, slang, or technical; is not inflected, derived, or compound; and is listed in major dictionaries.

Although Dupuy did not list the basic words in English, he established a way to identify them. He estimated there are 12,300 basic words in English, 7,800 of which are necessary for educational purposes in kindergarten through twelfth grade. To teach 7,800 words would require direct instruction of less than 650 words per year. Theoretically, such instruction could hold the key to understanding most of the estimated 240,000 words in English (Dupuy, 1974).

Using Dupuy's criteria Becker, Dixon, and Anderson-Inman (1980) identified 8,109 basic words. We cross referenced each word in Appendix A with their list. Of the 7,230 words in Appendix A, 4,505 were also on the Becker, Dixon, and Anderson-Inman list. We then analyzed those words using the suggestions of Nagy and Anderson (1984). Specifically, they noted that Becker, Dixon, and Anderson-Inman's use of a morphographically based system for identifying basic words produced a set of words with little practical validity. For example, in the Becker list, *annual* is considered a basic word for *millenium* on the grounds that both are derived from the Latin *annus*. As Nagy and Anderson (1984, p. 309) note, "A historical linguist can certainly see the relationship in form between these two words, but it is dubious that the normal speaker of English, armed only with such knowledge of morphology which can be gained from words currently in the language, would find any but a semantic relationship between them." In short, Nagy and Anderson found the Becker list inadequate on the grounds that it excluded many words that are truly basic in the sense that a knowledge of them would lead a reader to understand other derived and related words. Consequently, the words in Appendix A not identified as basic from the Becker list were reviewed by two raters. Words judged by both raters as fundamental (not being derived from other words in the common use of English) were then designated as basic. For example, *luggage* was not included on the Becker list on the grounds that it is derived from *lug*. However, both raters agreed that in the common use of English, *luggage* is not thought of as derived from *lug*. So *luggage* was added to the list of basics. Similarly, some words on the Becker list were dropped from the basic designation on the grounds that they do have commonly understood derived forms. For example, *congresswoman* was on the Becker list of basics, but both raters agreed that in the common use of the language, *congresswoman* is considered a derived form of *congressman*. Twenty-six words were dropped from the Becker list and 605 were added. This process of adding and deleting increased the number of basic words in Appendix A to 5,084. (A more thorough description of the process used to add and delete basic words from the Becker list is provided in Marzano & Marzano, 1987.)

**Figure 3**
**Cluster with Basic Words**

Cluster name:    Joining Actions
Cluster number: 2v

| Minicluster | Grade Level | Part of Speech |
|---|---|---|
| 2v.1 **Connection** | | |
| connection (connect) | 4 | N |
| b bond | 5 | N, V |
| 2v.2 **Join** | | |
| b join | 3 | V |
| b marry | 3 | V |
| b wed | 3 | V |
| b link | 4 | N, V |
| b connect | 5 | V |
| unite (union) | 5 | V |
| b fuse | 6 | V |
| b combine | 6 | V |
| adjoin (join) | 6 | V |
| b merge | 6 | V |

Any word not classified as basic in Appendix A has the basic word from which (in the opinion of the raters) it is commonly considered derived written in parentheses to its right. For ease of discussion, in Figure 2 we presented words without identifying basic words. Figure 3 illustrates how that cluster appears in Appendix A with basic word designations and with basic words in parentheses. Notice that of the twelve words in the two miniclusters, nine are basic (preceded by the letter *b*) and three are not. The three nonbasic words have the basic words written in parentheses to the right.

## Using the Clusters to Organize Vocabulary Instruction

Rather than systematically teaching the words in each of the superclusters in Appendix A, readers are advised to develop instructional clusters tailored to the needs of students and the specific content being studied. To do this, teachers should identify the words they wish to teach. As Beck, McKeown, and Omanson (1987, p. 158) note in their discussion of how to select words for direct instruction:

> The selection of words for the program and whether they would be taught in a narrow or rich way cannot be determined independent of the classroom curriculum. Rather, those decisions would be made based on the classroom lessons, opportunities that arose spontaneously, such as community or news events, and contributions from the children themselves.

To illustrate how words could be selected, the teacher might first consider what students will be reading, then try to identify words central to understanding that content using the guides to important words provided in most textbooks and basals. From these lists, the teacher could select important words and add words not identified by the text but known to cause problems for students.

Once these words are identified, the teacher can organize them into instructional clusters by using Appendix B, which contains all of the words in Appendix A alphabetized and identified by supercluster, cluster, and minicluster. For example, if a teacher identified *parch* to teach to students, he or she could consult Appendix B and find that *parch* has the cluster designation 52a.4. The number 52 indicates that *parch* is found in supercluster 52, Temperature/Fire. Within that supercluster, the word is found in cluster *a* and minicluster 4. Turning to cluster 52a, the teacher would find that *parch* is a verb form recommended for introduction at the sixth grade level. Looking through that cluster, the teacher could identify other related concepts to introduce at the same time. Hence, the clusters can be used as a tool for expanding the number of concepts a teacher might introduce to students. Instead of teaching *parch* in isolation, the teacher could introduce *swelter* and *temperate* at the same time, using students' knowledge of one term to help them understand the meaning of others.

Once teachers have organized target words into instructional clusters, they will have a powerful tool with which to teach important content related concepts and to expand student vocabulary in a relatively efficient manner. In the next chapter we consider how the clusters can be used in various instructional activities.

## References

Beck, Isabel, McKeown, Margaret, and Omanson, Richard. The effects and uses of diverse vocabulary instructional techniques. In Margaret McKeown and Mary Curtis (Eds.), *The nature of vocabulary acquisition*. Hillsdale, NJ: Erlbaum, 1987.

Beck, Isabel, Perfetti, Charles, and McKeown, Margaret. Effects of long-term vocabulary instruction on lexical access and reading comprehension. *Journal of Educational Psychology*, 1982, *74* (4), 506-521.

Becker, Wesley C., Dixon, Robert, and Anderson-Inman, Lynne. *Morphographic and root word analysis of 26,000 high frequency words*. Eugene, OR: University of Oregon College of Education, 1980.

Carroll, John, Davies, Peter, and Richman, Barry. *The American Heritage word frequency book*. Boston, MA: Houghton Mifflin, 1971.

Dahl, Hartvig. *Word frequencies of spoken American English*. Essex, CT: Verbatim, 1979.

Dupuy, H.P. *The rationale, development and standardization of a basic word vocabulary test*. DHEW Publication No. HRA 74-1334. Washington, DC: U.S. Government Printing Office, 1974.

Harris, Albert, and Jacobson, Milton. *Basic elementary reading vocabularies*. New York: Macmillan, 1972.

Marzano, Robert J., and Marzano, Jana S. *A study of basic words in elementary school textbooks*. Aurora, CO: Mid-Continent Regional Educational Laboratory, 1987.

MALASPINA COLLEGE LIBRARY

McKeown, Margaret. The acquisition of word meaning from context by children of high and low ability. *Reading Research Quarterly,* 1985, *20,* 482-496.

McKeown, Margaret, Beck, Isabel, Omanson, Richard, and Perfetti, Charles. The effects of long-term vocabulary instruction on reading comprehension: A replication. *Journal of Reading Behavior,* 1983, *15* (1), 3-18.

Mervis, Carolyn B. Category structure and the development of categorization. In Rand J. Spiro, Bertram C. Bruce, and William F. Brewer (Eds.), *Theoretical issues in reading comprehension.* Hillsdale, NJ: Erlbaum, 1980.

Nagy, William, and Anderson, Richard. How many words are there in printed school English? *Reading Research Quarterly,* 1984, *19,* 303-330.

Thorndike, Robert L., and Lorge, Irving. *The teacher's word book of 30,000 words.* New York: Teachers College Press, 1943.

# Chapter 3
# Some Instructional Uses of the Clusters

In this chapter we consider ways the clusters can be used to enhance vocabulary instruction by (1) establishing a frame of reference, (2) teaching words as labels, (3) teaching words at the experiential level, and (4) teaching words at the attribute level.

## Establishing a Frame of Reference for New Words

The most obvious use of the clusters is to establish a frame of reference for new words by presenting the clusters as general categories around which vocabulary learning will occur. The teacher might examine upcoming lessons to identify words central to the content or to understanding the story and then organize the words using Appendix B as a guide.

Suppose a teacher identifies five categories in which to organize words to be taught. The teacher explains to students that they will be studying a number of new words related to the upcoming unit or stories, then tells them the categories but not the vocabulary words. For example, the teacher might say that many of the new words will fall into the Occupations category, while others will be part of the Vehicles Used in Work category. Next, the teacher discusses the categories with the students and identifies example words for each category.

At this point it would be useful to identify anchor concepts for each category. Anchor concepts are words students already know that are representative of concepts in the category. For example, if a social studies teacher identified the Games that Are Popular in the United States category, some anchor concepts might be *baseball, football,* and *basketball.* As new concepts are introduced, students can relate them to the more familiar anchor concepts. They can ask themselves how the new words are similar to or different from the anchor words and use their knowledge of known words to help them understand related new words.

Students can keep individual vocabulary notebooks arranged by categories with anchor concepts displayed at the beginning of each category. As new words

**Figure 4**
**Sample Page from Student Vocabulary Notebook**

Category: Types of Mental Actions

Anchor Concepts: think, forget, remember, guess, wonder, solve

| Word | Similar Words | What It Probably Means |
|------|---------------|------------------------|
| ponder | wonder, examine | when you think deeply about something |
| derive | solve, predict, figure out | when you figure out something from something else |
| | | |

are identified, students enter them in the appropriate category with notes regarding their meaning. Figure 4 shows how a page might look.

The form of individual vocabulary notebooks may vary. Students might represent information about new words in different ways. It is only important that the notebook help students make connections between known and unknown words by using the categories.

## Teaching New Words as Labels

As we pointed out in Chapter 1, there are many ways of knowing a word, so different instructional strategies should be used to coincide with the different types of word knowledge.

Words can be labels for familiar concepts. Suppose students know the concepts *home* and *house*. Since they already have an experiential base for those concepts, learning *domicile* would require them only to associate a set of familiar experiences with an unfamiliar label.

Since experiences can be stored as mental pictures, kinesthetic associations, smells, or feelings, the teacher might ask students to create a mental picture of their house or some idealized version of a home. The teacher might then explain that *domicile* is another word with a meaning similar to *house* and *home* and is in the same general category.

To help reinforce the phonological label for domicile, students might repeat the word to themselves, a form of phonological rehearsal. If the phonological label is rehearsed enough it can be retrieved easily.

To reinforce the orthographic label, students might picture the word as if it were spelled on a mental screen. This form of orthographic or visual rehearsal often is used in visually based spelling strategies. The technique develops a strong mental picture of the spelling of the word.

In general, then, new words that are synonyms for known words can be approached as new labels rather than as new concepts. In this case, the instructional task is not so much that of developing an experiential base for words but of associating phonological and orthographic labels with known experiences that can be cued by known words within a cluster. The teacher's main task is to help students identify known words that are synonyms for or very similar to a new word. The new word is treated as a new phonological and orthographic label.

## Teaching New Words at the Experiential Level

Instructional clusters also can be used to teach new concepts — those words for which students do not have a readily available experiential base. Whether a new word is a new concept or a new label for a known concept is a very important distinction for instructional purposes. Teaching a new label for a known concept is a fairly straightforward process, but teaching a new concept can be a difficult and time consuming task. Recall from Chapter 1 that Klausmeier (1985) identified four stages of learning a concept. Teaching a concept at the experiential level might be likened to Klausmeier's concrete and identity stages, in which he emphasizes the need to have available the actual item or pictorial or other representation of the concept. We have chosen to use the term experiential level to emphasize that when students first learn a concept it is essential to create many experientially based associations with the new word.

The simplest way to establish an experiential base for a new concept is to have students do something directly related to the concept. For example, a teacher trying to establish an experiential base for *merge* might have students merge two or more objects. The teacher might demonstrate how various elements merge (e.g., two colors of paint merging to make a third) or provide students with materials they could merge.

If a direct experience is not possible, an indirect experience should be provided. Words in clusters are useful in providing indirect experiences. A teacher who wants to provide students with an indirect experience for *merge* could have them recall experiences they have had with words in the cluster where *merge* appears. *Merge* appears in minicluster 2v.2, which includes *join, marry, wed, link, connect, unite, fuse, combine, adjoin, merge*. Through discussion, the teacher can help students recall their experiences by saying "Can you think of a time when you joined two or more objects together? Describe to the person sitting next to you a time when you joined or connected something."

As students recount their memories, the teacher can add additional information. For example, "Sally, your description of joining two pieces of rope to make one long piece was good. Now, to merge the two pieces of rope you might have unraveled the ends and braided them together so they became like a single piece of rope rather than two pieces tied together."

Yuille and Marschark (1983) say that many of the concepts we know have indi-

rect experiential bases. For example, most adults have a rich understanding of *parachuting* even though they have never actually parachuted. This is because they have looked down from high places; they have jumped from a diving board into a swimming pool; they have experienced jolting sensations. All of these direct experiences are put together to form an indirect experiential base for *parachuting*.

**Figure 5**
**Types of Graphic Organizers**

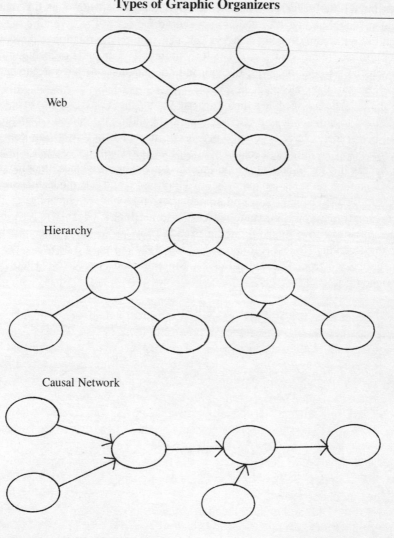

Once a direct or indirect experiential base is established for a new concept, students can begin to develop a mental representation for it. To do so, they make a point of remembering cues they will associate with the new concept. Their mental representations can take a number of forms, including episodic, semantic, and symbolic.

For an episodic representation, students rememeber specific events with which they associate the concept. For example, students might rehearse (replay in their minds) the experiment with the different colored paints done while developing an experiential base for *merge*. The teacher might talk students through this mental rehearsal, highlighting information they should include: "Try to picture the different colors coming together. See if you can picture in your mind the colors starting to merge into one. Try to smell the paint." The intent is to include many rich sensory associations with the episode so students will have a number of strong cues for the concept.

If students did not receive a direct experience for the new concept, the teacher might have to provide guidance, describing and building the episodic representation since students have no direct episodes from which to draw: "I'm going to describe a way of thinking about the concept *merge*. I will try to paint a picture you can see in your minds. One time I merged two things together. Imagine...."

A semantic representation involves words, phrases, and statements that are descriptors for the concept. A useful strategy here is to have students use graphic organizers to develop a semantic representation. Graphic organizers have been shown to be effective in tasks ranging from vocabulary learning to comprehension to notetaking (Jones, Amiran, & Katims, 1985). Figure 5 depicts a few organizers drawn from Dansereau (1985), Marzano and Arredondo (1986), and McTighe (1987).

**Figure 6**
**Sample Web**

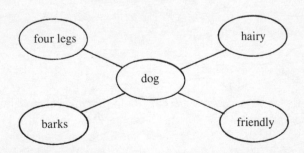

Although the type of graphic organizer used is arbitrary, certain types of organizers are most useful for certain types of concepts. For example, the web is best used for fairly concrete concepts. Figure 6 depicts a web for *dog*.

Hierarchies are most effective with general concepts with a number of subordinate concepts. Figure 7 is a hierarchic organizer for *woman*.

**Figure 7**
**Sample Hierarchic Organizer**

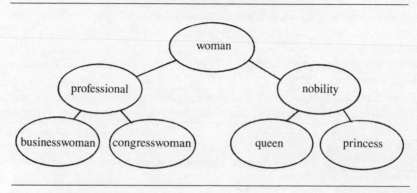

Causal network organizers are most effective with concepts involving actions or processes. Figure 8 is an organizer for *bake*.

**Figure 8**
**Sample Causal Network**

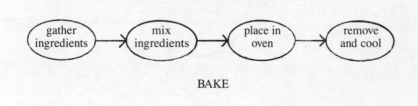

To use graphic organizers, a teacher would first present students with a direct or indirect experiential base for the concept. Then, instead of having students create a mental picture of the experience, the teacher would ask them to represent graphically the information they have learned about the concept as a result of the experience. For example, after students had witnessed the demonstration of the paints merging, the teacher might lead a discussion about the characteristics of

*merge*, listing them on the board. Students would be asked to represent graphically the information generated from the discussion. The teacher might provide a sample graphic organizer to help students get started.

**Figure 9**
**Semiconcrete Experience for 10 to 1**

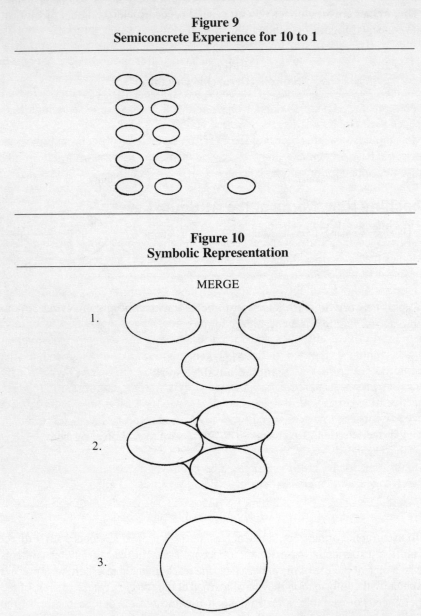

**Figure 10**
**Symbolic Representation**

Symbolic representations, the third type of mental representation, are something like the semiconcrete experiences described by Underhill, Uprichard, and Heddens (1980)—pictorial or pictographic representations of concrete experiences. Figure 9 is a semiconcrete experience of the ratio 10 to 1.

In a symbolic representation, the symbol system can be subjective, but not arbitrary. It should convey the meaning of the concept in a way that is appropriate to its socially understood meaning and understandable to the student. Figure 10 is a symbolic representation for *merge*. Once again, the teacher provides an experiential base for the concept and then asks students to generate a symbolic representation. Having students exhibit and explain their representations helps deepen their understanding.

In summary, teaching words at the experiential level involves providing an experiential base for students and then having them represent the information in an episodic, semantic, or symbolic fashion.

## Teaching New Words at the Attribute Level

Teaching words at the attribute level is a step up in complexity and sophistication from teaching them at the experiential level. Teaching at the attribute level assumes that an experiential base has been established. The emphasis is on making fine distinctions about the attributes of the concept.

Our notion of teaching words at the attribute level differs from Klausmeier's classificatory and formal levels in terms of the importance given to critical attributes. According to Smith and Medin (1981), vocabulary instruction techniques that stress critical attributes and formal definitions are basically Aristotelian. This is commonly referred to as the classical approach to word knowledge—that people do not know a concept until they can identify the class to which it belongs, its primary and secondary attributes, its definition, and so on. If this perspective were correct, most readers could claim to have a thorough knowledge of very few concepts. Anderson and Freebody (1981) report recent research indicating that literate adults are incapable of articulating the classical elements of even very basic English words.

Smith and Medin (1981) recommend a prototype rather than a classical approach to teaching attributes. An individual's prototypical knowledge for a well developed concept would certainly contain such classical elements as key attributes and examples of the concept, but probably these would not be exactly the same for any two individuals. However, there would be enough overlap between the elements known by two individuals to make their prototypes of the concept quite similar. This suggests that teachers should help students develop a large number of accurate classical elements for concepts rather than a few specific attributes considered to be critical.

If most concepts do not have critical attributes, then which attributes should be reinforced in instruction? The answer to this question rests with the teacher. That

is, the teacher should select attributes important to the concept and consistent with the students' backgrounds. The following list developed by Marzano and Arredondo (1986) can help teachers select attributes important to four classes of concepts: object, action, event, and state. These attributes are drawn from various case grammars and systems developed to describe the functions of words as used in propositions (Fillmore, 1968; Schlesinger, 1971; Shank & Abelson, 1977; Turner & Greene, 1977).

## Object Concepts

Object concepts usually are concrete and are expressed as nouns. Important attributes include

- the concept usually performs a specific action (an umpire)
- a specific action usually is performed on the concept (a punching bag)
- the concept commonly is used as an instrument or tool in a specific action (baseball bat)
- the concept is made in a specific way (wine)
- the concept is part of something (wheel)
- the concept has specific parts or can be divided up in specific ways (a country)
- the concept has specific characteristics relative to
    - taste (cake)
    - feel (silk)
    - smell (skunk)
    - sound (flute)
    - color (cloud)
    - number or quantity (ants)
    - location (Denver)
    - dimensionality (a diamond)
    - emotional states (a witch)
    - popularity (rock music)
    - commonality (a diamond)
    - danger (a gun)
    - value (a diamond)
    - freedom or ownership (a slave)

## Action Concepts

Action concepts usually take the form of verbs and express action. Important attributes include

- a specific person or thing usually performs the action (march)
- a specific instrument is used in the action (swing)
- something is produced as a result of the action (bake)
- as a result of the action, someone or something changes its state relative to

- smell (fumigate)
- taste (sweeten)
- feel (wrinkle)
- sound (tune)
- color (paint)
- number or quantity (multiply)
- direction (turn)
- location (send)
- dimensionality (lengthen)
- time or duration (stop)
- freedom or ownership (capture)
- emotional state (frighten)
- popularity (dislike)
- commonness (endanger)
- certainty (threaten)
- value (devalue)
- intensity (negate)
- there is a specific process or sequence of events involved in the action (bake)
- the concept involves
  - moving a specific body part (kick)
  - grasping an object (hold)
  - taking one object into another object (eat)
  - expelling an object (cry)
  - transferring information (speak)
  - acquiring information (listen)
  - focusing a sense organ toward a stimulus (look)

## Event Concepts

Event concepts are usually expressed as nouns, but they represent actions involving specific times, places, participants, and activities. Important attributes include

- the event has specific participants who are normally involved (a wedding)
- the event involves a specific process (football game)
- the event has a specific reason or causes specific results (a parade)
- the event occurs at a specific time (lunch)
- the event has a specific duration (dinner)
- the event occurs in specific locations (a dance)

## State Concepts

State concepts usually are expressed as adjectives or adverbs. Their basic function is to describe object, action, or event concepts. Common attributes include

- there are degrees of possessing the concept (angry)
- the state conveyed by the concept is acquired in a specific way (tired)
- the state conveyed by the concept excludes other states from existing simultaneously (dead)

These attributes are intended for teachers to use as guides for selecting attributes to emphasize with students. The best way to use the list is to read through it, selecting attributes important to the concept being taught. For example, a teacher who wants to reinforce specific attributes relative to *equilibrium* might read through the list of attributes, selecting those that appear most important to equilibrium. Rather than go through all the attributes, it is best to focus on the most appropriate ones for the general type of concept under study. It is a common mistake to use the part of speech of the concept to select its type (e.g., assume that all nouns are object concepts, all verbs are action concepts). Research and theory in linguistics (Chafe, 1970; Quirk et al., 1972) indicate that for many concepts the part of speech is not a good indicator of attributes. Some nouns are more like verbs than nouns; some verbs are more like nouns than verbs, etc. With this in mind, a teacher might go through the action concept attributes rather than the object concept attributes to identify important attributes relative to *equilibrium*. A useful technique is to change the attributes into relevant questions.

- Is there a specific person or thing that causes equilibrium?
- Is there a specific instrument used to produce equilibrium?
- Is something commonly produced as a result of equilibrium?
- As a result of equilibrium, does someone or something usually change its
    - smell, taste, feel, sound, color?
    - number or quantity?
    - direction?
    - location?
    - dimensionality?
    - time or duration?
    - freedom or ownership?
    - emotional state?
    - popularity?
    - commonness?
    - certainty?
    - danger?
    - value?
    - intensity?
    - truth?
- Is there a specific process to equilibrium?
- Does equilibrium involve
    - the movement of a body part?

- grasping an object?
- taking in an object?
- expulsion of an object?
- the acquisition of new information?
- focusing a sense organ?

*Based on these questions, the teacher might decide on two important attributes about equilibrium:* When two elements reach equilibrium, they have usually undergone a change of state relative to their dimensionality (they have changed shape or size), time or duration (they have shortened or lengthened their time or duration to become equal), or intensity (they have lessened or strengthened to become equal); and there is a specific process involved in reaching a state of equilibrium (the element greater than the other element on some dimension is lessened in that dimension, or the element lesser than the other element becomes greater in that dimension).

Going through the list of attributes is a tool to help teachers and students identify important attributes relative to a new concept. The list is not comprehensive and certainly is not meant to force teachers and students to think about concepts in specific ways. Teachers should feel free to select other attributes or to rephrase attributes whenever appropriate.

## Figure 11
### Semantice Features

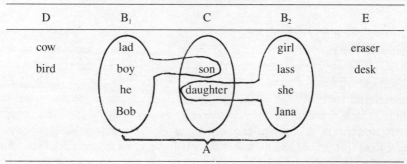

| D | B$_1$ | C | B$_2$ | E |
|---|---|---|---|---|
| cow | lad | | girl | eraser |
| bird | boy | son | lass | desk |
| | he | daughter | she | |
| | Bob | | Jana | |
| | | A | | |

Once important attributes for a concept have been identified, the next step is to reinforce the attributes with students. There are many useful techniques for doing this, all based on the notion of semantic feature analysis. Words are known at a semantic level by features they do or do not possess (Katz & Foder, 1963). Figure 11 illustrates semantic features. The words in set A are all human and two legged. These semantic features are important to understanding the words in the two groups. Of course, semantic features are simply a set of what we have re-

ferred to as characteristics or attributes. The words in B1 and B2 are differentiated because all B1 words contain the added semantic feature of being male; all B2 words have the semantic feature female. Words in set C do not share a male-female distinction, but they have a common semantic feature that might be labelled siblings.

Semantic feature theory posits that for each word we know we associate a number of features:

cow [animal] [concrete] [four legged] [milk producing]
girl [animal] [concrete] [two legged] [human] [female]
desk [not animal] [concrete] [four legged]

From this perspective, we might say that learning a word at the attribute level is a process of increasing the number of semantic features associated with a known word and making finer and finer distinctions among those features.

**Figure 12**
**Attribute Comparison Matrix**

|  | furry | barks | four legs |
|---|---|---|---|
| dogs | + | + | + |
| snakes | – | – | – |
| birds | – | – | – |
| horses | – | – | + |

To facilitate this, reading researchers (Johnson & Pearson, 1984) have developed what we call the attribute comparison matrix. To construct an attribute comparison matrix, the teacher lists a set of attributes in columns and a set of concepts along rows of a matrix (Figure 12). Words from clusters can be used to compare and contrast concepts by attributes. For example, a teacher might help students discover the important characteristics of *merge* by having them compare it with concepts in its minicluster (*marry, join, fuse*). They would identify (using check marks or pluses and minuses) the attributes of each concept. This can be followed by a number of additional activities. Students can suggest more words that share the same features as those in the matrix, then identify the shared features.

Next, students can analyze the matrix to develop some generalizations about the words. Students should discover that two words rarely, if ever, have the same pattern of semantic features. In other words, the pattern of attributes within a matrix eventually will differ when enough semantic features have been listed. In addition to discovering the uniqueness of words, students will learn the nature and structure of the categories into which words are grouped.

Finally, students can describe the similarities or differences among concepts in a matrix, developing simple descriptions or formal definitions. A simple description emphasizes any combination of attributes of particular interest to students. Some students might highlight the fact that two concepts share all but one attribute. Others might point out that two concepts share very few attributes yet still belong to the same general category.

A linguistic description that includes specific elements is a formal definition. Negin (1987) notes that a formal definition includes a superordinate category to which the word belongs, a subordinate category within the superordinate category, and the attributes that justify the word's inclusion in the subordinate category. For *merge,* students might note that it belongs in the supercluster Types of Motion and the cluster Joining Action, and then list some attributes from the attribute comparison matrix to justify its inclusion as a joining action.

In summary, the clusters can be used to facilitate instruction by providing a frame of reference, an experiential base for learning new labels and new concepts, and comparing new and known concepts.

The clusters provide a framework for basic vocabulary instruction. They also provide a structure for a number of enrichment activities. These are described in Chapter 4.

## References

Anderson, Richard, and Freebody, Peter. Vocabulary knowledge. In John T. Guthrie (Ed.), *Comprehension and teaching.* Newark, DE: International Reading Association, 1981.

Chafe, Wallace L. *Meaning and the structure of language.* Chicago: University of Chicago Press, 1970.

Dansereau, Donald. Learning strategies research. In Judith W. Segal, Susan F. Chipman, and Robert Glaser (Eds.), *Thinking and learning skills,* volume 1. Hillsdale, NJ: Erlbaum, 1985.

Fillmore, Charles J. The case for case. In E. Bach and R.T. Harms (Eds.), *Universals in linguistic theory.* New York: Holt, Rinehart & Winston, 1968.

Graves, Donald. The role of instruction in fostering vocabulary. In Margaret McKeown and Mary Curtis (Eds.), *The nature of vocabulary acquisition.* Hillsdale, NJ: Erlbaum, 1987.

Johnson, Dale D., and Pearson, P. David. *Teaching reading vocabulary.* New York: Holt, Rinehart & Winston, 1984.

Jones, Beau F., Amiran, MindaRae, and Katims, Michael. Teaching cognitive strategies and text structures within language arts programs. In Judith W. Segal, Susan F. Chipman, and Robert Glaser (Eds.), *Thinking and learning skills,* volume 1. Hillsdale, NJ: Erlbaum, 1985.

Katz, J., and Fodor, J. The structure of semantic theory. *Journal of Verbal Learning and Verbal Behavior,* 1963, *39,* 170-210.

Klausmeier, Herbert. *Educational psychology.* New York: Harper & Row, 1985.

Marzano, Robert J., and Arredondo, Daisy E. *Tactics for thinking.* Alexandria, VA: Association for Supervision and Curriculum Development, 1986.

McTighe, Jay. *Graphic organizers*. Baltimore, MD: Maryland State Department of Education, 1987.

Negin, Gary. *Inferential reasoning for teachers*. Dubuque, IA: Kendall/Hunt, 1987.

Quirk, Randolph, Greenbaum, Sidney, Leech, Geoffrey, and Svartvik, Jan. *A grammar of contemporary English*. London: Longman, 1972.

Schank, Roger, and Abelson, Robert. *Scripts, plans, goals and understanding*. Hillsdale, NJ: Erlbaum, 1977.

Schlesinger, I.M. Production of utterances and language acquisition. In Dan I. Slobin (Ed.), *The ontogenesis of grammar*. New York: Academic Press, 1971.

Smith, Edward E., and Medin, Douglas L. *Categories and concepts*. Cambridge, MA: Harvard University Press, 1981.

Turner, Althea, and Greene, Edith. *The construction of a propositional text base*. Boulder, CO: Institute for the Study of Intellectual Behavior, 1977.

Underhill, Bob, Uprichard, Ed, and Heddens, Jim. *Diagnosing mathematics difficulties*. Columbus, OH: Charles E. Merrill, 1980.

Yuille, John, and Marschark, Marc. Effects on memory: Theoretical perspectives. In Anees A. Sheikh (Ed.), *Imagery: Current theory, research and application*. New York: Wiley, 1983.

# Chapter 4

# Going Beyond the Clusters

Beck and colleagues (Beck, Perfetti, & McKeown, 1982; McKeown et al., 1983) found that having students involved in a wide variety of vocabulary activities improves vocabulary knowledge. Nagy and Anderson (1984) agreed that when students experience many different word learning activities their motivation and depth of word knowledge improves.

In this chapter, we consider six vocabulary development activities not tied directly to the cluster approach but that can be augmented by use of the categories: (1) making broad associations, (2) creating analogies and metaphors, (3) detecting errors in word use, (4) using morphology, (5) learning words from context, and (6) connecting reading and writing.

## Making Broad Associations

For students to understand words at a level deep enough to aid comprehension, they must make many and varied associations with the words (Nagy, 1985). This is supported by several theories (described in Chapter 1) claiming that word knowledge includes many ways of representing information.

Marzano et al. (1987) suggest asking students to make unusual associations with vocabulary words. If the vocabulary to be learned included *virtuoso, philanthropist, novice, hermit,* and *accomplice,* students might be asked to choose which word goes best with *crook* and which goes best with *monastery.* Similarly, students might be encouraged to respond affectively by signaling the emotions words elicit by saying yea or boo.

Underwood's (1969) nine memory cues (described in Chapter 1) can be used in guiding students to make associations. Questions to elicit these and other cues might include the following.

*Temporal.* Does the new word remind you of a specific event?
*Spatial.* Does the new word remind you of a particular spatial arrangement?
*Frequency.* Does the new word remind you of anything that happens over and
    over?

*Modality.* Does the new word remind you of a taste, smell, or sound?

*Acoustic.* Does the new word have a distinctive sound?

*Visual.* Does the new word remind you of an image?

*Affective.* Does the new word remind you of an emotion?

*Context.* Did you first read or hear the word in an unusual situation?

*Verbal.* Does the new word remind you of interesting information?

Students might ask themselves these questions about new vocabulary words and compare their answers, noting different ways individuals respond to words and different associations people make with words. They might also ask these questions about words in a supercluster, cluster, or minicluster, noting that closely related words often elicit similar reactions or that apparently similar words elicit very dissimilar reactions. To illustrate, consider the words in minicluster 4h.1: *whale, seal, shark, dolphin, walrus, porpoise, swordfish.* After students have answered the questions about each word, they might note that different emotional responses are elicited by *shark.* Where some students associate fear with the concept, others may associate fascination. Similarly, students may differ in the tastes, smells, and sounds they associate with the animals listed. By comparing their responses to words within a supercluster, cluster, or minicluster, students can deepen the number and types of associations they make with words and their knowledge of the words.

## Creating Analogies and Metaphors

In a broad sense, teachers use analogies whenever they relate known to unknown words. In a stricter sense, analogical reasoning is a specific type of thinking of the form *A is to B as C is to D.* According to Sternberg (1977), analogical reasoning includes four components: encoding, inferring, mapping, and applying. Encoding is identification of important attributes or characteristics within the analogy. Inferring is identification of the rule that relates adjacent concepts; for example, in the analogy feather is to bird as leaf is to tree, the relationship between adjacent concepts is part to whole. Mapping is identification of the relationship between nonadjacent terms—feather and leaf are parts, tree and bird are wholes. Applying is identifying the missing term, as in feather is to bird as _____ is to tree.

According to Lewis and Greene (1982), there are eight basic semantic relationships around which analogies are commonly built.

1. *Similar Concepts.* Adjacent concepts are synonyms or similar in meaning.
   jump: leap:: shout: _____
   a. whisper
   b. argue
   *c. scream

42

2. *Dissimilar Concepts.* Adjacent concepts are antonyms or dissimilar in meaning.
   this: that:: go: _____
      a. proceed
      b. run
     *c. come

3. *Class Membership.* Adjacent concepts belong to the same class or category.
   elephant: lion:: blue: _____
      a. bird
     *b. pink
      c. mood

4. *Class Name and Class Member.* One element in a set is a class name, the other is a member of the class.
   fork: utensil:: bee: _____
      a. flower
      b. spring
     *c. insect

5. *Part to Whole.* One element in a set is a part of the other element in the set.
   wheel: car:: heel: _____
      a. sidewalk
     *b. leg
      c. show

6. *Change.* One element in a set turns into the other element.
   plant: seed:: _____ : butterfly
      a. pollen
      b. wings
     *c. caterpillar

7. *Function.* One element in a set performs a function on or for another.
   tutor: student:: _____ : car:
      a. golf
      b. speed
     *c. driver

8. *Quantity/Size.* The two elements in the set are comparable in terms of quantity or size.
   valley: hole:: _____ : housecat:
      a. jungle
      b. mouse
     *c. lion

Students can use these relationships to form analogies among words within clusters. To illustrate, consider minicluster 1d.4—*boxer, runner, gymnast, fighter, diver, racer, wrestler, skier, lifeguard, skater, swimmer, acrobat, horseman.* Students might be given the following analogy and asked to create similar analogies using related words from the minicluster: gymnast is to gym as racer is to track. Once students have formed analogies, they should be asked to explain the relationships among the concepts in their analogies. What is the relationship between a gymnast and a gym? How is that similar to the relationship between a racer and a track?

A metaphor is similar to an analogy but the central tension in a metaphor is to identify how two seemingly different items are, in fact, similar (Ortony, 1980). The terms in a metaphor are usually called the topic and the vehicle. The topic is the principle subject to which the metaphorical term (or vehicle) is applied. Therefore, if one says that *A* is a *B* when *A* is not literally a *B*, then *A* would be the topic and *B* the vehicle.

Initially, teachers should provide students with a fairly clear representation of the nature and formation of metaphors. To illustrate, we will use the metaphor *love is a rose.* Here *love* is the topic and *rose* the vehicle. *Love* is not related to *rose* at a literal level, but rather at an abstract, attributional level. Literally, *love* and *rose* do not share any common attributes. However, if we consider their attributes in an abstract sense, we begin to see a relationship between the concepts. This is depicted in Figure 13. It is at the level of shared abstract attributes (desirable, double edged) that the connection or central tension between the two concepts can be seen. When presented with this sort of concrete representation of the nature of a metaphor, most students can learn to generate fairly sophisticated metaphors.

**Figure 13**
**Literal and Shared Attributes in a Metaphor**

| Literal Attributes of Love | Shared Abstract Attributes | Literal Attributes of Rose |
|---|---|---|
| an emotion | | a flower |
| sometimes pleasant | desirable | beautiful |
| can be associated with unpleasant experiences | double edged | has thorns |
| often occurs in adolescence | | comes in different colors |

Teachers can give students a metaphor using a word from a cluster (A skater is a ballerina on ice.), then ask the students to explain the tension of the metaphor using the structure shown in Figure 13. Then ask students to generate metaphors for the other words from the cluster. As with analogies, students should be asked to explain their metaphors, describing how the topic and vehicle are similar at the abstract attribute level.

Research indicates that the development of genuine metaphoric comprehension emerges long after a child has mastered the rudiments of language comprehension (Ortony, 1980). However, research also indicates that children have a capacity, although inadequately developed, to understand metaphoric relationships even before the age of five. Exercises requiring students to create metaphoric links between concepts are among the highest level cognitive activities that can take place in the classroom (Suhor, 1984).

Regardless of its apparent complexity and sophistication, developing vocabulary knowledge through metaphor is a skill well worth developing. As Ortony (1980, p. 361) states:

> It is more than a linguistic and psychological curiosity. It is more than rhetorical flourish. It is also a means of conveying and acquiring new knowledge and of seeing things in new ways. It may well be that metaphors are closely related to insight. Anecdotal evidence for this abounds in the history of science. Newton's apple and Kekule's snakes are but two famous examples.

## Detecting Errors in Word Use

One of the most powerful ways of reinforcing a deep understanding of words is to help students become aware of errors in word use and how the use and structure of language can change meaning. This was the basic reason behind Vosniadou and Brewer's (1987) recommendation that students engage in Socratic dialogue as an aid to understanding concepts. Several researchers have identified ways language use can affect the meaning of words (Lipman, Sharp, & Oscanyan, 1980; Toulmin, Rieke, & Janik, 1979). Negin (1987) describes ways teachers can help students develop an understanding of errors in language. Three common errors are ambiguity, vagueness, and use of confusing terms.

## Ambiguity

A word is ambiguous if it has more than one possible meaning and the reader cannot tell from context which is appropriate. The following statements are ambiguous:

Girls alone are permitted in the club.
Christine has a goldfish but she doesn't care for it.
How many records did he have?

Teachers can ask students to identify ambiguities in their own language. They also can identify ambiguous words in the clusters. For example, the following words could be ambiguous: *bright* (minicluster 38.a.4), *clear* (38a.4), *dull* (38e.2), *cheap* (28e.1), *broke* (28e.2). As an exercise, students might illustrate how words within clusters can be used ambiguously and tell the meaning implied in each situation.

## Vagueness

While ambiguous words can have several meanings in a context, a vague word has only one meaning, but it is not clear how it should be applied. Typically, vague words involve statements of quantity or degree. Each sentence below contains a vague word.

There were a lot of people at the beach.
Bill bought a new car.
Do you feel well?

Vague words are important. They are descriptive and are often easier to use than more precise terms. For example, we say "It is cold today" without specifying that it is thirty-one degrees. However, there are circumstances in which vagueness is out of place. In response to the question "When does water freeze?" a science teacher would not want to hear "When it gets very cold."

Teachers can have students identify vague words in clusters; the following have vague meanings: *small* (minicluster 3a.2), *tiny* (3a.2), *wee* (3a.2), *piece* (3f.3), *part* (3f.3), *more* (3g.8), *most* (3g.8), *long* (32f.1), *wide* (32f.1).

Students can illustrate how words are used vaguely and then tell a more precise way to say the same thing.

## Confusing Terms

Finally, some words or terms often are confused. For example

affect, effect: *Affect* is a verb meaning "to influence." *Effect* is used either as a verb or a noun. As a verb it means "to bring about" ("He effected a change through his persistance."). As a noun it means "result" ("The effect of the storm was felt for several days.").

already, all ready: *Already* is an adverb meaning that something has occurred prior to a stated time. ("He has already gone."). *All ready* is a phrase expresing a state of being prepared (He was all ready.).

Appendix C contains a number of commonly confused terms identified by Marzano and DiStefano (1981).

In addition to having students note these words and how they can be confused, the teacher might have students identify possible confusions between terms not

found in Appendix C. For example, students might note that *vow* and *oath* in minicluster 10i.1 are sometimes used synonymously when in fact they have different meanings. Similarly, they might note that *poise* and *grace* in minicluster 13b.2 are sometimes used incorrectly as synonyms. Making such fine distinctions in word use deepens students' knowledge of words being studied.

## Using Morphology

Knowledge of morphological relatedness among words is an important tool in determining the meaning of words from context (Nagy & Anderson, 1984). Sternberg (1985) stresses the importance of internal (verses external or contextual) cues to word meaning.

Nagy and Anderson (p. 326) note that internal approaches to word learning based on etymological or historical relationships among words are of little value in vocabulary instruction: "We remain highly skeptical of approaches to vocabulary that proceed on an etymological or historical approach which feigns that words such as *dialect, collect,* and *intellect* have some basic meaning in common." Similarly, Shepard (in Nagy & Anderson) has shown that knowledge of Latin roots is not strongly related to a knowledge of the meanings of words containing such roots.

Nagy and Anderson recommend teaching affixes that allow students to determine the various derived forms of a new word. They refer to a word and its derived form as a "word family." Teaching words together as families has a number of advantages. If the most frequent word in the family is known, this knowledge builds a bridge from familiar to new. For example, once the meaning of *drama* is taught, its derivations (*dramatist, dramatize, dramatization*) can be taught with little additional effort.

Teaching words in families calls students' attention to the process of word formation so they are more likely to take advantage of semantic relationships when learning new words on their own. In addition, covering a family of words familiarizes students with the changes in meaning that occur between related words, thus preparing them to deal with cases in which the semantic relationships among morphologically related words are not apparent.

Figure 14 lists suffixes that often change the part of speech of the words to which they are attached. This list can help to reinforce students' knowledge of word families. Students can apply these suffixes to the words in a cluster, noting changes in meaning that are produced. To illustrate, consider the words in minicluster 38b.1: *shine, sparkle, flash, glow, glitter, glisten, twinkle, shimmer, dazzle, radiate*. Students might experiment with the affixes in Figure 14, creating real and fabricated words and explaining their meaning. Some real words they might produce include *shiny, shiner, sparkly,* and *sparkler*. How do these words differ in meaning from their original forms? Some fabricated words they might produce include *flashable, glower,* and *glitterdom*. What might these words mean? (What would *glitterdom* be like?)

**Figure 14**
**Suffixes**

Suffixes marking nouns

| -acy | -ary | -ent | -ier | -ment | -tion |
|------|------|------|------|-------|-------|
| -age | -ate | -er | -ite | -mony | -tude |
| -an | -cy | -ery | -ism | -ness | -ty |
| -ance | -dom | -ess | -ist | -or | -ure |
| -ancy | -ee | -ette | -ity | -ory | -y |
| -ant | -eer | -hood | -ive | -ship | -yer |
| -ar | -ence | -ice | -kin | -ster | |
| -ard | -ency | -ie | -let | -teen | |

Suffixes marking verbs

| -ate | -en | -fy | -ify | -ise | -ize |
|------|-----|-----|------|------|------|

Suffixes marking adjectives

| -able | -ary | -escent | -ile | -ory | -wise |
|-------|------|---------|------|------|-------|
| -ac | -ate | -ful | -ine | -ose | -y |
| -aceous | -ble | -ible | -ish | -ous | |
| -al | -ent | -ic | -less | -some | |
| -am | -er | -ical | -like | -ty | |
| -ar | -ern | -id | -ly | -ulent | |

Suffixes marking adverbs

| -ally | -like | -ward | -wise |
|-------|-------|-------|-------|
| -fold | -ly | -ways | |

Johnson and Pearson (1984) recommend direct instruction in the following inflectional endings.

*Plural*
s — girls
es — watches

*Comparison*
er — taller
est — tallest

*Tense*
ed — jumped
ing — jumping
s — jumps

*Possessive*
's — Ann's, boy's

Ask students to use words in a cluster in their inflected forms. Similarly, give students activities in which they use prefixes. Some common Latin, Greek, and Anglo Saxon prefixes are listed in Figure 15.

Ideally, students will transfer the knowledge they gain from such word analysis activities to situations in which they are trying to determine the meaning of unknown words.

# Figure 15
## Prefixes

---

### Latin Prefixes

| | | |
|---|---|---|
| ab-, abs-, a- | from, away | abstain |
| ad- | to, toward | adjoin |
| ante- | before | antecedent |
| bene- | well, good | benefactor |
| bi- | two | bimodal |
| circum- | around, about | circumnavigate |
| con- | with | concurrent |
| contra- | against | contradistinction |
| de- | down | depress |
| dis- | apart, opposite of | dislike |
| ex- | out, from | excavate |
| extra- | beyond | extracurricular |
| in-, il-, im-, ir- | not | inept, illicit, immature, irrational |
| in-, im- | in | infringe, impede |
| inter- | between | intercede |
| intra- | within | intramural |
| intro- | within | introspection |
| juxta- | near | juxtapose |
| non- | not, opposite from | nonviolent |
| per- | through | perforate |
| post- | after | postmortem |
| pre- | before | predetermine |
| re- | again, back | reclaim, recoil |
| retro- | backward | retroflex |
| semi- | half, partly | semiskilled |
| sub- | under | submarine |
| super- | over | supersonic |
| trans- | across | transcontinental |
| ultra- | beyond, extremely | ultraconservative |

### Greek Prefixes

| | | |
|---|---|---|
| a-, an- | not | amorphous, anhydrous |
| ambi, amphi- | around, both | ambidextrous, amphibious |
| ana- | back, opposite | anaphase |
| anti- | against | antiwar |
| cata- | down | cataclysm |
| dia- | through | diatribe |
| dys- | bad | dysfunction |
| epi- | upon | epigram |
| eu- | good | euphemism |
| hyper- | beyond, excess | hyperactive |
| hypo- | under | hypotension |

**Figure 15**
**Prefixes (continued)**

| meta- | beyond, | metaphysics |
|---|---|---|
| | denoting change | metamorphosis |
| para- | side by side, near | paraphrase |
| peri- | around | perimeter |
| prot- | first | prototype |
| syn-, sym- | together | synchronize, symphony |

**Anglo-Saxon Prefixes**

| a- | in, on, of | ashore, akin |
|---|---|---|
| be- | near, about | beside |
| for- | off, to the uttermost | forswear, forbear |
| mis- | wrong, bad | misunderstand |
| out- | beyond, more than | outlaw |
| over- | too much | overcompensate |
| un- | not | unbeaten |
| with- | against | withstand |

Durkin (1976, pp. 54-55) has developed a two step method for teaching students to use information available from prefixes and suffixes as word analysis tools.

1. With derived and inflected words, prefixes and suffixes should be separated mentally from the root so that if the root is not familiar, its pronunciation can be worked out with the help of letter sound relationships.
2. Once a root is identified, the suffix immediately attached to it should be added. If there is a second suffix, that should be added next. The prefix is added last.

Durkin offers the following illustration of the analysis-synthesis process for derived and inflected words.

| *foretell* | *carelessness* | *unwanted* | *unenviable* |
|---|---|---|---|
| tell | careless | wanted | enviable |
| foretell | care | want | envy |
| | careless | wanted | enviable |
| | carelessness | unwanted | unenviable |

In addition to Durkin's generalized strategy, the following activities can be used to reinforce students' knowledge and use of prefixes and suffixes.

1. Select a root word to which many prefixes and suffixes can be added (e.g.,

*courage*). Have the students use a list of prefixes and suffixes and the dictionary to generate as many words as possible: *discourage, encourage, courageous.*

2. Have students create new words using common roots and affixes. Johnson and Pearson (1984, p. 102) illustrate this process using the following four sets of roots and affixes.

| trans | luno | graph | ological |
|-------|--------|-------|-----------|
| tele | helio | vis | ic (or al) |
| proto | stella | phon | ology |
| neo | terre | trop | phobia |

Students can select one prefix or suffix from each column to create such new words as *telelunophonology,* the study of sending sound across the moon.

3. Identify from the newspaper words that have roots and affixes. Have students break the words into their component parts.

4. Compound words also can help reinforce students' knowledge of morphological relationships among words. Compound words are usually defined as two words joined together to create a new word that has the combined meaning of the two root words. In many cases, this is an inaccurate definition. For example, consider *blackboard.* It means more than is suggested by the meaning of the two roots—*black* and *board.* Many instructional activities can be developed using a list of compound words.

   a. Separate compound words into their roots. Have students discuss the independent meanings of the roots and then the combined meaning in the compound word (for example, *afternoon, mailbox,* and *streetlight*).

   b. Make word puzzles by supplying students with definitions of root words for selected compound words. See if students can identify the compound words using these definitions.

   animal with wings + container used for bathing = (answer: birdbath)

   c. Have students separate compound words into their roots and discuss the meaning of those roots. This activity helps demonstrate that some compounds are truly composites of the meaning of both root words while others are not.

## Learning Words from Context

In Chapter 1, we noted that wide reading should be considered a primary vocabulary development technique. As students increase the amount and type of

reading they do, they increase the number of words they learn through context. Ekwall and Shanker (1983) say students should be taught the use of six basic contextual clues.

*Description clues.* A description of the word, often in a phrase set off by commas: The *general,* a great leader, was worried about the battle.

*Comparison/contrast clues.* A comparison or contrast of the unknown word to a known word: He was *upset* instead of happy about winning the election.

*Experience or familiar expressions clues.* A child's experience or knowledge of familiar expressions used to help determine the unknown word: She was as *quiet* as a mouse.

*Synonym clues.* A word with a similar meaning: Todd's *automobile* was one of the nicest cars on the block.

*Example clues.* An example given to provide the needed clues for identification: Cliff is extremely *competitive.* He will bet on almost anything.

*Definition clues.* A word directly defined in context: A *noun* is a person, place, or thing.

Sternberg (1985) offers a slightly different list of important contextual clues, which he calls external cues.

*Temporal.* Cues regarding the duration or frequency of the unknown word or when the unknown word can occur: A total *eclipse* of the sun occurs just a few times each century.

*Spatial.* Cues regarding the location of the unknown word or possible locations in which the unknown word can be found: The *biceps* are located above the elbow on the inner part of the arm.

*Value.* Cues regarding the worth or desirability of the unknown word or the types of affect the unknown word arouses: *Alcoholism* can cause great stress within a family.

*Stative descriptive.* Cues regarding the properties of the unknown word (size, shape, color, odor, feel): A *prairie* is flat and relatively dry with light but consistent vegetation.

*Functional descriptive.* Cues regarding possible purposes of the unknown word, actions the unknown word can perform, or probable uses of the unknown word: A *moped* can be used for daily transportation when the weather is not bad.

*Causal/enablement.* Cues regarding possible causes of or enabling conditions for the unknown word: A *tsunami* can occur in the South Pacific as a result of an earthquake at the bottom of the ocean.

*Class membership.* Cues regarding one or more classes of which the unknown word is a member or cues describing the general class to which the unknown word belongs: A tsunami is a type of *tidal wave* that has a particularly high speed.

*Equivalence.* Cues regarding the similarities or differences of the unknown word with known words: The *mode* is like the *mean* except that it is based on the most frequent score.

As students encounter unknown words in their reading, they can look for these and other clues and generate hypotheses as to what the unknown words mean. As students continue reading and gathering more information about an unknown word, they should shape their hypotheses, deleting inaccurate information and adding information not included in their initial guess. This is a process those involved in semiotic theory (Eco, 1976) and those interested in its application to language learning (Langer, 1983) refer to as *retroduction,* an initial "messy guess" as to what a word might mean. Eco notes that people routinely do this in activities ranging from everyday conversation to scientific inquiry. Highly creative acts of retroduction are involved in interpreting a complex literary text, solving criminal cases, and making new scientific paradigms (Eco, 1976).

It is during retroduction that clusters can be of use. When students encounter a new word and attempt to determine its meaning using contextual clues, they can also try to categorize the unknown word, identifing the cluster to which the unknown word logically belongs. Implicit in this categorization process is the comparison and contrast of the unknown word with known words. As students advance through the process of retroduction, gradually adding information to their understanding of a new word, they might also adjust the meanings of some of the known words in the category to which the unknown word has been assigned. This helps them look for new distinctions with which to differentiate words in a category.

Clusters can act as broad organizers in which to house words students learn through context as a result of their wide reading and language use. We believe that in a very direct sense this meets Nagy and Anderson's challenge (1984, p. 328) that "Vocabulary instruction ought...to teach skills and strategies that would help children become independent word learners."

Having students categorize new words they encounter in their reading and then compare and contrast them with known words in a category helps develop the priming function Jenkins, Stein, and Wysocki (1984) say is so important to learning words in context. Specifically, they found that repeated encounters with a new word do not insure that students will learn the word, even when the context is particularly rich for discovering the word's meaning. Instead, the word must be marked either in advance (e.g., the teacher primes students to the new words they will encounter in a passage) or after the fact (e.g., students record new words they encounter while reading).

## Connecting Reading and Writing

Researchers and theorists such as Applebee and Langer (1983) and Graves (1983) have noted that reading and writing are natural language activities and

should not be treated in isolation. Reading and writing reinforce one another. Duin and Graves (1987) found that focusing on vocabulary development during writing activities has a direct, positive effect on the quality of student writing.

Substantial research has been done on the writing process. Graves (1983) discribes the writing process in terms of choice, rehearsal, and composing. Cooper and O'Dell (1977) talk about writing as consisting of prewriting, writing, and revising. Glatthorn (1982) speaks of exploring, planning, drafting, and revising. Regardless of the terms used, writing is an identifiable process with phases or stages. Flower and Hayes (1980a, 1980b, 1981) have shown that these stages are not discrete or linear; when people write, they do not always explore, plan, draft, and revise. Instead, writing is much more iterative, with writers looping back to previous phases as they make decisions about content, form, and style. However, for instruction, it is useful to present students with a stage or phase model of writing.

The following description of how Hilary, a second grader, progresses through these stages, is based on Graves' model of choice, rehearsal, and composing (paraphrased from DiStefano, Dole, & Marzano, 1984, pp. 25-26).

*Choice.* Hilary talks to her teacher about seeing the movie *Bambi.* Her teacher encourages her to write something about the movie to share with her classmates. Hilary agrees and begins rehearsal.

*Rehearsal.* Hilary draws a deer in a forest with big bushes, trees, and other animals. When the teacher asks Hilary about the picture, Hilary says Bambi is looking for his mother, who died in the fire. Hilary begins to jot down words such as *fire, deer, Bambi,* and *mother.* Then she begins to compose.

*Composing.* Hilary asks her teacher for help. "I don't know where to begin," she says. "Should I start from when my mom and dad said they would take me?" "What do you think?" says her teacher. "I think I'll start with the fire in the forest." Hilary begins to write. "Once upon a time...." After three sentences, she stops. She asks her teacher to read what she has written. The teacher suggests that Hilary read her partial story to her friend Kim. When Hilary finishes, she says she will take the paper home and finish it. Kim tells her not to forget to say how the campers started the fire and offers a few more suggestions.

As the example illustrates, in the choice phase students select a topic to write about. During the rehearsal phase, they begin to shape the ideas they will express in their writing—transforming mental images to pictures, symbols, and words. During composing, students write, progressing through a series of drafts.

It is during the rehearsal phase that the clusters can be of most use. Once Hilary had decided to write about Bambi and had finished her drawing, the teacher could have guided her to some specific clusters that might contain useful concepts for Hilary to consider in her writing. For example, the teacher might have had Hilary examine the words in supercluster 4 (Animals) and respond to the question "What other types of animals might you want to mention in your story?"

Similarly the teacher might have asked Hilary to examine the words in supercluster 5 (Feelings/Emotions) to identify some emotions she might want to depict using her animal characters.

## Conclusion

In this book we have described various ways to use clusters to teach words and concepts while attempting to illustrate that such an approach has a sound theoretical and research base. Much research still must be done before such a system should be adopted on a large scale, but we believe there is enough evidence to justify field testing to determine the best audience for such instruction and the best words to teach. The techniques presented here and the clusters and basic words in Appendix A are one of the first steps in that effort. Readers are encouraged to adapt the techniques and categories to suit their own purposes.

### References

Applebee, Arthur, and Langer, Judith. Instructional scaffolding: Reading and writing as natural language activities. *Language Arts,* 1983, *60,* 168-175.

Beck, Isabel, Perfetti, Charles, and McKeown, Margaret. Effect of long-term vocabulary instruction on lexical access and reading comprehension. *Journal of Educational Psychology,* 1982, *74* (4), 506-521.

Cooper, Charles, and O'Dell, Lee (Eds.). *Evaluating writing: Describing, measuring, judging.* Urbana, IL: National Council of Teachers of English, 1977.

DiStefano, Philip, Dole, Janice, and Marzano, Robert. *Elementary language arts.* New York: Wiley, 1984.

Duin, Ann, and Graves, Michael. Intensive vocabulary instruction as a prewriting technique. *Reading Research Quarterly,* 1987, *22,* 311-330.

Durkin, Dolores. *Teaching word identification.* Boston: Allyn and Bacon, 1976.

Eco, Umberto. *A theory of semiotics.* Bloomington, IN: Indiana University, 1976.

Ekwall, Eldon E., and Shanker, James L. *Diagnosis and remediation of the disabled reader.* Boston: Allyn and Bacon, 1983.

Flower, Linda, and Hayes, John. A cognitive process theory of writing. *College Composition and Communication,* 1981, *32,* 365-387.

Flower, Linda, and Hayes, John. The cognition of discovery, defining a rhetorical problem. *College Composition and Communication,* 1980a, *13,* 21-32.

Flower, Linda, and Hayes, John. The dynamics of composing: Making plans and juggling constraints. In L.W. Gregg and E.R. Steinburg (Eds.), *Cognitive processes in writing.* Hillsdale, NJ: Erlbaum, 1980b.

Glatthorn, Allan. Demystifying the teaching of writing. *Language Arts,* 1982, *59,* 722-725.

Graves, Donald. *Teachers and children at work.* Exeter, NH: Heinemann, 1983.

Jenkins, Joseph, Stein, Marcy, and Wysocki, Katherine. Learning vocabulary through reading. *American Educational Research Journal,* 1984, *21* (4), 767-787.

Johnson, Dale D., and Pearson, P. David. *Teaching reading vocabulary.* New York: Holt, Rinehart & Winston, 1984.

Langer, Susanne K. Discursive and presentational forms. In Robert E. Innis (Ed.), *Semiotics.* Bloomington, IN: Indiana University, 1985.

Lewis, David, and Greene, James. *Thinking better.* New York: Holt, Rinehart & Winston, 1972.

Lipman, Matthew, Sharp, Ann Margaret, and Oscanyan, Frederick. *Philosophy in the classroom.* Philadelphia: Temple University Press, 1980.

Marzano, Robert J., and DiStefano, Philip. *The writing process.* New York: D. Van Nostrand, 1981.

Marzano, Robert J., Hagerty, Patricia, Valencia, Shelia, and DiStefano, Philip. *Reading diagnosis and instruction: Theory into practice.* Englewood Cliffs, NJ: Prentice Hall, 1987.

McKeown, Margaret, Beck, Isabel, Omanson, Richard, and Perfetti, Charles. The effects of long-term vocabulary instruction on reading comprehension: A replication. *Journal of Reading Behavior,* 1983, *15* (1), 3-18.

Nagy, William E. *Vocabulary instruction: Implications of the new research.* Paper presented at the conference of the National Council of Teachers of English, Philadelphia, 1985.

Nagy, William, and Anderson, Richard. How many words are there in printed school English? *Reading Research Quarterly,* 1984, *19,* 303-330.

Negin, Gary. *Inferential reasoning for teachers.* Dubuque, IA: Kendall/Hunt, 1987.

Ortony, Andrew. Metaphor. In Rand J. Spiro, Bertram C. Bruce, and William F. Brewer (Eds.), *Theoretical issues in reading comprehension.* Hillsdale, NJ: Erlbaum 1980.

Sternberg, Robert J. *Beyond IQ.* Cambridge, England: Cambridge University Press, 1985.

Sternberg, Robert J. *Intelligence, information processing and analogical reasoning: The computational analysis of human abilities.* Hillsdale, NJ: Erlbaum, 1977.

Suhor, Charles. Toward a semiotic-based curriculum. *Journal of Curriculum Studies,* 1984, *16,* 247-257.

Toulmin, Stephen, Rieke, Richard, and Janik, Allan. *An introduction to reasoning.* New York: Macmillan, 1979.

Underwood, B.J. Attributes of memory. *Psychological Review,* 1969, *76,* 559-573.

Vosniadou, Stella, and Brewer, William F. Theories of knowledge restructuring on development. *Review of Educational Research,* 1987, *57* (1), 51-67.

# Appendix A
# Words in Clusters

## Supercluster 1
## Occupations

### 1a Occupations (General)

| Minicluster | Grade Level | Part of Speech |
|---|---|---|
| **1a.1. Workmen** | | |
| workmen (workman) | 3 | N |
| worker (work) | 4 | N |
| b workman | 4* | N |
| laborer (labor) | 4* | N |
| professional (profession) | 5 | N |
| b craftsman | 5* | N |
| employee (employ) | 6 | N |
| **1a.2. Occupation** | | |
| b occupation | 3* | N |
| b career | 5 | N |
| b craft | 5 | N |
| b role | 5* | N |
| b profession | 6 | N |
| livelihood (life) | SS | N |
| employment (employ) | SS | N |
| **1a.3. Task** | | |
| b job | 2 | N |
| b housework | 3* | N |
| b task | 4 | N |
| b chore | 4 | N |
| b labor | 5 | N, V |
| production (produce) | 6 | N |

### 1b Supervisors/Assistants

| Minicluster | Grade Level | Part of Speech |
|---|---|---|
| **1b.1. Assistant** | | |
| assistant (assist) | 4* | N |
| attendant (attend) | 5 | N |
| b apprentice | 5 | N |
| b journeyman | SS | N |

---

**Key**

Basic words
  Basic words are preceded by *b*.
  All other words are followed by the basic word in parentheses.

Grade levels
  K-6   The grade level at which a word is introduced.
  *      Indicates a word does not appear frequently in student reading material, but when it does appear it is at the level indicated.
  –      Words or phrases for which a grade level could not be determined.

Content specific words are indicated by the content area in which they are used:
  SS   Social Studies
  EN   English
  MA   Math
  SC   Science

Part of Speech
  N          Noun
  V          Verb
  A          Adjective
  AV        Adverb
  AV (+ly) Adverb when suffix -ly is added
  PRO       Pronoun
  PREP     Preposition
  INT        Interjection
  DET       Determiner
  AX         Auxiliary verb
  RM         Relationship marker

For readers' convenience, this Key is repeated periodically throughout Appendix A.

Readers should note that many of the words on this list are sex stereotyped because the list is based on basals written before publishers began to reduce sex stereotyping in books for children.

## 1b.2. Boss

| Minicluster | Grade Level | Part of Speech |
|---|---|---|
| owner (own) | 3 | N |
| b boss | 4 | N |
| director (direct) | 4* | N |
| b foreman | 5 | N |
| manager (manage) | 5 | N |
| b landlord | 6 | N |
| employer (employ) | 6* | N |

## 1b.3. Supervisor

| | | |
|---|---|---|
| leader (lead) | 5 | N |
| b superintendent | 5 | N |
| supervisor (supervise) | 6 | N |
| overseer (oversee) | SS | N |
| b chairman | SS | N |
| administrator (administrate) | 6+ | N |

## 1b.4. Founder

| | | |
|---|---|---|
| producer (produce) | 5* | N |
| founder (found) | 6 | N |
| b sponsor | 6 | N |

## 1c Royalty/Statesmen

| Minicluster | Grade Level | Part of Speech |
|---|---|---|
| **1c.1. Governor** | | |
| b mayor | 4 | N |
| dignitary (dignity) | 4 | N |
| b official | 4 | N |
| governor (govern) | 5 | N |
| b congressman | 5* | N |
| ambassador (embassy) | 5* | N |
| b statesman | 5* | N |
| congresswoman (congressman) | 5 | N |
| b consul | 5* | N |
| b tribune | 6 | N |
| politician (politics) | 6 | N |
| senator (senate) | 6 | N |
| councilor (council) | 6 | N |
| b candidate | 6* | N |
| b delegate | 6* | N |
| **1c.2. Master** | | |
| b majesty | 3 | N |
| b master | 3 | N, V |
| b highness | 6 | N |
| b hidalgo | SS | N |
| **1c.2.1** _____ | | |
| b throne | 6 | N |
| **1c.3. King** | | |
| b king | 2 | N |
| b queen | 3 | N |
| princess (prince) | 3 | N |
| b prince | 3 | N |
| b knight | 5 | N |
| duchess (duke) | 5 | N |
| b duke | 5 | N |
| b sire | 5 | N |
| b earl | 5* | N |
| b baron | 5* | N |
| b sultan | 5 | N |
| b czar | 5* | N |
| b squire | 5* | N |
| b nobleman | SS | N |
| b sheik | SS | N |
| **1c.4. Emperor** | | |
| b lord | 3 | N, V |
| b chief | 3 | N |
| b monarch | 4 | N |
| b president | 4 | N |
| empress (empire) | 5 | N |
| emperor (empire) | 5 | N |
| b vice president | 6 | N |
| dictator (dictate) | SS | N |
| liberator (liberate) | SS | N |
| **1c.4.1** _____ | | |
| imperial (empire) | 5* | A |
| presidential (president) | 6* | A |

## 1d People in Sports

| Minicluster | Grade Level | Part of Speech |
|---|---|---|
| **1d.1 Winner** | | |
| winner (win) | 4* | N |
| loser (lose) | 6* | N |

## 1d.2. **Athlete**

| | | | |
|---|---|---|---|
| | player (play) | 4 | N |
| b | athlete | 6 | N |
| | contestant (contest) | 6 | N |

## 1d.3. **Fielder**

| | | | |
|---|---|---|---|
| | batter (bat) | 3 | N |
| b | baseman | 4 | N |
| | fielder (field) | 4* | N |
| | catcher (catch) | 5 | N |
| b | shortstop | 6 | N |

## 1d.4. **Wrestler**

| | | | |
|---|---|---|---|
| | boxer (box) | 1 | N |
| | runner (run) | 4 | N |
| | gymnast (gym) | 4 | N |
| | fighter (fight) | 4* | N |
| | diver (dive) | 4* | N |
| | racer (race) | 5* | N |
| | wrestler (wrestle) | 5* | N |
| | skier (ski) | 5* | N |
| b | lifeguard | 6 | N |
| | skater (skate) | 6 | N |
| | swimmer (swim) | 6 | N |
| b | acrobat | 6 | N |
| b | horseman | SS | N |

## 1d.5. **Coach**

| | | | |
|---|---|---|---|
| | trainer (train) | 2 | N |
| b | coach | 3 | N, V |
| b | umpire | 4 | N, V |
| b | referee | 6 | N, V |

## 1e Reporters/Writers

| Minicluster | Grade Level | Part of Speech |
|---|---|---|

### 1e.1. **Newscaster**

| | | | |
|---|---|---|---|
| | sportscaster (sportscast) | 4 | N |
| b | weatherman | 4* | N |
| | newscaster (newscast) | 5* | N |
| | announcer (announce) | 6 | N |

## 1e.2. **Writer**

| | | | |
|---|---|---|---|
| | reporter (report) | 3* | N |
| b | author | 4 | N |
| | poet (poem) | 4 | N |
| b | newspaperman | 4 | N |
| | writer (write) | 4* | N |
| | narrator (narrate) | 5 | N |
| | historian (history) | 6* | N |
| b | critic | 6* | N |
| | speaker (speak) | EN | N |

## 1f Outdoor Professions

| Minicluster | Grade Level | Part of Speech |
|---|---|---|

### 1f.1. **Hunter**

| | | | |
|---|---|---|---|
| | fisher (fish) | 4 | N |
| | hunter (hunt) | 4 | N |
| | trapper (trap) | 4* | N |
| b | fisherman | 5 | N |
| | camper (camp) | 5* | N |
| | tanner (tan) | 6 | N |
| b | gamesman | 6+ | N |
| b | sportsman | 6+ | N |

### 1f.2. **Miner**

| | | | |
|---|---|---|---|
| | miner (mine) | 4* | N |
| | digger (dig) | 5* | N |

### 1f.3. **Cowboy**

| | | | |
|---|---|---|---|
| b | cowhand | 2 | N |
| | cowboy (cowhand) | 2 | N |
| | ranger (range) | 4 | N |
| | rancher (ranch) | 4 | N |
| b | shepherd | 4 | N |
| b | scout | 4 | N, V |
| b | stockman | SS | N |
| b | herdsman | SS | N |
| | cowgirl (cowhand) | SS | N |

### 1f.4. **Farmer**

| | | | |
|---|---|---|---|
| | farmer (farm) | 2 | N |
| | gardener (garden) | 4 | N |
| | grower (grow) | 5* | N |
| b | serf | 6* | N |
| | picker (pick) | SS | N |
| | sharecropper (sharecrop) | SS | N |

## 1f.5. Logger

|   |   |   |   |
|---|---|---|---|
|   | logger (log) | 4* | N |
| b | lumberjack | 5 | N |
| b | woodcutter | 5 | N |
| b | woodsman | 5* | N |
|   | forester (forest) | 5* | N |
|   | cutter (cut) | 6* | N |
| b | lumberman | SS | N |

# 1g Artists

| Minicluster | Grade Level | Part of Speech |
|---|---|---|

## 1g.1. Painter

|   |   |   |   |
|---|---|---|---|
|   | painter (paint) | 4 | N |
|   | potter (pot) | 4* | N |
|   | artist (art) | 5 | N |
|   | designer (design) | 5* | N |
| b | architect | 6* | N |
|   | sculptor (sculpt) | 6 | N |
|   | photographer (photograph) | 6 | N |

## 1g.2. Musician

|   |   |   |   |
|---|---|---|---|
|   | musician (music) | 4 | N |
|   | conductor (conduct) | 5 | N |
|   | composer (compose) | 5* | N |
|   | singer (sing) | 6 | N |
|   | drummer (drum) | 6 | N |
|   | violinist (violin) | 6* | N |
|   | soloist (solo) | EN | N |

# 1h Entertainers

| Minicluster | Grade Level | Part of Speech |
|---|---|---|

## 1h.1. Actress

|   |   |   |   |
|---|---|---|---|
| b | model | 3 | N, V |
|   | dancer (dance) | 5* | N |
|   | actress (act) | 6 | N |
|   | actor (act) | 6 | N |

## 1h.2. Clown

|   |   |   |   |
|---|---|---|---|
| b | clown | 2 | N, V |
| b | barker | 4* | N |
|   | magician (magic) | 5 | N |
|   | comic (comedy) | 5 | N |
|   | juggler (juggle) | 5* | N |

## 1h.3. Entertainer

|   |   |   |   |
|---|---|---|---|
|   | entertainer (entertain) | 4 | N |
|   | performer (perform) | 5* | N |

# 1i Teachers/Advisors

| Minicluster | Grade Level | Part of Speech |
|---|---|---|

## 1i.1. Teacher

|   |   |   |   |
|---|---|---|---|
|   | teacher (teach) | 2 | N |
| b | professor | 3 | N |
| b | student | 4 | N |
| b | pupil | 4 | N |
|   | librarian (library) | 4 | N |
| b | principal | 5 | N |
|   | instructor (instruct) | 5* | N |
| b | tutor | 6 | N, V |

## 1i.2. Counselor

|   |   |   |   |
|---|---|---|---|
|   | counselor (counsel) | 6 | N |
|   | adviser (advise) | 6* | N |
|   | therapist (therapy) | 6+ | N |

# 1j Public Servants

| Minicluster | Grade Level | Part of Speech |
|---|---|---|

## 1j.1 Policeman

|   |   |   |   |
|---|---|---|---|
| b | fireman | 1* | N |
|   | firemen (fireman) | 1 | N |
| b | policeman | 2 | N |
|   | policewoman (policeman) | 2 | N |
|   | detective (detect) | 3 | N |
| b | officer | 4 | N |
| b | sheriff | 5 | N |
|   | inspector (inspect) | 5* | N |
| b | trooper | 6 | N |
|   | protector (protect) | 6* | N |

## 1k Scientists/Discoverers

| Minicluster | Grade Level | Part of Speech |
|---|---|---|
| **1k.1. Scientist** | | |
| scientist (science) | 3 | N |
| engineer (engine) | 3 | N |
| b astronaut | 4 | N |
| veterinarian (veterinary) | 4* | N |
| astronomer (astronomy) | 5 | N |
| archeologist (archeology) | 5 | N |
| biologist (biology) | 5* | N |
| mathematician (mathematics) | 6 | N |
| chemist (chemistry) | 6 | N |
| naturalist (nature) | 6 | N |
| geographer (geography) | SS | N |
| geologist (geology) | SC | N |
| meteorologist (meteorology) | SC | N |
| botanist (botany) | SC | N |
| **1k.2. Explorer** | | |
| inventor (invent) | 3 | N |
| explorer (explore) | 4 | N |
| discoverer (discover) | 5* | N |
| surveyor (survey) | 5* | N |
| researcher (research) | 6* | N |

## 1L Areas of Work

| Minicluster | Grade Level | Part of Speech |
|---|---|---|
| **1L.1. Business** | | |
| b business | 3 | N |
| b law | 4 | N |
| b military | 5 | N |
| education (educate) | 5 | N |
| b agriculture | 5* | N |
| b industry | 6 | N |
| b politics | 6 | N |
| b religion | 6 | N |

| **1L.2. Science** | | |
|---|---|---|
| b medicine | 3 | N |
| b science | 3 | N |
| b geography | 4 | N |
| b chemistry | 5 | N |
| b geology | 5* | N |
| b astronomy | 5* | N |
| b biology | 5* | N |
| b archeology | 6* | N |
| b architecture | 6 | N |
| b psychology | SC | N |
| b physics | SC | N |
| **1L.2.1 _____** | | |
| scientific (science) | 4 | A, AV (+ly) |
| geological (geology) | 6 | A, AV (+ly) |

---

### Key

**Basic words**

Basic words are preceded by *b*.
All other words are followed by the basic word in parentheses.

**Grade levels**

K-6   The grade level at which a word is introduced.

\*    Indicates a word does not appear frequently in student reading material, but when it does appear it is at the level indicated.

–    Words or phrases for which a grade level could not be determined.

Content specific words are indicated by the content area in which they are used:

SS   Social Studies
EN   English
MA   Math
SC   Science

**Part of Speech**

| | |
|---|---|
| N | Noun |
| V | Verb |
| A | Adjective |
| AV | Adverb |
| AV (+ly) | Adverb when suffix -ly is added |
| PRO | Pronoun |
| PREP | Preposition |
| INT | Interjection |
| DET | Determiner |
| AX | Auxiliary verb |
| RM | Relationship marker |

## 1m Occupations Related to Buying/Selling

| Minicluster | Grade Level | Part of Speech |
|---|---|---|
| **1m.1. Customer** | | |
| b customer | 3 | N |
| buyer (buy) | 5* | N |
| shopper (shop) | 6* | N |
| b patron | 6+ | N |
| **1m.2. Salesman** | | |
| peddler (peddle) | 3 | N |
| b merchant | 4 | N |
| b salesman | 4* | N |
| trader (trade) | 4* | N |
| seller (sell) | 5* | N |
| vendor (vend) | 6* | N |

## 1n Small Business

| Minicluster | Grade Level | Part of Speech |
|---|---|---|
| **1n.1. Blacksmith** | | |
| b goldsmith | 4* | N |
| b blacksmith | 5 | N |
| b shoemaker | 6 | N |
| cobbler (cobble) | 6 | N |
| **1n.2. Baker** | | |
| b butcher | 4 | N, V |
| baker (bake) | 4 | N |
| b grocer | 5* | N |
| b milkman | 6* | N |
| **1n.3. Tailor** | | |
| miller (mill) | 2 | N |
| b tailor | 4 | N, V |
| weaver (weave) | 4* | N |
| b tinker | 5 | N, V |
| florist (flower) | 6+ | N |

## 1o People Who Work in Offices

| Minicluster | Grade Level | Part of Speech |
|---|---|---|
| **1o.1. Businessman** | | |
| b businessman | 4* | N |
| businesswoman (businessman) | 4* | N |
| **1o.2. Secretary** | | |
| b secretary | 6 | N |
| typist (type) | 6* | N |
| receptionist (reception) | 6* | N |

## 1p Builders

| Minicluster | Grade Level | Part of Speech |
|---|---|---|
| **1p.1. Builder** | | |
| builder (build) | 3* | N |
| manufacturer (manufacture) | 5* | N |
| contractor (contract) | 6+ | N |

## 1q Printers

| Minicluster | Grade Level | Part of Speech |
|---|---|---|
| **1q.1. Publisher** | | |
| printer (print) | 3* | N |
| editor (edit) | 4* | N |
| publisher (publish) | 5* | N |
| b scribe | 5* | N |

## 1r People Who Clean Up

| Minicluster | Grade Level | Part of Speech |
|---|---|---|
| **1r.1. Janitor** | | |
| b garbageman | 4 | N |
| b janitor | 5 | N |
| custodian (custody) | 6+ | N |

## 1s Occupations Related to Money

| Minicluster | Grade Level | Part of Speech |
|---|---|---|
| **1s.1. Banker** | | |
| banker (bank) | 4 | N |
| b teller | 6* | N |
| cashier (cash) | 6+ | N |
| accountant (account) | 6+ | N |

## 1t Occupations Related to Prisons

| Minicluster | Grade Level | Part of Speech |
|---|---|---|
| 1t.1. **Prisoner** | | |
| prisoner (prison) | 4 | N |
| b slave | 5 | N |
| captive (capture) | 5 | N, A |
| warden (ward) | 6 | N |
| b inmate | 6+ | N |
| 1t.2. **Guard** | | |
| b guard | 3 | N, V |
| b watchman | 4* | N |
| b sentry | 6 | N |

## 1u Occupations Related to Medicine

| Minicluster | Grade Level | Part of Speech |
|---|---|---|
| 1u.1. **Doctor** | | |
| b doctor | 2 | N, V |
| b nurse | 3 | N |
| b patient | 3 | N |
| dentist (dental) | 4* | N |
| b physician | 5* | N |
| surgeon (surgery) | 6 | N |
| psychiatrist (psychiatry) | 6+ | N |

## 1v Occupations Related to Transportation

| Minicluster | Grade Level | Part of Speech |
|---|---|---|
| 1v.1. **Pilot** | | |
| b pilot | 3 | N, V |
| flier (fly) | 4 | N |
| b skipper | 5 | N |
| b porter | 5 | N |
| b seaman | 5* | N |
| copilot (pilot) | 6+ | N |
| b steward | 6+ | N |
| stewardess (steward) | 6+ | N |

## 1w Clergy/Religious

| Minicluster | Grade Level | Part of Speech |
|---|---|---|
| 1w.1. **Priest** | | |
| b cardinal | 3* | N |
| b minister | 5 | N |
| b priest | 6 | N |
| b bishop | 6 | N |
| b monk | 6 | N |
| abbot (abbey) | 6 | N |
| b prophet | 6 | N |
| missionary (mission) | 6 | N |
| b nun | 6* | N |
| b pope | 6+ | N |
| b deacon | 6+ | N |

## 1x Repairmen

| Minicluster | Grade Level | Part of Speech |
|---|---|---|
| 1x.1. **Carpenter** | | |
| b repairman | 3* | N |
| b plumber | 3* | N |
| b carpenter | 4 | N |
| b mason | 5 | N |
| mechanic (mechanics) | 6 | N |
| technician (technical) | 6 | N |

## 1y Legal Participants and Occupations

| Minicluster | Grade Level | Part of Speech |
|---|---|---|
| 1y.1. **Judge** | | |
| b judge | 3 | N, V |
| defendant (defend) | 4 | N |
| clerk (clerical) | 4* | N |
| b witness | 5 | N, V |
| lawyer (law) | 6 | N |
| b attorney | 6+ | N |
| prosecutor (prosecute) | 6+ | N |
| counselor (counsel) | 6+ | N |
| juror (jury) | 6+ | N |
| 1y.1.1 _____ | | |
| b trial | 4 | N |

## 1z Servants

| Minicluster | Grade Level | Part of Speech |
|---|---|---|
| 1z.1. **Maid** | | |
| b maid | 3 | N |
| servant (serve) | 3 | N |
| b butler | 3* | N |
| b usher | 5* | N, V |

## 1aa Occupations Related to Restaurants

| Minicluster | Grade Level | Part of Speech |
|---|---|---|
| 1aa.1. **Waitress** | | |
| b dishwasher | 2 | N |
| waiter (wait) | 4* | N |
| waitress (wait) | 4* | N |
| b chef | 5* | N |
| b busboy | 6+ | N |

## 1bb Messengers

| Minicluster | Grade Level | Part of Speech |
|---|---|---|
| 1bb.1. **Mailman** | | |
| operator (operate) | 4 | N |
| messenger (message) | 4 | N |
| b postmaster | 5* | N |
| telegrapher (telegraph) | SC | N |
| b mailman | 6+ | N |

## 1cc Occupations Usually Held by Youths

| Minicluster | Grade Level | Part of Speech |
|---|---|---|
| 1cc.1 **Babysitter** | | |
| babysitter (babysit) | 6+ | N |
| b paperboy | 6+ | N |

## 1dd Work Related Actions

| Minicluster | Grade Level | Part of Speech |
|---|---|---|
| 1dd.1. **Work** | | |
| b work | K | N, V |
| b struggle | 3 | N, V |
| b toil | 6 | N, V |
| b overwork | EN | V |
| 1dd.2. **Hire** | | |
| b hire | 5 | V |
| b employ | 5 | V |
| 1dd.2.1 _____ | | |
| b apply | 5 | V |
| 1dd.3. **Quit** | | |
| b quit | 4 | V |
| b resign | 5* | V |
| b retire | 6 | V |
| 1dd.4. **Usage** | | |
| usage (use) | 5* | N |
| b overuse | EN | N |

# Supercluster 2
## Types of Motion

### 2a General Motion

| Minicluster | Grade Level | Part of Speech |
|---|---|---|
| 2a.1. **Motion** | | |
| b motion | 4 | N, V |
| action (act) | 4 | N |
| movement (move) | 5 | N |
| activity (act) | 5 | N |
| 2a.1.1 _____ | | |
| movable (move) | 4* | A |
| motionless (motion) | 5 | A |
| b mobile | 5* | N, A, AV (+ly) |

## 2b Lack of Motion

| Minicluster | Grade Level | Part of Speech |
|---|---|---|
| 2b.1. **Stillness** | | |
| b stillness (still) | 4 | N |
| inertia (inert) | SC | N |
| b standstill | SS | N |
| 2b.1.1. _____ | | |
| b stationary | 5* | A |
| b static | SC | A, AV (+ly) |
| 2b.2. **Suspend** | | |
| b hang | 2 | V |
| b dangle | 4 | V |
| b suspend | 6 | V |
| 2b.2.1. _____ | | |
| suspension (suspend) | 6 | N |
| 2b.3. **Stay** | | |
| b stay | 1 | N, V |
| b wait | 2 | N, V |
| b remain | 4 | V |
| b hesitate | 4 | V |
| b pause | 4 | N, V |
| b linger | 4 | V |
| b falter | 4 | V |
| b putter | 4 | V |
| await (wait) | 4 | V |
| 2b.4. **Interrupt** | | |
| b interrupt | 4 | V |
| b delay | 5 | N, V |
| 2b.4.1 _____ | | |
| interruption (interrupt) | 6+ | N |
| 2b.5. **Rest** | | |
| b rest | 2 | N, V |
| b settle | 3 | V |
| b relax | 4 | V |
| b lounge | 6* | V |
| b bask | 6 | V |

## 2c Beginning Motion

| Minicluster | Grade Level | Part of Speech |
|---|---|---|
| 2c.1. **Begin** | | |
| b begin | 2 | V |
| b start | 2 | N, V |
| b introduce | 4 | V |
| originate (origin) | 6+ | V |
| 2c.1.1 _____ | | |
| beginning (begin) | 3 | N |
| introduction (introduce) | 4 | N |
| initiation (initiate) | 4 | N |
| 2c.1.2 _____ | | |
| beginner (begin) | 2 | N |
| 2c.1.3 _____ | | |
| b initial | 6 | A, AV (+ly) |
| introductory (introduce) | EN | A |

---

**Key**

Basic words
  Basic words are preceded by *b*.
  All other words are followed by the basic word in parentheses.

Grade levels
  K-6  The grade level at which a word is introduced.
  *    Indicates a word does not appear frequently in student reading material, but when it does appear it is at the level indicated.
  –    Words or phrases for which a grade level could not be determined.
Content specific words are indicated by the content area in which they are used:
  SS  Social Studies
  EN  English
  MA  Math
  SC  Science

Part of Speech
  N    Noun
  V    Verb
  A    Adjective
  AV    Adverb
  AV (+ly)  Adverb when suffix -ly is added
  PRO  Pronoun
  PREP  Preposition
  INT  Interjection
  DET  Determiner
  AX  Auxiliary verb
  RM  Relationship marker

## 2d The Act of Occurring

| Minicluster | Grade Level | Part of Speech |
|---|---|---|
| 2d.1. **Do** | | |
| b do | K | V |
| b commit | 6 | V |
| 2d.2. **Happen** | | |
| b happen | 2 | V |
| b undergo | 4* | V |
| b occur | 5 | V |
| 2d.3. **React** | | |
| react (act) | 4 | V |
| 2d.3.1 _____ | | |
| reaction (act) | 5* | N |

## 2e Completion

| Minicluster | Grade Level | Part of Speech |
|---|---|---|
| 2e.1. **Complete** | | |
| b end | 2 | N, V |
| b finish | 2 | N, V |
| b fulfill | 6 | V |
| b complete | 6 | V, A, AV (+ly) |
| b culminate | 6+ | V |
| 2e.1.1 _____ | | |
| completion (complete) | 6+ | N |

## 2f Halting/Stopping

| Minicluster | Grade Level | Part of Speech |
|---|---|---|
| 2f.1. **Stop** | | |
| b stop | 1 | N, V |
| b quit | 4 | V |
| b cease | 5 | V |
| b halt | 5 | V |
| 2f.2. **Prevent** | | |
| b prevent | 5 | V |
| b ban | 6* | V |
| b abolish | 6 | V |
| 2f.3. **Avoid** | | |
| b avoid | 5 | V |
| 2f.4. **Resist** | | |
| b resist | 5 | V |
| 2f.5. **Clog** | | |
| b filter | 3 | V |
| b smother | 5 | V |
| b clog | 5* | N, V |
| b muffle | 6 | V |
| b stifle | 6 | V |

## 2g General Actions Involving Coming/Going

| Minicluster | Grade Level | Part of Speech |
|---|---|---|
| 2g.1. **Arrival** | | |
| arrival (arrive) | 6 | N |
| departure (depart) | 6 | N |
| 2g.1.1 _____ | | |
| destination (destiny) | 6 | N |
| 2g.2. **Journey** | | |
| b trip | 2 | N |
| b travel | 3 | N, V |
| b journey | 4 | N, V |
| flight (fly) | 4 | N, V |
| b voyage | 5 | N |
| b expedition | 5 | N |
| b excursion | 5* | N |
| b safari | 5* | N |
| b tour | 6 | N, V |
| migration (migrate) | SC | N |
| 2g.3. **Adventure** | | |
| b adventure | 3 | N |
| b quest | 6 | N |
| 2g.3.1 _____ | | |
| exploration (explore) | 6 | N |
| 2g.4. **Leave** | | |
| b leave | 2 | V |
| b withdraw | 5* | V |
| b depart | 6 | V |
| b recede | SS | V |

| | | |
|---|---|---|
| 2g.5. **Vanish** | | |
| disappear (appear) | 3 | V |
| b vanish | 4 | V |
| 2g.5.1 ____________ | | |
| b appear | 3 | V |
| 2g.6. **Roam** | | |
| b wander | 3 | V |
| b roam | 4 | V |
| b stray | 5 | N, V |
| b migrate | 5 | V |
| b rove | 5 | V |
| 2g.7. **Come** | | |
| b come | K | V |
| b visit | 2 | V |
| b arrive | 3 | V |
| 2g.8. **Go** | | |
| b go | 2 | V |
| b approach | 4 | N, V |
| b proceed | 5 | V |
| b advance | 5 | N, V |
| b progress | 6 | N, V |

## 2h Pursuit

| Minicluster | Grade Level | Part of Speech |
|---|---|---|
| 2h.1. **Pursuit** | | |
| pursuit (pursue) | 6 | N |
| 2h.2. **Chase** | | |
| b chase | 2 | N, V |
| b track | 2 | V |
| b follow | 2 | V |
| b pursue | 5 | V |

## 2i Taking/Bringing

| Minicluster | Grade Level | Part of Speech |
|---|---|---|
| 2i.1. **Take** | | |
| b take | K | V |
| b bring | 1 | V |
| b move | 2 | N, V |
| b carry | 2 | V |
| b tote | 4 | V |
| b bear | 5 | V |
| 2i.2. **Return** | | |
| b return | 2 | V |
| 2i.3. **Get** | | |
| b get | 1 | V |
| b fetch | 4 | V |
| 2i.3.1 ____________ | | |
| b whisk | 3 | V |
| 2i.4. **Send** | | |
| b send | 2 | V |
| b mail | 2 | N, V |
| b ship | 2 | N |
| b relay | 5 | N |
| b dispatch | 5* | V |
| b transplant | 6 | N, V |
| b transfer | 6 | N, V |
| 2i.5. **Remove** | | |
| b rid | 3 | V |
| b remove | 4 | V |
| 2i.6. **Put** | | |
| b put | K | V |
| b give | 1 | V |
| b place | 2 | V |
| b set | 2 | V |
| 2i.7. **Deliver** | | |
| b present | 3 | V |
| b deliver | 3 | V |
| b deposit | 4 | V |
| b bestow | 5 | V |
| b distribute | 6 | V |
| 2i.8. **Import** | | |
| import (port) | 5* | N, V |
| export (port) | 6 | N, V |

## 2j Tossing Actions

| Minicluster | Grade Level | Part of Speech |
|---|---|---|
| 2j.1. **Throw** | | |
| b toss | 1 | N, V |
| b throw | 2 | N, V |
| b pass | 2 | N, V |
| b pitch | 3 | N, V |
| b flip | 4 | N, V |
| b heave | 4 | N, V |
| b cast | 4 | V |
| b fling | 4 | N, V |
| b thrust | 4 | N, V |
| b flick | 5 | N, V |

2j.2. **Catch**

| Minicluster | Grade Level | Part of Speech |
|---|---|---|
| b catch | 1 | N, V |

## 2k Pushing Actions

| Minicluster | Grade Level | Part of Speech |
|---|---|---|
| 2k.1. **Push** | | |
| b pull | 2 | N, V |
| b push | 2 | N, V |
| b drag | 3 | V |
| b haul | 4 | V |
| b tow | 4 | V |
| b yank | 5 | N, V |
| 2k.2. **Support** | | |
| b support | 4 | N, V |
| b prop | 4 | V |
| 2k.3. **Lean** | | |
| b lean | 3 | V |

## 2L Vibration

| Minicluster | Grade Level | Part of Speech |
|---|---|---|
| 2L.1 **Shake** | | |
| b shake | 2 | N, V |
| b tremble | 3 | V |
| b shiver | 4 | N, V |
| b quiver | 4 | N, V |
| b shudder | 5 | N, V |
| b twitch | 5 | N, V |
| b quake | 6 | N, V |
| 2L.2. **Flutter** | | |
| b flutter | 3 | N, V |
| b wiggle | 3 | N, V |
| b vibrate | 3* | V |
| b sputter | 4 | N, V |
| b flap | 4 | V |
| b throb | 5 | N, V |
| waver (wave) | 6 | N, V |
| 2L.2.1 _____ | | |
| vibration (vibrate) | 6 | N |
| 2L.3. Juggle | | |
| b juggle | 4 | V |
| b jumble | 6 | N, V |

## 2m Shifting Motion

| Minicluster | Grade Level | Part of Speech |
|---|---|---|
| 2m1.1 **Slide** | | |
| b slide | 2 | N, V |
| b shift | 4 | N, V |
| b skid | 4 | N, V |
| b slip | 4 | N, V |

## 2n Jerking Motion

| Minicluster | Grade Level | Part of Speech |
|---|---|---|
| 2n.1. **Jerk** | | |
| b bounce | 2 | N, V |
| b jerk | 3 | N, V |
| b snap | 3 | V |
| b jolt | 4 | V |
| b jut | 4 | V |
| b budge | 5 | V |
| b lurch | 5 | N, V |
| 2n.2. **Ajar** | | |
| b ajar | 3 | AV |

## 2o Ascending Motion

| Minicluster | Grade Level | Part of Speech |
|---|---|---|
| 2o.1. **Raise** | | |
| b raise | 3 | V |
| b lift | 3 | V |
| b load | 3 | V |
| b hoist | 5 | V |
| b boost | 6 | N, V |
| b elevate | 6* | V |
| 2o.2. **Rise** | | |
| b blast off | 1* | V |
| b rise | 4 | V |
| b mount | 4 | V |
| arise (rise) | 6 | V |
| b ascend | 6 | V |
| b clamber | 6 | N |
| 2o.2.1 _____ | | |
| ascent (ascend) | 6* | N |

## 2p Descending Motion (General)

| Minicluster | Grade Level | Part of Speech |
|---|---|---|
| 2p.1. **Fall** | | |
| b fall | 1 | N, V |
| b plunge | 3 | N, V |
| b collapse | 4 | V |
| b tumble | 4 | N, V |
| b topple | 5 | V |
| b descend | 5 | V |
| b plummet | 6* | V |
| 2p.1.1 _____ | | |
| descent (descend) | 6* | N |
| 2p.2. **Lower** | | |
| b drop | 1 | V |
| lower (low) | 2 | V |
| b lay | 2 | V |
| b dump | 4 | V |
| b fumble | 5 | N, V |
| 2p.3. **Sag** | | |
| b dip | 3 | N, V |
| b sag | 4 | N, V |
| b droop | 4 | V |
| b slump | 6 | N, V |
| b slouch | 6 | V |

## 2q Descending Motion Done by Human Beings

| Minicluster | Grade Level | Part of Speech |
|---|---|---|
| 2q.1. **Sit** | | |
| b sit | K | V |
| b squat | 4 | V |
| b crouch | 4 | N, V |
| b stoop | 5 | V |
| 2q.2. **Lie** | | |
| b lie | 3 | V |
| b flop | 3 | V |
| b sprawl | 5 | V |

## 2r Reduction

| Minicluster | Grade Level | Part of Speech |
|---|---|---|
| 2r.1. **Contraction** | | |
| contraction (contract) | 4 | N |
| compression (compress) | SC | N |
| b fission | SC | N |
| closure (close) | MA | N |

---

**Key**

Basic words
 Basic words are preceded by *b*.
 All other words are followed by the basic word in parentheses.

Grade levels
 K-6 The grade level at which a word is introduced.
 * Indicates a word does not appear frequently in student reading material, but when it does appear it is at the level indicated.
 – Words or phrases for which a grade level could not be determined.
 Content specific words are indicated by the content area in which they are used:
 SS Social Studies
 EN English
 MA Math
 SC Science

Part of Speech
 N Noun
 V Verb
 A Adjective
 AV Adverb
 AV (+ly) Adverb when suffix -ly is added
 PRO Pronoun
 PREP Preposition
 INT Interjection
 DET Determiner
 AX Auxiliary verb
 RM Relationship marker

### 2r.2. Shorten

| | | |
|---|---|---|
| b fade | 4 | V |
| shorten (short) | 4* | V |
| b compress | 4* | V |
| b condense | 4* | V |
| b shrink | 5 | V |
| b diminish | 5* | V |
| b wither | 6 | V |
| b dwindle | 6 | V |
| b shrivel | 6 | V |
| b reduce | 6 | V |

### 2r.3. Cram

| | | |
|---|---|---|
| b cram | 6 | V |
| b cramp | 6 | N, V |

### 2r.4. Crumple

| | | |
|---|---|---|
| b crumble | 5 | V |
| b crinkle | 6 | V |
| b crumple | 6 | V |

## 2s Expansion

| Minicluster | Grade Level | Part of Speech |
|---|---|---|
| **2s.1. Explosion** | | |
| explosion (explode) | 5 | N |
| expansion (expand) | 5* | N |
| extension (extend) | 6* | N |
| diffusion (diffuse) | SC | N |
| **2s.2. Enlarge** | | |
| b swell | 4 | V |
| enlarge (large) | 5* | V |
| b magnify | 5* | V |
| b expand | 6 | V |
| b inflate | SC | V |
| **2s.3. Billow** | | |
| b fluff | 4 | V |
| b billow | 4 | V |
| b bulge | 5 | N, V |
| **2s.4. Explode** | | |
| b burst | 3 | V |
| b blast | 4 | N, V |
| b erupt | 4* | V |
| b explode | 5 | V |
| b discharge | 6* | V |
| **2s.5. Scatter** | | |
| b scatter | 3 | V |
| b scramble | 4 | N, V |

### 2s.6. Uproot

| | | |
|---|---|---|
| b uproot | 6* | V |

## 2t Force

| Minicluster | Grade Level | Part of Speech |
|---|---|---|
| **2t.1. Pressure** | | |
| b force | 3 | N |
| pressure (press) | 5 | N, V |
| propulsion (propel) | SC | N |

## 2u Closing/Opening Actions

| Minicluster | Grade Level | Part of Speech |
|---|---|---|
| **2u.1. Close** | | |
| b close | 2 | V |
| b open | 2 | V, A, AV (+ly) |
| b shut | 2 | V, A |
| b slam | 4 | N, V |

## 2v Joining Actions

| Minicluster | Grade Level | Part of Speech |
|---|---|---|
| **2v.1. Connection** | | |
| connection (connect) | 4* | N |
| b bond | 5 | N, V |
| **2v.2. Join** | | |
| b join | 3 | V |
| b marry | 3 | V |
| b wed | 3* | V |
| b link | 4 | N, V |
| b connect | 5 | V |
| unite (union) | 5* | V |
| b fuse | 6 | V |
| b combine | 6 | V |
| adjoin (join) | 6* | V |
| b merge | 6* | V |
| **2v.2.1 _____** | | |
| fusion (fuse) | SC | N |

2v.3. **Wedding**

| | | |
|---|---|---|
| wedding (wed) | 4 | N |
| marriage (marry) | 6 | N |

2v.4. **Include**

| | | |
|---|---|---|
| b include | 5 | V |
| b involve | 5 | V |
| b assign | 5 | V |

2v.5. **Intersect**

| | | |
|---|---|---|
| b intersect | MA | V |

2v.6. **Meet**

| | | |
|---|---|---|
| b meet | 2 | V |
| b accompany | 5 | V |
| b encounter | 6 | V |
| b mingle | 6 | V |

2v.7. **Fasten**

| | | |
|---|---|---|
| b stick | 2 | V |
| b fasten | 3 | V |
| b hitch | 3 | V |
| tighten (tight) | 4* | V |

## 2w Separating Actions

| Minicluster | Grade Level | Part of Speech |
|---|---|---|
| 2w.1. **Separate** | | |
| b separate | 4 | V |
| b split | 4 | N, V |
| disconnect (connect) | SC | V |
| 2w.2. **Loosen** | | |
| unfasten (fasten) | 3* | V |
| loosen (loose) | 4 | V |
| unscrew (screw) | 5* | V |
| unwind (wind) | 6* | V |

## 2x Circular Motions

| Minicluster | Grade Level | Part of Speech |
|---|---|---|
| 2x.1. **Rotation** | | |
| rotation (rotate) | 5* | N |
| circulation (circle) | SC | N |

2x.2. **Spin**

| | | |
|---|---|---|
| b spin | 3 | N, V |
| b twirl | 4 | V |
| b orbit | 4 | N, V |
| b whirl | 5 | V |
| b rotate | 5 | V |
| b revolve | 6 | V |

2x.2.1 _____

| | | |
|---|---|---|
| orbital (orbit) | 6 | A |

2x.3. **Invert**

| | | |
|---|---|---|
| b reverse | 4 | V |
| b invert | SC | V |

2x.4. **Turn**

| | | |
|---|---|---|
| b turn | 2 | N, V |
| b sway | 3 | N, V |
| b swirl | 3 | V |
| b twist | 4 | N, V |
| b swerve | 6 | V |
| b pivot | 6 | V |

2x.5. **Surround**

| | | |
|---|---|---|
| b surround | 3 | V |
| enclose (close) | 6 | V |
| encircle (circle) | 6 | V |
| imprison (prison) | 6* | V |
| b encompass | 6* | V |

2x.6. **Around**

| | | |
|---|---|---|
| around (round) | K | PREP |
| b about | K | PREP |

2x.7. **Clockwise**

| | | |
|---|---|---|
| counterclockwise (clock) | 6 | AV |
| clockwise (clock) | 6* | AV |

# Supercluster 3
## Size/Quantity

### 3a Size (Small/Large)

| Minicluster | Grade Level | Part of Speech |
|---|---|---|
| 3a.1. **Size** | | |
| b size | 3 | N |

### 3a.2. **Small**

| | | |
|---|---|---|
| b little | K | A |
| b small | 2 | A |
| b tiny | 2 | A |
| microscopic (scope) | 4* | A |
| stubby (stub) | 5 | A |
| b wee | 5* | A |
| b compact | 5* | A |
| b miniature | 5* | A |

### 3a.3. **Large**

| | | |
|---|---|---|
| b big | K | A |
| b huge | 2 | A |
| b great | 2 | A, AV (+ly) |
| b giant | 2 | A |
| b large | 2 | A |
| b enormous | 3 | A, AV (+ly) |
| b grand | 4 | A |
| b vast | 5 | A, AV (+ly) |
| b mammoth | 6 | A |
| massive (mass) | 6 | A, AV (+ly) |
| b immense | 6 | A, AV (+ly) |
| monstrous (monster) | 6 | A, AV (+ly) |

### 3a.3.1 _____

| | | |
|---|---|---|
| b colossus | 6 | N |

## 3b Measurement Actions

| Minicluster | Grade Level | Part of Speech |
|---|---|---|

### 3b.1. **Measure**

| | | |
|---|---|---|
| b measure | 3 | N, V |
| b weigh | 3 | V |
| b order | 3 | N, V, AV (+ly) |
| measurement (measure) | 4 | N |
| b rank | 5 | N, V |
| b rate | 5 | N, V |
| b monitor | 6 | N, V |
| b sequence | 6* | N, V |

### 3b.1.1 _____

| | | |
|---|---|---|
| weight (weigh) | 3 | N |

## 3c Measurement Devices

| Minicluster | Grade Level | Part of Speech |
|---|---|---|

### 3c.1. **Ruler**

| | | |
|---|---|---|
| ruler (rule) | 4 | N |
| b scale | 4 | N, V |
| b thermometer | 5 | N |
| b compass | 5 | N |
| b yardstick | 5* | N |
| b gauge | 6 | N, V |
| protractor (protract) | MA | N |
| b abacus | MA | N |
| galvanometer (galvanism) | SC | N |
| seismograph (seismology) | SC | N |
| speedometer (speed) | 6* | N |

## 3d Things Commonly Measured

| Minicluster | Grade Level | Part of Speech |
|---|---|---|

### 3d.1. **Address**

| | | |
|---|---|---|
| b address | 3 | N, V |
| b longitude | 3 | N |
| b latitude | 3 | N |

### 3d.2. **Angle**

| | | |
|---|---|---|
| b meridian | 5* | N |
| b angle | 6 | N |
| b diameter | 6 | N |
| circumference (circle) | 6* | N |
| b radius | MA | N |
| vertex (vertical) | MA | N |

### 3d.3. **Census**

| | | |
|---|---|---|
| b countdown | 6 | N |
| b census | SS | N |

## 3e Specific Units of Measurement

| Minicluster | Grade Level | Part of Speech |
|---|---|---|
| 3e.1. **Mile** | | |
| b mile | 2 | N |
| b yard | 2 | N |
| b foot | 2 | N |
| b inch | 3 | N, V |
| kilometer (meter) | MA | N |
| decimeter (meter) | MA | N |
| centimeter (meter) | MA | N |
| 3e.2. **Watt** | | |
| b watt | 4* | N |
| b volt | SC | N |
| b ohm | SC | N |
| 3e.3. **Pound** | | |
| b pound | 3 | N |
| b ton | 5 | N |
| b gram | 5* | N |
| b ounce | 6 | N |
| kilogram (gram) | 6* | N |
| 3e.4. **Degree** | | |
| b degree | 4 | N |
| b grade | 5 | N, V |
| b metric | 6* | N, A |
| 3e.5. **Handful** | | |
| handful (hand) | 3 | N |
| cupful (cup) | 3* | N |
| b gallon | 4 | N |
| b bushel | 4 | N |
| b quart | 4 | N |
| mouthful (mouth) | 4 | N |
| b boatload | 4* | N |
| teaspoonful (teaspoon) | 4* | |
| spoonful (spoon) | 4* | N |
| b pint | 6 | N |
| b tablespoonful (tablespoon) | 6 | N |
| b pinch | 6 | N |

## 3f Partitives

| Minicluster | Grade Level | Part of Speech |
|---|---|---|
| 3f.1. **Speck** | | |
| b dot | 1 | N, V |
| b bit | 2 | N |
| b speck | 4 | N |
| b splinter | 4 | N, V |
| speckle (speck) | 4* | N |
| b particle | 6 | N |
| b fleck | 6 | N |
| 3f.2. **Type** | | |
| b type | 5 | N |
| b version | 6 | N |

### Key

Basic words
  Basic words are preceded by *b*.
  All other words are followed by the basic word in parentheses.

Grade levels
  K-6  The grade level at which a word is introduced.
  *    Indicates a word does not appear frequently in student reading material, but when it does appear it is at the level indicated.
  –    Words or phrases for which a grade level could not be determined.
  Content specific words are indicated by the content area in which they are used:
  SS   Social Studies
  EN   English
  MA   Math
  SC   Science

Part of Speech

| | |
|---|---|
| N | Noun |
| V | Verb |
| A | Adjective |
| AV | Adverb |
| AV (+ly) | Adverb when suffix -ly is added |
| PRO | Pronoun |
| PREP | Preposition |
| INT | Interjection |
| DET | Determiner |
| AX | Auxiliary verb |
| RM | Relationship marker |

## 3f.3. Part

| | | | |
|---|---|---|---|
| b | part | 2 | N |
| b | piece | 3 | N, V |
| b | member | 4 | N |
| b | section | 4 | N, V |
| b | factor | 4* | N, V |
| b | item | 5 | N |
| b | segment | 5* | N |
| b | ration | 6* | N, V |
| b | fragment | 6 | N, V |
| b | element | 6 | N |
| b | portion | 6 | N |
| | subset (set) | MA | N |

## 3f.4. Sample

| | | | |
|---|---|---|---|
| b | sample | 4 | N, V |
| b | specimen | 6 | N |

## 3f.5. Slice

| | | | |
|---|---|---|---|
| b | slab | 4 | N |
| b | chunk | 4 | N, V |
| b | sliver | 5* | N |
| b | scrap | 5 | N |
| b | crumb | 5 | N |
| b | slice | 5 | N, V |
| b | wisp | 6 | N |

## 3f.6. Category

| | | | |
|---|---|---|---|
| b | department | 4 | N |
| b | category | 6* | N |

## 3g General Amounts

| Minicluster | Grade Level | Part of Speech |
|---|---|---|

### 3g.1. Amount

| | | | |
|---|---|---|---|
| b | amount | 4 | N, V |
| b | quantity | 6 | N |
| | extent (extend) | 6* | N |

### 3g.2. Variety

| | | | |
|---|---|---|---|
| b | lot | 2 | N |
| b | number | 2 | N |
| | variety (vary) | 5 | N |

### 3g.2.1 _____

| | | | |
|---|---|---|---|
| | various (vary) | 4 | A |

### 3g.3. All

| | | | |
|---|---|---|---|
| b | all | K | N |
| b | whole | 3 | A, AV (+ly) |
| b | entire | 3 | A, AV (+ly) |

### 3g.4. Numerous

| | | | |
|---|---|---|---|
| | countless (count) | 4* | A, AV (+ly) |
| | numerous (number) | 5* | A |
| | infinite (finite) | 5* | N, A, AV (+ly) |
| b | abundant | 6 | A, AV (+ly) |
| | unlimited (limit) | 6* | A |
| | extensive (extend) | 6* | A, AV (+ly) |

### 3g.5 Several

| | | | |
|---|---|---|---|
| b | several | 3 | N, A |
| b | dozen | 4 | N, A |
| b | plenty | 5 | N |
| | abundance (abundant) | 5* | N |
| b | majority | 5* | N |

### 3g.6. Another

| | | | |
|---|---|---|---|
| b | another | 1 | N, A |
| b | other | 1 | N, A |
| b | extra | 3 | N, A |
| | additional (add) | 5* | A |

### 3g.7. Increase/Decrease

| | | | |
|---|---|---|---|
| b | increase | 4 | N, V |
| b | decrease | 6 | N, V |
| b | abound | 6* | V |

### 3g.8. Many

| | | | |
|---|---|---|---|
| b | many | 1 | N, A |
| b | more | 1 | N, A |
| b | most | 2 | N, A |

### 3g.9. Pair

| | | | |
|---|---|---|---|
| b | both | 2 | N, A |
| | twice (two) | 2 | N, A |
| b | pair | 2 | N, V |
| b | half | 3 | N, A |
| b | couple | 4 | N, A |
| b | double | 5 | N, A |
| b | two | 5* | N, A |
| b | twain | 5 | N, A |

### 3g.9.1 _____

| | | | |
|---|---|---|---|
| b | medium | 4* | A |

### 3g.10. Little

| | | | |
|---|---|---|---|
| b | little | K | N, A |
| b | few | 2 | N, A |
| b | less | 3 | N, A |

## 3g.11. Lack

| | Grade Level | Part of Speech |
|---|---|---|
| b lack | 4 | N, V |
| shortage (short) | 4* | N |
| scarcity (scarce) | 6* | N |

## 3g.12. Single

| | | |
|---|---|---|
| b only | 2 | A |
| b single | 3 | A |
| b lone | 4* | A |

## 3g.13. Partial

| | | |
|---|---|---|
| partial (part) | 5* | A, AV (+ly) |
| b scant | 6* | A, AV (+ly) |
| b finite | 6* | A |
| b sparse | 6* | A, AV (+ly) |
| fractional (fraction) | MA | A, AV (+ly) |

## 3g.14. Singular/Plural

| | | |
|---|---|---|
| b plural | 4* | A |
| singular (single) | 6* | A |

# 3h Cardinal/Ordinal Numbers

| Minicluster | Grade Level | Part of Speech |
|---|---|---|

## 3h.1. First

| | | |
|---|---|---|
| b first | 1 | N, A |
| b second | 2 | N, A |
| third (three) | 2 | N, A |
| fourth (four) | 2 | N, A |
| tenth (ten) | 3 | N, A |
| fifth (five) | 3 | N, A |
| sixth (six) | 3* | N, A |
| eighth (eight) | 3* | N, A |
| eighteenth (eighteen) | 3* | N, A |
| seventh (seven) | 4 | N, A |
| ninth (nine) | 4 | N, A |
| fiftieth (fifty) | 4* | N, A |
| thirteenth (thirteen) | 5* | N, A |
| fourteenth (fourteen) | 5* | N, A |
| sixteenth (sixteen) | 5* | N, A |
| thousandth (thousand) | 5* | N, A |
| seventeenth (seventeen) | | |
| nineteenth (nineteen) | 6* | N, A |
| fifteenth (fifteen) | 6 | N, A |
| twentieth (twenty) | 6* | N, A |
| twelfth (twelve) | 6* | N, A |
| eleventh (eleven) | 6+ | N, A |
| sixtieth (sixty) | 6+ | N, A |
| eightieth (eighty) | 6+ | N, A |
| ninetieth (ninety) | 6+ | N, A |
| millionth (million) | 6+ | N, A |

## 3h.1.1 _____

| | | |
|---|---|---|
| secondary (second) | 5* | A, AV (+ly) |

## 3h.2. Number

| | | |
|---|---|---|
| b number | 2 | N, V |
| b data | 4* | N |
| numeral (number) | 5 | N |
| b decimal | 5* | N |
| b digit | 6* | N |
| numeration (number) | MA | N |

## 3h.3. One

| | | |
|---|---|---|
| b two | K | N, A |
| b one | 1 | N, A |
| b three | 1 | N, A |
| b four | 1 | N, A |
| b five | 1 | N, A |
| b six | 2 | N, A |
| b seven | 2 | N, A |
| b eight | 2 | N, A |
| b ten | 2 | N, A |
| b thirty | 3 | N, A |
| b nine | 3 | N, A |
| b forty | 3 | N, A |
| b eleven | 3 | N, A |
| b fifty | 3 | N, A |
| b twelve | 3 | N, A |
| b hundred | 3 | N, A |
| b sixteen | 3 | N, A |
| b million | 3 | N, A |
| b twenty | 3 | N, A |
| b sixteen | 3 | N, A |
| b eighteen | 3 | N, A |
| b sixty | 4 | N, A |
| b thirteen | 4 | N, A |
| b seventy | 4 | N, A |
| b fifteen | 4 | N, A |
| b eighty | 4 | N, A |

| | | | |
|---|---|---|---|
| b | nineteen | 4* | N, A |
| b | ninety | 4* | N, A |
| b | fourteen | 5 | N, A |
| b | seventeen | 6 | N, A |
| b | billion | 6 | N, A |
| b | trillion | 6* | N, A |

## 3i Specifiers

| Minicluster | Grade Level | Part of Speech |
|---|---|---|
| **3i.1. No** | | |
| b no | K | DET |
| b a | K | DET |
| b an | K | DET |
| b the | K | DET |
| b every | 2 | DET |
| b each | 2 | DET |
| b either | 3 | DET |
| **3i.2. This** | | |
| b this | K | N, A |
| b that | K | N, A |
| b these | K | N, A |
| b those | K | N, A |

## 3j Diminishers

| Minicluster | Grade Level | Part of Speech |
|---|---|---|
| **3j.1. Generally** | | |
| b general (ly) | 4 | A, AV |
| roughly (rough) | 4 | AV |
| broadly (broad) | 5 | AV |
| approximate (ly) (proximate) | 5* | A, AV |
| **3j.2. Precisely** | | |
| b just | 1 | AV |
| alone (lone) | 2 | AV |
| b only | 2 | AV |
| exactly (exact) | 3 | AV |
| purely (pure) | 3 | AV |
| particularly (particular) | 4 | AV |
| simply (simple) | 4 | AV |
| precisely (precise) | 6 | AV |
| exclusively (exclude) | 6* | AV |
| specifically (specific) | 6* | AV |
| b in particular | – | AV |

| Minicluster | Grade Level | Part of Speech |
|---|---|---|
| **3j.3. Mostly** | | |
| largely (large) | 2 | AV |
| mostly (most) | 2 | AV |
| mainly (main) | 3 | AV |
| especially (special) | 4 | AV |
| notably (note) | 6* | AV |
| b at least | 6* | AV |
| **3j.4. Sufficiently** | | |
| b enough | 2 | AV |
| b rather | 3 | AV |
| sufficiently (suffice) | 6 | AV |
| b kind of | – | AV |
| b sort of | – | AV |
| b more or less | – | AV |
| **3j.5. Slightly** | | |
| partly (part) | 2 | AV |
| b mild (ly) | 4 | AV |
| slightly (slight) | 4 | A, AV |
| b mere (ly) | 4 | A, AV |
| b somewhat | 6 | AV |
| b moderate (ly) | 6* | AV |
| b in part | – | AV |
| b in some respect | – | AV |
| b to some extent | – | AV |
| **3j.6. Scarcely** | | |
| b hardly | 1 | AV |
| scarcely (scarce) | 4 | AV |
| barely (bare) | 6* | AV |
| b a bit | – | AV |
| b a little | – | AV |
| b in the least | – | AV |
| b in the slightest | – | AV |
| b in the least bit | – | AV |
| **3j.7. Almost** | | |
| b almost | 2 | AV |
| practically (practical) | 4 | AV |
| nearly (near) | 6* | AV |
| virtually (virtual) | 6* | AV |
| b as good as | – | AV |

## 3k Intensifiers

| Minicluster | Grade Level | Part of Speech |
|---|---|---|
| 3k.1. **Absolutely** | | |
| b most | 2 | AV |
| widely (wide) | 2 | AV |
| b quite | 2 | AV |
| fully (full) | 3 | AV |
| b complete (ly) | 3 | A, AV |
| perfectly (perfect) | 3 | AV |
| b entire (ly) | 4 | A, AV |
| totally (total) | 4 | AV |
| b absolute (ly) | 5 | A, AV |
| b utter (ly) | 5 | A, AV |
| b extreme (ly) | 5 | A, AV |
| b thorough (ly) | 6 | AV |
| b altogether | 6 | AV |
| exceedingly (exceed) | 6 | AV |
| exceptionally (except) | 6* | AV |
| b in all respects | – | AV |
| 3k.2. **Greatly** | | |
| b too | K | AV |
| b so | K | AV |
| b very | 1 | AV |
| b more | 1 | AV |
| b such | 2 | AV |
| badly (bad) | 2 | AV |
| deeply (deep) | 2 | AV |
| greatly (great) | 2 | AV |
| highly (high) | 2 | AV |
| b much | 2 | AV |
| b well | 2 | AV |
| b sure | 2 | AV |
| terribly (terror) | 4 | AV |
| intense (ly) (tense) | 6 | AV |
| b by far | – | AV |
| b a great deal | – | AV |

# Supercluster 4
# Animals

## 4a Animals (General)

| Minicluster | Grade Level | Part of Speech |
|---|---|---|
| 4a.1. **Pet** | | |
| b pet | 1 | N, V |
| b animal | 1 | N |
| b creature | 4 | N |
| b beast | 4 | N |
| b critter | 6+ | N |

---

**Key**

Basic words
> Basic words are preceded by *b*.
> All other words are followed by the basic word in parentheses.

Grade levels
> K-6   The grade level at which a word is introduced.
> *   Indicates a word does not appear frequently in student reading material, but when it does appear it is at the level indicated.
> –   Words or phrases for which a grade level could not be determined.

Content specific words are indicated by the content area in which they are used:

| | |
|---|---|
| SS | Social Studies |
| EN | English |
| MA | Math |
| SC | Science |

Part of Speech

| | |
|---|---|
| N | Noun |
| V | Verb |
| A | Adjective |
| AV | Adverb |
| AV (+ly) | Adverb when suffix -ly is added |
| PRO | Pronoun |
| PREP | Preposition |
| INT | Interjection |
| DET | Determiner |
| AX | Auxiliary verb |
| RM | Relationship marker |

## 4a.2. Mammal

| | Grade Level | Part of Speech |
|---|---|---|
| b mammal | 3* | N |
| b amphibian | 6* | N |
| invertebrate (vertebrae) | SC | N |
| b feline | 6* | N |
| b primate | 6* | N |

## 4a.2.1 _____.

| | | |
|---|---|---|
| b fossil | 4 | N |

# 4b Cats/Dogs

| Minicluster | Grade Level | Part of Speech |
|---|---|---|
| **4b.1. Lion** | | |
| b cat | 1 | N |
| b lion | 2 | N |
| b tiger | 2 | N |
| b panther | 4 | N |
| b leopard | 5 | N |
| b cougar | 5 | N |
| b wildcat | 5* | N |
| lioness (lion) | 6 | N |
| b puma | 6 | N |
| **4b.2. Wolf** | | |
| b wolf | 2 | N |
| b coyote | 4 | N |
| b dingo | 5 | N |
| b jackal | 6 | N |
| b hyena | 6* | N |
| **4b.3. Dog** | | |
| b dog | K | N |
| b bulldog | 4 | N |
| b mutt | 4 | N |
| b hound | 4 | N |
| b spaniel | 5 | N |
| b poodle | 5 | N |
| b terrier | 5 | N |
| b beagle | 5* | N |
| b collie | 5* | N |
| b greyhound | 6 | N |
| doggie (dog) | 6* | N |

# 4c Reptiles/Mythical Animals

| Minicluster | Grade Level | Part of Speech |
|---|---|---|
| **4c.1. Snake** | | |
| b rattlesnake | 3* | N |
| b snake | 4 | N |
| b serpent | 5 | N |
| b reptile | 5 | N |
| b anaconda | 5* | N |
| **4c.2. Dragon** | | |
| b dragon | 2 | N |
| b dinosaur | 4 | N |
| b unicorn | 5 | N |
| b monster | 5 | N |
| b nymph | 5* | N |
| b satyr | 6* | N |
| **4c.3. Alligator** | | |
| b turtle | 1 | N |
| b crocodile | 4 | N |
| b lizard | 4 | N |
| b alligator | 5 | N |
| b tortoise | 6 | N |

# 4d Baby Animals

| Minicluster | Grade Level | Part of Speech |
|---|---|---|
| **4d.1. Kitten** | | |
| b kitten | 2 | N |
| puppy (pup) | 2 | N |
| b bunny | 2 | N |
| b calf | 2 | N |
| b pup | 2 | N |
| kitty (kitten) | 3 | N |
| b colt | 3 | N |
| b cub | 4 | N |
| b tadpole | 4* | N |
| chick (chicken) | 4 | N |
| b fawn | 5 | N |
| b yearling | 5 | N |
| duckling (duck) | 6 | N |

## 4e Large Land Animals

| Minicluster | Grade Level | Part of Speech |
|---|---|---|
| **4e.1. Deer** | | |
| b deer | 2 | N |
| b reindeer | 5 | N |
| b doe | 5 | N |
| b antelope | 5 | N |
| b caribou | 6 | N |
| b elk | 6 | N |
| b gazelle | 6* | N |
| **4e.2. Horse** | | |
| b horse | 1 | N |
| b pony | 1 | N |
| b donkey | 3 | N |
| b mare | 5 | N |
| b burro | 5 | N |
| b stallion | 5 | N |
| b steed | 5 | N |
| b racehorse | 5* | N |
| b pinto | 6 | N |
| b stag | 6 | N |
| b bronco | 6* | N |
| b mustang | 6* | N |
| **4e.3. Cow** | | |
| b cow | 1 | N |
| b steer | 3 | N |
| b cattle | 3 | N |
| b ox | 4 | N |
| b longhorn | 5* | N |
| b bison | 6* | N |
| **4e.4. Goat** | | |
| b goat | K | N |
| b sheep | 2 | N |
| b lamb | 2 | N |
| b llama | 5 | N |
| b ram | 5 | N |
| **4e.5. Pig** | | |
| b pig | 1 | N |
| b sow | 3* | N |
| b hog | 4* | N |
| **4e.6. Anteater** | | |
| b anteater | 4 | N |
| b opossum | 4* | N |
| b sloth | 6* | N |

| Minicluster | Grade Level | Part of Speech |
|---|---|---|
| **4g.7. Bear** | | |
| b bear | 1 | N |
| b buffalo | 3 | N |
| b giraffe | 3 | N |
| b zebra | 4 | N |
| b camel | 5 | N |
| b yak | 5* | N |
| b bull | 6 | N |
| **4e.8. Fox** | | |
| b fox | 1 | N |
| b raccoon | 3 | N |
| b skunk | 3 | N |
| b weasel | 6 | N |

## 4f Rodents

| Minicluster | Grade Level | Part of Speech |
|---|---|---|
| **4f.1. Rabbit** | | |
| b rabbit | 1 | N |
| b kangaroo | 4 | N |
| b hare | 6 | N |
| **4f.2. Mouse** | | |
| b mouse | 2 | N |
| b hamster | 3* | N |
| b rat | 4 | N |
| b mole | 4* | N |
| b muskrat | 5* | N |
| b mink | 5* | N |
| **4f.3. Squirrel** | | |
| b squirrel | 2 | N |
| b porcupine | 3 | N |
| b chipmunk | 3 | N |
| b beaver | 4 | N |
| b woodchuck | 4 | N |
| b rodent | 6 | N |

## 4g Primates

| Minicluster | Grade Level | Part of Speech |
|---|---|---|
| **4g.1. Monkey** | | |
| b monkey | 2 | N |
| b chimpanzee | 4 | N |
| b baboon | 4* | N |
| b gorilla | 6 | N |
| b ape | 6 | N |

## 4h Sea Animals

| Minicluster | Grade Level | Part of Speech |
|---|---|---|
| **4h.1. Whale** | | |
| b whale | 3 | N |
| b seal | 4 | N |
| b shark | 4 | N |
| b dolphin | 4 | N |
| b walrus | 6 | N |
| b porpoise | 6 | N |
| b swordfish | 6 | N |
| **4h.2. Fish** | | |
| b fish | K | N, V |
| b snapper | 2* | N |
| b perch | 3 | N |
| b trout | 4 | N |
| b tuna | 4* | N |
| b sardine | 4* | N |
| b flounder | 5 | N |
| b cod | 5* | N |
| b salmon | 5* | N |
| b herring | 6 | N |
| b bass | 6 | N |
| b pike | 6 | N |
| b catfish | 6 | N |
| b halibut | SS | N |
| **4h.3. Minnow** | | |
| b minnow | 4 | N |
| b goldfish | 4 | N |
| b guppy | 5 | N |

## 4i Shellfish and Others

| Minicluster | Grade Level | Part of Speech |
|---|---|---|
| **4i.1. Jellyfish** | | |
| b starfish | 4* | N |
| b sponge | 6 | N |
| b lungfish | SC | N |
| b jellyfish | SC | N |
| b eel | 5* | N |
| **4i.2. Crab** | | |
| b shrimp | 4 | N |
| b lobster | 4* | N |
| b shellfish | 4* | N |
| b crab | 5 | N |
| b crayfish | 6* | N |
| **4i.3. Oyster** | | |
| b shell | 3 | N |
| b oyster | 4* | N |
| b clam | 5 | N |
| b barnacle | 5* | N |
| b mollusk | SC | N |
| b scallop | SS | N |
| **4i.4. Snail** | | |
| b slug | 5* | N |
| b snail | 6 | N |
| **4i.5. Octopus** | | |
| b octopus | 6 | N |
| b squid | 6 | N |

## 4j Birds

| Minicluster | Grade Level | Part of Speech |
|---|---|---|
| **4j.1. Robin** | | |
| b bird | 1 | N |
| b robin | 2 | N |
| b jay | 2 | N |
| b crow | 2 | N, V |
| b parrot | 3 | N, V |
| b wren | 3* | N |
| b canary | 4 | N |
| b sparrow | 4 | N |
| b bluebird | 4* | N |
| b lark | 4* | N |
| b pigeon | 5 | N |
| b parakeet | 5* | N |
| b woodpecker | 6* | N |
| **4j.2. Finch** | | |
| b hummingbird | 3* | N |
| b starling | 3* | N |
| b songbird | 4 | N |
| b cuckoo | 5 | N |
| b oriole | 5 | N |
| b dove | 5 | N |
| b raven | 5 | N |
| b mockingbird | 5* | N |
| b finch | 5* | N |
| b nightingale | 6* | N |
| b plover | SC | N |

### 4j.3. **Chicken**

| | | |
|---|---|---|
| b hen | 1 | N |
| b turkey | 3 | N |
| b rooster | 3 | N |
| b cock | 5 | N |
| b chicken | 5 | N |
| b fowl | 5* | N |

### 4j.4. **Ostrich**

| | | |
|---|---|---|
| b crane | 5 | N |
| b ostrich | 6 | N |
| b swan | 6 | N |

### 4j.5. **Hawk**

| | | |
|---|---|---|
| b owl | 2 | N |
| b eagle | 3 | N |
| b hawk | 4 | N |
| b falcon | 5* | N |
| b vulture | 6 | N |

### 4j.6. **Pheasant**

| | | |
|---|---|---|
| b partridge | 5* | N |
| b quail | 6 | N |
| b pheasant | 6 | N |

### 4j.7. **Duck**

| | | |
|---|---|---|
| b duck | 1 | N |
| b goose | 2 | N |
| b mallard | 4* | N |
| b gull | 5 | N |
| b drake | 5* | N |
| b gannet | 6 | N |
| b albatross | 6* | N |
| b platypus | 6* | N |
| b gander | 6* | N |

## 4k Insects

| Minicluster | Grade Level | Part of Speech |
|---|---|---|
| **4k.1. Mosquito** | | |
| b fly | 1 | N, V |
| b bee | 1 | N |
| b butterfly | 3 | N |
| b insect | 3 | N |
| b bug | 3 | N, V |
| b grasshopper | 3* | N |
| b dragonfly | 3* | N |
| b flea | 4 | N |
| b mosquito | 4 | N |
| b firefly | 4 | N |

| | | |
|---|---|---|
| b mantis | 4* | N |
| b wasp | 5 | N |
| b drone | 5 | N |
| b gnat | 5 | N |
| b hornet | 5 | N |
| b moth | 6 | N |
| b mite | 6 | N |
| b cicada | 6 | N |
| b ladybug | 6 | N |

### 4k.2. **Spider**

| | | |
|---|---|---|
| b caterpillar | 2* | N |
| b spider | 3 | N |
| b ant | 4 | N |
| b worm | 4 | N |
| b cricket | 4 | N |
| b silkworm | 4* | N |
| b termite | 4* | N |
| b cockroach | 5 | N |
| b beetle | 5 | N |
| b earthworm | 5 | N |
| b roundworm | SC | N |

---

**Key**

Basic words

    Basic words are preceded by *b*.
    All other words are followed by the basic word in parentheses.

Grade levels

  K-6  The grade level at which a word is introduced.

   *    Indicates a word does not appear frequently in student reading material, but when it does appear it is at the level indicated.

  –    Words or phrases for which a grade level could not be determined.

Content specific words are indicated by the content area in which they are used:

| | |
|---|---|
| SS | Social Studies |
| EN | English |
| MA | Math |
| SC | Science |

Part of Speech

| | |
|---|---|
| N | Noun |
| V | Verb |
| A | Adjective |
| AV | Adverb |
| AV (+ly) | Adverb when suffix -ly is added |
| PRO | Pronoun |
| PREP | Preposition |
| INT | Interjection |
| DET | Determiner |
| AX | Auxiliary verb |
| RM | Relationship marker |

## 4L Parts of Animals

| Minicluster | Grade Level | Part of Speech |
|---|---|---|
| **4L.1. Hide** | | |
| b hide | 2 | N |
| b deerskin | 5 | N |
| b goatskin | 5 | N |
| b pelt | 6 | N |
| b fleece | 6 | N |
| **4L.2. Mane** | | |
| b fur | 3 | N |
| b whisker | 3 | N |
| b mane | 4 | N |
| **4L.3. Feather** | | |
| b quill | 4* | N |
| b plume | 6 | N |
| b feather | 6 | N |
| **4L.4. Beak** | | |
| b beak | 4 | N |
| b snout | 6 | N |
| b duckbill | 6 | N |
| b bill | 6 | N |
| **4L.5. Tail** | | |
| b tail | 2 | N |
| b paw | 2 | N, V |
| b flipper | 3* | N |
| b claw | 4 | N, V |
| b fin | 4 | N |
| b hoof | 4 | N |
| **4L.6. Tusk** | | |
| b tusk | 4 | N |
| b ivory | 5 | N |
| b antler | 5 | N |
| b antenna | 5* | N |
| **4L.7. Gill** | | |
| b sac | SC | N |
| b pouch | SC | N |
| b gill | SC | N |

## 4m Animal Dwellings

| Minicluster | Grade Level | Part of Speech |
|---|---|---|
| **4m.1. Kennel** | | |
| b zoo | 1 | N |
| b stall | 3 | N |
| b doghouse | 3* | N |
| b kennel | 4 | N |
| b stable | 4 | N |
| b corral | 5 | N |
| aquarium (aqua) | 5 | N |
| b coop | 5* | N |
| b livery | SS | N |
| b stockyard | SS | N |
| **4m.2. Nest** | | |
| b nest | 2 | N, V |
| b beehive | 4 | N |
| b cocoon | 4* | N |
| b hive | 5* | N |

## 4n Animal Equipment

| Minicluster | Grade Level | Part of Speech |
|---|---|---|
| **4n.1. Saddle** | | |
| b rein | 3 | N |
| b saddle | 3 | N, V |
| b horseshoe | 3* | N |
| b harness | 4 | N, V |
| b collar | 4 | N, V |
| b bridle | 4 | N, V |
| b leash | 4 | N |
| b stirrup | 5 | N |
| b yoke | 6 | N, V |
| b muzzle | 6 | N, V |

## 4o Animal Actions

| Minicluster | Grade Level | Part of Speech |
|---|---|---|
| **4o.1. Swoop** | | |
| b fly | 1 | V |
| b swoop | 4 | V |
| b soar | 4 | V |
| b swarm | 4 | N, V |
| b sting | 4 | N, V |

**4o.2. Graze**

| | | |
|---|---|---|
| b graze | 4 | V |

**4o.3. Gallop**

| | | |
|---|---|---|
| b buck | 4 | V |
| b gallop | 4 | N, V |
| b stampede | 5 | N, V |
| b canter | 6 | N, V |

**4o.4. Hunt**

| | | |
|---|---|---|
| b trap | 2 | N, V |
| b hunt | 2 | N, V |
| b snare | 6 | N, V |

**4o.5. Horseback**

| | | |
|---|---|---|
| b horseback | 4* | A |
| b bareback | 5 | A |
| horseless (horse) | SS | A |

# Supercluster 5
## Feelings/Emotions

### 5a Names for Feelings (General)

| Minicluster | Grade Level | Part of Speech |
|---|---|---|
| **5a.1. Mood** | | |
| feeling (feel) | 4 | N |
| b mood | 4 | N |
| b emotion | 5 | N |
| b impluse | 5 | N |
| impression (impress) | 6 | N |
| sensation (sense) | 6 | N |

### 5b Fear

| Minicluster | Grade Level | Part of Speech |
|---|---|---|
| **5b.2. Fright** | | |
| b alarm | 3 | N, V |
| b fright | 3 | N |
| b fear | 4 | N, V |
| b shock | 4 | N, V |
| b terror | 4 | N |
| b horror | 5 | N |
| b panic | 5 | N |
| b agony | 6 | N |
| desperation (despair) | 6 | N |

**5b.2. Startle**

| | | |
|---|---|---|
| b scare | 2 | N, V |
| frighten (fright) | 2 | V |
| b startle | 3 | V |
| b haunt | 4 | V |
| b petrify | 4* | V |
| terrify (terror) | 5 | V |
| horrify (horror) | 5 | V |

**5b.3. Afraid**

| | | |
|---|---|---|
| b afraid | 2 | A |
| fearful (fear) | 3 | A, AV (+ly) |
| cautious (caution) | 4 | A, AV (+ly) |
| desperate (despair) | 4 | A, AV (+ly) |
| b frantic | 5 | A, AV (+ly) |
| b eerie | 6 | A |
| frightful (fright) | 6* | A, AV (+ly) |

### 5c Actions Associated with Fear

| Minicluster | Grade Level | Part of Speech |
|---|---|---|
| **5c.1. Cower** | | |
| b cower | 6 | V |
| b wince | 6 | V |
| b flinch | 6 | V |

### 5d Worry/Guilt

| Minicluster | Grade Level | Part of Speech |
|---|---|---|
| **5d.1. Guilt** | | |
| b guilt | 5 | N |
| b shame | 6 | N, V |
| humiliation (humiliate) | 6 | N |
| embarrassment (embarrass) | 6 | N |
| **5d.1.1** _____ | | |
| guilty (guilt) | 6 | A |
| **5d.2. Worry** | | |
| b worry | 3 | N, V |
| b suspense | 5 | N |
| b concern | 5* | N, V |
| anxiety (anxious) | 6 | N |
| tension (tense) | 6 | N |

## 5d.3. **Anxious**

| Minicluster | Grade Level | Part of Speech |
|---|---|---|
| b anxious | 3 | A, AV (+ly) |
| uncomfortable (comfort) | 4* | A, AV (+ly) |
| b tense | 5 | A |
| uneasy (easy) | 5* | A |
| dissatisfied (satisfy) | 5* | A |
| discontent (content) | 6 | A |

## 5e Anger

| Minicluster | Grade Level | Part of Speech |
|---|---|---|
| **5e.1. Rage** | | |
| b rage | 3 | N |
| dislike (like) | 3* | N, V |
| b anger | 4 | N, V |
| b temper | 4 | N |
| b spite | 4 | N |
| b disgust | 5 | N |
| b wrath | 5* | N |
| b revenge | 6 | N |
| hatred (hate) | 6 | N |
| b disdain | 6 | N, V |
| **5e.2. Indignation** | | |
| b scorn | 6 | N, V |
| indignation (indignant) | 6 | N |
| b fury | 6 | N |
| b grudge | 6* | N |
| bitterness (bitter) | 6* | N |
| **5e.3. Despise** | | |
| b hate | 3 | N, V |
| b despise | 6 | V |
| b seethe | 6 | V |
| b gloat | 6 | V |
| b resent | 6* | V |
| **5e.4. Enrage** | | |
| enrage (rage) | 4 | V |
| arouse (rouse) | 4 | V |
| displease (please) | 4* | V |
| b outrage | 6 | N, V |
| b irritate | 6* | V |

## 5e.5. **Hostile**

| Minicluster | Grade Level | Part of Speech |
|---|---|---|
| angry (anger) | 2 | A, AV (+ly) |
| b hostile | 4 | A |
| furious (fury) | 4 | A, AV (+ly) |
| b indignant | 6 | A, AV (+ly) |

## 5f Cruelty/Fierceness

| Minicluster | Grade Level | Part of Speech |
|---|---|---|
| **5f.1. Cruelty** | | |
| cruelty (cruel) | 6 | N |
| meanness (mean) | 6 | N |
| **5f.1.1 _____** | | |
| b mean | 2 | A |
| b cruel | 3 | A, AV (+ly) |
| b wicked | 4 | A, AV (+ly) |
| b vicious | 4 | A, AV (+ly) |
| merciless (mercy) | 6* | A, AV (+ly) |
| abusive (abuse) | 6* | A, AV (+ly) |
| **5f.2. Fierce** | | |
| b fierce | 2 | A, AV (+ly) |
| b violent | 6 | A, AV (+ly) |
| ferocious (fierce) | 6* | A, AV (+ly) |
| warlike (war) | 6* | A |
| destructive (destroy) | 6* | A, AV (+ly) |

## 5g Irritability

| Minicluster | Grade Level | Part of Speech |
|---|---|---|
| **5g.1. Grumpy** | | |
| b grumpy | 2 | A, AV (+ly) |
| scornful (scorn) | 4 | A, AV (+ly) |
| b gruff | 4 | A, AV (+ly) |
| unkind (kind) | 4 | A |
| b rude | 4 | A, AV (+ly) |
| unfriendly (friend) | 5 | A |
| unpleasant (please) | 5* | A, AV (+ly) |
| disagreeable (agree) | 5* | A, AV (+ly) |
| irritable (irritate) | 6* | A, AV (+ly) |

## 5h Sadness

| Minicluster | Grade Level | Part of Speech |
|---|---|---|
| **5h.1. Sorrow** | | |
| b despair | 4 | N, V |
| sadness (sad) | 4 | N |
| b woe | 4 | N |
| b sorrow | 4* | N |
| disappointment (disappoint) | 5 | N |
| b distress | 5 | N |
| b dismay | 6 | N |
| unrest (rest) | 6* | N |
| **5h.2. Sad** | | |
| b sad | 2 | A, AV (+ly) |
| b sorry | 2 | A |
| unhappy (happy) | 2 | A, AV (+ly) |
| sorrowful (sorrow) | 5 | A, AV (+ly) |
| b wistful | 5 | A, AV (+ly) |
| b forlorn | 6 | A |

## 5h.3. Suffer

| | | |
|---|---|---|
| b suffer | 4 | V |
| b mourn | 4 | V |
| b grieve | 6 | V |
| b regret | 6 | N, V |

## 5i Upset/Misery

| Minicluster | Grade Level | Part of Speech |
|---|---|---|
| **5i.1. Disturb** | | |
| b upset | K | N, V |
| b bother | 3 | N, V |
| b disturb | 4 | V |
| b exasperate | 5 | V |
| b frustrate | 6* | V |
| b depress | 6* | V |

---

**Key**

Basic words
   Basic words are preceded by *b*.
   All other words are followed by the basic word in parentheses.

Grade levels
   K-6   The grade level at which a word is introduced.
   *       Indicates a word does not appear frequently in student reading material, but when it does appear it is at the level indicated.
   –       Words or phrases for which a grade level could not be determined.
   Content specific words are indicated by the content area in which they are used:
   SS        Social Studies
   EN        English
   MA        Math
   SC        Science

Part of Speech
   N            Noun
   V            Verb
   A            Adjective
   AV          Adverb
   AV (+ly)   Adverb when suffix -ly is added
   PRO        Pronoun
   PREP       Preposition
   INT         Interjection
   DET        Determiner
   AX          Auxiliary verb
   RM          Relationship marker

## 5i.2. Solemn

| | | Grade Level | Part of Speech |
|---|---|---|---|
| b | serious | 3 | A, AV (+ly) |
| b | solemn | 3 | A, AV (+ly) |
| b | sullen | 5 | A, AV (+ly) |
| b | sober | 6 | A, AV (+ly) |
| b | somber | 6* | A, AV (+ly) |

## 5i.3. Miserable

| | | Grade Level | Part of Speech |
|---|---|---|---|
| | miserable (misery) | 5 | A, AV (+ly) |
| | wretched (wretch) | 5 | A, AV (+ly) |

## 5i.4. Lonely

| | | Grade Level | Part of Speech |
|---|---|---|---|
| | alone (lone) | 2 | A |
| | lonely (lone) | 4 | A |
| b | homesick | 5* | A |

# 5j Excitement

| Minicluster | Grade Level | Part of Speech |
|---|---|---|

## 5j.1. Excitement

| | | Grade Level | Part of Speech |
|---|---|---|---|
| | excitement (excite) | 3 | N |
| | amazement (amaze) | 5 | N |
| | astonishment (astonish) | 6 | N |
| b | awe | 6 | N |
| b | passion | 6 | N |
| | disbelief (belief) | 6 | N |
| b | ecstasy | 6* | N |
| | jubilation (jubilant) | 6* | N |

## 5j.2. Surprise

| | | Grade Level | Part of Speech |
|---|---|---|---|
| b | surprise | 1 | N, V |
| b | amaze | 3 | V |
| b | astonish | 4 | V |
| b | marvel | 4 | V |
| b | fascinate | 5 | V |
| | astound (astonish) | 5 | V |

## 5j.3. Excite

| | | Grade Level | Part of Speech |
|---|---|---|---|
| b | excite | 2 | V |
| b | thrill | 4 | N, V |
| b | enchant | 4 | V |
| | rejoice (joy) | 6 | V |
| | enliven (life) | 6* | V |
| b | enthrall | 6* | V |

# 5k Fun/Humor

| Minicluster | Grade Level | Part of Speech |
|---|---|---|

## 5k.1. Fun

| | | Grade Level | Part of Speech |
|---|---|---|---|
| b | fun | K | N |
| b | joy | 2 | N |
| | happiness (happy) | 3 | N |
| b | delight | 3 | N, V |
| | pleasure (please) | 4 | N |
| | enjoyment (joy) | 4 | N |
| b | glee | 4* | N |

## 5k.2. Happy

| | | Grade Level | Part of Speech |
|---|---|---|---|
| b | happy | 1 | A, AV (+ly) |
| b | merry | 2 | A, AV (+ly) |
| b | silly | 2 | A |
| b | gay | 3 | A, AV (+ly) |
| | cheerful (cheer) | 3 | A, AV (+ly) |
| b | glad | 3 | A, AV (+ly) |
| b | jolly | 4 | A |
| | enjoyable (joy) | 4* | A, AV (+ly) |
| | joyous (joy) | 5 | A, AV (+ly) |
| b | bonny | 5* | A |
| | joyful (joy) | 6 | A, AV (+ly) |
| | gleeful (glee) | 6 | A, AV (+ly) |
| b | giddy | 6 | A |

## 5k.3. Humor

| | | Grade Level | Part of Speech |
|---|---|---|---|
| b | please | 1 | V |
| b | amuse | 4 | V |
| b | humor | 4 | N, V |
| b | entertain | 4 | V |

## 5k.4. Play

| | | Grade Level | Part of Speech |
|---|---|---|---|
| b | play | K | N, V |
| b | frolic | 5* | V |

## 5k.5. Joke

| | | Grade Level | Part of Speech |
|---|---|---|---|
| b | joke | 2 | N, V |

# 5L Comfort/Contentment

| Minicluster | Grade Level | Part of Speech |
|---|---|---|
| **5L.1. Comfort** | | |
| contentment (content) | 3 | N |
| b comfort | 4 | N |
| b relief | 5 | N |
| **5L.2. Pity** | | |
| b pity | 4 | N, V |
| b sympathy | 6 | N |
| b empathy | 6* | N |
| **5L.3. Calm** | | |
| b calm | 3 | V, A AV (+ly) |
| b satisfy | 4 | V |
| b tame | 4 | V |
| civilize (civil) | 4* | V |
| becalm (calm) | 6* | V |
| **5L.4. Soothe** | | |
| b soothe | 5 | V |
| b console | 6 | V |
| sympathize (sympathy) | 6 | V |
| empathize (empathy) | 6* | V |
| **5L.5. Content** | | |
| comfortable (comfort) | 3 | A, AV (+ly) |
| b content | 3 | A, AV (+ly) |
| b cozy | 4 | A |
| b snug | 4 | A, AV (+ly) |
| undisturbed (disturb) | 4* | A |
| peaceful (peace) | 5 | A, AV (+ly) |
| b mellow | 6 | A |

# 5m Jealousy/Envy

| Minicluster | Grade Level | Part of Speech |
|---|---|---|
| **5m.1. Envy** | | |
| b envy | 4 | N, V |
| b lust | 6* | N, V |
| b greed | 6* | N |

| Minicluster | Grade Level | Part of Speech |
|---|---|---|
| **5m.2. Jealous** | | |
| b jealous | 4 | A, AV (+ly) |
| defensive (defend) | 5 | A, AV (+ly) |
| protective (protect) | 6 | A |
| possessive (possess) | EN | A, AV (+ly) |
| **5m.2.1** _____ | | |
| jealousy (jealous) | 4 | N |

# 5n Hope/Doubt

| Minicluster | Grade Level | Part of Speech |
|---|---|---|
| **5n.1. Hope** | | |
| b hope | 2 | N, V |
| b trust | 4 | N, V |
| b faith | 5 | N |
| b belief | 6 | N |
| **5n.2. Hopeless** | | |
| hopeless (hope) | 4 | A, AV (+ly) |
| hopeful (hope) | 4* | A, AV (+ly) |
| **5n.3. Doubt** | | |
| b doubt | 4 | N, V |
| confusion (confuse) | 5 | N |
| suspicion (suspect) | 6 | N |

# 5o Liking/Believing

| Minicluster | Grade Level | Part of Speech |
|---|---|---|
| **5o.1. Like** | | |
| b like | K | V |
| b care | 2 | N, V |
| b love | 2 | N, V |
| b respect | 3 | N, V |
| enjoy (joy) | 3 | V |
| b favor | 4 | N, V |
| b admire | 4 | V |
| b cherish | 4* | V |
| b prefer | 5 | V |
| b appreciate | 5 | V |
| b regard | 5 | N, V |
| b revere | 5* | V |
| b value | 6 | V |
| b adore | 6 | V |

### 5o.2. **Gratitude**

| | | |
|---|---|---|
| admiration (admire) | 4 | N |
| gratitude (grateful) | 5 | N |
| b affection | 5 | N |
| appreciation (appreciate) | 6 | N |

### 5o.3. **Believe**

| | | |
|---|---|---|
| b believe | 2 | V |
| b accept | 4 | V |
| b support | 4 | N, V |
| b pardon | 5 | N, V |
| b approve | 6 | V |
| b forgive | 6 | V |
| b devote | 6 | V |
| entrust (trust) | 6 | V |
| dignify (dignity) | 6 | V |

### 5o.3.1 _____

| | | |
|---|---|---|
| approval (approve) | 6 | N |

## 5p Neglecting Actions

| Minicluster | Grade Level | Part of Speech |
|---|---|---|
| **5p.1. Neglect** | | |
| b neglect | 5 | N, V |
| b omit | 5 | V |
| b overlook | 6 | V |
| **5p.2. Isolate** | | |
| b isolate | 6 | V |
| b maroon | 6 | V |

## 5q Desire

| Minicluster | Grade Level | Part of Speech |
|---|---|---|
| **5q.1. Want** | | |
| b want | K | N, V |
| b wish | 1 | N, V |
| b miss | 1 | V |
| b need | 2 | N, V |
| b deserve | 3 | V |
| b expect | 3 | V |
| b seek | 4 | V |
| b desire | 4 | N, V |
| b yearn | 6 | V |
| b crave | 6 | V |

### 5q.2. **Greedy**

| | | |
|---|---|---|
| greedy (greed) | 3 | A, AV (+ly) |
| selfish (self) | 4 | A, AV (+ly) |

## 5r Human Traits (General)

| Minicluster | Grade Level | Part of Speech |
|---|---|---|
| **5r.1. Ability** | | |
| ability (able) | 4 | N |
| b skill | 4 | N |
| capability (capable) | 5 | N |
| b talent | 5 | N |
| b attribute | 6* | N |
| **5r.2. Behavior** | | |
| b manner | 3 | N |
| b attitude | 5 | N |
| behavior (behave) | 5 | N |
| b bearing | 5* | N |
| personality (person) | 6 | N |
| appearance (appear) | 6 | N |
| **5r.3. Trait** | | |
| b quality | 5 | N |
| characteristic (character) | 5 | N |
| b trait | 6 | N |
| b aspect | 6* | N |

# Supercluster 6
## Food/Meals

### 6a Types of Meals

| Minicluster | Grade Level | Part of Speech |
|---|---|---|
| **6a.1. Meal** | | |
| b supper | 2 | N |
| dinner (dine) | 2 | N |
| b lunch | 2 | N |
| b meal | 3 | N |
| b chow | 6* | N |
| b brunch | 6* | N |

| 6a.2. **Feast** | | |
|---|---|---|
| b picnic | 1 | N |
| b feast | 3 | N, V |
| b banquet | 5* | N |

| 6a.3. **Dessert** | | |
|---|---|---|
| b treat | 3 | N, V |
| b dessert | 4 | N |
| b tidbit | 5 | N |
| refreshment (refresh) | 5* | N |
| b snack | 5* | N, V |

## 6b Food Types

| Minicluster | Grade Level | Part of Speech |
|---|---|---|
| **6b.1. Food** | | |
| b food | 1 | N |
| nourishment (nourish) | 6 | N |
| b nutrition | 6 | N |
| delicacy (delicate) | 6 | N |
| **6b.2. Provisions** | | |
| b stuffs | 3 | N |
| b crop | 3 | N |
| provisions (provide) | 5 | N |
| merchandise (merchant) | 5 | N |
| supplies (supply) | 6* | N |
| **6b.3. Fruits/Vegetables** | | |
| b fruit | 2 | N |
| b meat | 3 | N |
| b vegetable(s) | 3 | N |
| b seafood | 4* | N |
| **6b.4. Diet** | | |
| b diet | 5 | N, V |

## 6c Sweets

| Minicluster | Grade Level | Part of Speech |
|---|---|---|
| **6c.1. Jam** | | |
| b honey | 2 | N |
| b jam | 3 | N |
| b syrup | 3* | N |
| b molasses | 6 | N |

| 6c.2. **Cake** | | |
|---|---|---|
| b cake | K | N |
| b cupcake | 2 | N |
| b cookie | 2 | N |
| b gingerbread | 3 | N |
| b doughnut | 4 | N |
| b brownie | 4* | N |
| b tart | 5 | N, A |
| b pastry | 6 | N |

| 6c.3. **Candy** | | |
|---|---|---|
| sweets (sweet) | 2 | N |
| b gum | 3 | N |
| b candy | 3 | N |
| b lollipop | 3* | N |
| b pudding | 4 | N |
| b marshmallow | 5* | N |
| b custard | 6* | N |

---

### Key

Basic words
  Basic words are preceded by *b*.
  All other words are followed by the basic word in parentheses.

Grade levels
  K-6    The grade level at which a word is introduced.
  *      Indicates a word does not appear frequently in student reading material, but when it does appear it is at the level indicated.
  –      Words or phrases for which a grade level could not be determined.

Content specific words are indicated by the content area in which they are used:
  SS    Social Studies
  EN    English
  MA    Math
  SC    Science

Part of Speech
  N           Noun
  V           Verb
  A           Adjective
  AV          Adverb
  AV (+ly)    Adverb when suffix -ly is added
  PRO         Pronoun
  PREP        Preposition
  INT         Interjection
  DET         Determiner
  AX          Auxiliary verb
  RM          Relationship marker

## 6c.4. Flavor

| | | | |
|---|---|---|---|
| b | cocoa | 4 | N |
| b | flavor | 4 | N, V |
| b | chocolate | 4 | N |
| b | licorice | 5* | N |
| b | vanilla | 6* | N |

## 6d Prepared Foods

| Minicluster | Grade Level | Part of Speech |
|---|---|---|
| **6d.1. Noodles** | | |
| b noodles | 5* | N |
| b spaghetti | 5* | N |
| b macaroni | 5* | N |
| **6d.2. Cereal** | | |
| b oatmeal | 3* | N |
| b mush | 4 | N |
| b porridge | 5 | N |
| b cereal | 6 | N |
| **6d.3. Bread** | | |
| b bread | 3 | N |
| b pancake | 4 | N |
| b tortilla | 4 | N |
| b muffin | 4* | N |
| b loaf | 5 | N |
| b toast | 5 | N, V |
| b biscuit | 5 | N |
| b bun | 6 | N |
| loaves (loaf) | 6* | N |
| **6d.4. Cracker** | | |
| b chip(s) | 3 | N |
| b cracker | 5* | N |
| **6d.5. Sandwich** | | |
| b sandwich | 3 | N |
| b hamburger | 4 | N |
| b frankfurter | 5* | N |
| **6d.6. Salad** | | |
| b salad | 4 | N |

## 6e Meats

| Minicluster | Grade Level | Part of Speech |
|---|---|---|
| **6e.1. Beef** | | |
| b ham | 4 | N |
| b sausage | 4 | N |
| b beef | 4 | N |
| b bacon | 4 | N |
| b poultry | 5* | N |
| b mutton | 6 | N |
| b pork | 6 | N |
| b steak | 6 | N |

## 6f Dairy Products

| Minicluster | Grade Level | Part of Speech |
|---|---|---|
| **6f.1. Butter** | | |
| b egg | 2 | N |
| b butter | 2 | N |
| b cream | 2 | N |
| b cheese | 4 | N |
| b margarine | 5* | N |
| b yolk | SC | N |

## 6g Ingredients Used to Prepare Foods

| Minicluster | Grade Level | Part of Speech |
|---|---|---|
| **6g.1. Flour** | | |
| b flour | 3 | N |
| b batter | 3 | N |
| b mix | 3 | N, V |
| b dough | 4 | N |
| b yeast | 4* | N |
| b sourdough | 5 | N |
| gelatin (gel) | 5* | N |
| b starch | 6 | N, V |

## 6g.2. Spice

| | | | |
|---|---|---|---|
| b | salt | 2 | N, V |
| b | sugar | 3 | N |
| b | pepper | 3* | N, V |
| b | cinnamon | 4 | N |
| b | vinegar | 4 | N |
| b | cloves | 4 | N |
| b | ginger | 5 | N |
| b | parsley | 5 | N |
| b | catsup | 5 | N |
| b | nutmeg | 5* | N |
| b | mustard | 6 | N |
| b | curry | 6 | N |
| b | spice | 6 | N |
| b | garlic | 6* | N |

## 6g.3. Ingredient

| | | | |
|---|---|---|---|
| b | ingredient | 6 | N |

# 6h Things to Drink

| Minicluster | Grade Level | Part of Speech |
|---|---|---|
| **6h.2. Soda** | | |
| b milk | 2 | N, V |
| b pop | 2 | N |
| lemonade (lemon) | 2 | N |
| b coffee | 3 | N |
| b tea | 3 | N |
| b nectar | 3 | N |
| b soda | 4 | N |
| b juice | 4 | N |
| b cider | 4 | N |
| **6h.2. Wine** | | |
| b wine | 5* | N |
| b beer | 5* | N |
| b mead | 5* | N |
| b gin | 5* | N |
| b ale | 5* | N |
| b alcohol | SC | N |
| b liquor | SC | N |
| **6h.3. Soup** | | |
| b soup | 2 | N |
| b broth | 6 | N |

# 6i Fruits

| Minicluster | Grade Level | Part of Speech |
|---|---|---|
| **6i.1. Apple** | | |
| b apple | 2 | N |
| b pear | 4 | N |
| b watermelon | 4* | N |
| b peach | 5 | N |
| b apricot | 5 | N |
| b melon | 6 | N |
| **6i.2. Plum** | | |
| b grape | 4 | N |
| b fig | 5 | N |
| b plum | 5 | N |
| b prune | 5 | N |
| b raisin | 5 | N |
| **6i.3. Berry** | | |
| b cherry | 2 | N |
| b blueberry | 2 | N |
| b strawberry | 3* | N |
| b raspberry | 4 | N |
| b cranberry | 4* | N |
| **6i.4. Orange** | | |
| b lemon | 2* | N |
| b orange | 3 | N |
| b lime | 5 | N |
| b grapefruit | 5* | N |
| b tangerine | 5* | N |
| **6i.5. Banana** | | |
| b banana | 2 | N |
| b pineapple | 4* | N |
| b coconut | 5 | N |
| b copra | SS | N |

## 6j Vegetables

| Minicluster | Grade Level | Part of Speech |
|---|---|---|
| 6j.1. **Tomato** | | |
| b radish | 2 | N |
| b turnip | 3 | N |
| b carrot | 3 | N |
| b bean | 3 | N |
| b potato | 3 | N |
| b beet | 3* | N |
| b tomato | 4 | N |
| b onion | 4 | N |
| b olive | 4 | N |
| b yam | 4* | N |
| b pickle | 5 | N |
| b celery | 5 | N |
| b peas | 5 | N |
| b spinach | 5* | N |
| b hominy | 5* | N |
| b cucumber | 5* | N |
| 6j.2. **Cabbage** | | |
| b pumpkin | 2 | N |
| b squash | 3 | N |
| b lettuce | 3 | N |
| b cabbage | 6 | N |
| 6j.3. **Rice** | | |
| b popcorn | 2* | N |
| b corn | 2 | N |
| b grain | 3 | N |
| b rice | 3 | N |
| b wheat | 4 | N |
| b barley | 4* | N |
| b rye | 4* | N |
| b oats | 5* | N |
| b kernel | 5* | N |
| b soybean | 5 | N |
| b maize | 6 | N |
| b malt | 6* | N |
| 6j.4. **Nut** | | |
| b peanut | 1 | N |
| b seed | 3 | N, V |
| b acorn | 4 | N |
| b nut | 4 | N |
| b chestnut | 4* | N |
| b walnut | 6 | N |
| b pecan | 6* | N |
| b cashew | 6* | N |
| b almond | 6* | N |
| b filbert | 6* | N |

## 6k Actions Done to/with Food

| Minicluster | Grade Level | Part of Speech |
|---|---|---|
| 6k.1. **Cook** | | |
| b cook | 2 | N, V |
| b bake | 3 | V |
| b fry | 3 | V |
| b roast | 3 | N, V |
| b grill | 4 | N, V |
| b boil | 4 | N, V |
| b barbecue | 5* | N, V |
| b brew | 6 | V |
| b simmer | 6* | V |
| 6k.2. **Serve** | | |
| b serve | 3 | V |
| b blend | 4 | V |
| b churn | 4 | V |
| b knead | 5* | V |
| b sift | 5* | V |
| b shuck | 6 | V |
| 6k.3. **Spoil** | | |
| b spoil | 3 | V |
| ripen (ripe) | 4* | V |
| b rot | 6 | V |
| b decay | 6 | N, V |
| perishable (perish) | 6 | A |

## 6L Food Tastes

| Minicluster | Grade Level | Part of Speech |
|---|---|---|
| 6L.1. **Taste** | | |
| b taste | 3 | N, V |
| 6L.2. **Sweet** | | |
| b sweet | 2 | A |
| b bitter | 4 | A |
| b delicious | 3 | A |
| tasty (taste) | 3* | A |
| b sour | 6 | A |
| 6L.2.1 _____ | | |
| bitterness (bitter) | 6 | N |
| sweetness (sweet) | 6 | N |
| 6L.3. **Ripe** | | |
| b ripe | 3 | A |
| juicy (juice) | 4 | A |

## 6L.4. **Rotten**

|  |  |  |  |
|---|---|---|---|
| | greasy (grease) | 5* | A |
| b | stale | 5* | A |
| | rotten (rot) | 6 | A |
| b | raw | 6 | A |

## 6m Eating/Drinking Actions

| Minicluster | Grade Level | Part of Speech |
|---|---|---|
| **6m.1. Chew** | | |
| b chew | 3 | V |
| b swallow | 3 | N, V |
| b taste | 3 | N, V |
| b nibble | 3 | N, V |
| b bite | 3 | N, V |
| b gnaw | 4 | V |
| b munch | 5 | V |
| **6m.2. Eat** | | |
| b eat | K | V |
| b feed | 2 | V |
| b dine | 3 | V |
| b devour | 6 | V |
| b gorge | 6 | V |
| b consume | 6 | V |
| **6m.3. Drink** | | |
| b drink | 2 | N, V |
| b sip | 6 | N, V |
| b gargle | 6 | V |

## 6n Hunger/Thirst

| Minicluster | Grade Level | Part of Speech |
|---|---|---|
| **6n.1. Hunger** | | |
| b hunger | 4 | N, V |
| b thirst | 4* | N, V |
| b appetite | 6 | N |
| **6n.1.1** _____ | | |
| hungry (hunger) | 2 | A, AV (+ly) |
| thirsty (thirst) | 4 | A |
| b ravenous | 6* | A, AV (+ly) |
| **6n.2. Starve** | | |
| b starve | 4 | V |

## 6n.3. **Carnivorous**

| | | | |
|---|---|---|---|
| carnivorous (carnivore) | | SC | A |

## 6o Smoking

| Minicluster | Grade Level | Part of Speech |
|---|---|---|
| **6o.1. Pipe** | | |
| b pipe | 3 | N |
| b cigar | 3* | N |
| b cigarette | 6 | N |

---

**Key**

Basic words
  Basic words are preceded by *b*.
  All other words are followed by the basic word in parentheses.

Grade levels
  K-6  The grade level at which a word is introduced.
  *  Indicates a word does not appear frequently in student reading material, but when it does appear it is at the level indicated.
  –  Words or phrases for which a grade level could not be determined.

Content specific words are indicated by the content area in which they are used:
  SS  Social Studies
  EN  English
  MA  Math
  SC  Science

Part of Speech
  N  Noun
  V  Verb
  A  Adjective
  AV  Adverb
  AV (+ly)  Adverb when suffix -ly is added
  PRO  Pronoun
  PREP  Preposition
  INT  Interjection
  DET  Determiner
  AX  Auxiliary verb
  RM  Relationship marker

# Supercluster 7
## Time

### 7a Time (General)

| Minicluster | Grade Level | Part of Speech |
|---|---|---|
| **7a.1. Time** | | |
| b time | 1 | N, V AV (+ly) |
| b daytime | 3 | N |
| b springtime | 3* | N |
| b summertime | 3* | N |
| b lifetime | 4* | N |
| b dinnertime | 4* | N |
| b bedtime | 4* | N |
| b wintertime | 4* | N |
| b mealtime | 5* | N |
| b peacetime | SS | N |
| 7a.1.1 _____ | | |
| b date | 4 | N |

### 7b Devices Used to Measure Time

| Minicluster | Grade Level | Part of Speech |
|---|---|---|
| **7b.1. Clock** | | |
| b clock | 2 | N, V |
| b watch | 2 | N |
| b calendar | 5 | N |
| b wristwatch | 6 | N |
| b sundial | 6 | N |
| 7b.1.1 _____ | | |
| b o'clock | 3 | N |

### 7c Parts of a Day

| Minicluster | Grade Level | Part of Speech |
|---|---|---|
| **7c.1. Day** | | |
| b day | 1 | N |
| b morning | 1 | N |
| b noon | 3 | N |
| b afternoon | 4 | N |
| b dawn | 4 | N |
| b sunrise | 4 | N |
| b midday | 6 | N |

| | Grade Level | Part of Speech |
|---|---|---|
| **7c.2. Night** | | |
| b night | 1 | N |
| b tonight | 2 | N |
| b evening | 2 | N |
| b dusk | 4 | N |
| b eve | 4 | N |
| b nightfall | 4 | N |
| b sunset | 4 | N |
| b midnight | 5 | N |
| b twilight | 5 | N |
| b sundown | 5* | N |
| b overnight | 6 | N |
| **7c.3. Minute** | | |
| b minute | 2 | N |
| b second | 2 | N |
| b hour | 3 | N |
| b instant | 3 | N |
| b moment | 4 | N |

### 7d Periods of Time Longer than a Day

| Minicluster | Grade Level | Part of Speech |
|---|---|---|
| **7d.1. Age** | | |
| b season | 3 | N, V |
| b age | 3 | N, V |
| b period | 4 | N |
| b cycle | 4 | N, V |
| b term | 6 | N |
| b phase | 6 | N, V |
| b generation | 6 | N |
| b interval | 6* | N |
| b interim | 6* | N |
| **7d.2. Season** | | |
| b fall | 1 | N |
| b summer | 2 | N |
| b winter | 2 | N |
| b spring | 2 | N |
| b autumn | 4 | N |
| **7d.3. Week** | | |
| b week | 2 | N |
| b year | 2 | N |
| b month | 3 | N |
| b century | 4 | N |
| b weekend | 4 | N |
| b decade | 4* | N |
| centennial (century) | 6* | N |
| b millennium | 6* | N |

## 7e Months and Days

| Minicluster | Grade Level | Part of Speech |
|---|---|---|
| **7e.1. January** | | |
| b January | 2 | N |
| b February | 2 | N |
| b March | 2 | N |
| b April | 2 | N |
| b May | 2 | N |
| b June | 2 | N |
| b July | 2 | N |
| b August | 2 | N |
| b September | 2 | N |
| b October | 2 | N |
| b November | 2 | N |
| b December | 2 | N |
| **7e.2. Monday** | | |
| b Monday | 1 | N |
| b Tuesday | 1 | N |
| b Wednesday | 1 | N |
| b Thursday | 1 | N |
| b Friday | 1 | N |
| b Saturday | 1 | N |
| b Sunday | 1 | N |

## 7f Relative Time

| Minicluster | Grade Level | Part of Speech |
|---|---|---|
| **7f.1. Tomorrow** | | |
| b tomorrow | 1 | N |
| b today | 2 | N |
| b yesterday | 3 | N |
| b someday | 4 | N |
| b everyday | 4 | N |
| b morrow | 5* | N |
| **7f.2. Past** | | |
| past (pass) | 2 | N, A |
| b present | 3 | N, A |
| b future | 4 | N, A |
| eternity (eternal) | 6 | N |
| **7f.3. Childhood** | | |
| childhood (child) | 5 | N |
| boyhood (boy) | 5* | N |
| adolescence (adolescent) | 6* | N |

| 7f.4. Old | | |
|---|---|---|
| **7f.4. Old** | | |
| b old | 1 | A |
| worn (wear) | 3 | A |
| b ancient | 4 | A |
| b antique | 6 | N, A |
| **7f.5. Historic** | | |
| historical (history) | 4* | A, AV (+ly) |
| historic (history) | 4* | A |
| b extinct | 5* | A |
| prehistoric (history) | 5* | A |
| colonial (colony) | 6 | A |
| b primitive | 6 | A, AV (+ly) |
| b medieval | 6 | A |
| **7f.5.1 _____** | | |
| b history | 3 | N |
| ancestry (ancestor) | 6 | N |

## 7g Prior Action (Relationship Markers)

| Minicluster | Grade Level | Part of Speech |
|---|---|---|
| **7g.1. Early** | | |
| b early | 1 | AV |
| b ago | 2 | AV |
| lately (late) | 2 | AV |
| b already | 3 | AV |
| **7g.1.1 _____** | | |
| earlier (early) | 2 | RM |
| **7g.2. Initially** | | |
| initially (initial) | 6 | RM |
| b beforehand | 6 | RM |
| b in the beginning | – | RM |
| b at first | – | RM |
| b before that | – | RM |
| b before now | – | RM |
| b until then | – | RM |
| b up to now | – | RM |
| **7g.3. Previous** | | |
| original (origin) | 4 | A, AV (+ly) |
| b former | 4 | A, AV (+ly) |
| b previous | 6 | A, AV (+ly) |
| b initial | 6* | A, AV (+ly) |

## 7g.4. New

| Minicluster | Grade Level | Part of Speech |
|---|---|---|
| b new | K | A |
| b current | 3 | A, AV (+ly) |
| b fresh | 3 | A, AV (+ly) |
| b modern | 4 | A |
| b recent | 5 | A, AV (+ly) |
| b brand new | 5 | A |

### 7g.4.1 _____

| | | |
|---|---|---|
| b ready | 1 | A |

## 7g.5. After

| | | |
|---|---|---|
| b after | 1 | RM |
| b prior to | – | RM |
| b subsequent to | – | RM |

# 7h Subsequent Action (Relationship Markers)

| Minicluster | Grade Level | Part of Speech |
|---|---|---|
| **7h.1. Soon** | | |
| b soon | K | AV |
| eventually (event) | 5 | AV |
| momentarily (moment) | 6 | AV |
| **7h.2. Later** | | |
| b then | K | AV |
| b next | 1 | AV |
| later (late) | 2 | AV |
| shortly (short) | 2 | AV |
| afterwards (after) | 5 | AV |
| latter (late) | 6 | AV |
| b hitherto | 6* | AV |
| subsequently (sequence) | 6* | AV |
| b after that | – | AV |
| b in the end | – | AV |
| b so far | – | AV |
| b as yet | – | AV |
| **7h.2.1 _____** | | |
| b late | 2 | A |
| eventual (event) | 5 | A |
| **7h.3. Before** | | |
| b before | 1 | PREP |
| until (til) | 2 | PREP |
| b since | 3 | PREP |

# 7i Concurrent Action (Relationship Markers)

| Minicluster | Grade Level | Part of Speech |
|---|---|---|
| **7i.1. Now** | | |
| b now | K | AV |
| presently (present) | 3 | AV |
| immediately (immediate) | 3 | AV |
| b nowadays | 4 | AV |
| b at this point | – | AV |
| **7i.2. At** | | |
| b at | K | PREP |
| b on | K | PREP |
| **7i.3. When** | | |
| b as | 1 | RM |
| b when | 1 | RM |
| b while | 2 | RM |
| whilst (while) | 6* | RM |
| **7i.4. Meanwhile** | | |
| b meanwhile | 5 | AV |
| simultaneously (simultaneous) | 6 | AV |
| concurrently (concur) | 6* | AV |
| contemporaneously (contemporary) | 6* | AV |
| b in the meantime | – | AV |
| b in the interim | – | AV |
| b at the same time | – | AV |

# 7j Speed

| Minicluster | Grade Level | Part of Speech |
|---|---|---|
| **7j.1. Speed** | | |
| b speed | 4 | N, V |
| b velocity | SC | N |
| **7j.2. Frenzy** | | |
| b fuss | 4 | N, V |
| b flurry | 6 | N |
| b frenzy | 6 | N |
| b haste | 6* | N |

## 7j.3. Hurry

| | | | |
|---|---|---|---|
| b | hurry | 1 | N, V |
| b | race | 1 | N, V |
| b | rush | 3 | N, V |
| b | dash | 3 | N, V |
| b | charge | 4 | N, V |
| b | hustle | 5 | N, V |
| b | hurtle | 5 | N, V |
| b | scurry | 6 | V |
| b | hasten | 6* | V |

## 7j.4. Quick

| | | | |
|---|---|---|---|
| b | fast | K | A |
| b | quick | 2 | A, AV (+ly) |
| b | swift | 3 | A, AV (+ly) |
| b | rapid | 4 | A, AV (+ly) |
| | speedy (speed) | 4* | A, AV (+ly) |
| b | brisk | 5 | A, AV (+ly) |
| b | fleet | 6 | A, AV (+ly) |

## 7j.5. Sudden

| | | | |
|---|---|---|---|
| b | sudden | 2 | A, AV (+ly) |
| b | immediate | 3 | A, AV (+ly) |
| b | instant | 4 | A, AV (+ly) |
| b | prompt | 4 | A, AV (+ly) |
| b | abrupt | 5 | A, AV (+ly) |
| b | brief | 5 | A, AV (+ly) |
| b | automatic | 6 | A, AV (+ly) |
| | hasty (haste) | 6* | A, AV (+ly) |

## 7j.5.1 _____

| | | | |
|---|---|---|---|
| | hastily (haste) | 4 | AV |
| | automatically (automatic) | 5* | AV |

## 7j.5.2 _____

| | | | |
|---|---|---|---|
| b | helter skelter | 4 | AV |
| b | sluggish | 4 | A |
| b | headlong | 6 | AV |

## 7j.6 Slow

| | | | |
|---|---|---|---|
| b | slow | K | A, AV (+ly) |

---

**Key**

Basic words
    Basic words are preceded by *b*.
    All other words are followed by the basic word in parentheses.

Grade levels
  K-6  The grade level at which a word is introduced.
  *    Indicates a word does not appear frequently in student reading material, but when it does appear it is at the level indicated.
  –    Words or phrases for which a grade level could not be determined.

Content specific words are indicated by the content area in which they are used:
  SS    Social Studies
  EN    English
  MA    Math
  SC    Science

Part of Speech
  N      Noun
  V      Verb
  A      Adjective
  AV    Adverb
  AV (+ly)  Adverb when suffix -ly is added
  PRO  Pronoun
  PREP  Preposition
  INT  Interjection
  DET  Determiner
  AX  Auxiliary verb
  RM  Relationship marker

## 7k Duration

| Minicluster | Grade Level | Part of Speech |
|---|---|---|
| **7k.1. Permanent** | | |
| b long | 1 | A |
| b common | 3 | A, AV (+ly) |
| b usual | 3 | A, AV (+ly) |
| b constant | 4 | A, AV (+ly) |
| b regular | 4 | A, AV (+ly) |
| b permanent | 5 | A, AV (+ly) |
| b frequent | 5 | A, AV (+ly) |
| continual (continue) | 6 | A, AV (+ly) |
| b continuous (continue) | 6* | A, AV (+ly) |
| b eternal | 6* | A, AV (+ly) |
| endless (end) | 6* | A, AV (+ly) |
| b annual | 6* | A, AV (+ly) |
| incessant (cease) | 6* | A, AV (+ly) |
| invariable (vary) | 6* | A, AV (+ly) |
| customary (custom) | 6* | A, AV (+ly) |
| b general | 6* | A, AV (+ly) |
| habitual (habit) | 6* | A, AV (+ly) |

| **7k.2. Temporary** | | |
|---|---|---|
| b rare | 4 | A, AV (+ly) |
| indefinite (define) | 4* | A, AV (+ly) |
| occasional (occasion) | 5 | A, AV (+ly) |
| b temporary | 5* | A, AV (+ly) |
| momentary (moment) | 6 | A, AV (+ly) |
| irregular (regular) | 6 | A, AV (+ly) |
| infrequent (frequent) | 6* | A, AV (+ly) |
| periodic (period) | 6* | A, AV (+ly) |

| **7k.3. Duration** | | |
|---|---|---|
| b duration | 6* | N |
| longevity (long) | 6* | N |

| **7k.4. Again** | | |
|---|---|---|
| b again | 1 | AV |
| once (one) | 2 | AV |
| twice (two) | 2 | AV |
| b often | 2 | AV |

| **7k.5. Weekly** | | |
|---|---|---|
| nightly (night) | 1 | AV |
| weekly (week) | 2 | AV |
| hourly (hour) | 3 | AV |
| daily (day) | 6 | AV |
| (1, 2, 3) times | 6* | AV |
| quarterly (quarter) | 6* | AV |

| 7k.5.1 _____ | | |
|---|---|---|
| b always | 2 | AV |
| b forever | 4 | AV |

| **7k.6. Never** | | |
|---|---|---|
| never (ever) | 1 | AV |
| b sometimes | 2 | AV |
| b seldom | 4 | AV |
| b awhile | 4 | AV |
| b anymore | 6 | AV |

| **7k.7. Continue** | | |
|---|---|---|
| b continue | 3 | V |
| b persist | 6 | V |
| b relent | 6 | V |

| 7k.7.1 _____ | | |
|---|---|---|
| b repeat | 4 | V |

# Supercluster 8
## Machines/Engines/Tools

### 8a Machines

| Minicluster | Grade Level | Part of Speech |
|---|---|---|
| 8a.1. **Machine** | | |
| b machine | 3 | N |
| equipment (equip) | 4 | N |
| machinery (machine) | 5 | N |
| mechanism (mechanics) | 6 | N |
| 8a.1.1 _____ | | |
| b equip | 4* | V |
| 8a.1.2 _____ | | |
| mechanical (mechanics) | 5 | A, AV (+ly) |
| 8a.2. **Hardware** | | |
| b hardware | 4* | N |
| b apparatus | 6 | N |
| b contraption | 6 | N |
| b gadget | 6* | N |

### 8b Engines and Parts of Engines

| Minicluster | Grade Level | Part of Speech |
|---|---|---|
| 8b.1. **Engine** | | |
| b engine | 3 | N |
| b motor | 3 | N |
| 8b.2. **Gear** | | |
| b brake | 4 | N |
| b gear | 5 | N |
| transmission (transmit) | 5* | N |
| starter (start) | 5* | N |
| generator (generate) | 5* | N |
| b throttle | 6 | N |
| b piston | SC | N |
| compressor (compress) | SC | N |
| 8b.3. **Jet** | | |
| b jet | 3 | N, A |
| b diesel | 6 | N, A |
| b turbine | 6* | N |

### 8c Fuels

| Minicluster | Grade Level | Part of Speech |
|---|---|---|
| 8c.1. **Oil** | | |
| b oil | 2 | N, V |
| b gas | 3 | N |
| b fuel | 5 | N, V |
| gasoline (gas) | 5 | N |
| b grease | 5 | N, V |
| b petroleum | 5* | N |
| b kerosene | 5* | N |
| lubrication (lubricate) | 6+ | N |

### 8d Appliances

| Minicluster | Grade Level | Part of Speech |
|---|---|---|
| 8d.1. **Stove** | | |
| b oven | 2 | N |
| b stove | 3 | N |
| toaster (toast) | 4* | N |
| b griddle | 5 | N |
| 8d.2. **Furnace** | | |
| b furnace | 4 | N |
| radiator (radiate) | 4* | N |
| boiler (boil) | 5* | N |
| heater (heat) | SC | N |
| 8d.3. **Freezer** | | |
| refrigerator (frigid) | 3 | N |
| b icebox | 4* | N |
| freezer (freeze) | 4* | N |
| 8d.4. **TV** | | |
| TV (television) | 1 | N |
| b radio | 3 | N |
| b television | 3 | N |
| b phonograph | 4* | N |
| b stereo | – | N |

### 8e Tools (General)

| Minicluster | Grade Level | Part of Speech |
|---|---|---|
| 8e.1. **Tools** | | |
| b tool | 3 | N |
| b aid | 4 | N |
| b device | 6 | N |
| b utensil | 6* | N |

## 8e.2. Drill

| | Grade Level | Part of Speech |
|---|---|---|
| b drill | 3 | N, V |
| b screwdriver | 4* | N |
| b wrench | 6 | N, V |
| pliers (ply) | 6 | N |

## 8e.3. Lever

| | | |
|---|---|---|
| b lever | 4 | N |
| b wedge | 4* | N, V |
| b crowbar | 4* | N |

## 8e.4. Hammer

| | | |
|---|---|---|
| b hammer | 3 | N, V |
| b anvil | 5 | N |
| b sledge | 6 | N |

## 8e.5. Saw

| | | |
|---|---|---|
| b saw | K | N, V |
| clipper (clip) | 4 | N |
| b jigsaw | 4* | N |
| b scissors | 5 | N |
| b sickle | 5* | N |
| b scythe | 5* | N |
| b awl | 6 | N |
| mower (mow) | 6 | N |
| trimmer (trim) | 6 | N |
| b lawnmower | 6 | N |

## 8e.6. Shovel

| | | |
|---|---|---|
| b shovel | 2 | N, V |
| b hoe | 4 | N, V |
| b spade | 6 | N, V |
| b rake | 6 | N, V |

## 8e.7. Chisel

| | | |
|---|---|---|
| b chisel | 3 | N, V |
| b sandpaper | 4 | N |
| b rasp | 6 | N |
| scraper (scrape) | 6 | N |

# 8f Tools Used for Cutting

| Minicluster | Grade Level | Part of Speech |
|---|---|---|
| **8f.1. Axe** | | |
| b axe | 4 | N, V |
| b tomahawk | 5* | N |
| b hatchet | 6* | N |

## 8f.2. Knife

| | | |
|---|---|---|
| b knife | 3 | N, V |
| b spear | 3 | N, V |
| b sword | 4 | N |
| b harpoon | 4 | N, V |
| b lance | 5 | N, V |
| b dagger | 6 | N |
| b razor | 6 | N |

## 8f.3. Blade

| | | |
|---|---|---|
| b blade | 4 | N |
| b arrowhead | 5* | N |
| b barb | 6 | N |

# 8g Cutting Actions

| Minicluster | Grade Level | Part of Speech |
|---|---|---|
| **8g.1. Chop** | | |
| b chop | 3 | N, V |
| b peck | 4 | N, V |
| b prick | 4 | V |
| b pierce | 5 | V |
| b hack | 6 | V |
| **8g.2. Scrape** | | |
| b scratch | 3 | N, V |
| b mow | 4 | V |
| b shave | 5 | N, V |
| b scrape | 5 | N, V |
| b whittle | 5 | V |
| b chafe | 6 | V |
| b scuff | 6 | V |
| **8g.3. Grind** | | |
| b carve | 4 | V |
| b grind | 4 | V |
| b peel | 4 | N, V |
| b pare | 4* | V |
| b shred | 5 | V |
| b snip | 5 | V |
| b grate | 6 | V |
| b mince | 6 | V |
| **8g.4. Cut** | | |
| b cut | 1 | N, V |
| b slit | 5 | N, V |
| b slash | 5 | N, V |
| b stab | 6 | V |
| b slice | 6 | N, V |

## 8g.5. Dig

| Minicluster | Grade Level | Part of Speech |
|---|---|---|
| b dig | 2 | V |
| b burrow | 4 | V |
| b bury | 4 | V |
| b scoop | 4 | N, V |
| b furrow | 6 | N, V |
| b excavate | 6 | V |

## 8h Fasteners

| Minicluster | Grade Level | Part of Speech |
|---|---|---|
| **8h.1. Hook** | | |
| b hook | 3 | N, V |
| b nail | 3 | N, V |
| b hinge | 4 | N |
| b fishhook | 4* | N |
| b screw | 5 | N, V |
| b peg | 5 | N |
| b spike | 6 | N |
| b rivet | 6 | N, V |
| **8h.2. Clamp** | | |
| b clamp | 5 | N, V |
| b clothespin | 6* | N |
| **8h.3. Needle** | | |
| b pin | 3 | N, V |
| b needle | 3 | N, V |
| b tack | 4 | N, V |
| b thumbtack | 5* | N, V |
| **8h.4. String** | | |
| b string | 2 | N, V |
| b rope | 2 | N, V |
| b strap | 4 | N, V |
| b chain | 4 | N, V |
| b cable | 5 | N |
| b lasso | 5 | N, V |
| b cord | 5* | N |
| b thong | 6 | N |
| b tether | 6 | N, V |
| **8h.4.1** _____ | | |
| b knot | 4 | N, V |
| **8h.5. Lock** | | |
| b lock | 3 | N, V |
| b key | 3 | N |
| b bolt | 5 | N, V |

## 8i Handles

| Minicluster | Grade Level | Part of Speech |
|---|---|---|
| **8i.1. Handle** | | |
| b handle | 2 | N |
| b latch | 4 | N, V |
| b doorknob | 4* | N |
| b grip | 4 | N, V |
| b dial | 5 | N, V |
| b knob | 6 | N |

## 8j Miscellaneous Devices

| Minicluster | Grade Level | Part of Speech |
|---|---|---|
| **8j.1. Lever** | | |
| b switch | 3 | N, V |
| b lever | 4 | N |
| b trigger | 6 | N, V |

---

**Key**

Basic words
Basic words are preceded by *b*.
All other words are followed by the basic word in parentheses.

Grade levels
K-6    The grade level at which a word is introduced.
*    Indicates a word does not appear frequently in student reading material, but when it does appear it is at the level indicated.
–    Words or phrases for which a grade level could not be determined.
Content specific words are indicated by the content area in which they are used:
SS    Social Studies
EN    English
MA    Math
SC    Science

Part of Speech
N    Noun
V    Verb
A    Adjective
AV    Adverb
AV (+ly)    Adverb when suffix -ly is added
PRO    Pronoun
PREP    Preposition
INT    Interjection
DET    Determiner
AX    Auxiliary verb
RM    Relationship marker

## 8j.2. Pedal

| | | | |
|---|---|---|---|
| b | crank | 6 | N, V |
| b | pedal | 6 | N, V |

## 8j.3. Pulley

| | | | |
|---|---|---|---|
| | roller (roll) | 2* | N |
| | pulley (pull) | 3 | N |
| b | spool | 3* | N |
| | spindle (spin) | 5 | N |

## 8j.4. Platform

| | | | |
|---|---|---|---|
| b | ladder | 2 | N |
| b | platform | 2 | N |
| b | gantry | 6 | N |
| b | tripod | 6* | N |

## 8j.5. Pointer

| | | | |
|---|---|---|---|
| | pointer (point) | 3* | N |
| b | wand | 4 | N |
| b | baton | 6 | N |

# 8k Equipment Related to Vision

| Minicluster | | Grade Level | Part of Speech |
|---|---|---|---|
| **8k.1. Telescope** | | | |
| | telescope (scope) | 3 | N, V |
| | microscope (scope) | 4* | N |
| b | binoculars | 6 | N |
| | periscope (scope) | 6 | N |
| b | eyepiece | SC | N |
| | electroscope (scope) | SC | N |
| **8k.2. Camera** | | | |
| b | camera | 3 | N |
| b | film | 6 | N, V |
| b | lens | 6 | N |

# 8L Electronic Equipment

| Minicluster | | Grade Level | Part of Speech |
|---|---|---|---|
| **8L.1. Transmitter** | | | |
| | transmitter (transmit) | 5* | N |
| | wireless (wire) | 5* | N |
| b | transistor | 6* | N |

## 8L.2. Computer

| | | | |
|---|---|---|---|
| b | robot | 4* | N |
| | computer (compute) | 6* | N |
| | teletype (type) | 6* | N |
| b | terminal | 6+ | N |

# 8m Utensils Used for Cooking/Eating

| Minicluster | | Grade Level | Part of Speech |
|---|---|---|---|
| **8m.1. Silverware** | | | |
| b | fork | 3 | N |
| b | knife | 3 | N, V |
| b | teaspoon | 3 | N |
| b | spoon | 4 | N, V |
| b | silverware | 5* | N |
| b | tablespoon | 6* | N |
| b | chopsticks | 6* | N |
| **8m.2. Pan** | | | |
| b | pan | 1 | N |
| b | pot | 3 | N |
| b | kettle | 3 | N |
| b | teakettle | 4* | N |
| b | teapot | 4* | N |
| b | saucepan | 5* | N |
| **8m.3. Ladle** | | | |
| b | sieve | 5* | N |
| | dipper (dip) | 5* | N |
| b | tong | 5* | N |
| b | ladle | 6 | N, V |
| **8m.4. Opener** | | | |
| | opener (open) | 6* | N |
| b | corkscrew | SC | N |
| **8m.5. Bowl** | | | |
| b | glass | 2 | N |
| b | bowl | 2 | N |
| b | cup | 2 | N |
| b | mug | 4 | N |
| **8m.6. Dish** | | | |
| b | dish | 2 | N |
| b | saucer | 4 | N |
| | platter (plate) | 4 | N |
| b | tray | 4 | N |
| b | chinaware | SS | N |

## 8m.7. **Beater**

| Minicluster | Grade Level | Part of Speech |
|---|---|---|
| beater (beat) | 3* | N |

## 8n Weapons

| Minicluster | Grade Level | Part of Speech |
|---|---|---|
| **8n.1. Weapon** | | |
| b weapon | 5 | N |
| b arms | 6+ | N |
| b firearms | SS | N |
| **8n.2. Missile** | | |
| b missile | 5 | N |
| b torpedo | 5 | N, V |
| b bullet | 5 | N |
| b bomb | 5* | N, V |
| b pellet | 6* | N |
| **8n.3. Gun** | | |
| b gun | 2 | N |
| b rifle | 4 | N, V |
| b cannon | 4 | N |
| b pistol | 6 | N |
| b musket | 6 | N |
| b revolver | 6* | N |
| b shotgun | 6+ | N |
| **8n.4. Explosive** | | |
| b gunpowder | 4* | N |
| b dynamite | 5 | N, V |
| explosive (explode) | 6 | N, A, AV(+ly) |
| b ammunition | 6 | N |
| b firecracker | 6* | N |
| **8n.5. Bow** | | |
| b bow | 3 | N |
| b arrow | 3 | N |
| b dart | 4 | N |
| b sling | 4 | N |
| b boomerang | SS | N, V |
| b slingshot | SS | N |
| **8n.6. Whip** | | |
| b whip | 4 | N, V |
| **8n.7. Noose** | | |
| b noose | 5 | N |

# Supercluster 9
## Types of People

### 9a People (General Names)

| Minicluster | Grade Level | Part of Speech |
|---|---|---|
| **9a.1. Fellow** | | |
| b person | 2 | N |
| b fellow | 3 | N |
| b character | 4 | N |
| b human | 4 | N |
| b being | 4 | N |
| b individual | 5 | N, A AV (+ly) |
| b buster | 5 | N |
| b self | 5 | N |
| **9a.1.1 _____** | | |
| b people | 2 | N |
| b folk | 3 | N |
| mankind (man) | 4* | N |

### 9b Names for Women

| Minicluster | Grade Level | Part of Speech |
|---|---|---|
| **9b.1. Lady** | | |
| b woman | 2 | N |
| b lady | 3 | N |
| b widow | 4 | N |
| b mistress | 4 | N |
| b squaw | 4* | N |
| female (male) | 4* | N |
| ma'am (madame) | 5 | N |
| hostess (host) | 5* | N |
| b madame | 6* | N |
| b dame | 6 | N |
| b housewife | 6* | N |
| b virgin | SS | N |
| b spinster | – | N |
| **9b.2. Girl** | | |
| b girl | 1 | N |
| b lass | 3* | N |
| maiden (maid) | 4* | N |
| b tomboy | 6* | N |

## 9c Names for Men

| Minicluster | Grade Level | Part of Speech |
|---|---|---|
| **9c.1. Boy** | | |
| b boy | 1 | N |
| b lad | 3 | N |
| **9c.2. Guy** | | |
| b guy | K | N |
| b man | K | N, V |
| b sir | 3 | N |
| b male | 3 | N |
| b mister | 4 | N |
| gentlemen (gentleman) | 4 | N |
| b gentleman | 4* | N |
| b host | 6 | N |
| b señor | 6 | N |
| b bachelor | – | N |

## 9d Names Indicating Age

| Minicluster | Grade Level | Part of Speech |
|---|---|---|
| **9d.1. Baby** | | |
| b baby | 1 | N, V |
| babe (baby) | 4 | N |
| b newborn | 4* | N |
| b infant | 6 | N |
| b papoose | 6 | N |
| b embryo | SC | N |
| b tot | 6+ | N |
| toddler (toddle) | 6+ | N |
| **9d.2. Kid** | | |
| b child | 3 | N |
| b youth | 4 | N |
| b kid | 4 | N |
| b orphan | 5 | N |
| b urchin | 5* | N |
| youngster (young) | 6 | N |
| b junior | 6 | N |
| b minor | 6 | N |
| **9d.3. Grown-up** | | |
| elder (old) | 5 | N |
| b veteran | 6 | N |
| b grown-up | 6* | N |
| b senior | – | N |

## 9e Names Indicating Friendship/ Camaraderie

| Minicluster | Grade Level | Part of Speech |
|---|---|---|
| **9e.1. Friend** | | |
| b friend | 1 | N |
| b neighbor | 2 | N |
| b classmate | 3* | N |
| b pal | 4 | N |
| b partner | 4 | N |
| b teammate | 5 | N |
| b ally | 6 | N |
| b playmate | 6 | N |
| b comrade | 6 | N |
| b chum | – | N |
| b buddy | – | N |
| acquaintance (acquaint) | – | N |
| **9e.2. Lover** | | |
| b mate | 6 | N |
| b darling | 6 | N |
| lover (love) | 6* | N |
| b girlfriend | – | N |
| b boyfriend | – | N |

## 9f Names for Spiritual or Mythological Characters

| Minicluster | Grade Level | Part of Speech |
|---|---|---|
| **9f.1. Fairy** | | |
| b fairy | 2 | N |
| b elf | 4* | N |
| elves (elf) | 5* | N |
| b mermaid | 5* | N |
| **9f.2. Spirit** | | |
| b spirit | 3 | N |
| b ghost | 4 | N |
| b soul | 5 | N |
| **9f.3. Angel** | | |
| b God | 4 | N |
| b angel | 4* | N |
| b saint | 5 | N |
| **9f.4. Demon** | | |
| b goblin | 3* | N |
| b phantom | 5 | N |
| b demon | 5 | N |
| b devil | 5* | N |

9f.5. **Witch**

| | | | |
|---|---|---|---|
| b | witch | 4 | N |
| b | wizard | 4 | N |

## 9g Names Indicating Negative Characteristics about People

| Minicluster | Grade Level | Part of Speech |
|---|---|---|
| 9g.1. **Liar** | | |
| b storyteller | 4* | N |
| liar (lie) | 5 | N |
| b gossip | 6 | N |
| 9g.2. **Rascal** | | |
| b rascal | 5 | N |
| b nuisance | 5 | N |
| b pest | 6 | N |
| b dolt | 6 | N |
| b fool | 6 | N |
| 9g.3. **Enemy** | | |
| b enemy | 3 | N |
| b foe | 4* | N |
| b bully | 5 | N, V |
| b opponent | 5* | N |
| b rival | 6 | N, V |
| 9g.4. **Grouch** | | |
| b grouch | 5 | N |
| b hermit | 6* | N |
| 9g.5. **Outlaw** | | |
| thief (thievery) | 3 | N |
| b bandit | 4 | N |
| b pirate | 4 | N |
| killer (kill) | 4* | N |
| b outlaw | 5 | N |
| robber (rob) | 5 | N |
| rustler (rustle) | 5 | N |
| b burglar | 5* | N |
| criminal (crime) | 6 | N |
| b villain | 6 | N |
| b tyrant | 6 | N |
| b fiend | 6* | N |
| b victim | 6 | N |

## 9h Names Indicating Lack of Permanence for People

| Minicluster | Grade Level | Part of Speech |
|---|---|---|
| 9h.1. **Stranger** | | |
| visitor (visit) | 3 | N |
| stranger (strange) | 4 | N |
| b guest | 4 | N |
| tourist (tour) | 6 | N |
| vacationer (vacation) | SS | N |

---

**Key**

Basic words
  Basic words are preceded by *b*.
  All other words are followed by the basic
  word in parentheses.

Grade levels
  K-6   The grade level at which a word is
          introduced.
  *      Indicates a word does not appear
          frequently in student reading
          material, but when it does appear it
          is at the level indicated.
  –      Words or phrases for which a grade
          level could not be determined.
  Content specific words are indicated by
  the content area in which they are used:
  SS     Social Studies
  EN     English
  MA     Math
  SC     Science

Part of Speech
  N           Noun
  V           Verb
  A           Adjective
  AV          Adverb
  AV (+ly)    Adverb when suffix -ly is
                added
  PRO         Pronoun
  PREP        Preposition
  INT         Interjection
  DET         Determiner
  AX          Auxiliary verb
  RM          Relationship marker

## 9h.2. Rover

| | | | |
|---|---|---|---|
| | rover (rove) | 3* | N |
| b | runaway | 4* | N |
| | beggar (beg) | 5 | N |
| b | gypsy | 6 | N |
| b | vagabond | 6 | N |
| b | nomad | 6* | N |
| | wanderer (wander) | 6* | N |
| b | wayfarer | 6* | N |

## 9h.3. Spectator

| | | | |
|---|---|---|---|
| | passenger (passenger) | 4 | N |
| | spectator (spectacle) | 6 | N |

# 9i Names Indicating Permanence for People

| Minicluster | Grade Level | Part of Speech |
|---|---|---|

## 9i.1. Settler

| | | | |
|---|---|---|---|
| | settler (settle) | 4 | N |
| b | pioneer | 4 | N |
| b | pilgrim | 4* | N |
| | colonist (colony) | 5 | N |
| | puritan (pure) | 5* | N |

## 9i.2. Inhabitant

| | | | |
|---|---|---|---|
| | villager (village) | 4 | N |
| | dweller (dwell) | 4* | N |
| | inhabitant (inhabit) | 5 | N |
| b | townspeople | 5* | N |
| b | tenant | 5 | N |
| | resident (reside) | 5 | N |
| b | tribesman | SS | N |
| b | bushman | SS | N |

## 9i.3. Native

| | | | |
|---|---|---|---|
| b | native | 4 | N |
| | foreigner (foreign) | 4* | N |
| b | citizen | 5 | N |

## 9i.3.1 _____

| | | | |
|---|---|---|---|
| b | foreign | 4 | A |
| | immigrant (immigrate) | 6 | N, A |

## 9i.4. Patriot

| | | | |
|---|---|---|---|
| b | traitor | 5 | N |
| b | patriot | 6 | N |
| b | countryman | SS | N |

# 9j Names Indicating Size of People

| Minicluster | Grade Level | Part of Speech |
|---|---|---|

## 9j.1. Giant

| | | | |
|---|---|---|---|
| b | giant | 2 | N |
| b | dwarf | 4* | N |
| b | midget | 6 | N |
| b | runt | 6 | N |
| b | pygmy | 6* | N |

# 9k Names Indicating Fame

| Minicluster | Grade Level | Part of Speech |
|---|---|---|

## 9k.1. Celebrity

| | | | |
|---|---|---|---|
| b | star | 2 | N |
| | celebrity (celebrate) | 4 | N |
| b | hero | 4 | N |
| b | champion | 4 | N |
| | heroine (hero) | 6 | N |
| b | idol | 6* | N |
| | savior (save) | SS | N |

# 9L Names Indicating Knowledge of a Topic

| Minicluster | Grade Level | Part of Speech |
|---|---|---|

## 9L.1. Expert

| | | | |
|---|---|---|---|
| b | expert | 4 | N |
| b | scholar | 5 | N |
| b | genius | 5 | N |
| | specialist (special) | 6 | N |
| b | amateur | 6 | N |
| b | novice | 6 | N |
| b | sage | 6* | N |

## 9m Names Indicating Financial Status

| Minicluster | Grade Level | Part of Speech |
|---|---|---|
| **9m.1. Millionaire** | | |
| millionaire (million) | 5* | N |
| b peasant | 5* | N |
| b miser | 6 | N |
| pauper (poor) | 6* | N |

## 9n Family Relations

| Minicluster | Grade Level | Part of Speech |
|---|---|---|
| **9n.1. Family** | | |
| b family | 3 | N |
| b household | 4 | N |
| **9n.2. Relative** | | |
| b ancestor | 4 | N |
| relative (relate) | 5 | N |
| descendant (descend) | 5* | N |
| b heir | 6* | N |
| **9n.3. Father** | | |
| daddy (dad) | K | N |
| b father | K | N, V |
| b dad | 2 | N |
| papa (pa) | 4 | N |
| b pa | 4 | N |
| **9n.4. Parent** | | |
| b parent | 3 | N |
| b ward | 4 | N |
| b offspring | 5 | N |
| guardian (guard) | 5* | N |
| **9n.5. Mother** | | |
| b mother | K | N, V |
| mamma (mom) | 3 | N |
| mama (mom) | 3 | N |
| ma (mom) | 4 | N |
| b mom | 4 | N |
| **9n.6. Sister** | | |
| b sister | 1 | N |
| b brother | 2 | N |
| b son | 2 | N |
| b daughter | 3 | N |
| b sibling | 6 | N |

| Minicluster | Grade Level | Part of Speech |
|---|---|---|
| **9n.7. Spouse** | | |
| b wife | 2 | N |
| b husband | 3 | N |
| b bride | 3 | N |
| b groom | 6 | N |
| b spouse | 6 | N |
| **9n.8. Grandparent** | | |
| b grandfather | 2 | N, V |
| b grandmother | 2 | N |
| b granny | 3 | N |
| b grandpa | 4 | N |
| grandma (grandmother) | 4 | N |
| b grandparent | 4* | N |
| b grandson | 4* | N |
| b granddaughter | 4* | N |
| grandchildren (grandchild) | 5* | N |
| **9n.9. Aunt** | | |
| b aunt | 2 | N |
| b uncle | 2 | N |
| b cousin | 6 | N |
| b nephew | 6 | N |
| b niece | 6 | N |

## 9o Names Indicating Political Disposition

| Minicluster | Grade Level | Part of Speech |
|---|---|---|
| **9o.1. Communist** | | |
| confederate (confederacy) | 5* | N, A |
| socialist (social) | SS | N, A |
| communist (common) | SS | N, A |
| nationalist (nation) | SS | N, A |
| **9o.2. Feudalism** | | |
| feudalism (feudal) | SS | N |
| b feudal | SS | A |
| **9o.3. Democratic** | | |
| democratic (democracy) | 5* | A, AV (+ly) |
| republican (republic) | SS | A |
| **9o.3.1 _____** | | |
| b civic | 6 | A |

# Supercluster 10
## Communication

### 10a Oral Communication (General)

| Minicluster | Grade Level | Part of Speech |
|---|---|---|
| **10.a.1. Statement** | | |
| statement (state) | 4 | N |
| expression (express) | 4 | N |
| b remark | 4 | N, V |
| resolution (resolute) | 5 | N |
| demonstration (demonstrate) | 5* | N |
| declaration (declare) | 5* | N |
| b comment | 6 | N, V |
| exclamation (claim) | 6 | N |
| b testimony | 6 | N |
| proclamation (proclaim) | SS | N |
| **10a.2. Talk** | | |
| b talk | 1 | N, V |
| b speak | 3 | V |
| b utter | 5 | V |
| b discuss | 5 | V |
| b communicate | 5 | V |
| b correspond | 5* | V |
| b chat | 6 | N, V |
| b converse | 6* | V |
| **10a.3. Conversation** | | |
| conversation (converse) | 4 | N |
| b lecture | 5* | N, V |
| discussion (discuss) | 6 | N |
| b dialogue | 6* | N |
| **10a.4. Talkative** | | |
| vocal (voice) | 5* | A, AV (+ly) |
| talkative (talk) | 6 | A |
| verbose (verbiage) | 6* | A, AV (+ly) |

### 10b Communications Involving Confrontation or Negative Information

| Minicluster | Grade Level | Part of Speech |
|---|---|---|
| **10b.1. Argue** | | |
| b argue | 4 | V |
| disobey (obey) | 5* | V |
| b rebel | 5* | V |
| b revolt | 5* | N, V |
| disagree (agree) | 6 | V |
| discount (count) | MA | V |
| **10b.2. Oppose** | | |
| b oppose | K | V |
| b complain | 3 | V |
| b object | 4 | V |
| b protest | 4 | N, V |
| **10b.3. Betray** | | |
| b disappoint | 3 | V |
| b betray | 5 | V |
| disguise (guise) | 5 | V |
| b exaggerate | 6 | V |
| b deceive | 6 | V |
| **10b.4. Swear** | | |
| b swear | 5* | V |
| b curse | 6 | N, V |
| **10b.5. Complaint** | | |
| argument (argue) | 2 | N |
| b quarrel | 3 | N, V |
| b debate | 5* | N, V |
| criticism (critic) | 5* | N |
| complaint (complain) | 6 | N |
| objection (object) | 6 | N |
| **10b.6. Warn** | | |
| b warn | 3 | V |
| b correct | 4 | V |
| b remind | 4 | V |
| beware (wary) | 4* | V |
| b confront | 6 | V |
| **10b.7. Threat** | | |
| warning (warn) | 4* | N |
| prediction (predict) | 4* | N |
| b threat | 5 | N |
| prophecy (prophet) | 6 | N |
| b omen | 6* | N |

## 10h.8. **Accuse**

| | | | |
|---|---|---|---|
| b | blame | 4 | V |
| b | accuse | 4 | V |
| b | denounce | 6 | V |
| b | condemn | 6 | V |

## 10b.9. **Insult**

| | | | |
|---|---|---|---|
| b | scold | 3 | V |
| b | tease | 3 | N, V |
| | disgrace (grace) | 4 | N, V |
| b | insult | 5 | N, V |
| b | embarrass | 5 | V |
| b | jeer | 6 | N, V |
| b | ridicule | 6 | V |
| b | scoff | 6 | N, V |

## 10b.10. **Dare**

| | | | |
|---|---|---|---|
| b | dare | 3 | N, V |
| | threaten (threat) | 4 | V |

## 10b.11. **Falsehood**

| | | | |
|---|---|---|---|
| b | lie | 3 | N, V |
| | foolishness (fool) | 4 | N |
| | nonsense (sense) | 4 | N |
| | exaggeration (exaggerate) | 6 | N |
| b | rumor | 6 | N |
| b | sham | EN | N |
| b | falsehood | 6 | N |

# 10c Communication Involving General Presentation of Information

| Minicluster | Grade Level | Part of Speech |
|---|---|---|
| **10c.1. Show** | | |
| b show | K | N, V |
| b tell | 1 | V |
| b explain | 3 | V |
| b describe | 4 | V |
| b exhibit | 6 | N, V |
| b notify | 6 | V |
| b expose | 6* | V |
| b demonstrate | 6 | V |

## 10c.2. **Mention**

| | | | |
|---|---|---|---|
| b | say | K | V |
| b | state | 3 | V |
| b | mention | 3 | N, V |
| b | relate | 4 | V |
| b | pronounce | 4 | V |
| b | indicate | 6 | V |
| b | convey | 6 | V |

## 10c.3. **Broadcast**

| | | | |
|---|---|---|---|
| b | transmit | 5* | V |
| b | broadcast | 5* | N, V |
| | telecast (cast) | EN | N, V |

---

**Key**

Basic words
> Basic words are preceded by *b*.
> All other words are followed by the basic word in parentheses.

Grade levels
> K-6   The grade level at which a word is introduced.
> *   Indicates a word does not appear frequently in student reading material, but when it does appear it is at the level indicated.
> –   Words or phrases for which a grade level could not be determined.

Content specific words are indicated by the content area in which they are used:
| | |
|---|---|
| SS | Social Studies |
| EN | English |
| MA | Math |
| SC | Science |

Part of Speech
| | |
|---|---|
| N | Noun |
| V | Verb |
| A | Adjective |
| AV | Adverb |
| AV (+ly) | Adverb when suffix -ly is added |
| PRO | Pronoun |
| PREP | Preposition |
| INT | Interjection |
| DET | Determiner |
| AX | Auxiliary verb |
| RM | Relationship marker |

## 10c.4. Exclaim

| | | |
|---|---|---|
| exclaim (claim) | 3 | V |
| b declare | 3 | V |
| b present | 3 | V |
| b boast | 4 | N, V |
| b announce | 4 | V |
| b claim | 4 | N, V |
| b brag | 5 | V |
| b herald | 6 | V |
| proclaim (claim) | 6 | V |

## 10c.5. Stress

| | | |
|---|---|---|
| b stress | 6 | V |
| b emphasize | 6* | V |

## 10d Communication Involving Positive Information

| Minicluster | Grade Level | Part of Speech |
|---|---|---|
| **10d.1. Greeting** | | |
| greeting (greet) | 2* | N |
| b apology | 6 | N |
| b truce | 6* | N |
| **10d.2. Assure** | | |
| b assure | 5 | V |
| b encourage | 5 | V |
| b charm | 5 | V |
| b inspire | 6 | V |
| b soothe | 6 | V |
| **10d.3. Praise** | | |
| b support | 4 | N, V |
| b praise | 5 | N, V |
| congratulations (congratulate) | 6 | N |
| **10d.4. Congratulate** | | |
| b congratulate | 6 | V |
| acknowledge (know) | 6 | V |
| **10d.5. Welcome** | | |
| b invite | 3 | V |
| b welcome | 3 | V |
| b offer | 3 | V |
| b greet | 4 | V |

## 10d.6. Pray

| | | |
|---|---|---|
| b worship | 5 | V |
| b pray | 5 | V |
| b preach | 5* | V |
| b dedicate | 5* | V |
| b bless | 6 | V |

## 10d.6.1 _____

| | | |
|---|---|---|
| prayer (pray) | 4 | N |
| blessing (bless) | 5 | N |

## 10e Persuasion

| Minicluster | Grade Level | Part of Speech |
|---|---|---|
| **10e.1. Convince** | | |
| b convince | 4 | V |
| b tempt | 4 | V |
| b persuade | 4 | V |
| b bait | 4 | V |
| b influence | 5 | V |
| b bribe | 5 | N, V |
| b discourage | 5 | V |
| b convert | 5* | V |
| b enlist | 5* | V |
| **10e.2. Plead** | | |
| b urge | 4 | V |
| b appeal | 4 | N, V |
| plead (plea) | 5 | V |
| b coax | 6 | V |
| **10e.3. Suggest** | | |
| b suggest | 4 | V |
| b advise | 5 | V |
| b hint | 5 | N, V |
| b imply | 6 | V |
| recommend (commend) | 6 | V |

## 10f Questions

| Minicluster | Grade Level | Part of Speech |
|---|---|---|
| **10f.1. Answer** | | |
| b answer | 2 | N, V |
| b reply | 3 | N, V |
| b respond | 5 | V |
| b retort | 6 | N, V |

## 10f.2. Question

| | | Grade Level | Part of Speech |
|---|---|---|---|
| b | call | K | N, V |
| b | ask | K | V |
| b | question | 2 | N, V |
| b | bid | 4 | N, V |
| b | beckon | 5 | V |
| b | interview | 5 | N, V |
| b | summon | 5 | V |
| b | inquire | 6 | V |
| b | consult | 6 | V |

## 10f.3. Test

| | | | |
|---|---|---|---|
| b | test | 3 | N, V |
| b | quiz | 5* | N, V |
| | examination (exam) | 6 | N |

## 10f.4. Suspect

| | | | |
|---|---|---|---|
| b | suspect | 4 | N, V |

# 10g Communications Involving Supervision/Commands

| Minicluster | Grade Level | Part of Speech |
|---|---|---|

## 10g.1. Instruction

| | | | |
|---|---|---|---|
| b | direction | 3 | N |
| | advice (advise) | 4 | N |
| | suggestion (suggest) | 4 | N |
| | instruction (instruct) | 5 | N |

## 10g.2. Command

| | | | |
|---|---|---|---|
| b | insist | 3 | V |
| b | command | 4 | N, V |
| b | demand | 4 | N, V |
| b | require | 5 | V |

## 10g.3. Allow

| | | | |
|---|---|---|---|
| b | let | K | V |
| b | allow | 3 | V |
| b | support | 4 | V |
| b | excuse | 4 | V |
| b | permit | 5 | N, V |

## 10g.4. Obey

| | | | |
|---|---|---|---|
| b | obey | 3 | V |
| b | agree | 3 | V |
| b | consent | 5 | N, V |
| b | submit | 6 | V |
| b | yield | 6 | V |
| b | cooperate | 6 | V |
| b | participate | 6* | V |

## 10g.5. Regulate

| | | | |
|---|---|---|---|
| b | direct | 3 | V |
| b | control | 4 | N, V |
| b | supervise | 5* | V |
| b | regulate | 5* | V |
| b | govern | 5* | V |
| b | manage | 6* | V |
| b | dominate | 6* | V |

## 10g.5.1 _____

| | | | |
|---|---|---|---|
| b | force | 3 | N, V |
| | enforce (force) | 5 | V |
| b | exploit | 6* | N, V |
| | supervision (supervise) | 6 | N |

## 10g.6. Authority

| | | | |
|---|---|---|---|
| b | authority | 6 | N |
| | leadership (lead) | 6* | N |

## 10g.7. Refuse

| | | | |
|---|---|---|---|
| b | refuse | 3 | V |
| b | deny | 5 | V |
| | forbid (forbade) | 5* | V |
| b | decline | 6 | V |
| b | reject | 6 | V |

# 10h Giving Out Information Previously Withheld

| Minicluster | Grade Level | Part of Speech |
|---|---|---|

## 10h.1. Confide

| | | | |
|---|---|---|---|
| b | confess | 4 | V |
| b | confide | 6 | V |

## 10h.2. Admit

| | | | |
|---|---|---|---|
| b | admit | 4 | V |
| | apologize (apology) | 5 | V |

# 10i Promises

| Minicluster | Grade Level | Part of Speech |
|---|---|---|

## 10i.1. Plea

| | | | |
|---|---|---|---|
| b | promise | 3 | N, V |
| b | plea | 5 | N, V |
| b | vow | 5 | N, V |
| b | oath | 5* | N |
| b | pledge | 6 | N, V |

## 10j Recording or Translating Information

| Minicluster | Grade Level | Part of Speech |
|---|---|---|
| **10j.1. Quotation** | | |
| b quote | 5* | N, V |
| quotation (quote) | 6 | N |
| translation (translate) | 6 | N |
| interpretation (intepret) | 6 | N |
| recording (record) | 6* | N |
| **10j.1.1 _____** | | |
| b record | 3 | N, V |
| **10j.1.2 _____** | | |
| b translate | 6 | V |

## 10k Exclamations (General)

| Minicluster | Grade Level | Part of Speech |
|---|---|---|
| **10k.1. Ha** | | |
| b oh | 1 | INT |
| b ho | 3 | INT |
| b ah | 3 | INT |
| b hurrah | 3 | INT |
| b ow | 3* | INT |
| b pooh | 4 | INT |
| b ha | 4 | INT |
| b hey | 4 | INT |
| b aha | 4 | INT |
| b aw | 4 | INT |
| b wow | 5 | INT |
| b ooh | 5 | INT |
| b gee | 5 | INT |
| b alas | 5 | INT |
| b ay | 5* | INT |
| b olé | 6 | INT |
| b ugh | 6 | INT |
| b bravo | 6 | INT |
| **10k.2. No/Yes** | | |
| b no | K | INT |
| b yes | K | INT |
| b maybe | 1 | INT |
| b aye | 4 | INT |
| ok (okay) | 4 | INT, A |
| b okay | 4 | INT, A |

## 10k.3. Hello

| | Grade Level | Part of Speech |
|---|---|---|
| goodby (good-bye) | 1 | INT |
| b hello | 1 | INT |
| hi (hello) | 2 | INT |
| b good-bye | 4 | INT |
| b farewell | 5 | INT |
| b howdy | 5 | INT |

# Supercluster 11
# Transporation

## 11a Types of Transporation

| Minicluster | Grade Level | Part of Speech |
|---|---|---|
| **11a.1. Car** | | |
| b car | K | N |
| automobile (auto) | 3 | N |
| b auto | 4* | N |
| b vehicle | 5 | N |
| **11a.2. Truck** | | |
| b truck | 1 | N, V |
| b van | 4 | N |
| b jeep | 4 | N |
| b sedan | 6 | N |
| b pickup | 6 | N |
| **11a.3. Bus** | | |
| b bus | 1 | N, V |
| b taxicab | 3 | N |
| b taxi | 4 | N |
| b cab | 4 | N |
| b subway | 5 | N |
| b ambulance | 5* | N |
| b stagecoach | SS | N |
| **11a.4. Bike** | | |
| bike (bicycle) | K | N, V |
| b bicycle | 3 | N, V |
| scooter (scoot) | 5 | N |
| unicycle (bicycle) | 6* | N |
| tricycle (bicycle) | 6* | N |
| **11a.5. Train** | | |
| b train | K | N |
| b streetcar | 4* | N |
| b locomotive | 4* | N |
| b caboose | 5 | N |

### 11a.6. **Cart**

| | | | |
|---|---|---|---|
| b | wagon | 1 | N |
| b | cart | 2 | N, V |
| b | buggy | 4 | N |
| b | carriage | 4 | N |
| | trailer (trail) | 5 | N |
| b | chariot | 6 | N |

## 11b Work Related Vehicles

| Minicluster | Grade Level | Part of Speech |
|---|---|---|

### 11b.1. **Tractor**

| | | | |
|---|---|---|---|
| b | tractor | 2 | N |
| b | dredge | 5* | N |
| b | bulldozer | 5* | N |
| b | harrow | 6* | N |
| | reaper (reap) | SS | N |

### 11b.2. **Wheelbarrow**

| | | | |
|---|---|---|---|
| b | wheelbarrow | 5* | N |
| b | barrow | 5* | N |

### 11b.3. **Elevator**

| | | | |
|---|---|---|---|
| | elevator (elevate) | 2 | N |
| | escalator (escalate) | 3* | N |
| | conveyor (convey) | 5* | N |
| b | derrick | 5* | N |

## 11c Vehicles Used in Snow

| Minicluster | Grade Level | Part of Speech |
|---|---|---|

### 11c.1. **Sled**

| | | | |
|---|---|---|---|
| b | sled | 2 | N, V |
| b | toboggan | 6 | N, V |
| b | dogsled | 6 | N |
| b | snowplow | 6 | N, V |

## 11d Vehicles Used for Air Transporation

| Minicluster | Grade Level | Part of Speech |
|---|---|---|

### 11d.1. **Airplane**

| | | | |
|---|---|---|---|
| b | airplane | 1 | N, V |
| b | helicopter | 3 | N |
| b | plane | 4 | N |
| b | airship | 4* | N |
| b | airline | 4* | N |
| | airliner (airline) | 4* | N |
| b | aircraft | 6 | N |

### 11d.1.1 _____

| | | |
|---|---|---|
| aerial (air) | 5* | A |

---

**Key**

**Basic words**

Basic words are preceded by *b*.
All other words are followed by the basic word in parentheses.

**Grade levels**

K-6  The grade level at which a word is introduced.

\*  Indicates a word does not appear frequently in student reading material, but when it does appear it is at the level indicated.

–  Words or phrases for which a grade level could not be determined.

Content specific words are indicated by the content area in which they are used:

| | |
|---|---|
| SS | Social Studies |
| EN | English |
| MA | Math |
| SC | Science |

**Part of Speech**

| | |
|---|---|
| N | Noun |
| V | Verb |
| A | Adjective |
| AV | Adverb |
| AV (+ly) | Adverb when suffix -ly is added |
| PRO | Pronoun |
| PREP | Preposition |
| INT | Interjection |
| DET | Determiner |
| AX | Auxiliary verb |
| RM | Relationship marker |

### 11d.2. Balloon

| | | |
|---|---|---|
| b balloon | 1 | N, V |
| b kite | 2 | N |
| glider (glide) | 4 | N |
| b blimp | 6 | N |
| b dirigible | 6* | N |

### 11d.3. Rocket

| | | |
|---|---|---|
| b rocket | 1 | N, V |
| b spacecraft | 4* | N |
| b skyrocket | SC | N |

## 11e Vehicles Used for Sea Transporation

| Minicluster | Grade Level | Part of Speech |
|---|---|---|

### 11e.1. Ship

| | | |
|---|---|---|
| b boat | K | N, V |
| b ship | 2 | N, V |
| b hulk | 5 | N |
| b vessel | 5 | N |

### 11e.2. Ferry

| | | |
|---|---|---|
| liner (ocean liner) | 4* | N |
| b ferry | 5 | N, V |
| tanker (tank) | 5* | N |
| freighter (freight) | SS | N |
| b ocean liner | SS | N |

### 11e.3. Battleship

| | | |
|---|---|---|
| b warship | 4* | N |
| b submarine | 5 | N |
| sub (submarine) | 5* | N |
| carrier (carry) | 5* | N |
| b battleship | 5* | N |
| b flagship | 5* | N |
| destroyer (destroy) | 6* | N |

### 11e.4. Steamship

| | | |
|---|---|---|
| b steamship | 4* | N |
| b steamboat | 5* | N |
| steamer (steam) | SS | N |

### 11e.5. Tug

| | | |
|---|---|---|
| b tug | 3 | N |
| b barge | 4 | N |
| b tugboat | 4* | N |
| b scow | 5 | N |

### 11e.6. Sailboat

| | | |
|---|---|---|
| b sailboat | 2* | N |
| b yacht | 4* | N |
| b schooner | 5 | N |
| b galleon | 6 | N |
| b caravel | 6 | N |

### 11e.7. Canoe

| | | |
|---|---|---|
| b keelboat | 4* | N |
| b canoe | 4 | N, V |
| b raft | 5 | N, V |
| b rowboat | 6 | N |
| b gondola | 6* | N |
| b flatboat | SS | N |

### 11e.8. Shipwreck

| | | |
|---|---|---|
| b shipwreck | 6 | N, V |
| b shipbuilding | SS | N |

### 11e.9. Seagoing

| | | |
|---|---|---|
| b seagoing | 5* | A |
| b seafaring | 5* | A |

## 11f Parts of Vehicles

| Minicluster | Grade Level | Part of Speech |
|---|---|---|

### 11f.1. Wheel

| | | |
|---|---|---|
| b wheel | 2 | N |
| b tire | 2 | N |
| b axle | 6 | N |
| b hub | 6 | N |

### 11f.2. Seatbelt

| | | |
|---|---|---|
| b trunk | 2 | N |
| b mirror | 3 | N |
| b windshield | 4 | N |
| b headlight | 6 | N |
| b seatbelt | 6* | N |

### 11f.3. Deck

| | | |
|---|---|---|
| b deck | 4 | N |
| b mast | 4 | N |
| b anchor | 4 | N, V |
| b hull | 5 | N |
| b keel | 6 | N |
| b helm | 6 | N |
| b gunwale | 6 | N |
| b galley | 6 | N |
| b gangplank | 6 | N |

### 11f.3.1 _____

| | | |
|---|---|---|
| b oar | 4 | N |
| b paddle | 4 | N, V |
| b rudder | 5 | N |

## 11f.4. Wing

| | | Grade Level | Part of Speech |
|---|---|---|---|
| b | wing | 2 | N |
| b | tail | 2 | N |
| b | cockpit | 4 | N |
| | propeller (propel) | 5 | N |
| | rotor (rotate) | 5 | N |
| b | fuselage | 6* | N |

## 11f.4.1 _____

| | | | |
|---|---|---|---|
| b | wingspan | SC | N |

# 11g Actions and Characteristics of Vehicles

| Minicluster | Grade Level | Part of Speech |
|---|---|---|

## 11g.1. Ride

| | | | |
|---|---|---|---|
| b | ride | K | N, V |
| b | fly | 1 | V |
| b | row | 2 | V |
| b | drive | 2 | N, V |
| b | sail | 3 | N, V |
| b | glide | 4 | V |
| b | scuttle | 5 | V |
| b | launch | 5 | N, V |
| b | navigate | 5* | V |
| b | cruise | 6 | N, V |
| | refuel (fuel) | SS | V |
| b | lubricate | SS | V |

## 11g.1.1 _____

| | | | |
|---|---|---|---|
| | navigable (navigate) | SS | A |

## 11g.2. Driver

| | | | |
|---|---|---|---|
| | driver (drive) | 3 | N |
| | rider (ride) | 4 | N |
| b | passenger | 4 | N |

## 11g.3. Transport

| | | | |
|---|---|---|---|
| b | transport | 6 | N, V |

## 11g.3.1 _____

| | | | |
|---|---|---|---|
| | transportation (transport) | 6 | N |

# 11h Things Traveled On

| Minicluster | Grade Level | Part of Speech |
|---|---|---|

## 11h.1. Road

| | | | |
|---|---|---|---|
| b | road | 1 | N |
| b | street | 1 | N |
| b | roadway | 1 | N |
| b | highway | 4 | N |
| b | freeway | 5* | N |
| b | turnpike | 5* | N |
| | detour (tour) | 5* | N, V |
| b | avenue | 6 | N |
| b | expressway | 6* | N |
| b | boulevard | 6* | N |

## 11h.1.1 _____

| | | | |
|---|---|---|---|
| b | roadside | 6* | N |

## 11h.2. Intersection

| | | | |
|---|---|---|---|
| b | crossroad | 5* | N |
| | intersection (intersect) | 5* | N |

## 11h.3. Route

| | | | |
|---|---|---|---|
| b | way | 1 | N |
| b | pass | 2 | N, V |
| b | route | 4 | N, V |
| | passage (pass) | 5 | N |
| b | passageway | 6 | N |

## 11h.4. Alley

| | | | |
|---|---|---|---|
| b | alley | 4* | N |
| b | lane | 4 | N |
| b | driveway | 6* | N |

## 11h.5. Bridge

| | | | |
|---|---|---|---|
| b | bridge | 2 | N |
| b | tunnel | 3 | N, V |
| b | span | 5 | N, V |
| b | drawbridge | SS | N |

## 11h.6. Track

| | | | |
|---|---|---|---|
| b | track | 2 | N, V |
| b | rail | 3 | N |
| b | railroad | 4 | N |
| b | railway | 5* | N |

## 11h.7. Ramp

| | | | |
|---|---|---|---|
| b | chute | 5 | N |
| b | ramp | 5 | N |

## 11h.8. Path

| | | |
|---|---|---|
| b sidewalk | 2 | N |
| b path | 3 | N |
| b trail | 3 | N, V |
| b course | 3 | N |
| b pathway | 6* | N |

## 11h.9. Seaway

| | | |
|---|---|---|
| b seaway | SS | N |
| b waterway | SS | N |

## 11h.9.1 _____

| | | |
|---|---|---|
| aqueduct (aqua) | 5* | N |

## 11h.9.2 _____

| | | |
|---|---|---|
| mooring (moor) | 6 | N |

## 11h.10. Airport

| | | |
|---|---|---|
| b airport | 4 | N |
| b airfield | 4* | N |
| b runway | 6 | N |

# Supercluster 12
## Mental Actions/Thinking

### 12a Thought/Memory (General)

| Minicluster | Grade Level | Part of Speech |
|---|---|---|
| **12a.1. Memory** | | |
| b thought | 2 | N, V |
| imagination (imagine) | 4 | N |
| b memory | 4 | N |
| b conscience | 6 | N |
| contemplation (contemplate) | 6* | N |
| **12a.2. Memorize** | | |
| memorize (memory) | 6 | V |
| visualize (visual) | EN | V |

### 12a.3. Think

| | | |
|---|---|---|
| b think | 1 | V |
| b wonder | 2 | N, V |
| b suppose | 3 | V |
| b consider | 4 | V |
| b muse | 5 | V |
| b reckon | 5 | V |
| b deliberate | 6 | V |
| b ponder | 6 | V |
| b survey | 6 | N, V |

### 12a.4. Remember

| | | |
|---|---|---|
| b remember | 3 | V |
| b forget | 3 | V |
| recall (call) | 5 | N, V |

### 12b Subjects/Topics

| Minicluster | Grade Level | Part of Speech |
|---|---|---|
| **12b.1. Topic** | | |
| b subject | 4 | N |
| b topic | 5 | N |
| b theme | 6 | N |
| **12b.2. Plan** | | |
| b plan | 2 | N, V |
| b scheme | 6 | N, V |
| objective (object) | 6 | N |

### 12c Mental Exploration

| Minicluster | Grade Level | Part of Speech |
|---|---|---|
| **12c.1. Investigation** | | |
| b experiment | 3 | N, V |
| investigation (investigate) | 5* | N |
| inspection (inspect) | 5* | N |
| examination (exam) | 6 | N |
| experimentation (experiment) | SC | N |

12c.2. **Explore**

| | Grade Level | Part of Speech |
|---|---|---|
| b explore | 3 | V |
| b search | 3 | V |
| b research | 4 | N, V |
| examine (exam) | 4 | V |
| b pry | 5 | V |
| b inspect | 5 | V |
| b probe | 6 | N, V |
| b investigate | 6 | V |

12c.3. **Assignment**

| | | |
|---|---|---|
| b lesson | 3 | N |
| assignment (assign) | 5* | N |
| b homework | 6 | N |

# 12d Mental Actions Involving Conclusions

| Minicluster | Grade Level | Part of Speech |
|---|---|---|

12d.1. **Solve**

| | | |
|---|---|---|
| b solve | 3 | V |
| b invent | 3 | V |
| b resolve | 4 | N, V |
| b design | 4 | V |
| b compose | 5* | V |
| b derive | 5* | V |
| b create | 6 | V |
| b compute | 6 | V |

12d.2. **Conclude**

| | | |
|---|---|---|
| b determine | 5 | V |
| b conclude | 6 | V |
| b comprehend | 6 | V |

12d.3. **Prove**

| | | |
|---|---|---|
| b prove | 3 | V |
| b predict | 5 | V |
| b calculate | 6 | V |
| b forecast | 6 | N, V |
| b foresee | 6* | V |

12d.3.1 _____

| | | |
|---|---|---|
| prediction (predict) | 4* | N |
| b proof | 6 | N |
| calculation (calculate) | 6* | N |

12d.4. **Guess**

| | | |
|---|---|---|
| b guess | 1 | N, V |
| b estimate | 6 | V |
| b assume | 6 | V |

12d.5. **Discovery**

| | | |
|---|---|---|
| invention (invent) | 3 | N |
| b fact | 3 | N |
| discovery (discover) | 4 | N |
| b theory | 4 | N |
| information (inform) | 4 | N |
| b clue | 4 | N |
| b principle | 5* | N |
| b evidence | 6 | N |
| b proof | 6 | N |
| indicator (indicate) | 6* | N |
| indication (indicate) | SC | N |

12d.5.1 _____

| | | |
|---|---|---|
| b mystery | 3 | N |

**Key**

Basic words
  Basic words are preceded by *b*.
  All other words are followed by the basic word in parentheses.

Grade levels
  K-6  The grade level at which a word is introduced.
  *    Indicates a word does not appear frequently in student reading material, but when it does appear it is at the level indicated.
  –    Words or phrases for which a grade level could not be determined.

Content specific words are indicated by the content area in which they are used:
  SS    Social Studies
  EN    English
  MA    Math
  SC    Science

Part of Speech
  N         Noun
  V         Verb
  A         Adjective
  AV        Adverb
  AV (+ly)  Adverb when suffix -ly is added
  PRO       Pronoun
  PREP      Preposition
  INT       Interjection
  DET       Determiner
  AX        Auxiliary verb
  RM        Relationship marker

## 12e Consciousness

| Minicluster | Grade Level | Part of Speech |
|---|---|---|
| 12e.1. **Awake** | | |
|   awake (wake) | 3 | V, A |
| b  conscious | 6* | A, AV (+ly) |
| 12e.2. **Asleep** | | |
|   asleep (sleep) | 3 | A |
| b  weary | 5 | A, AV (+ly) |
| b  drowsy | 5* | A |
|   unconcious (conscious) | 6* | A, AV (+ly) |
| 12e.3. **Dream** | | |
| b  dream | 2 | N, V |
| b  daydream | 3 | N, V |
| b  nap | 3 | N, V |
| b  nightmare | 5 | N |
| b  daze | 5 | N, V |
| b  vision | 5 | N |
| b  fantasy | 6 | N |
|   hallucination (hallucinate) | 6* | N |
| b  illusion | 6* | N |
| 12e.4. **Sleep** | | |
| b  sleep | 1 | N, V |
| b  doze | 4 | V |
| b  slumber | 6 | N, V |
| b  snooze | 6 | N, V |
| 12e.5. **Awaken** | | |
|   awaken (wake) | 3 | V |
| b  wake | 3 | V |
|   waken (wake) | 5 | V |
| 12e.6. **Fantasize** | | |
| b  pretend | 3 | V |
|   fantasize (fantasy) | 6* | V |
| b  hallucinate | 6* | V |

## 12f Interest

| Minicluster | Grade Level | Part of Speech |
|---|---|---|
| 12f1.1 **Curiosity** | | |
| b  interest | 3 | N, V |
| b  attention | 3 | N |
|   curiosity (curious) | 5 | N |
| b  intrigue | 6* | N, V |
|   concentration (concentrate) | 6* | N |

## 12g Teaching/Learning

| Minicluster | Grade Level | Part of Speech |
|---|---|---|
| 12g.1. **Instruction** | | |
|   direction (direct) | 3 | N |
|   advice (advise) | 4 | N |
|   suggestion (suggest) | 5 | N |
|   instruction (instruct) | 5 | N |
| 12g.2. **Teach** | | |
| b  coach | 3 | N, V |
| b  teach | 3 | V |
| b  educate | 5 | V |
| b  instruct | 5* | V |
| b  enlighten | 5* | V |
| 12g.3. **Learn** | | |
| b  learn | 1 | V |
| b  realize | 3 | V |
| b  discover | 3 | V |
| b  detect | 5* | V |
| b  analyze | 6 | V |
| 12g.4. **Outsmart** | | |
| b  trick | 2 | N, V |
| b  outwit | 5 | N |
| b  outsmart | 5 | N |
| 12g.5. **Confuse** | | |
| b  confuse | 4 | V |
| b  perplex | 5 | V |
| b  bewilder | 5 | V |
| b  baffle | 5 | V |
| b  mystify | 6 | V |

## 12g.6. **Know**

| Minicluster | Grade Level | Part of Speech |
|---|---|---|
| b know | K | V |
| b understand | 3 | V |
| 12g.6.1 _____ | | |
| knowledge (know) | 5 | N |

## 12h Processes and Procedures

| Minicluster | Grade Level | Part of Speech |
|---|---|---|
| 12h.1. **Procedure** | | |
| b process | 5 | N, V |
| b method | 5 | N |
| procedure (proceed) | 6* | N |
| b technique | 6* | N |
| b maneuver | 6* | N, V |

## 12i Definition

| Minicluster | Grade Level | Part of Speech |
|---|---|---|
| 12i.1. **Definition** | | |
| definition (define) | 5 | N |
| meaning (mean) | 5 | N |
| 12i.2. **Symbolize** | | |
| b represent | 4 | V |
| b define | 4* | V |
| b interpret | 5 | V |
| symbolize (symbol) | 5* | V |

## 12j Choice

| Minicluster | Grade Level | Part of Speech |
|---|---|---|
| 12j.1. **Choose** | | |
| b pick | 2 | N, V |
| b choose | 2 | V |
| b decide | 3 | V |
| b select | 5 | V |
| 12j.1.1 _____ | | |
| b choice | 4 | N |
| selection (select) | 4* | N |
| decision (decide) | 5 | N |
| judgment (judge) | 6 | N |
| b verdict | 6 | N |

## 12j.2. **Judge**

| | Grade Level | Part of Speech |
|---|---|---|
| b judge | 3 | V |
| b suspect | 4 | N, V |
| misjudge (judge) | 5* | V |
| criticize (critic) | 6 | V |
| 12j.3. **Appoint** | | |
| b appoint | 6 | V |
| b ratify | SS | V |
| b repeal | SS | V |

## 12k Intelligence

| Minicluster | Grade Level | Part of Speech |
|---|---|---|
| 12k.1. **Wisdom** | | |
| wisdom (wise) | 4 | N |
| ignorance (ignorant) | 4* | N |
| b wit | 5 | N |
| intelligence (intelligent) | 5 | N |
| stupidity (stupid) | 6 | N |
| 12k.1.1 _____ | | |
| b wise | 2 | A, AV (+ly) |
| b smart | 3 | A, AV (+ly) |
| b sly | 4 | A, AV (+ly) |
| b brilliant | 5 | A, AV (+ly) |
| b shrewd | 5 | A, AV (+ly) |
| b intelligent | 5 | A, AV (+ly) |
| b cunning | 6 | A, AV (+ly) |
| 12k.1.2 _____ | | |
| b stupid | 3 | A, AV (+ly) |
| b dumb | 4 | A, AV (+ly) |
| uneducated (educate) | 5 | A |
| b ignorant | 6 | A, AV (+ly) |

## 12k.2. Alert

| | Grade Level | Part of Speech |
|---|---|---|
| b alert | 4 | A, AV (+ly) |
| b aware | 4 | A, AV (+ly) |

## 12k.3. Logical

| | | |
|---|---|---|
| sensible (sense) | 5 | A, AV (+ly) |
| logical (logic) | 6 | A, AV (+ly) |

## 12k.4. Clever

| | | |
|---|---|---|
| b clever | 2 | A, AV (+ly) |
| b able | 2 | A, AV (+ly) |
| skillful (skill) | 6 | A, AV (+ly) |
| b apt | 6* | A, AV (+ly) |
| unskilled (skill) | SS | A |
| b adept | 6* | A, AV (+ly) |

## 12k.5. Imaginative

| | | |
|---|---|---|
| imaginative (imagine) | 5* | A, AV (+ly) |
| creative (create) | 6* | A, AV (+ly) |

## 12L Beliefs

| Minicluster | Grade Level | Part of Speech |
|---|---|---|
| **12L.1. Custom** | | |
| b custom | 4 | N |
| b ideal | 5 | N |
| b belief | 6 | N |
| b superstition | 6 | N |
| b tradition | 6 | N |
| b philosophy | 6* | N |
| **12L.2. Habit** | | |
| b habit | 4 | N |
| b instinct | 6 | N |

# Supercluster 13
## Nonemotional Traits

### 13a Kindness/Goodness

| Minicluster | Grade Level | Part of Speech |
|---|---|---|
| **13a.1. Goodness** | | |
| goodness (good) | 3 | N |
| patience (patient) | 4 | N |
| kindness (kind) | 5 | N |
| b charity | 6 | N |
| b mercy | 6 | N |
| forgiveness (forgive) | 6 | N |
| **13a.2. Courtesy** | | |
| courtesy (courteous) | 5* | N |
| hospitality (hospitable) | 6 | N |
| consideration (consider) | 6* | N |
| **13a.3. Tender** | | |
| b tender | 3 | A, AV (+ly) |
| b gentle | 3 | A, AV (+ly) |
| thoughtful (thought) | 4 | A, AV (+ly) |
| b sensitive | 4* | A, AV (+ly) |
| sympathetic (sympathy) | 6 | A, AV (+ly) |
| b lenient | 6* | AV (+ly) |
| **13a.4. Grateful** | | |
| b grateful | 3 | A, AV (+ly) |
| thankful (thank) | 3 | A, AV (+ly) |
| **13a.5. Kind** | | |
| b kind | 1 | A, AV (+ly) |
| b nice | 2 | A, AV (+ly) |
| pleasant (please) | 3 | A, AV (+ly) |

### 13a.6. **Affectionate**

| | | | |
|---|---|---|---|
| affectionate (affection) | 5 | A, AV (+ly) | |
| attentive (attention) | 6* | A, AV (+ly) | |

### 13a.7. **Generous**

| | | | |
|---|---|---|---|
| willing (will) | 3 | A, AV (+ly) | |
| unselfish (self) | 4* | A, AV (+ly) | |
| b generous | 5 | A, AV (+ly) | |

### 13a.8. **Gracious**

| | | | |
|---|---|---|---|
| b polite | 3 | A, AV (+ly) | |
| b civil | 5 | A, AV (+ly) | |
| gracious (grace) | 6 | A, AV (+ly) | |
| respectful (respect) | 6 | A, AV (+ly) | |
| b courteous | 6* | A, AV (+ly) | |
| chivalrous (chivalry) | 6* | A, AV (+ly) | |
| tactful (tact) | 6* | A, AV (+ly) | |

## 13b Eagerness/Dependability

| Minicluster | Grade Level | Part of Speech |
|---|---|---|

### 13b.1. **Eagerness**

| | | |
|---|---|---|
| eagerness (eager) | 4 | N |
| reliability (rely) | 6* | N |
| dependability (depend) | 6* | N |
| trustworthiness (trustworthy) | 6* | N |
| sincerity (sincere) | 6* | N |

### 13b.2. **Poise**

| | | |
|---|---|---|
| b poise | 5 | N, V |
| b grace | 5 | N, V |
| determination (determine) | 5 | N |
| enthusiasm (enthuse) | 5 | N |
| b conceit | 6 | N |
| b ambition | 6* | N |

### 13b.3. **Duty**

| | | |
|---|---|---|
| b duty | 4 | N |
| service (serve) | 4 | N, V |
| responsibility (responsible) | 4 | N |

### 13b.4. **Effective**

| | | |
|---|---|---|
| b efficient | 4 | A, AV (+ly) |
| effective (effect) | 5* | A, AV (+ly) |

### 13b.5. **Dependable**

| | | |
|---|---|---|
| dependable (depend) | 4* | A, AV (+ly) |
| b sincere | 4* | A, AV (+ly) |
| b responsible | 6 | A, AV (+ly) |
| reliable (rely) | 6 | A, AV (+ly) |
| b trustworthy | 6 | A |

### Key

**Basic words**
Basic words are preceded by *b*.
All other words are followed by the basic word in parentheses.

**Grade levels**
K-6   The grade level at which a word is introduced.
\*   Indicates a word does not appear frequently in student reading material, but when it does appear it is at the level indicated.
–   Words or phrases for which a grade level could not be determined.

Content specific words are indicated by the content area in which they are used:
SS   Social Studies
EN   English
MA   Math
SC   Science

**Part of Speech**
N   Noun
V   Verb
A   Adjective
AV   Adverb
AV (+ly)   Adverb when suffix -ly is added
PRO   Pronoun
PREP   Preposition
INT   Interjection
DET   Determiner
AX   Auxiliary verb
RM   Relationship marker

13b.6. **Busy**

| | Grade Level | Part of Speech |
|---|---|---|
| b busy | 2 | A, AV (+ly) |
| b eager | 3* | A, AV (+ly) |
| lively (life) | 3 | A |
| playful (play) | 3* | A, AV (+ly) |
| active (act) | 5 | A, AV (+ly) |
| energetic (energy) | 5* | A, AV (+ly) |
| enthusiastic (enthuse) | 5* | A, AV (+ly) |
| adventurous (adventure) | 5* | A, AV |
| vigorous (vigor) | 6 | A, AV (+ly) |

13b.7. **Ambitious**

| | | |
|---|---|---|
| b earnest | 4 | A, AV (+ly) |
| b diligent | 5* | A, AV (+ly) |
| productive (produce) | 5* | A, AV |
| b thorough | 6 | A, AV (+ly) |
| industrious (industry) | 6* | A, AV (+ly) |
| ambitious (ambition) | 6* | A, AV (+ly) |
| compulsive (compulsion) | 6* | A, AV (+ly) |

## 13c Lack of Initiative

| Minicluster | Grade Level | Part of Speech |
|---|---|---|
| 13c.1. **Lazy** | | |
| b slow | K | A, AV (+ly) |
| b lazy | 2 | A |
| b casual | 5 | A, AV (+ly) |
| inactive (act) | 5* | A, AV (+ly) |
| b idle | 6 | A, AV (+ly) |
| b passive | 6 | A, AV (+ly) |
| b sluggish | 6 | A |

13c.2. **Aimless**

| | | |
|---|---|---|
| aimless (aim) | 4* | A, AV (+ly) |
| restless (rest) | 4* | A, AV (+ly) |
| nomadic (nomad) | SS | A |

## 13d Freedom/Independence

| Minicluster | Grade Level | Part of Speech |
|---|---|---|
| 13d.1. **Free** | | |
| b free | 3 | A, AV (+ly) |
| independent (depend) | 5* | A, AV (+ly) |
| 13d.2. **Dependent** | | |
| obedient (obey) | 5 | A, AV (+ly) |
| dependent (depend) | 6 | A, AV (+ly) |

## 13e Confidence/Pride

| Minicluster | Grade Level | Part of Speech |
|---|---|---|
| 13e.1. **Sure** | | |
| b sure | 2 | A |
| b proud | 2 | A, AV (+ly) |
| b certain | 3 | A |
| confident (confide) | 5 | A, AV (+ly) |
| b vain | 6 | A, AV (+ly) |
| b dominant | 6* | A, AV (+ly) |
| 13e.1.1 _____ | | |
| b pride | 4 | N |
| confidence (confide) | 6 | N |

## 13f Patience

| Minicluster | Grade Level | Part of Speech |
|---|---|---|
| 13f.1. **Patient** | | |
| b patient | 3 | A, AV (+ly) |
| impatient (patient) | 3 | A, AV (+ly) |
| expectant (expect) | 6 | A, AV (+ly) |

## 13g Luck/Prosperity

| Minicluster | Grade Level | Part of Speech |
|---|---|---|
| 13g.1. **Fortune** | | |
| lucky (luck) | 2 | A, AV (+ly) |
| fortunate (fortune) | 4 | A, AV (+ly) |
| successful (succeed) | 4 | A, AV (+ly) |
| prosperous (prosper) | 5* | A, AV (+ly) |
| 13g.1.1 _____ | | |
| b luck | 2 | N |
| success (succeed) | 4 | N |
| b fate | 5 | N |

## 13h Strictness

| Minicluster | Grade Level | Part of Speech |
|---|---|---|
| 13h.1. **Stern** | | |
| b stern | 4 | A, AV (+ly) |
| b stubborn | 4 | A, AV (+ly) |
| b strict | 5 | A, AV (+ly) |
| b steadfast | 5* | A, AV (+ly) |
| b staunch | 6 | A, AV (+ly) |

## 13i Humor

| Minicluster | Grade Level | Part of Speech |
|---|---|---|
| 13i.1. **Funny** | | |
| funny (fun) | K | A |
| witty (wit) | 5 | A |
| b wry | 6 | A, AV (+ly) |
| humorous (humor) | 6 | A, AV (+ly) |
| 13i.1.1 _____ | | |
| b fun | K | N, A |
| b humor | 4 | N |

## 13j Spirituality

| Minicluster | Grade Level | Part of Speech |
|---|---|---|
| 13j.1. **Religious** | | |
| religious (religion) | 5 | A, AV (+ly) |
| glorious (glory) | 5 | A, AV (+ly) |
| spiritual (spirit) | 6 | A, AV (+ly) |
| miraculous (miracle) | 6 | A, AV (+ly) |
| b holy | 6 | A |
| b sacred | 6 | A, AV (+ly) |
| b divine | 6* | A, AV (+ly) |

## 13k Prudence

| Minicluster | Grade Level | Part of Speech |
|---|---|---|
| 13k.1. **Prudence** | | |
| prudence (prude) | 4* | N |
| modesty (modest) | 5 | N |
| 13k.1.1 _____ | | |
| b modest | 5 | N |

## 13L Shyness

| Minicluster | Grade Level | Part of Speech |
|---|---|---|
| 13L.1. **Meek** | | |
| b shy | 3 | A, AV (+ly) |
| helpless (help) | 3 | A, AV (+ly) |
| b meek | 4 | A, AV (+ly) |
| b mild | 4 | A, AV (+ly) |
| b timid | 5 | A, AV (+ly) |
| needy (need) | 5* | A |
| b reluctant | 6 | A, AV (+ly) |

## 13m Dishonesty

| Minicluster | Grade Level | Part of Speech |
|---|---|---|
| 13m.1. **Dishonest** | | |
| tricky (trick) | 5 | A |
| b naughty | 5 | A |
| unfair (fair) | 5 | A, AV (+ly) |
| dishonest (honest) | 6* | A, AV (+ly) |
| mischievous (mischief) | 6* | A, AV (+ly) |
| b phony | 6* | A |
| unscrupulous (scruples) | 6* | A, AV (+ly) |
| unfaithful (faith) | 6* | A, AV (+ly) |
| 13m.1.1 _____ | | |
| b mischief | 5 | N |

## 13n Loyalty/Courage

| Minicluster | Grade Level | Part of Speech |
|---|---|---|
| 13n.1 **Allegiance** | | |
| b allegiance | 3* | N |
| friendship (friend) | 4 | N |
| obedience (obey) | 5* | N |
| loyalty (loyal) | 6* | N |
| devotion (devote) | 6* | N |
| 13n.1.1 _____ | | |
| b treason | 6 | N |
| disloyalty (loyal) | 6* | N |
| 13n.2. **Courage** | | |
| b courage | 3 | N |
| bravery (brave) | 4 | N |
| 13n.3. **Brave** | | |
| b brave | 2 | A, AV (+ly) |
| b bold | 4 | A, AV (+ly) |
| fearless (fear) | 4* | A, AV (+ly) |
| 13n.4. **Heroic** | | |
| heroic (hero) | 5 | A, AV (+ly) |
| b gallant | 5* | A, AV (+ly) |
| courageous (courage) | 6 | A, AV (+ly) |
| 13n.5. **Honorable** | | |
| honorable (honor) | 4 | A, AV (+ly) |
| b noble | 5 | A, AV (+ly) |
| b moral | 5 | A, AV (+ly) |
| faithful (faith) | 5 | A, AV (+ly) |
| patriotic (patriot) | 5* | A, AV (+ly) |
| 13n.6. **Glory** | | |
| b honor | 3 | N, V |
| b power | 3 | N |
| b glory | 6 | N |

## 13n.7. **Fair**

| Minicluster | Grade Level | Part of Speech |
|---|---|---|
| b just | 1 | A, AV (+ly) |
| b fair | 2 | A, AV (+ly) |
| b honest | 4 | A, AV (+ly) |
| b loyal | 5 | A, AV (+ly) |
| impartial (partial) | SS | A, AV (+ly) |

## 13o Instability

| Minicluster | Grade Level | Part of Speech |
|---|---|---|
| **13o.1. Wild** | | |
| b wild | 3 | A, AV (+ly) |
| crazy (craze) | 3 | A |
| careless (care) | 4 | A, AV (+ly) |
| b frantic | 5 | A, AV (+ly) |
| reckless (reck) | 5* | A, AV (+ly) |
| unsettled (settle) | 5* | A |
| fanatical (fanatic) | 6 | A, AV (+ly) |
| unstable (stable) | 6* | A, AV (+ly) |
| feverish (fever) | 6* | A, AV (+ly) |
| unsteady (steady) | 6* | A, AV (+ly) |
| wasteful (waste) | SS | A, AV (+ly) |
| uncontrolled (control) | SC | A |

## 13p Caution

| Minicluster | Grade Level | Part of Speech |
|---|---|---|
| **13p.1. Careful** | | |
| careful (care) | 2 | A, AV (+ly) |
| b curious | 3 | A, AV (+ly) |
| watchful (watch) | 4 | A, AV (+ly) |
| cautious (caution) | 4 | A, AV (+ly) |
| suspicious (suspect) | 5 | A, AV (+ly) |
| **13p.1.1** _____ | | |
| b caution | 6 | A, AV (+ly) |

---

### Key

**Basic words**
Basic words are preceded by *b*.
All other words are followed by the basic word in parentheses.

**Grade levels**

K-6   The grade level at which a word is introduced.

\*     Indicates a word does not appear frequently in student reading material, but when it does appear it is at the level indicated.

–     Words or phrases for which a grade level could not be determined.

Content specific words are indicated by the content area in which they are used:

| | |
|---|---|
| SS | Social Studies |
| EN | English |
| MA | Math |
| SC | Science |

**Part of Speech**

| | |
|---|---|
| N | Noun |
| V | Verb |
| A | Adjective |
| AV | Adverb |
| AV (+ly) | Adverb when suffix -ly is added |
| PRO | Pronoun |
| PREP | Preposition |
| INT | Interjection |
| DET | Determiner |
| AX | Auxiliary verb |
| RM | Relationship marker |

# Supercluster 14
## Location/Direction

### 14a Location (General)

| Minicluster | Grade Level | Part of Speech |
|---|---|---|
| **14a.1. Direction** | | |
| direction | 3 | N |
| (direct) | | |
| distance (distant) | 3 | N |
| b position | 4 | N |
| location (locate) | 6 | N |
| b altitude | 6 | N |
| **14a.2. Place** | | |
| b place | 2 | N, V |
| b spot | 2 | N, V |
| b point | 2 | N, V |
| b axis | 4 | N |
| b pinpoint | 6 | N, V |

### 14b Boundaries

| Minicluster | Grade Level | Part of Speech |
|---|---|---|
| **14b.1. Edge** | | |
| b corner | 2 | N, V |
| b side | 2 | N |
| b edge | 3 | N, V |
| b rim | 4 | N |
| b ridge | 4 | N |
| b limit | 4 | N, V |
| b border | 5 | N |
| b brim | 5 | N |
| boundary (bound) | 5 | N |
| b perimeter | 5* | N |
| b margin | 5* | N |
| b outskirts | 5* | N |
| b exterior | 5* | N |
| b brink | 6 | N |

### 14c Planes

| Minicluster | Grade Level | Part of Speech |
|---|---|---|
| **14c.1. Diagonal** | | |
| b diagonal | 5* | N, A, AV (+ly) |
| b vertical | 6 | A, AV (+ly) |
| horizontal (horizon) | 6 | A, AV (+ly) |
| b perpendicular | 6* | A, AV (+ly) |
| **14c.2. Sideways** | | |
| b sideways | 4* | AV |
| b broadside | 5 | AV |

### 14d Nonspecific Locations

| Minicluster | Grade Level | Part of Speech |
|---|---|---|
| **14d.1. Somewhere** | | |
| b here | K | PRO |
| b there | 1 | PRO |
| b where | 1 | PRO |
| b anywhere | 3 | PRO |
| b somewhere | 4 | PRO |
| b everywhere | 4 | PRO |
| b nowhere | 4 | PRO |
| b elsewhere | 4* | PRO |

### 14e Compass Directions

| Minicluster | Grade Level | Part of Speech |
|---|---|---|
| **14e.1. North** | | |
| b west | 3 | N |
| b south | 3 | N |
| b north | 3 | N |
| b east | 3 | N |
| b northeast | 3* | N |
| b northwest | 3* | N |
| b southwest | 3* | N |
| b southeast | 3* | N |
| b midwest | 6 | N |

14e.1.1 _____

|  | | |
|---|---|---|
| southern (south) | 4 | A |
| western (west) | 4 | A |
| northwestern (northwest) | 4* | A |
| b westward | 4* | A, AV |
| southwestern (southwest) | 4* | A |
| eastern (east) | 5 | A |
| northern (north) | 5 | A |
| b eastward | 5* | A, AV |
| northeastern (northeast) | 5* | A |
| b southward | 5* | A, AV |
| southeastern (southeast) | 5* | A |
| b northward | 5* | A, AV |
| b northernmost | 5* | A |
| northerly (north) | 6* | A, AV |
| b westernmost | 6 | A |
| b southernmost | 6 | A |
| b easternmost | 6 | A |

14e.2. **Right**

|  | | |
|---|---|---|
| b right | 1 | N, A |
| b left | 2 | N, A |

## 14f Back-Front-Middle

| Minicluster | Grade Level | Part of Speech |
|---|---|---|
| 14f.1. **Back** | | |
| b back | 1 | N, A, AV |
| b end | 2 | N, A |
| b rear | 3 | N, A |
| b hind | 3 | A |
| b background | 4 | N, A |
| b endpoint | MA | N |
| 14f.1.1 _____ | | |
| b backward | 3 | AV |
| b backwards | 3 | AV |
| b astern | 6* | AV |
| 14f.1.2 _____ | | |
| b behind | K | AV, PREP |

14f.2. **Front**

|  | | |
|---|---|---|
| b front | 2 | N, A |

14f.2.1 _____

|  | | |
|---|---|---|
| b ahead | 2 | AV |

14f.2.2 _____

|  | | |
|---|---|---|
| b ahead of | – | PREP |

14f.3. **Center**

|  | | |
|---|---|---|
| b center | 3 | N, A |
| b middle | 3 | N, A |
| midst (mid) | 5 | N |
| b midway | 5* | N |

14f.3.1 _____

|  | | |
|---|---|---|
| b mid | 5 | A |
| central (center) | 6 | A |

## 14g Direction To/From

| Minicluster | Grade Level | Part of Speech |
|---|---|---|
| 14g.1. **To** | | |
| b to | K | PREP |
| b at | K | PREP |
| b from | K | PREP |

## 14h Inward/Outward Direction

| Minicluster | Grade Level | Part of Speech |
|---|---|---|
| 14h.1. **In** | | |
| b interior | 6 | N, A |
| 14h.1.1 _____ | | |
| b in | K | AV, PREP |
| b inside | 2 | AV, PREP |
| b indoors | 2* | AV |
| b inward | 4 | AV |
| b inland | 4 | AV |
| 14h.1.2 _____ | | |
| b internal | 5* | A |
| b incoming | SS | A |

## 14h.2. Outward

| | | Grade Level | Part of Speech |
|---|---|---|---|
| b | out | K | AV, PREP |
| b | outside | 2 | AV, PREP |
| b | outdoor(s) | 3 | AV |
| b | outward | 6 | AV |

## 14h.3. Through

| | | | |
|---|---|---|---|
| b | through | 2 | AV, PREP |
| b | throughout | 4 | AV, PREP |

## 14h.4. Enter

| | | | |
|---|---|---|---|
| b | enter | 3 | V |
| b | insert | 5* | N, V |
| b | inject | 6* | V |

# 14i Up/On

| Minicluster | | Grade Level | Part of Speech |
|---|---|---|---|
| **14i.1. On** | | | |
| b | on | K | PREP |
| **14i.1.1** _____ | | | |
| | atop (top) | 5* | PREP |
| b | on top of | – | PREP |
| **14i.1.2** _____ | | | |
| b | abroad | 3 | AV, PREP |
| **14i.2. Over** | | | |
| b | over | 1 | AV, PREP |
| b | above | 2 | AV, PREP |
| b | overhead | 3 | AV |
| **14i.2.1** _____ | | | |
| b | off | 1 | AV, PREP |
| **14i.3. Top** | | | |
| b | tip | 2 | N |
| b | top | 2 | N, A |
| **14i.3.1** _____ | | | |
| b | bottom | 1 | N, A |

## 14i.4. High

| | | Grade Level | Part of Speech |
|---|---|---|---|
| b | high | 2 | A |
| b | low | 2 | A |
| | upper (up) | 4 | A |

## 14i.5. Upright

| | | | |
|---|---|---|---|
| b | upright | 1* | A |
| b | upside down | 2 | A |

## 14i.6. Up

| | | | |
|---|---|---|---|
| b | up | K | AV, PREP |
| b | upward | 3 | A, AV |
| b | upstairs | 3 | AV |
| b | skyward | 3* | A, AV |
| b | uphill | 3* | A, AV |
| b | upland | SS | AV |

## 14i.7. Overland

| | | | |
|---|---|---|---|
| b | overland | 5* | A, AV |

# 14j Down/Under

| Minicluster | | Grade Level | Part of Speech |
|---|---|---|---|
| **14j.1. Under** | | | |
| b | under | 1 | AV, PREP |
| b | below | 3 | AV, PREP |
| b | beneath | 3 | PREP |
| b | underneath | 5 | AV, PREP |
| **14j.1.1** _____ | | | |
| b | underside | 4* | N |
| **14j.1.2** _____ | | | |
| b | underground | 4 | N, A |
| b | underfoot | 4 | N |
| **14j.2. Down** | | | |
| b | down | K | AV |
| b | downstairs | 3 | A, AV |
| b | downhill | 4* | A, AV |
| b | downward | 6 | A, AV |
| b | downtown | 6 | A, AV |

## 14k Distances

| Minicluster | Grade Level | Part of Speech |
|---|---|---|
| 14k.1. **Distant** | | |
| b distant | 3 | A |
| b remote | 6 | A |
| outer (out) | 6 | A |
| b outlying | 6* | A |
| 14k.1.1 _____ | | |
| b away | K | AV |
| b far | 1 | A, AV |
| b faraway | 3* | A, AV |
| 14k.1.2 _____ | | |
| b abroad | 5 | AV |
| b overseas | 5* | AV |
| 14k.1.3 _____ | | |
| past (pass) | 2 | A, AV, PREP |
| b beyond | 3 | PREP |
| 14k.2. **Close** | | |
| closeness (close) | 6* | N |
| 14k.2.1 _____ | | |
| b beside | K | AV |
| b with | K | PREP |
| b close | 2 | A, AV |
| b near | 2 | A, PREP |
| b along | 2 | A, PREP |
| b nearby | 2 | A, AV |
| b alongside | 4 | AV, PREP |
| aside (side) | 4 | AV, PREP |
| opposite (oppose) | 4 | AV, PREP |
| b local | 5 | A |
| b abreast | 6 | AV |
| 14k.3. **Homeward** | | |
| b homeward | 5 | AV |
| 14k.4. **Between** | | |
| b by | 1 | PREP |
| b between | 2 | PREP |

## 14L Presence/Absence

| Minicluster | Grade Level | Part of Speech |
|---|---|---|
| 14L.1. **Present** | | |
| presence (present) | 6 | N |
| absence (absent) | 6 | N |
| 14L.1.1 _____ | | |
| b present | 3 | A |
| b absent | 6 | A |
| 14L.2. **Available** | | |
| available (avail) | 5 | A |
| unavailable (avail) | 6 | A |

**Key**

Basic words
   Basic words are preceded by *b*.
   All other words are followed by the basic word in parentheses.

Grade levels
   K-6   The grade level at which a word is introduced.
   *   Indicates a word does not appear frequently in student reading material, but when it does appear it is at the level indicated.
   –   Words or phrases for which a grade level could not be determined.
   Content specific words are indicated by the content area in which they are used:
   SS   Social Studies
   EN   English
   MA   Math
   SC   Science

Part of Speech
   N   Noun
   V   Verb
   A   Adjective
   AV   Adverb
   AV (+ly)   Adverb when suffix -ly is added
   PRO   Pronoun
   PREP   Preposition
   INT   Interjection
   DET   Determiner
   AX   Auxiliary verb
   RM   Relationship marker

# Supercluster 15
## Literature/Writing

### 15a Names/Titles

| Minicluster | Grade Level | Part of Speech |
|---|---|---|
| **15a.1. Name** | | |
| b name | 1 | N, V |
| b brand | 5 | N, V |
| b title | 5 | N, V |
| b nickname | 6 | N, V |
| b euphemism | EN | N |
| **15a.1.1 _____** | | |
| rename (name) | 5* | V |
| entitle (title) | 6* | V |
| **15a.2. Label** | | |
| b tag | 3 | N, V |
| b label | 4 | N, V |
| heading (head) | 4 | N |
| signature (sign) | 4* | N |
| b autograph | 5* | N, V |
| b caption | 5* | N, V |
| inscription (script) | 6 | N |
| subheading (heading) | EN | N |

### 15b Types of Literature

| Minicluster | Grade Level | Part of Speech |
|---|---|---|
| **15b.1. Literature** | | |
| b writing | 3 | N |
| literature (literate) | 5 | N |
| b composition | 6 | N |
| **15b.2. Story** | | |
| b story | 1 | N |
| b tale | 3 | N |
| b myth | 4 | N |
| b fiction | 5 | N |
| b comedy | 5 | N |
| b fable | 5 | N |
| b script | 6 | N |
| b mythology | 6* | N |
| nonfiction (fiction) | EN | N |

### 15c Types of Books

| Minicluster | Grade Level | Part of Speech |
|---|---|---|
| **15c.1. Book** | | |
| b book | K | N |
| b textbook | 4* | N |
| b catalogue | 4* | N |
| b text | 5* | N |
| primer (prime) | 5* | N |
| booklet (book) | 5* | N |
| b manual | 6 | N |
| b anthology | EN | N |
| **15c.2. Novel** | | |
| b novel | 5* | N |
| b biography | 5* | N |
| autobiography (biography) | 5* | N |
| **15c.3. Cookbook** | | |
| b cookbook | 4* | N |
| b menu | 5 | N |
| b recipe | 6 | N |
| **15c.4. Encyclopedia** | | |
| dictionary (diction) | 4 | N |
| b encyclopedia | 4 | N |
| b atlas | 5* | N |
| b almanac | 6 | N |
| b testament | SS | N |
| b scripture | SS | N |
| b Bible | SS | N |
| b Koran | SS | N |
| **15c.5. Magazine** | | |
| b article | 3 | N |
| b magazine | 4 | N |
| b newspaper | 4 | N |
| b headline | 5* | N |
| publication (publish) | 5* | N |
| b journal | 5* | N |
| **15c.6. Edition** | | |
| b volume | 3* | N |
| b index | 5 | N, V |
| b issue | 5 | N, V |
| edition (edit) | 5* | N |
| summary (sum) | 6* | N |

## 15d Poems/Songs

| Minicluster | Grade Level | Part of Speech |
|---|---|---|
| 15d.1. **Poem** | | |
| b poem | 3 | N |
| b rhyme | 4 | N, V |
| b verse | 5 | N |
| · b limerick | 5* | N |
| b sonnet | 6 | N |
| poetry (poem) | 6 | N |
| b stanza | 6 | N |
| 15d.1.1 _____ | | |
| poetic (poem) | 6* | A, AV (+ly) |
| 15d.2. **Song** | | |
| song (sing) | 2 | N |
| b music | 3 | N |
| b tune | 3 | N, V |
| b anthem | 5* | N |
| b psalm | 5 | N |
| b melody | 5 | N |
| b hymn | 6* | N |
| b ballad | EN | N |
| lullaby (lull) | EN | N |
| b carol | EN | N |
| 15d.2.1 _____ | | |
| b sing | 1 | V |
| b recite | 4 | V |

## 15e Drawings/Illustrations

| Minicluster | Grade Level | Part of Speech |
|---|---|---|
| 15e.1. **Drawings** | | |
| drawing (draw) | 4 | N |
| b chart | 4 | N, V |
| illustration (illustrate) | 4* | N |
| b diagram | 5 | N, V |
| b blueprint | 5 | N |
| b graph | 6 | N, V |

## 15f Messages

| Minicluster | Grade Level | Part of Speech |
|---|---|---|
| 15f.1. **Letter** | | |
| b letter | 1 | N, V |
| b note | 2 | N, V |
| b postcard | 2* | N |
| b message | 3 | N |
| b telegram | 3 | N |
| b report | 3 | N, V |
| b valentine | 3 | N |
| b envelope | 4 | N |
| b telegraph | 4 | N |
| b diary | 5 | N |
| correspondence (respond) | 5* | N |
| 15f.2. **Advertisement** | | |
| b ad | 3* | N |
| b bulletin | 3* | N |
| poster (post) | 4 | N |
| b billboard | 5* | N |
| advertisement (advertise) | 5* | N |
| announcement (announce) | 5* | N |
| commercial (commerce) | 6 | N |
| b slogan | 6* | N |

## 15g Things to Write On/With

| Minicluster | Grade Level | Part of Speech |
|---|---|---|
| 15g.1. **Notebook** | | |
| b notebook | 3 | N |
| b scrapbook | 3 | N |
| b document | 5* | N |
| manuscript (script) | 6* | N |

## 15g.2. **Pen**

| | | |
|---|---|---|
| b pen | 2 | N |
| b crayon | 2* | N |
| b pencil | 3 | N |
| b brush | 3 | N, V |
| b press | 3 | N, V |
| eraser (erase) | 3 | N |
| b ink | 4 | N |
| typewriter (typewrite) | 4 | N |
| b chalk | 5 | N |

## 15g.3. **Paper**

| | | |
|---|---|---|
| b paper | 2 | N |
| b parchment | 4 | N |
| b scroll | 4 | N |
| b blackboard | 4* | N |
| b tablet | 6 | N |
| b chalkboard | 6* | N |

## 15h Rules/Laws

| Minicluster | Grade Level | Part of Speech |
|---|---|---|
| **15h.1. Rule** | | |
| b rule | 3 | N, V |
| b law | 4 | N |
| regulation (regulate) | 5 | N |
| commandment (command) | SS | N |
| **15h.1.1** _____ | | |
| lawless (law) | 5* | A, AV (+ly) |
| lawful (law) | 5* | A, AV (+ly) |
| **15h.2. Treaty** | | |
| proposal (propose) | 5* | N |
| b treaty | 5* | N |
| b constitution | 5 | N |
| b contract | 6 | N, V |
| amendment (amend) | SS | N |
| b policy | SS | N |
| charter (chart) | SS | N |
| **15h.2.1** _____ | | |
| constitutional (constitution) | SS | N |

## 15i Reading/Writing/Drawing Actions

| Minicluster | Grade Level | Part of Speech |
|---|---|---|
| **15i.1. Scribble** | | |
| b doodle | 3* | N, V |
| b trace | 5 | N, V |
| b scribble | 5* | V |
| b jot | 5* | V |
| **15i.2. Write** | | |
| b sign | 2 | N, V |
| b write | 2 | V |
| b spell | 4 | V |
| b copy | 4 | N, V |
| b publish | 4 | V |
| rewrite (write) | 4* | V |
| b indent | 5* | V |
| misspell (spell) | 6* | V |
| **15i.3. Paint** | | |
| b paint | K | N, V |
| b color | 1 | N, V |
| b draw | 3 | V |
| b draft | 5 | N, V |
| b etch | 5 | V |
| b inscribe | 6 | V |
| b sketch | 6 | N, V |
| b illustrate | 6 | V |
| b engrave | 6* | V |
| **15i.4. Punctuate** | | |
| b punctuate | EN | V |
| b underline | EN | V |
| italicize (italics) | EN | V |
| capitalize (capital) | EN | V |
| **15i.5. Read** | | |
| b read | 1 | V |
| b skim | 4 | V |
| b scan | 6 | V |
| preview (view) | EN | N, V |
| b proofread | EN | V |
| **15i.6. Handwriting** | | |
| b handwriting | 3 | N |
| b penmanship | 5 | N |
| **15i.6.1** _____ | | |
| handwritten (handwrite) | EN | A |

# Supercluster 16
## Water/Liquids

### 16a Different Forms of Water

| Minicluster | Grade Level | Part of Speech |
|---|---|---|
| **16a.1. Water** | | |
| b water | 1 | N, V |
| b liquid | 4 | N |
| b fluid | 6 | N, A |
| **16a.2. Rain** | | |
| b rain | 1 | N, V |
| b rainfall | 3 | N |
| b raindrop | 4* | N |
| b hail | 5 | N, V |
| b sleet | 5 | N, V |
| **16a.2.1** _____ | | |
| b rainbow | 1* | N |
| **16a.3. Snow** | | |
| b snow | 2 | N, V |
| b flake | 4 | N |
| b snowfall | 5* | N |
| b snowflake | 6 | N |
| **16a.3.1** _____ | | |
| b snowman | 2 | N |
| b snowball | 6 | N |
| **16a.4. Ice** | | |
| b ice | 1 | N |
| b frost | 3 | N |
| b glacier | 5 | N |
| b floe | 5 | N |
| b slush | 6 | N |
| icicle (ice) | 6 | N |
| b iceberg | 6 | N |

### 16b Actions Related to Water

| Minicluster | Grade Level | Part of Speech |
|---|---|---|
| **16b.1. Drip** | | |
| b drip | 4 | N, V |
| b sprinkle | 4 | N, V |
| b ripple | 4 | N, V |
| b seep | 4* | V |
| b trickle | 5 | N, V |
| b excrete | SC | V |
| **16b.2. Splash** | | |
| b splash | 2 | N, V |
| b spray | 4 | N, V |
| b overflow | 4* | N, V |
| b gush | 4* | V |
| b spatter | 5 | V |
| b slosh | 5 | V |
| b cascade | 5* | N, V |
| b spurt | 6 | N, V |
| b squirt | 6 | N, V |
| b surge | 6 | N, V |
| **16b.3. Spill** | | |
| b spill | 3 | N, V |
| b flush | 4 | V |
| b leak | 4 | N, V |
| b flow | 4 | V |
| b drain | 5 | N, V |
| b ebb | 6 | V |

## Key

**Basic words**

Basic words are preceded by *b*.
All other words are followed by the basic word in parentheses.

**Grade levels**

K-6   The grade level at which a word is introduced.

\*   Indicates a word does not appear frequently in student reading material, but when it does appear it is at the level indicated.

–   Words or phrases for which a grade level could not be determined.

Content specific words are indicated by the content area in which they are used:

| | |
|---|---|
| SS | Social Studies |
| EN | English |
| MA | Math |
| SC | Science |

**Part of Speech**

| | |
|---|---|
| N | Noun |
| V | Verb |
| A | Adjective |
| AV | Adverb |
| AV (+ly) | Adverb when suffix -ly is added |
| PRO | Pronoun |
| PREP | Preposition |
| INT | Interjection |
| DET | Determiner |
| AX | Auxiliary verb |
| RM | Relationship marker |

**16b.4. Pour**

| | | | |
|---|---|---|---|
| b | pour | 3 | N, V |
| b | stir | 4 | N, V |

**16b.5. Boil**

| | | | |
|---|---|---|---|
| b | melt | 3 | V |
| b | bubble | 3 | N, V |
| b | boil | 4 | V |
| b | freeze | 5 | V |
| b | dissolve | 5 | V |
| b | thaw | 5 | N, V |
| | evaporate (vapor) | 5 | V |

**16b.6. Swim**

| | | | |
|---|---|---|---|
| b | swim | 2 | N, V |
| b | float | 2 | V |
| b | dive | 3 | N, V |
| b | drown | 3 | V |
| b | drift | 3 | N, V |
| b | wade | 4 | V |
| b | sink | 4 | V |

**16b.7. Soak**

| | | | |
|---|---|---|---|
| b | soak | 5 | V |
| b | drench | 5 | V |
| b | absorb | 5 | V |
| | moisten (moist) | 5 | V |
| b | dilute | SC | V |
| b | saturate | 6* | V |

**16b.8. Wet**

| | | | |
|---|---|---|---|
| b | wet | 1 | V, A |
| b | dry | 2 | V, A |
| | slippery (slip) | 4 | A |
| b | moist | 4* | A |
| b | damp | 5 | A |
| b | soggy | 5 | A |
| b | slick | 6 | A |

## 16c Equipment Used with Liquids

| Minicluster | Grade Level | Part of Speech |
|---|---|---|

**16c.1. Fountain**

| | | | |
|---|---|---|---|
| b | fountain | 3 | N |
| b | hydrant | 4* | N |
| | sprinkler (sprinkle) | 6 | N |

**16c.2. Hose**

| | | | |
|---|---|---|---|
| b | pump | 3 | N, V |
| b | hose | 3 | N |
| b | faucet | 4 | N |
| b | spout | 6· | N, V |
| b | valve | 6 | N |
| b | funnel | 6 | N, V |
| b | nozzle | SC | N |

## 16d Moisture

| Minicluster | Grade Level | Part of Speech |
|---|---|---|

**16d.1. Dew**

| | | | |
|---|---|---|---|
| b | dew | 5 | N |
| b | dewdrop | 5 | N |
| | moisture (moist) | 6 | N |
| | droplet (drop) | SC | N |

**16d.2. Evaporation**

| | | | |
|---|---|---|---|
| | evaporation (vapor) | 4* | N |
| | condensation (condense) | SC | N |

**16d.3. Mist**

| | | | |
|---|---|---|---|
| b | cloud | 3 | N |
| b | mist | 4 | N |
| b | haze | 5 | N |
| b | smog | 5* | N |

## 16e Slime

| Minicluster | Grade Level | Part of Speech |
|---|---|---|

**16e.1. Sediment**

| | | | |
|---|---|---|---|
| b | slime | SC | N |
| b | silt | SC | N |
| b | sediment | SC | N |

**16e.2. Foam**

| | | | |
|---|---|---|---|
| b | scum | 3* | N |
| b | foam | 5 | N |
| b | froth | 6* | N |

## 16f Bodies of Water

| Minicluster | Grade Level | Part of Speech |
|---|---|---|
| **16f.1. River** | | |
| b river | 2 | N |
| b stream | 2 | N |
| b brook | 2 | N |
| b pond | 2 | N |
| b marsh | 3 | N |
| b waterfall | 3* | N |
| b creek | 4 | N |
| b puddle | 4 | N |
| b swamp | 4 | N |
| b bog | 5 | N |
| b geyser | 5* | N |
| b tributary | 6* | N |
| gusher | SS | N |
| **16f.2. Lagoon** | | |
| b reef | 4 | N |
| b moor | 5 | N |
| b lagoon | 6 | N |
| b shoal | 6 | N |
| b delta | 6 | N |
| b fjord | 6* | N |
| b watershed | SC | N |
| b headwaters | SC | N |
| **16f.3. Ocean** | | |
| b sea | 2 | N |
| b ocean | 3 | N |
| b cove | 4 | N |
| b bay | 5 | N |
| b inlet | 5 | N |
| b gulf | 6 | N |
| **16f.4. Tide** | | |
| b current | 3 | N |
| b tide | 4 | N |
| b surf | 5 | N, V |
| b tidewater | SS | N |
| **16f.4.1** _____ | | |
| tidal (tide) | SC | A |

## 16g Places Near Water

| Minicluster | Grade Level | Part of Speech |
|---|---|---|
| **16g.1. Island** | | |
| b island | 5 | N |
| b peninsula | 5* | N |
| b isle | 6 | N |
| **16g.2. Shore** | | |
| b beach | 3 | N, V |
| b shore | 3 | N |
| b coast | 4 | N |
| b seacoast | 4* | N |
| b seashore | 4* | N |
| b riverside | 4* | N |
| b mainland | 4* | N |
| b strand | 5 | N |
| b lakeside | 5* | N |

## 16h Directions Related to Water

| Minicluster | Grade Level | Part of Speech |
|---|---|---|
| **16h.1. Inland** | | |
| b underwater | 4 | A, AV |
| ashore (shore) | 4 | AV |
| b inland | 4 | A, AV |
| b upstream | 4* | AV |
| b overboard | 5* | AV |
| b downstream | 6 | AV |
| b midstream | 6 | AV |
| afloat (float) | 6* | AV |
| b offshore | 6* | A, AV |
| b undersea | 6* | AV |
| b upriver | SS | AV |

## 16i Manmade Places Near Water

| Minicluster | Grade Level | Part of Speech |
|---|---|---|
| **16i.1. Harbor** | | |
| b harbor | 3 | N |
| b shipyard | 4 | N |
| b seaport | 4* | N |

| 16i.2. **Lighthouse** | | |
|---|---|---|
| b lighthouse | 4 | N |

| 16i.3. **Dock** | | |
|---|---|---|
| b dock | 3 | N, V |
| b wharf | 5 | N |
| b pier | 6 | N |

| 16i.4. **Pool** | | |
|---|---|---|
| b pool | 2 | N |
| b reservoir | 4* | N |
| b dike | 4* | N |
| b dam | 5 | N, V |
| b canal | 5 | N |
| b channel | 5 | N, V |
| aquarium (aqua) | 5 | N |
| b breakwater | 6 | N |
| b moat | SS | N |

# Supercluster 17
# Clothing

## 17a Clothing (General)

| Minicluster | Grade Level | Part of Speech |
|---|---|---|
| 17a.1. **Suit** | | |
| b suit | 2 | N |
| b uniform | 4 | N |
| b costume | 4 | N |
| b clothing | 5 | N |
| b outfit | 5 | N, V |
| b clothes | 5* | N |
| b garment | 6 | N |
| b apparel | 6* | N |
| 17a.2. **Style** | | |
| b style | 4 | N, V |
| b fashion | 4 | N, V |

## 17b Parts of Clothing

| Minicluster | Grade Level | Part of Speech |
|---|---|---|
| 17b.1. **Button** | | |
| b button | 2 | N, V |
| zipper (zip) | 3 | N |

| 17b.2. **Seam** | | |
|---|---|---|
| b seam | 5* | N |
| lining (line) | 5* | N |
| b hem | 6* | N, V |

| 17b.3. **Pocket** | | |
|---|---|---|
| b pocket | 1 | N |
| b sleeve | 4 | N |
| b collar | 4 | N |
| b ruffle | 5 | N, V |
| b cuff | 6 | N |

## 17c Shirts/Pants/Skirts

| Minicluster | Grade Level | Part of Speech |
|---|---|---|
| 17c.1. **Shirt** | | |
| b shirt | 2 | N |
| b sweater | 5 | N |
| b blouse | 6 | N |
| b tunic | 6 | N |
| 17c.2. **Pants** | | |
| b shorts | 2 | N |
| b trousers | 3 | N |
| b tights | 3 | N |
| b jeans | 5 | N |
| b pants | 5 | N |
| 17c.3. **Dress** | | |
| b dress | 1 | N, V |
| b skirt | 3 | N |
| b apron | 3 | N |
| b robe | 3 | N |
| b petticoat | 6 | N |
| b kimono | 6 | N |
| b gown | 6 | N |

## 17d Things Worn on the Head

| Minicluster | Grade Level | Part of Speech |
|---|---|---|
| 17d.1. **Hat** | | |
| b hat | 1 | N |
| b cap | 3 | N |
| b bonnet | 3 | N |
| b crown | 3 | N |
| b headdress | 3* | N |
| b helmet | 4 | N |
| b hood | 4 | N |
| b fez | SS | N |

## 17d.2. **Glasses**

| | Grade Level | Part of Speech |
|---|---|---|
| b glasses | 2 | N |
| b eyeglasses | 2* | N |
| b spectacles | 5 | N |
| b goggles | 5 | N |
| b visor | 6* | N |

## 17e Things Worn on the Hands/Feet

| Minicluster | Grade Level | Part of Speech |
|---|---|---|
| **17e.1. Shoe** | | |
| b shoe | 1 | N, V |
| b boot | 2 | N, V |
| b skate | 2 | N, V |
| b moccasin | 4 | N |
| b sock | 5 | N |
| b ski | 5 | N |
| b sandal | 5 | N |
| slipper (slip) | 6 | N |
| b stocking | 6 | N |
| **17e.1.1 _____** | | |
| b spur | 5 | N, V |
| **17e.2. Gloves** | | |
| b gloves | 2 | N |
| mittens (mitt) | 4 | N |
| b mitt | 5 | N |

## 17f Coats

| Minicluster | Grade Level | Part of Speech |
|---|---|---|
| **17f.1. Coat** | | |
| b coat | 1 | N, V |
| b jacket | 3 | N |
| b overcoat | 4 | N |
| b raincoat | 4* | N |
| **17f.2. Shawl** | | |
| b cape | 3 | N |
| b shawl | 4 | N |
| b cloak | 5 | N |
| b mantle | 5* | N |
| b shroud | 6 | N |

## 17g Accessories to Clothing

| Minicluster | Grade Level | Part of Speech |
|---|---|---|
| **17g.1. Scarf** | | |
| b tie | 2 | N, V |
| b belt | 3 | N |
| b ribbon | 3 | N |
| b handkerchief | 3 | N |
| b sash | 4 | N |
| b scarf | 4* | N |
| muffler (muff) | 4* | N |
| b necktie | 4* | N |
| b kerchief | 5 | N |
| b tassel | 6 | N |
| **17g.2. Umbrella** | | |
| b umbrella | 4 | N |
| b cane | 4 | N |
| b parasol | 4* | N |

---

## Key

**Basic words**

Basic words are preceded by *b*.
All other words are followed by the basic word in parentheses.

**Grade levels**

K-6 The grade level at which a word is introduced.

\* Indicates a word does not appear frequently in student reading material, but when it does appear it is at the level indicated.

– Words or phrases for which a grade level could not be determined.

Content specific words are indicated by the content area in which they are used:

SS Social Studies
EN English
MA Math
SC Science

**Part of Speech**

| N | Noun |
|---|---|
| V | Verb |
| A | Adjective |
| AV | Adverb |
| AV (+ly) | Adverb when suffix -ly is added |
| PRO | Pronoun |
| PREP | Preposition |
| INT | Interjection |
| DET | Determiner |
| AX | Auxiliary verb |
| RM | Relationship marker |

## 17k.2. **Thread**

| | | | |
|---|---|---|---|
| b | thread | 3 | N |
| b | yarn | 5 | N |
| b | fiber | 6 | N |

## 17k.3. **Silk**

| | | | |
|---|---|---|---|
| b | silk | 2 | N |
| b | felt | 2 | N |
| b | leather | 3 | N |
| b | terry | 3 | N |
| b | buckskin | 3 | N |
| b | wool | 4 | N |
| b | velvet | 4 | N |
| b | cotton | 5 | N |
| b | linen | 5 | N |
| b | plaid | 5 | N |
| b | satin | 5 | N |
| b | nylon | 6 | N |
| b | calico | 6 | N |
| b | flannel | 6 | N |
| b | khaki | 6 | N |
| b | rayon | 6* | N |

## 17k.3.1 _____

| | | |
|---|---|---|
| woolen (wool) | 6 | A |

## 17L Smell/Scent

| Minicluster | Grade Level | Part of Speech |
|---|---|---|

### 17L.1. **Scent**

| | | | |
|---|---|---|---|
| b | smell | 2 | N, V |
| b | scent | 4 | N |
| b | fragrance (fragrant) | 5* | N |
| b | odor | 6 | N |

### 17L.2. **Vapor**

| | | | |
|---|---|---|---|
| b | vapor | 6 | N |
| b | fume | 6 | N |

# Supercluster 18
## Places—Where People Live/Dwell

### 18a Where People Live

| Minicluster | Grade Level | Part of Speech |
|---|---|---|

#### 18a.1. **Neighborhood**

| | | | |
|---|---|---|---|
| | neighborhood (neighbor) | 3 | N |
| b | birthplace | 5* | N |
| b | homeland | SS | N |

#### 18a.2. **Paradise**

| | | | |
|---|---|---|---|
| b | heaven | 4 | N |
| b | paradise | 6 | N |
| b | wonderland | 6* | N |

#### 18a.3. **Town**

| | | | |
|---|---|---|---|
| b | town | 1 | N |
| b | city | 2 | N |
| b | village | 3 | N |
| b | capital | 3* | N |
| b | colony | 4 | N |
| | settlement (settle) | 4 | N |
| b | resort | 5* | N |
| | Capitol | 5 | N |

#### 18a.4. **Camp**

| | | | |
|---|---|---|---|
| b | camp | 2 | N, V |

#### 18a.5. **Slum**

| | | | |
|---|---|---|---|
| b | slum | 6 | N |
| b | suburb | 6 | N |

#### 18a.6. **State**

| | | | |
|---|---|---|---|
| b | state | 3 | N |
| | kingdom (king) | 3 | N |
| b | empire | 6 | N |
| | dominion (domain) | SS | N |

### 18b Continents/Countries

| Minicluster | Grade Level | Part of Speech |
|---|---|---|

#### 18b.1. **Country**

| | | | |
|---|---|---|---|
| b | country | 4 | N |
| b | nation | 4 | N |

#### 18b.2. **Continent**

| | | | |
|---|---|---|---|
| b | continent | 5 | N |

### 18b.2. Continent

| Minicluster | Grade Level | Part of Speech |
|---|---|---|
| b continent | 5 | N |

### 18b.2.1 _____

| | | |
|---|---|---|
| continental | 4* | N |
| (continent) | | |

### 18b.3. Africa

| | | |
|---|---|---|
| b Antarctica | SS | N |
| b South America | SS | N |
| b North America | SS | N |
| b Africa | SS | N |
| b Asia | SS | N |
| b Australia | SS | N |
| b Greenland | SS | N |

### 18b.4. United States

| | | |
|---|---|---|
| b United States | SS | N |
| b America | SS | N |
| b China | SS | N |
| b Japan | SS | N |
| b France | SS | N |
| b Spain | SS | N |
| b Italy | SS | N |
| b Germany | SS | N |
| b Brazil | SS | N |
| b Israel | SS | N |
| b Iran | SS | N |
| b Holland | SS | N |
| b Mexico | SS | N |
| b Canada | SS | N |

## 18c States

| Minicluster | Grade Level | Part of Speech |
|---|---|---|

### 18c.1. Alabama

| | | |
|---|---|---|
| b Alabama | SS | N |
| b Alaska | SS | N |
| b Arizona | SS | N |
| b Arkansas | SS | N |
| b California | SS | N |
| b Colorado | SS | N |
| b Connecticut | SS | N |
| b Delaware | SS | N |
| b Florida | SS | N |
| b Georgia | SS | N |
| b Hawaii | SS | N |
| b Idaho | SS | N |
| b Illinois | SS | N |
| b Indiana | SS | N |
| b Iowa | SS | N |
| b Kansas | SS | N |
| b Kentucky | SS | N |
| b Louisiana | SS | N |
| b Maine | SS | N |
| b Maryland | SS | N |
| b Massachusetts | SS | N |
| b Michigan | SS | N |
| b Minnesota | SS | N |
| b Mississippi | SS | N |
| b Missouri | SS | N |
| b Montana | SS | N |
| b Nebraska | SS | N |
| b Nevada | SS | N |
| b New Hampshire | SS | N |
| b New Jersey | SS | N |
| b New Mexico | SS | N |
| b New York | SS | N |
| b North Carolina | SS | N |
| b North Dakota | SS | N |
| b Ohio | SS | N |
| b Oklahoma | SS | N |
| b Oregon | SS | N |
| b Pennsylvania | SS | N |
| b Rhode Island | SS | N |
| b South Carolina | SS | N |
| b South Dakota | SS | N |
| b Tennessee | SS | N |
| b Texas | SS | N |
| b Utah | SS | N |
| b Vermont | SS | N |
| b Virginia | SS | N |
| b Washington | SS | N |
| b West Virginia | SS | N |
| b Wisconsin | SS | N |
| b Wyoming | SS | N |

## 18d Cities

| Minicluster | Grade Level | Part of Speech |
|---|---|---|

### 18d.1. Seattle

| | | |
|---|---|---|
| b Cheyenne | SS | N |
| b Chicago | SS | N |
| b Cincinnati | SS | N |
| b Cleveland | SS | N |
| b Columbus | SS | N |

| | | |
|---|---|---|
| b Dallas | SS | N |
| b Denver | SS | N |
| b Des Moines | SS | N |
| b Detroit | SS | N |
| b Duluth | SS | N |
| b Harrisburg | SS | N |
| b Hartford | SS | N |
| b Helena | SS | N |
| b Houston | SS | N |
| b Indianapolis | SS | N |
| b Jackson | SS | N |
| b Jacksonville | SS | N |
| b Kansas City | SS | N |
| b Lansing | SS | N |
| b Los Angeles | SS | N |
| b Louisville | SS | N |
| b Memphis | SS | N |
| b Miami | SS | N |
| b Milwaukee | SS | N |
| b Montgomery | SS | N |
| b Nashville | SS | N |
| b New Orleans | SS | N |
| b New York City | SS | N |
| b Oklahoma City | SS | N |
| b Omaha | SS | N |
| b Peoria | SS | N |
| b Philadelphia | SS | N |
| b Phoenix | SS | N |
| b Pittsburgh | SS | N |
| b Portland | SS | N |
| b Providence | SS | N |
| b Reno | SS | N |
| b Richmond | SS | N |
| b St. Louis | SS | N |
| b Salt Lake City | SS | N |
| b San Antonio | SS | N |
| b San Francisco | SS | N |
| b Sante Fe | SS | N |
| b Seattle | SS | N |
| b Spokane | SS | N |
| b Springfield | SS | N |
| b Tampa | SS | N |
| b Toledo | SS | N |
| b Topeka | SS | N |
| b Trenton | SS | N |
| b Washington, DC | SS | N |
| b Wichita | SS | N |

# Supercluster 19
## Noises/Sounds

### 19a Noises (General)

| Minicluster | Grade Level | Part of Speech |
|---|---|---|
| **19a.1. Sound** | | |
| b sound | 2 | N, V |
| b noise | 2 | N |
| silence (silent) | 3 | N |
| **19a.2. Hush** | | |
| b hush | 4 | N, V |
| b lull | 6* | N, V |
| **19a.3. Clatter** | | |
| b clatter | 4 | N, V |
| b commotion | 5 | N |
| b peal | 6 | N |

---

**Key**

Basic words
  Basic words are preceded by *b*.
  All other words are followed by the basic word in parentheses.

Grade levels
  K-6  The grade level at which a word is introduced.
  *    Indicates a word does not appear frequently in student reading material, but when it does appear it is at the level indicated.
  –    Words or phrases for which a grade level could not be determined.

Content specific words are indicated by the content area in which they are used:
SS   Social Studies
EN   English
MA   Math
SC   Science

Part of Speech
N        Noun
V        Verb
A        Adjective
AV      Adverb
AV (+ly) Adverb when suffix -ly is added
PRO    Pronoun
PREP   Preposition
INT    Interjection
DET    Determiner
AX     Auxiliary verb
RM    Relationship marker

### 19a.4. Hear

| | Grade Level | Part of Speech |
|---|---|---|
| b hear | 1 | V |
| b listen | 2 | V |
| b hark | 6 | V |

### 19a.5. Noisy

| | Grade Level | Part of Speech |
|---|---|---|
| b quiet | 2 | A, AV (+ly) |
| b loud | 2 | A, AV (+ly) |
| b silent | 3 | A, AV (+ly) |
| b shrill | 4 | A, AV (+ly) |
| noisy (noise) | 4 | A, AV (+ly) |
| b hoarse | 4 | A, AV (+ly) |
| breathless (breath) | 4 | A, AV (+ly) |
| b harsh | 4 | A, AV (+ly) |
| deafening (deaf) | 5 | A, AV (+ly) |
| voiceless (voice) | EN | A |

### 19a.6. Pitch

| | Grade Level | Part of Speech |
|---|---|---|
| b pitch | 3 | N |
| b tone | 6 | N |
| intensity (intense) | SC | N |

## 19b Devices that Produce Sound

| Minicluster | Grade Level | Part of Speech |
|---|---|---|
| **19b.1. Phone** | | |
| telephone (phone) | 2 | N, V |
| b phone | 4 | N, V |
| receiver (receive) | 4* | N |
| b loudspeaker | 5 | N |
| b earphone | 6* | N |
| **19b.2. Horn** | | |
| b horn | 2 | N |
| b bell | 2 | N |
| b alarm | 3 | N, V |
| b doorbell | 3 | N |
| b gong | 4 | N, V |
| b siren | 4 | N |
| b chime | 5 | N, V |

## 19c Noises Made by People

| Minicluster | Grade Level | Part of Speech |
|---|---|---|
| **19c.1. Roar** | | |
| b roar | 2 | N, V |
| b cheer | 3 | N, V |
| laughter (laugh) | 3 | N |
| b uproar | 4 | N |
| applause (applaud) | 6 | N |
| b applaud | 6 | V |
| **19c.2. Snore** | | |
| b gasp | 3 | N, V |
| b gulp | 4 | N, V |
| b yawn | 4 | N, V |
| b wheeze | 5 | N, V |
| b snore | 6 | N, V |
| b cough | 6 | N, V |
| b belch | 6 | N, V |
| b hiccup | 6 | N, V |
| b burp | 6* | N, V |
| **19c.3. Yell** | | |
| b yell | 2 | N, V |
| b shout | 2 | N, V |
| b whoop | 2 | N, V |
| b whistle | 2 | N, V |
| b squeal | 3 | N, V |
| b bellow | 4 | V |
| b blurt | 4 | V |
| b chant | 4 | N, V |
| b shriek | 5 | N, V |
| b screech | 5 | N, V |
| b holler | 6 | N, V |
| b blare | 6 | V |
| **19c.4. Giggle** | | |
| b laugh | 1 | N, V |
| b chuckle | 3 | N, V |
| b giggle | 4 | N, V |
| b snicker | 6 | N, V |
| **19c.5. Cry** | | |
| b cry | 1 | N, V |
| b sob | 3 | N, V |
| b groan | 3 | N, V |
| b sigh | 3 | N, V |
| b moan | 4 | N, V |
| b wail | 4 | N, V |
| b grumble | 4 | N, V |
| b whimper | 4 | N, V |
| b whine | 4 | N, V |
| b bawl | 6 | V |

## 19c.6. Mumble

| | Grade Level | Part of Speech |
|---|---|---|
| b whisper | 2 | N, V |
| b mutter | 3 | N, V |
| b hum | 3 | N, V |
| b stammer | 4 | N, V |
| b mumble | 4 | N, V |
| b murmur | 4 | N, V |
| chatter (chat) | 4 | N, V |
| b stutter | 5 | N, V |

## 19d Animal Noises

| Minicluster | Grade Level | Part of Speech |
|---|---|---|
| **19d.1. Gobble** | | |
| b quack | 2 | N, V |
| b peep | 2 | N, V |
| b growl | 3 | N, V |
| b howl | 3 | N, V |
| b buzz | 3 | N, V |
| b bark | 3 | N, V |
| b gobble | 3 | N, V |
| b squawk | 3 | N, V |
| b honk | 3 | N, V |
| b croak | 3* | N, V |
| b cheep | 3* | N, V |
| b chirp | 4 | N, V |
| b hoot | 4 | N, V |
| b bleat | 4 | N, V |
| whinny (whine) | 4 | N, V |
| b grunt | 4 | N, V |
| b snarl | 4 | N, V |
| b snort | 4 | N, V |
| b hiss | 4 | N, V |
| b yelp | 4 | N, V |
| b neigh | 5 | N, V |
| b meow | 5 | N, V |
| b caw | 5 | N, V |
| b purr | 5 | N, V |
| b moo | 5 | N, V |
| b cluck | 5 | N, V |
| b bray | 5* | N, V |
| b cackle | 5* | N, V |
| b yap | 6 | N, V |
| b yowl | 6* | N, V |

## 19e Noises Made by Objects

| Minicluster | Grade Level | Part of Speech |
|---|---|---|
| **19e.1. Tick** | | |
| b ring | 2 | N, V |
| b swish | 2 | N, V |
| b clop | 3 | N, V |
| b thud | 3 | N, V |
| b thump | 3 | N, V |
| b squeak | 3 | N, V |
| b tick | 3 | N, V |
| b whir | 3* | N, V |
| b rattle | 4 | N, V |
| b rustle | 4 | N, V |
| b slam | 4 | N, V |
| b click | 4 | N, V |
| b clank | 4 | N, V |
| b creak | 4 | N, V |
| b jingle | 4 | N, V |
| b gurgle | 4 | N, V |
| b crunch | 4 | N, V |
| b ping | 4* | N, V |
| **19e.2. Clang** | | |
| crackle (crack) | 5 | N, V |
| b clang | 5 | N, V |
| b chug | 5 | N, V |
| b fizz | 5* | N, V |
| b zoom | 6 | V |
| b plop | 6 | V |
| b clink | 6 | N, V |
| b plunk | 6 | N, V |
| b tinkle | 6 | N, V |

# Supercluster 20
## Land/Terrain

### 20a Areas of Land

| Minicluster | Grade Level | Part of Speech |
|---|---|---|
| **20a.1. Acre** | | |
| b lot | 2 | N |
| b acre | 4 | N |
| b plot | 4 | N |
| b tract | 5* | N |
| acreage (acre) | 6 | N |

## 20a.2. Location

| | | | |
|---|---|---|---|
| b | place | 2 | N |
| b | surface | 3 | N |
| b | area | 4 | N |
| b | premises | 6 | N |
| | expanse (expand) | 6 | N |
| b | site | 6 | N |
| | location (locate) | 6 | N |
| | clearing (clear) | SS | N |

## 20a.3. Territory

| | | | |
|---|---|---|---|
| b | territory | 4 | N |
| b | property | 4 | N |
| b | frontier | 4 | N |
| b | zone | 4* | N, V |
| b | region | 5 | N |
| b | horizon | 5 | N |
| b | district | 6 | N |
| b | terrain | 6* | N |

# 20b Characteristics of Places

| Minicluster | Grade Level | Part of Speech |
|---|---|---|

## 20b.1. Geographic

| | | | |
|---|---|---|---|
| | geographic (geography) | 5* | A |
| | geographical (geography) | 5* | A, AV (+ly) |

## 20b.2. Tropical

| | | | |
|---|---|---|---|
| | tropical (tropics) | 4 | A, AV (+ly) |
| | polar (pole) | 5 | A |

## 20b.3. Coastal

| | | | |
|---|---|---|---|
| | coastal (coast) | 4* | A |
| | mountainous (mountain) | 5 | A |

## 20b.3.1 _____

| | | | |
|---|---|---|---|
| | volcanic (volcano) | 5* | A |

## 20b.4. Rural

| | | | |
|---|---|---|---|
| | developed (develop) | 4 | A |
| b | rural | 5* | A |
| | metropolitan (metropolis) | 6* | A |
| | underdeveloped (underdevelop) | SC | A |

## 20b.5. Barren

| | | | |
|---|---|---|---|
| b | bleak | 5 | A |
| b | barren | 6 | A |
| b | desolate | 6* | A |
| | treeless (tree) | 6* | A |

# 20c Valleys/Craters

| Minicluster | Grade Level | Part of Speech |
|---|---|---|

## 20c.1. Valley

| | | | |
|---|---|---|---|
| b | cave | 3 | N |
| b | valley | 3 | N |
| b | canyon | 4 | N |
| | cavern (cave) | 4* | N |
| b | ravine | 6 | N |
| b | gully | 6 | N |
| b | gulch | 6* | N |

## 20c.2. Hole

| | | | |
|---|---|---|---|
| b | hole | 2 | N |
| b | shaft | 4 | N |
| b | ditch | 5 | N |
| b | pit | 6 | N |
| b | trench | 6 | N |
| | cavity (cave) | 6* | N |

## 20c.3. Groove

| | | | |
|---|---|---|---|
| b | crack | 3 | N, V |
| b | notch | 4 | N, V |
| b | crease | 5 | N, V |
| b | gap | 5 | N |
| b | cleft | 6 | N |
| b | rift | 6 | N |
| b | rut | 6 | N |
| b | groove | 6 | N |
| b | fissure | 6* | N |

## 20c.4. Crater

| | | | |
|---|---|---|---|
| b | crater | 6 | N |
| b | chasm | 6 | N |
| b | crevice | 6* | N |
| | crevasse (crevice) | 6* | N |

## 20d Mountains/Hills

| Minicluster | Grade Level | Part of Speech |
|---|---|---|
| **20d.1. Mountain** | | |
| b hill | 1 | N |
| b mountain | 2 | N |
| b cliff | 3 | N |
| b dune | 4 | N |
| b hump | 4 | N |
| b peak | 4 | N |
| b range | 4 | N |
| b foothill | 5* | N |
| **20d.1.1 _____** | | |
| b lowland | 4* | N |
| b highland | 4* | N |
| **20d.2. Ridge** | | |
| b hillside | 4 | N |
| b slope | 4 | N |
| b ridge | 4 | N |
| b mountaintop | 4* | N |
| b crest | 5 | N |
| b mountainside | 5 | N |
| b bluff | 5 | N |
| b crag | 5 | N |
| b hilltop | 6 | N |
| b jag | 6 | N |
| embankment (bank) | 6 | N |
| b precipice | 6 | N |

## 20e Forests/Woodlands

| Minicluster | Grade Level | Part of Speech |
|---|---|---|
| **20e.1. Forest** | | |
| b forest | 2 | N |
| b jungle | 3 | N |
| b grassland | 3* | N |
| b meadow | 4 | N |
| b mesa | 4 | N |
| b grove | 4 | N |
| thicket (thick) | 4 | N |
| wilderness (wild) | 4 | N |
| b glen | 5 | N |
| b dale | 5 | N |
| b woodland | 5* | N |
| b tropics | 5* | N |

## 20f Fields/Pastures

| Minicluster | Grade Level | Part of Speech |
|---|---|---|
| **20f.1. Field** | | |
| b orchard | 2 | N |
| b field | 2 | N |
| b cornfield | 2 | N |
| b pasture | 3 | N |
| b vineyard | 5* | N |
| b farmland | 5* | N |
| b paddy | 5* | N |
| b battleground | 5* | N |
| b battlefield | 5* | N |

---

### Key

**Basic words**

Basic words are preceded by *b*.
All other words are followed by the basic word in parentheses.

**Grade levels**

| K-6 | The grade level at which a word is introduced. |
|---|---|
| * | Indicates a word does not appear frequently in student reading material, but when it does appear it is at the level indicated. |
| – | Words or phrases for which a grade level could not be determined. |

Content specific words are indicated by the content area in which they are used:

| SS | Social Studies |
|---|---|
| EN | English |
| MA | Math |
| SC | Science |

**Part of Speech**

| N | Noun |
|---|---|
| V | Verb |
| A | Adjective |
| AV | Adverb |
| AV (+ly) | Adverb when suffix -ly is added |
| PRO | Pronoun |
| PREP | Preposition |
| INT | Interjection |
| DET | Determiner |
| AX | Auxiliary verb |
| RM | Relationship marker |

## 20g Yards/Parks

| Minicluster | Grade Level | Part of Speech |
|---|---|---|
| **20g.1. Yard** | | |
| b yard | 2 | N |
| b garden | 2 | N |
| b park | 2 | N |
| b backyard | 3 | N |
| b barnyard | 3 | N |
| b patio | 4* | N |
| b courtyard | 4* | N |
| b schoolyard | 4* | N |
| b plaza | 5 | N |
| b terrace | 6 | N |
| b playground | 6 | N |

## 20h Bodies in Space

| Minicluster | Grade Level | Part of Speech |
|---|---|---|
| **20h.1. Earth** | | |
| b world | 2 | N |
| b earth | 2 | N |
| b globe | 2 | N |
| **20h.1.1 _____** | | |
| global | SS | A |
| **20h.2. Sky** | | |
| b sky | 3 | N |
| b space | 3 | N |
| b universe | 5 | N |
| b galaxy | SC | N |
| **20h.3. Sun/Moon** | | |
| b sun | 1 | N, V |
| b moon | 3 | N |
| b planet | 3 | N |
| b Mercury | SC | N |
| b Earth | SC | N |
| b Mars | SC | N |
| b Venus | SC | N |
| b Saturn | SC | N |
| b Jupiter | SC | N |
| b Uranus | SC | N |
| b Pluto | SC | N |
| b Neptune | SC | N |
| **20h.3.1 _____** | | |
| b solar | 6 | A |
| b lunar | SC | A |

| Minicluster | Grade Level | Part of Speech |
|---|---|---|
| **20h.4. Star** | | |
| b star | 2 | N |
| b constellation | 4* | N |
| b nova | 5* | N |
| **20h.5. Meteor** | | |
| b meteor | 4* | N |
| b comet | 4* | N |
| b satellite | 4* | N |
| **20h.6. Eclipse** | | |
| b eclipse | 5* | N, V |

# Supercluster 21
## Dwellings/Shelters

### 21a Man Made Structures

| Minicluster | Grade Level | Part of Speech |
|---|---|---|
| **21a.1. Building** | | |
| b tower | 2 | N, V |
| b skyscraper | 3 | N |
| building (build) | 4 | N |
| b structure | 4 | N, V |
| b shelter | 4 | N, V |
| construction (construct) | 6 | N |
| **21a.2. Establishment** | | |
| establishment (establish) | SS | N |
| installation (install) | SS | N |

## 21b Places to Live

| Minicluster | Grade Level | Part of Speech |
|---|---|---|
| 21b.1. **House** | | |
| b house | K | N, V |
| b home | K | N |
| b apartment | 2 | N |
| b cottage | 3 | N |
| b cabin | 3 | N |
| b farmhouse | 3* | N |
| b homestead | 5 | N |
| b hogan | 5 | N |
| b pueblo | 5* | N |
| b haven | 5* | N |
| dwelling (dwell) | 6 | N |
| habitat (habit) | 6* | N |
| 21b.2. **Mansion** | | |
| b mansion | 5* | N |
| b estate | 6 | N |
| b manor | SS | N |
| 21b.3. **Tent** | | |
| b tent | 2 | N |
| b tepee | 3* | N |
| b igloo | 6 | N |
| b wigwam | 6 | N |
| 21b.4. **Motel** | | |
| b inn | 3 | N |
| b motel | 3* | N |
| b lodge | 4 | N, V |
| b bunkhouse | 5 | N |

## 21c Places of Protection/Incarceration

| Minicluster | Grade Level | Part of Speech |
|---|---|---|
| 21c.1. **Fort** | | |
| b fort | 4 | N |
| b retreat | 4 | N, V |
| b refuge | 5 | N |
| b stronghold | SS | N |
| fortification (fort) | SS | N |
| fortress (fort) | SS | N |
| b outpost | SS | N |

| Minicluster | Grade Level | Part of Speech |
|---|---|---|
| 21c.2. **Jail** | | |
| b cage | 1 | N, V |
| b cell | 3 | N |
| b jail | 3 | N, V |
| b prison | 4 | N, V |
| stockade (stock) | 4 | N |
| b dungeon | 6 | N |
| reformatory (reform) | 6 | N |

## 21d Places Where Goods Are Bought and Sold

| Minicluster | Grade Level | Part of Speech |
|---|---|---|
| 21d.1. **Drugstore** | | |
| b drugstore | 4 | N |
| b barbershop | 5 | N |
| b bookstore | 5* | N |
| 21d.2. **Market** | | |
| b store | 1 | N, V |
| b market | 3 | N |
| grocery (grocer) | 3 | N |
| b supermarket | 5 | N |
| bakery (bake) | 5 | N |
| 21d.3. **Cafe** | | |
| b restaurant | 5 | N |
| b cafe | 5* | N |
| cafeteria (cafe) | 5* | N |
| b tavern | 6 | N |

## 21e Mills/Factories

| Minicluster | Grade Level | Part of Speech |
|---|---|---|
| 21e.1. **Shop** | | |
| b shop | 2 | N, V |
| b office | 3 | N |
| b headquarters | 4 | N |
| b booth | 4 | N |
| b workshop | 5* | N |
| studio (study) | 6 | N |
| 21e.2. **Factory** | | |
| b mill | 3 | N, V |
| b factory | 4 | N |
| b sawmill | 4 | N |
| tannery (tan) | SS | N |
| refinery (refine) | SS | N |

### 21e.3. Windmill

| Minicluster | Grade Level | Part of Speech |
|---|---|---|
| b windmill | 4* | N |

## 21f Places for Learning/ Experimentation

| Minicluster | Grade Level | Part of Speech |
|---|---|---|
| **21f.1. School** | | |
| b school | 1 | N, V |
| b classroom | 2* | N |
| b schoolhouse | 3* | N |
| b schoolroom | 4 | N |
| b kindergarten | 4* | N |
| academy (academic) | 6 | N |
| b college | 6 | N |
| b university | 6 | N |
| **21f.2. Library** | | |
| b library | 2 | N |
| b museum | 3 | N |
| b gallery | 6 | N |
| b archive | 6* | N |
| **21f.3. Lab** | | |
| b laboratory | 4 | N |
| planetarium (planet) | 4* | N |
| lab (laboratory) | 5* | N |
| observatory (observe) | 5* | N |
| reactor (act) | SC | N |

## 21g Places for Sports

| Minicluster | Grade Level | Part of Speech |
|---|---|---|
| **21g.1. Stadium** | | |
| b stadium | 4* | N |
| b arena | 6 | N |
| b auditorium | 6* | N |
| **21g.2. Gym** | | |
| b court | 4 | N |
| b gym | 4 | N |
| b rink | 5 | N |

## 21h Medical Facilities

| Minicluster | Grade Level | Part of Speech |
|---|---|---|
| **21h.1. Hospital** | | |
| b hospital | 3 | N |
| b ward | 4 | N |
| b clinic | 6* | N |
| infirmary (infirm) | 6* | N |
| **21h.2. Cemetery** | | |
| b cemetery | 6 | N |
| b morgue | 6 | N |
| b mortuary | 6 | N |

## 21i Places for Worship

| Minicluster | Grade Level | Part of Speech |
|---|---|---|
| **21i.1. Church** | | |
| b church | 3 | N |
| b mission | 5 | N |
| b chapel | 5* | N |
| b monastery | 5* | N |
| b temple | 6 | N |
| b cathedral | 6 | N |
| b shrine | 6* | N |
| b pantheon | SS | N |
| b convent | SS | N |
| b seminary | SS | N |

## 21j Places Related to Transportation

| Minicluster | Grade Level | Part of Speech |
|---|---|---|
| **21j.1. Airport** | | |
| b station | 2 | N |
| b airport | 4 | N |
| b terminal | 4* | N |
| b depot | 6* | N |

## 21k Places Used for Storage

| Minicluster | Grade Level | Part of Speech |
|---|---|---|
| 21k.1. **Shed** | | |
| b barn | 1 | N |
| b shed | 2 | N, V |
| b hut | 3 | N |
| b storehouse | 4* | N |
| b boathouse | 4* | N |
| b warehouse | 5 | N |
| b shack | 5 | N |
| b storeroom | 5* | N |
| 21k.1.1 _____ | | |
| b greenhouse | 6* | N |
| b hothouse | SS | N |

## 21L Farms/Ranches

| Minicluster | Grade Level | Part of Speech |
|---|---|---|
| 21L.1. **Farm** | | |
| b farm | 1 | N, V |
| b ranch | 2 | N, V |
| b dairy | 2* | N |
| plantation (plant) | 5 | N |
| 21L.1.1 _____ | | |
| fishery (fish) | SS | N |

## 21m Monuments

| Minicluster | Grade Level | Part of Speech |
|---|---|---|
| 21m.1. **Landmark** | | |
| b monument | 5 | N |
| b landmark | 5* | N |
| b totem | 5* | N |
| memorial (memory) | 6 | N |

# Supercluster 22
## Materials

### 22a Containers

| Minicluster | Grade Level | Part of Speech |
|---|---|---|
| 22a.1. **Container** | | |
| packet (pack) | 4 | N |
| b carton | 4 | N |
| folder (fold) | 4* | N |
| holder (hold) | 4* | N |
| container (contain) | 4* | N |
| 22a.2. **Capsule** | | |
| b capsule | 5 | N |
| b compartment | 5 | N |
| b cartridge | 6 | N |

---

### Key

**Basic words**

Basic words are preceded by *b*.
All other words are followed by the basic word in parentheses.

**Grade levels**

K-6  The grade level at which a word is introduced.

\*    Indicates a word does not appear frequently in student reading material, but when it does appear it is at the level indicated.

−    Words or phrases for which a grade level could not be determined.

Content specific words are indicated by the content area in which they are used:

| | |
|---|---|
| SS | Social Studies |
| EN | English |
| MA | Math |
| SC | Science |

**Part of Speech**

| | |
|---|---|
| N | Noun |
| V | Verb |
| A | Adjective |
| AV | Adverb |
| AV (+ly) | Adverb when suffix -ly is added |
| PRO | Pronoun |
| PREP | Preposition |
| INT | Interjection |
| DET | Determiner |
| AX | Auxiliary verb |
| RM | Relationship marker |

## 22a.3. **Box**

| | | |
|---|---|---|
| b box | 1 | N, V |
| b case | 3 | N, V |
| b crate | 4* | N, V |
| b tinderbox | 6 | N |

## 22a.4. **Test tube**

| | | |
|---|---|---|
| b test tube | SC | N |
| dropper (drop) | SC | N |

## 22a.5. **Package**

| | | |
|---|---|---|
| package (pack) | 3 | N, V |
| b freight | 4 | N |
| b cargo | 5 | N |
| b parcel | 6 | N |

## 22a.5.1 _____

| | | |
|---|---|---|
| shipment (ship) | SS | N |
| b shipload | SS | N |

## 22a.6. **Barrel**

| | | |
|---|---|---|
| b barrel | 4 | N |
| b cask | 5 | N |
| b keg | 5 | N |
| b bin | 6 | N |
| b hopper | SS | N |

## 22a.7. **Bag**

| | | |
|---|---|---|
| b bag | 1 | N, V |
| b basket | 2 | N |
| b sack | 3 | N |
| b breadbasket | SS | N |

## 22a.8. **Bottle**

| | | |
|---|---|---|
| b bottle | 2 | N, V |
| b jar | 2 | N, V |
| b pail | 2 | N |
| b pitcher | 3 | N |
| b jug | 4 | N |
| b bucket | 4 | N |

## 22a.9. **Tub**

| | | |
|---|---|---|
| b tank | 4 | N |
| b bathtub | 5 | N |
| b tub | 5 | N |
| b vat | 5* | N |
| b trough | 5* | N |
| b basin | 5* | N |
| b bath | 6 | N |

## 22a.10. **Luggage**

| | | |
|---|---|---|
| b luggage | 4* | N |
| b suitcase | 4* | N |
| baggage (bag) | 5 | N |
| b knapsack | 6* | N |

## 22b Materials/Objects Used to Cover Things

| Minicluster | Grade Level | Part of Speech |
|---|---|---|
| **22b.1. Lid** | | |
| b cover | 2 | N, V |
| b lid | 4 | N |
| b cork | 4 | N, V |
| b plug | 5 | N, V |
| wrapper (wrap) | 5* | N |
| stopper (stop) | SC | N |
| **22b.2. Canvas** | | |
| b canvas | 5 | N |
| b tarpaulin | 6 | N |
| **22b.3. Cardboard** | | |
| b cardboard | 4 | N |
| b cellophane | 5 | N |
| b foil | SC | N |

## 22c Wooden Building Material

| Minicluster | Grade Level | Part of Speech |
|---|---|---|
| **22c.1. Lumber** | | |
| b wood | 2 | N |
| b lumber | 4 | N |
| b timber | 4 | N |
| b plywood | 5* | N |
| b teakwood | SS | N |
| **22c.2. Board** | | |
| b stick | 2 | N |
| b board | 3 | N |
| b log | 3 | N |
| b plank | 5 | N |
| b panel | 6 | N, V |
| b slat | 6 | N |
| b shingle | 6 | N, V |

## 22d Nonwooden Building Material

| Minicluster | Grade Level | Part of Speech |
|---|---|---|
| **22d.1. Tin** | | |
| b brick | 3 | N, V |
| b tin | 3 | N |
| b cement | 4 | N, V |
| b concrete | 4 | N |
| b tile | 5* | N, V |
| b adobe | 5* | N |
| b asbestos | 5* | N |
| pavement (pave) | 6 | N |
| b porcelain | 6 | N |
| b ceramic | SC | N |
| **22d.1.1** _____ | | |
| b cornerstone | 6* | N |
| **22d.1.2** _____ | | |
| b pave | 4* | V |
| **22d.2. Pipe** | | |
| b pipe | 3 | N |
| b wire | 3 | N, V |
| b tube | 3 | N |
| b pipeline | 3 | N |
| **22d.3. Pole** | | |
| b bar | 2 | N |
| b pole | 3 | N |
| b rod | 4 | N |
| b post | 4 | N |
| b flagpole | 5 | N |
| b staff | 5 | N |
| b brace | 5 | N, V |
| b bracket | 6* | N, V |
| **22d.4. Hoop** | | |
| b hoop | 4 | N |
| b stilt | 5* | N |

## 22e General Names for Objects

| Minicluster | Grade Level | Part of Speech |
|---|---|---|
| **22e.1. Object** | | |
| b thing | 1 | N |
| b material | 4 | N |
| b object | 4 | N |
| b substance | 6 | N |

## 22f Building Actions

| Minicluster | Grade Level | Part of Speech |
|---|---|---|
| **22f.1. Construction** | | |
| construction (construct) | 6 | N |
| **22f.2. Accomplishment** | | |
| b accomplishment (accomplish) | 6 | N |
| **22f.2.1** _____ | | |
| b accomplish | 6 | V |
| **22f.3. Make** | | |
| b make | K | V |
| b build | 1 | V |
| b manufacture | 5 | V |
| b establish | 5 | V |
| b produce | 5 | V |
| b construct | 5 | V |
| b forge | 5 | V |
| b generate | 5* | V |
| **22f.4. Shape** | | |
| b shape | 2 | N, V |
| b form | 3 | N, V |
| b pare | 3 | V |
| b develop | 4 | V |
| b mold | 4 | N, V |
| b install | 5 | V |
| **22f.4.1** _____ | | |
| development (develop) | 5* | N |

## 22f.5. **Repair**

| Miniheading | | Grade Level | Part of Speech |
|---|---|---|---|
| b | fix | 2 | V |
| b | repair | 3 | N, V |
| | replace (place) | 4 | V |
| b | adjust | 4 | V |
| | rebuild (build) | 5* | V |
| | rearrange (arrange) | 5* | V |
| | strengthen (strong) | 5* | V |
| b | preserve | 5 | V |
| b | restore | 6 | V |
| b | adapt | 6 | V |
| b | maintain | 6 | V |
| b | modify | 6* | V |
| | modernize (modern) | SS | V |

### 22f.5.1 _____

| | maintenance (maintain) | 6* | N |
|---|---|---|---|

## 22g Wrapping/Packing Actions

| Minicluster | | Grade Level | Part of Speech |
|---|---|---|---|
| **22g.1.** | **Wrap** | | |
| b | glue | 2 | N, V |
| b | tape | 2 | N, V |
| b | wrap | 3 | N, V |
| b | pack | 3 | V |
| b | bind | 4* | V |
| **22g.2.** | **Unwrap** | | |
| | untie (tie) | 3 | V |
| | unlock (lock) | 3 | V |
| | uncover (cover) | 3* | V |
| | unload (load) | 4 | V |
| | unroll (roll) | 4* | V |
| | unpack (pack) | 5* | V |
| | unravel (ravel) | 6 | V |

# Supercluster 23
# The Human Body

## 23a The Body (General)

| Minicluster | | Grade Level | Part of Speech |
|---|---|---|---|
| **23a.1.** | **Body** | | |
| b | trunk | 2 | N |
| b | body | 3 | N |
| b | carcass | 6 | N |
| b | torso | SC | N |
| **23a.1.1** | _____ | | |
| b | physical | 5 | A, AV (+ly) |
| **23a.2.** | **Chest** | | |
| b | chest | 3 | N |
| b | shoulders | 3 | N |
| b | hips | 3 | N |
| b | lap | 4 | N |
| b | limb(s) | 5 | N |
| b | belly | 5* | N |

## 23b Body Coverings

| Minicluster | | Grade Level | Part of Speech |
|---|---|---|---|
| **23b.1.** | **Skin** | | |
| b | skin | 3 | N, V |
| b | flesh | 5 | N |
| b | scalp | 5 | N, V |
| b | tissue | 5* | N |
| b | blubber | 6 | N |
| b | membrane | SC | N |
| **23b.2.** | **Complexion** | | |
| b | complexion | 6 | N |
| **23b.3.** | **Beard** | | |
| b | hair | 1 | N |
| b | beard | 3 | N |
| b | mustache | 4 | N |
| b | pigtail | 4* | N |
| b | tuft | 6 | N |
| b | wig | 6 | N |
| b | toupee | 6* | N |
| b | hairline | 6* | N |
| **23b.3.1** | _____ | | |
| | bearded (beard) | 3 | A |

## 23b.4. **Scar**

| Minicluster | Grade Level | Part of Speech |
|---|---|---|
| b bump | 2 | N, V |
| b lump | 3 | N, V |
| b scar | 4 | N, V |
| b freckle | 4 | N |
| b bruise | 4 | N, V |
| b wart | 6 | N |
| b tumor | 6 | N |
| b birthmark | 6 | N |

## 23c The Head

| Minicluster | Grade Level | Part of Speech |
|---|---|---|
| **23c.1. Brain** | | |
| b head | 1 | N |
| b mind | 2 | N, V |
| b brain | 4 | N |
| b skull | 5* | N |
| **23c.2. Face** | | |
| b face | 2 | N, V |
| b cheek | 3 | N |
| b chin | 3 | N |
| forehead (head) | 4 | N |
| **23c.3. Cerebellum** | | |
| b auricle | SC | N |
| b cerebellum | SC | N |
| b cerebrum | SC | N |
| b medula | SC | N |

## 23d Mouth/Throat

| Minicluster | Grade Level | Part of Speech |
|---|---|---|
| **23d.1. Mouth** | | |
| b mouth | 2 | N |
| teeth (tooth) | 2* | N |
| b tooth | 2* | N |
| b tongue | 3 | N |
| b lip | 4 | N |
| b gums | 5 | N |
| b fang | 6 | N |
| **23d.1.1 _____** | | |
| b oral | 5 | A, AV (+ly) |

## 23d.2. **Throat**

| | Grade | Part of Speech |
|---|---|---|
| b voice | 2 | N, V |
| b throat | 4 | N |
| b windpipe | SC | N |

## 23e Eyes/Ears/Nose

| Minicluster | Grade Level | Part of Speech |
|---|---|---|
| **23e.1. Ear** | | |
| b ear | 2 | N |
| b eardrum | 3* | N |
| b earlobe | 5 | N |

---

### Key

**Basic words**

Basic words are preceded by *b*.
All other words are followed by the basic word in parentheses.

**Grade levels**

K-6  The grade level at which a word is introduced.

\*  Indicates a word does not appear frequently in student reading material, but when it does appear it is at the level indicated.

–  Words or phrases for which a grade level could not be determined.

Content specific words are indicated by the content area in which they are used:

| | |
|---|---|
| SS | Social Studies |
| EN | English |
| MA | Math |
| SC | Science |

**Part of Speech**

| | |
|---|---|
| N | Noun |
| V | Verb |
| A | Adjective |
| AV | Adverb |
| AV (+ly) | Adverb when suffix -ly is added |
| PRO | Pronoun |
| PREP | Preposition |
| INT | Interjection |
| DET | Determiner |
| AX | Auxiliary verb |
| RM | Relationship marker |

### 23e.2. **Eye**

| | Grade Level | Part of Speech |
|---|---|---|
| b eye | 2 | N, V |
| b eyebrow | 4 | N |
| b eyelid | 6 | N |
| b brow | 6 | N |
| b eyelash | 6 | N |
| b retina | SC | N |

### 23e.3. **Nose**

| | | |
|---|---|---|
| b nose | 2 | N |
| nostril (nose) | 5 | N |

## 23f Limbs

| Minicluster | Grade Level | Part of Speech |
|---|---|---|
| **23f.1. Arm** | | |
| b arm | 2 | N |
| b wrist | 5 | N |
| b elbow | 5 | N |
| b bicep | SC | N |
| **23f.2. Hand** | | |
| b hand | 1 | N, V |
| b thumb | 2 | N, V |
| b finger | 2 | N, V |
| b nail(s) | 3 | N |
| b fist | 4 | N |
| b palm | 4 | N, V |
| b knuckle | 6* | N |
| b fingernail | SC | N |

## 23g Legs/Feet

| Minicluster | Grade Level | Part of Speech |
|---|---|---|
| **23g.1. Foot** | | |
| b foot | 2 | N |
| b toe | 3 | N |
| b heel | 3 | N |
| b ankle | 4 | N |
| b arch | 4 | N, V |
| **23g.2. Leg** | | |
| b leg | 1 | N |
| b knee | 3 | N, V |
| calves (calf) | 5 | N |
| b thigh | 5* | N |
| b haunch | 6 | N |

## 23h Internal Organs

| Minicluster | Grade Level | Part of Speech |
|---|---|---|
| **23h.1. Stomach** | | |
| b stomach | 3 | N |
| b heart | 3* | N |
| b liver | 4* | N |
| b lung | 5 | N |
| b diaphragm | SC | N |
| b ovary | SC | N |
| b kidney | SC | N |
| b intestine | SC | N |

## 23i Internal Bodily Fluids

| Minicluster | Grade Level | Part of Speech |
|---|---|---|
| **23i.1. Blood** | | |
| b tear | 3 | N |
| b blood | 4 | N |
| b sweat | 5 | N, V |
| perspiration (perspire) | 6 | N |
| b saliva | SC | N |
| b mucus | SC | N |
| b hemoglobin | SC | N |
| **23i.2. Vein** | | |
| b vein | 4 | N |
| b vessel | 5 | N |
| b artery | 5* | N |
| b ventricle | SC | N |
| b capillary | SC | N |
| **23i.3. Bleed** | | |
| bleed (blood) | 5 | V |
| b digest | 5* | V |
| circulate (circle) | SC | V |

## 23j Bones/Muscles/Nerves

| Minicluster | Grade Level | Part of Speech |
|---|---|---|
| **23j.1. Bone** | | |
| b bone | 3 | N |
| b spine | 4 | N |
| b rib | 5 | N |
| b backbone | 5* | N |
| b vertebrae | SC | N |
| **23j.1.1** _____ | | |
| spinal (spine) | SC | A, AV (+ly) |
| **23j.2. Muscle** | | |
| b muscle | 4 | N, V |
| b sinew | 5* | N |
| b ligament | SC | N |
| b cartilage | SC | N |
| b tendon | SC | N |
| **23j.3. Nerve** | | |
| b gland | 5* | N |
| b nerve | 6 | N |
| b marrow | 6* | N |
| b neuron | SC | N |

## 23k Bodily Systems

| Minicluster | Grade Level | Part of Speech |
|---|---|---|
| **23k.1. Respiratory** | | |
| reproductive (produce) | 5* | A |
| salivary (saliva) | SC | A |
| respiratory | SC | A |
| (respire) | SC | A |
| sensory (sense) | SC | A |
| skeletal (skeleton) | SC | A |
| digestive (digest) | SC | A |
| circulatory (circle) | SC | A |
| **23k.1.1** _____ | | |
| digestion (digest) | SC | N |
| circulation (circle) | SC | N |

# Supercluster 24
# Vegetation

## 24a Vegetation (General)

| Minicluster | Grade Level | Part of Speech |
|---|---|---|
| **24a.1. Tree** | | |
| b tree | K | N, V |
| b bush | 3 | N |
| b plant | 6 | N, V |
| b shrub | 6 | N |
| **24a.2. Vegetation** | | |
| growth (grow) | 4* | N |
| b vegetation | 6 | N |
| b undergrowth | 6 | N |
| b underbrush | 6* | N |
| b humus | SC | N |
| b flora | SC | N |
| greenery (green) | SC | N |

## 24b Types of Trees

| Minicluster | Grade Level | Part of Speech |
|---|---|---|
| **24b.1. Oak** | | |
| b oak | 2 | N |
| b pine | 3 | N |
| b birch | 4 | N |
| b cottonwood | 4 | N |
| b mulberry | 4* | N |
| b locust | 4* | N |
| b evergreen | 4* | N |
| b fir | 5 | N |
| b aspen | 5 | N |
| b maple | 5 | N |
| b elm | 5 | N |
| b redwood | 5* | N |
| b sequoia | 5* | N |
| b mahogany | 5* | N |
| b hickory | 5* | N |
| b citrus | 5* | N |
| b spruce | 6 | N |
| b hemlock | 6 | N |
| b beech | 6 | N |
| b poplar | 6 | N |
| b cedar | 6 | N |
| b teak | SS | N |
| b balsa | SS | N |

## 24c Parts of Trees

| Minicluster | Grade Level | Part of Speech |
|---|---|---|
| **24c.1. Bark** | | |
| b bark | 1 | N |
| b branch | 2 | N, V |
| b twig | 3 | N |
| b leaf | 4 | N, V |
| b stump | 4 | N |
| b treetop | 4* | N |
| b limb | 5* | N |
| b bough | 5 | N |
| **24c.2. Sap** | | |
| b rubber | 3 | N |
| b balsam | 4* | N |
| b pith | 5* | N |
| b sap | 6 | N |
| b chlorophyll | SC | N |
| b resin | SS | N |

## 24d Flowers

| Minicluster | Grade Level | Part of Speech |
|---|---|---|
| **24d.1. Blossom** | | |
| b flower | 2 | N, V |
| b blossom | 3 | N, V |
| b bud | 3 | N |
| b pod | 3* | N |
| b petal | 5 | N |
| **24d.2. Seed** | | |
| b seed | 2 | N, V |
| b bulb | 4 | N |
| b sprout | 5 | N, V |
| b spore | SC | N |
| b stamen | SC | N |
| b pistil | SC | N |
| b pollen | SC | N |

| 24d.3. **Rose** | | |
|---|---|---|
| b rose | 3 | N |
| b tulip | 3* | N |
| b flax | 3* | N |
| b gardenia | 4 | N |
| b marigold | 4* | N |
| b lavender | 4* | N |
| b sunflower | 4* | N |
| b daffodil | 4* | N |
| b dandelion | 4* | N |
| b aster | 4* | N |
| b lily | 5 | N |
| b daisy | 5 | N |
| b lilac | 5* | N |
| b geranium | 5* | N |
| b anemone | 5* | N |
| b poppy | 6 | N |
| b petunia | 6* | N |
| b chrysanthemum | 6* | N |
| b carnation | 6* | N |
| 24d.4. **Holly** | | |
| b holly | 4 | N |
| b huckleberry | 5 | N |
| b brier | 5 | N |
| 24d.5. **Hemp** | | |
| b hemp | 6* | N |
| b jute | SS | N |
| b sisal | SS | N |

## 24e Other Vegetation

| Minicluster | Grade Level | Part of Speech |
|---|---|---|
| **24e.1. Moss** | | |
| b algae | 3* | N |
| b moss | 4 | N |
| b seaweed | 4* | N |
| b mushroom | 5 | N |
| b lichen | 6 | N |
| b kelp | SC | N |
| b fungus | SC | N |
| **24e.2. Vine** | | |
| b stalk | 4 | N |
| b vine | 4 | N |
| b root | 4 | N |
| b beanstalk | 4* | N |
| b cob | 5* | N |
| b grapevine | 6 | N |

| 24e.3. **Pollinate** | | |
|---|---|---|
| pollinate (pollen) | SC | V |
| 24e.3.1 _____ | | |
| pollination (pollen) | SC | N |
| 24e.4. **Grass** | | |
| b grass | 1 | N |
| b hay | 3 | N |
| b straw | 3 | N |
| b bamboo | 4 | N |
| b reed | 4 | N |
| b clover | 5 | N |
| b alfalfa | 5* | N |
| b thatch | 6 | N |

| 25a.2. **Mixture** | | |
|---|---|---|
| mixture (mix) | 4 | N |
| b compound | 4 | N, V |
| combination (combine) | 5 | N |
| composite (compose) | MA | N |
| 25a.3. **Grid** | | |
| b web | 4 | N, V |
| b grid | 6* | N |
| b network | 6* | N, V |

# Supercluster 25
# Groups

## 25a General Names for Groups of Things

| Minicluster | Grade Level | Part of Speech |
|---|---|---|
| 25a.1. **Group** | | |
| b group | 3 | N, V |
| b list | 3 | N, V |
| b file | 4 | N, V |
| collection (collect) | 4 | N |
| arrangement (arrange) | 4* | N |
| b series | 5 | N |
| b system | 5 | N |
| b assortment | 5* | N |
| classification (classify) | 5* | N |
| b directory (direct) | 5* | N |
| 25a.1.1 _____ | | |
| collector (collect) | 4* | N |
| 25a.1.2 _____ | | |
| collective (collect) | 6* | A, AV (+ly) |

**Key**

Basic words
> Basic words are preceded by *b*.
> All other words are followed by the basic word in parentheses.

Grade levels
> K-6   The grade level at which a word is introduced.
> *       Indicates a word does not appear frequently in student reading material, but when it does appear it is at the level indicated.
> –       Words or phrases for which a grade level could not be determined.

Content specific words are indicated by the content area in which they are used:

| | |
|---|---|
| SS | Social Studies |
| EN | English |
| MA | Math |
| SC | Science |

Part of Speech

| | |
|---|---|
| N | Noun |
| V | Verb |
| A | Adjective |
| AV | Adverb |
| AV (+ly) | Adverb when suffix -ly is added |
| PRO | Pronoun |
| PREP | Preposition |
| INT | Interjection |
| DET | Determiner |
| AX | Auxiliary verb |
| RM | Relationship marker |

## 25a.4. Bundle

| | | | |
|---|---|---|---|
| b | pile | 2 | N, V |
| b | bundle | 3 | N, V |
| b | stack | 4 | N, V |
| b | heap | 4 | N, V |
| b | clump | 4 | N, V |
| b | bunch | 4 | N, V |
| b | bale | 5 | N, V |
| b | cluster | 5 | N, V |
| b | wad | 6 | N, V |
| b | horde | 6 | N, V |

## 25a.5. Gather

| | | | |
|---|---|---|---|
| b | gather | 3 | V |
| b | arrange | 4 | V |
| b | collect | 4 | V |
| b | organize | 5 | V |
| | classify (class) | 6 | V |
| b | assemble | 6 | V |
| | summarize (sum) | EN | V |

## 25b Groups of People/Animals

| Minicluster | | Grade Level | Part of Speech |
|---|---|---|---|
| **25b.1. Crowd** | | | |
| b | crowd | 3 | N, V |
| b | gang | 4 | N |
| b | mass | 4 | N |
| b | throng | 6 | N |
| b | mob | 6 | N, V |
| **25b.2. Band** | | | |
| b | band | 3 | N, V |
| b | chorus | 5 | N |
| b | trio | 6 | N |
| b | quartet | 6 | N |
| **25b.3. Herd** | | | |
| b | herd | 3 | N, V |
| b | pod | 3* | N |
| b | flock | 4 | N, V |
| b | brood | 5 | N |
| b | gaggle | 6* | N |
| **25b.4. Class** | | | |
| b | class | 2 | N |
| b | club | 3 | N |
| b | sorority | 6* | N |
| | fraternity (fraternal) | 6* | N |
| | brotherhood (brother) | 6* | N |

## 25b.5. Team

| | | | |
|---|---|---|---|
| b | team | 3 | N, V |
| b | crew | 4 | N, V |
| b | huddle | 4 | N, V |

## 25c Political/Social Groups

| Minicluster | | Grade Level | Part of Speech |
|---|---|---|---|
| **25c.1. Republic** | | | |
| b | republic | 4* | N |
| b | democracy | 5 | N |
| b | commonwealth | SS | N |
| | confederacy (confederate) | SS | N |
| | federation (federate) | SS | N |
| | protectorate (protect) | SS | N |
| **25c.2. Country** | | | |
| b | country | 2 | N |
| b | nation | 4 | N |
| **25c.2.1** _____ | | | |
| | national (nation) | 4 | A, AV (+ly) |
| | international (nation) | 5 | A, AV (+ly) |
| **25c.3. Government** | | | |
| | government (govern) | 4 | N |
| | legislature (legislate) | 5 | N |
| b | parliament | 5* | N |
| b | congress | 6 | N |
| **25c.4. Political** | | | |
| | political (politics) | 6 | A, AV (+ly) |
| | federal (federate) | 6 | A, AV (+ly) |
| | legislative (legislate) | SS | A, AV (+ly) |
| **25c.5. Society** | | | |
| b | society | 4 | N |
| b | culture | 5 | N |
| | community (commune) | 5 | N |
| | civilization (civil) | 6 | N |
| b | caste | SS | N |

| Minicluster | Grade Level | Part of Speech |
|---|---|---|
| 25c.6. **Family** | | |
| b family | 2 | N |
| b tribe | 3 | N |
| b cult | 6* | N |
| 25c.6.1 ________ | | |
| tribal (tribe) | 5* | A |

### 25d Military Groups

| Minicluster | Grade Level | Part of Speech |
|---|---|---|
| 25d.1. **Army** | | |
| army (arms) | 3 | N |
| b police | 3 | N |
| b marines | 5 | N |
| b navy | 5 | N |
| b air force | 6 | N |
| 25d.1.1 ________ | | |
| naval (navy) | 6 | A |
| 25d.2. **Troop** | | |
| b troop | 4 | N, V |
| b detail | 5 | N |
| b corps | 5* | N |
| b patrol | 5 | N, V |
| b squadron | 6 | N |
| b regiment | 6* | N |
| b platoon | 6* | N |
| b legion | 6* | N |
| b brigade | 6* | N |

### 25e Social/Business Groups

| Minicluster | Grade Level | Part of Speech |
|---|---|---|
| 25e.1. **Organization** | | |
| b council | 4 | N |
| b committee | 4 | N |
| b institute | 5 | N |
| b league | 5 | N |
| organization (organize) | 5 | N |
| association | 6 | N |
| (associate) | 6 | N |
| foundation (found) | 6 | N |
| b commission | 6 | N |
| 25e.2. **Conference** | | |
| conference (confer) | 6 | N, V |
| b session | 6 | N |
| b convention | SS | N |
| 25e.3. **Gathering** | | |
| b gathering | 4 | N |
| b audience | 4 | N |
| attendance (attend) | 4* | N |
| assembly (assemble) | 6 | N |
| congregation (congregate) | 6 | N |
| 25e.4. **Membership** | | |
| membership (member) | 6* | N |
| partnership (partner) | 6* | N |

# Supercluster 26
## Value/Correctness

### 26a Right/Wrong

| Minicluster | Grade Level | Part of Speech |
|---|---|---|
| 26a.1. **Truth** | | |
| truth (true) | 3 | N |
| justice (just) | 4 | N |
| b virtue | 6 | N |
| reality (real) | 6* | N |
| 26a.1.1 ________ | | |
| b just | 1 | A |
| realistic (real) | 6* | A, AV (+ly) |
| 26a.2. **Mistake** | | |
| b mistake | 3 | N, V |
| error (err) | 5 | N, V |
| b blunder | 5 | N, V |
| b flaw | 5 | N, V |
| b crime | 6 | N |

## 26a.3. Right

| | Grade Level | Part of Speech |
|---|---|---|
| b right | 1 | A, AV (+ly) |
| b true | 2 | A, AV (+iy) |
| b correct | 4 | A, AV (+ly) |
| b legal | 5 | A, AV (+ly) |
| rightful (right) | 6 | A, AV (+ly) |

## 26a.4. Proper

| | Grade Level | Part of Speech |
|---|---|---|
| b proper | 3 | A, AV (+ly) |
| b appropriate | 5 | A, AV (+ly) |
| satisfactory (satisfy) | 5* | A, AV (+ly) |
| suitable (suit) | 5* | A, AV (+ly) |
| acceptable (accept) | EN | A, AV (+ly) |

## 26a.5. Wrong

| | Grade Level | Part of Speech |
|---|---|---|
| b wrong | 2 | A, AV (+ly) |
| incorrect (correct) | 4* | A, AV (+ly) |
| b false | 5 | A, AV (+ly) |
| guilty (guilt) | 6 | A |

## 26a.6. Honesty

| | Grade Level | Part of Speech |
|---|---|---|
| honesty (honest) | 4 | N |
| innocence (innocent) | 6* | N |
| fairness (fair) | 6* | N |

## 26a.6.1 _____

| | Grade Level | Part of Speech |
|---|---|---|
| b honest | 4 | A, AV (+ly) |
| b innocent | 4 | A, AV (+ly) |

# 26b Success

| Minicluster | Grade Level | Part of Speech |
|---|---|---|
| 26b.1. **Success** | | |
| success (succeed) | 4 | N |
| failure (fail) | 6 | N |
| 26b.1.1 _____ | | |
| b succeed | 4 | V |
| b fail | 4 | V |

# 26c Importance/Value

| Minicluster | Grade Level | Part of Speech |
|---|---|---|
| 26c.1. **Essential** | | |
| b important | 3 | A, AV (+ly) |
| elementary (element) | 3* | A |
| b primary | 3* | A, AV (+ly) |
| b necessary | 4 | A, AV (+ly) |
| basic (base) | 5 | A, AV (+ly) |
| b essential | 6 | A, AV (+ly) |
| critical (critic) | 6 | A, AV (+ly) |
| underlying (underlie) | SC | A |
| 26c.2. **Supreme** | | |
| b best | 2 | A |
| b perfect | 2 | A, AV (+ly) |
| favorite (favor) | 3 | A |
| b main | 3 | A, AV (+ly) |
| b super | 5 | A |
| b supreme | 5* | A, AV (+ly) |
| superb (super) | 6 | A, AV (+ly) |
| b major | 6 | A |
| b superior | 6 | A |
| b foremost | 6 | A |

**26c.3. Desirable**

| | | | |
|---|---|---|---|
| | beloved (love) | 4 | A |
| | desirable (desire) | 5* | A, AV (+ly) |
| | memorable (memory) | 5* | A, AV (+ly) |
| b | noteworthy | 6 | A |

**26c.4. Good**

| | | | |
|---|---|---|---|
| b | good | K | A |
| b | better | 1 | A |
| b | fine | 2 | A |
| b | dandy | 5 | A |
| | delightful (delight) | 5* | A, AV (+ly) |
| b | worthwhile | 6* | A |
| | impressive (impress) | 6* | A, AV (+ly) |

**26c.5. Terrific**

| | | | |
|---|---|---|---|
| | wonderful (wonder) | 2 | A, AV (+ly) |
| | remarkable (remark) | 4 | A, AV (+ly) |
| | excellent (excel) | 4 | A, AV (+ly) |
| b | magnificent | 4 | A, AV (+ly) |
| | fantastic (fantasy) | 5 | A, AV (+ly) |
| b | terrific | 5 | A, AV (+ly) |
| b | fabulous | 6 | A, AV (+ly) |
| | marvelous (marvel) | 6 | A, AV (+ly) |
| b | outstanding | 6 | A, AV (+ly) |
| | spectacular (spectacle) | 6 | A, AV (+ly) |
| b | extraordinary | 6 | A, AV (+ly) |
| | incredible (credible) | 6 | A, AV (+ly) |
| | exceptional (except) | 6* | A, AV (+ly) |
| b | tremendous | 6* | A, AV (+ly) |
| | invaluable (value) | 6* | A, AV (+ly) |

**26c.6. Precious**

| | | | |
|---|---|---|---|
| b | dear | 2 | A, AV (+ly) |
| b | precious | 3 | A, AV (+ly) |
| | valuable (value) | 4 | N, A |

**26c.6.1** _____

| | | | |
|---|---|---|---|
| | greatness (great) | 5* | N |

**26c.7. Usable**

| | | | |
|---|---|---|---|
| | useful (use) | 3 | A, AV (+ly) |
| b | usable (use) | 6 | A |

**26c.7.1** _____

| | | | |
|---|---|---|---|
| | usefulness (use) | 5 | N |

---

**Key**

Basic words

    Basic words are preceded by *b*.
All other words are followed by the basic word in parentheses.

Grade levels

    K-6  The grade level at which a word is introduced.

    \*    Indicates a word does not appear frequently in student reading material, but when it does appear it is at the level indicated.

    –    Words or phrases for which a grade level could not be determined.

Content specific words are indicated by the content area in which they are used:

| | |
|---|---|
| SS | Social Studies |
| EN | English |
| MA | Math |
| SC | Science |

Part of Speech

| | |
|---|---|
| N | Noun |
| V | Verb |
| A | Adjective |
| AV | Adverb |
| AV (+ly) | Adverb when suffix -ly is added |
| PRO | Pronoun |
| PREP | Preposition |
| INT | Interjection |
| DET | Determiner |
| AX | Auxiliary verb |
| RM | Relationship marker |

## 26d Lack of Value

| Minicluster | Grade Level | Part of Speech |
|---|---|---|
| **26d.1. Useless** | | |
| b spare | 3 | A |
| useless (use) | 4 | A, AV (+ly) |
| worthless (worth) | 5 | A, AV (+ly) |
| insignificant (signify) | 6 | A, AV |
| pitiful (pity) | 6 | A, AV (+ly) |
| unimportant (important) | 6 | A, AV (+ly) |
| nonessential (essential) | 6* | A |
| **26d.2. Bad** | | |
| b bad | 2 | A, AV (+ly) |
| terrible (terror) | 3 | A, AV (+ly) |
| b faulty (fault) | 3 | A |
| b awful | 3 | A, AV (+ly) |
| b dreadful (dread) | 4 | A, AV (+ly) |
| b horrible (horror) | 5 | A, AV (+ly) |
| b evil | 5 | A, AV (+ly) |
| negative (negate) | 6* | A, AV (+ly) |
| ghostly (ghost) | 6* | A |
| **26d.3. Unfavorable** | | |
| unbearable (bear) | 5* | A, AV (+ly) |
| unfavorable (favor) | 6* | A, AV (+ly) |
| unfit (fit) | 6 | A |
| **26d.4. Foul** | | |
| b foul | 5 | N, V, A |
| b grim | 5 | AV (+ly) |
| b tragic | 6 | A, AV (+ly) |
| unfortunate (fortune) | 6 | A, AV (+ly) |

## 26d.5. Foolish

| | Grade Level | Part of Speech |
|---|---|---|
| foolish (fool) | 3 | A, AV (+ly) |
| ridiculous (ridicule) | 5 | A, AV (+ly) |
| b absurd | 6 | A, AV (+ly) |

# Supercluster 27
## Similarity/Dissimilarity

### 27a Likeness

| Minicluster | Grade Level | Part of Speech |
|---|---|---|
| **27a.1. Likeness** | | |
| likeness (like) | 4* | N |
| equality (equal) | 5* | N |
| resemblance (resemble) | 6 | N |
| similarity (similar) | 6* | N |
| **27a.2. Concord** | | |
| b concord | 3 | N |
| agreement (agree) | 4* | N |
| b harmony | 6 | N |
| **27a.3. Same** | | |
| b like | 2 | A, PREP |
| b same | 2 | A |
| twin (two) | 2 | A |
| b exact | 3 | A, AV (+ly) |
| b alike (like) | 4* | A |
| related (relate) | 4* | A |
| b equal | 4* | A, AV (+ly) |
| b parallel | 5 | V, A |
| b identical | 6 | A, AV (+ly) |
| comparative (compare) | 6 | A, AV (+ly) |
| equivalent (equal) | 6* | A, AV (+ly) |
| b literal | 6* | A, AV (+ly) |
| b similar | 6* | A, AV (+ly) |

## 27a.4. Resemble

| | | | |
|---|---|---|---|
| b | match | 3 | N. V |
| | approximate (proximate) | 5* | V |
| b | resemble | 6 | V |

## 27a.5. Imitation

| | | | |
|---|---|---|---|
| b | substitute | 6 | N, V |
| | replacement (place) | 6* | N |
| | imitation (imitate) | 6* | V |

## 27a.6. Copy

| | | | |
|---|---|---|---|
| | replace (place) | 3 | V |
| b | imitate | 4 | V |
| b | copy | 4 | N, V |
| | mimic (mime) | 4* | V |
| b | duplicate | 6* | N, V |

# 27b Addition (Relationship Markers)

| Minicluster | Grade Level | Part of Speech |
|---|---|---|

### 27b.1. Coordinates

| | | | |
|---|---|---|---|
| b | with | K | RM |
| b | and | K | RM |
| b | as well as | – | RM |

### 27b.2. Similarity

| | | | |
|---|---|---|---|
| b | too | K | RM |
| b | also | 2 | RM |
| | besides (side) | 2 | RM |
| | equally (equal) | 4 | RM |
| | further (far) | 4 | RM |
| b | moreover | 5* | RM |
| b | furthermore | 6 | RM |
| b | likewise | 6* | RM |
| b | as well | – | RM |
| b | in addition | – | RM |
| b | for example | – | RM |

### 27b.3. Restatement

| | | | |
|---|---|---|---|
| b | indeed | 3 | RM |
| | actually (actual) | 4 | RM |
| | namely (name) | 6 | RM |
| b | that is | – | RM |

# 27c Difference

| Minicluster | Grade Level | Part of Speech |
|---|---|---|

### 27c.1. Difference

| | | |
|---|---|---|
| difference (differ) | 3 | N |
| comparison (compare) | 6 | N |
| variation (vary) | 6 | N |
| inequality (equal) | MA | N |

### 27c.2. Unlike

| | | | |
|---|---|---|---|
| | different (differ) | 2 | A, AV (+ly) |
| b | separate | 4 | A, AV, V, (+ly) |
| | unlike (like) | 4 | A, AV (+ly) |
| b | opposite (oppose) | 4 | A, AV (+ly) |
| b | unequal (equal) | 6* | A, AV (+ly) |

### 27c.2.1 _____

| | | | |
|---|---|---|---|
| b | differ | 6 | V |

### 27c.3. Change

| | | | |
|---|---|---|---|
| b | change | 2 | N, V |
| b | develop | 4 | V |
| b | undergo | 5 | V |
| | transform (form) | 5* | V |
| | reform (form) | 6 | N, V |
| b | vary | 6 | V |

# 27d Contrast (Relationship Markers)

| Minicluster | Grade Level | Part of Speech |
|---|---|---|

### 27d.1. Antithesis

| | | | |
|---|---|---|---|
| b | not | K | RM |
| b | but | K | RM |
| b | yet | 2 | RM |
| b | without | 2 | RM |

## 27d.2. Comparison

| | | | |
|---|---|---|---|
| b | than | 1 | RM |
| b | else | 2 | RM |
| b | otherwise | 5 | RM |
| | alternately (alternate) | 6 | RM |
| | alternatively (alternate) | 6* | RM |
| b | whereas | 6* | RM |
| | contrariwise (contrary) | 6* | RM |
| | contrastingly (contrast) | 6* | RM |
| | conversely (converse) | 6* | RM |
| | oppositely (oppose) | 6* | RM |
| b | or rather | – | RM |
| b | on the contrary | – | RM |
| b | in comparison | – | RM |
| b | on the other hand | – | RM |
| b | by comparison | – | RM |
| b | by way of contrast | – | RM |

## 27d.3. Alternative

| | | | |
|---|---|---|---|
| b | or | K | RM |
| b | either...or | – | RM |
| | neither...nor (either...or) | – | RM |

## 27d.4. Concession

| | | | |
|---|---|---|---|
| b | still | 1 | RM |
| | besides (side) | 2 | RM |
| b | only | 2 | RM |
| | although (though) | 3 | RM |
| b | though | 3 | RM |
| b | anyway | 3 | RM |
| b | however | 4 | RM |
| b | nevertheless | 5* | RM |
| | despite (spite) | 6 | RM |
| b | anyhow | 6* | RM |
| b | in any case | – | RM |
| b | in any event | – | RM |
| b | at any rate | – | RM |
| b | except for | – | RM |
| b | regardless of | – | RM |

# Supercluster 28
## Money/Finance

### 28a Money/Goods You Receive

| Minicluster | Grade Level | Part of Speech |
|---|---|---|
| **28a.1. Savings** | | |
| savings (save) | 2 | N |
| account (count) | 4 | N, V |
| **28a.2. Fortune** | | |
| b fortune | 3 | N |
| b treasure | 3 | N |
| b worth | 3 | N |
| b wealth | 4 | N |
| **28a.3. Salary** | | |
| b salary | 5 | N |
| allowance (allow) | 5* | N |
| b wage | 6 | N |
| b income | 6* | N |
| **28a.4. Gift** | | |
| b gift | 3 | N |
| contribution (contribute) | 5 | N |
| payment (pay) | 5* | N |
| b tribute | 6 | N |
| **28a.5. Scholarship** | | |
| b grant | 3 | N, V |
| b reward | 3 | N, V |
| scholarship (scholar) | 6 | N |
| b fund | 6 | N, V |
| inheritance (inherit) | 6* | N |
| **28a.6. Profit** | | |
| b gain | 5 | N, V |
| b profit | 5 | N, V |
| b credit | 5 | N, V |
| dividend (divide) | MA | N |
| **28a.7. Trophy** | | |
| b prize | 1 | N, V |
| b medal | 4 | N |
| b trophy | 6 | N |
| b award | 6 | N, V |
| **28a.8. Insurance** | | |
| insurance (insure) | 6 | N |

## 28b Money/Goods Paid Out

| Minicluster | Grade Level | Part of Speech |
|---|---|---|
| **28b.1. Fee** | | |
| b tax | 5 | N, V |
| b fee | 5 | N, V |
| b fare | 5 | N |
| b toll | 5* | N, V |
| b tariff | 5* | N |
| taxation (tax) | 5* | N |
| b bail | 6 | N, V |
| **28b.2. Price** | | |
| b cost | 3 | N, V |
| loss (lost) | 4 | N |
| b price | 5 | N |
| b due(s) | 5 | N |
| b expense | 5 | N |
| b debt | 6 | N |
| **28b.3. Poverty** | | |
| poverty (poor) | 6 | N |
| b blight | 6 | N |

## 28c Types of Money

| Minicluster | Grade Level | Part of Speech |
|---|---|---|
| **28c.1. Money** | | |
| b money | 1 | N |
| economics (economy) | 5 | N |
| b capital | 5 | N |
| b cash | 5 | N, V |
| b commerce | 5* | N |
| b economy | 5* | N |
| b finance | 6* | N, V |
| b revenue | 6* | N |
| **28c.2. Penny** | | |
| b penny | 1 | N |
| b cent | 3 | N |
| b dollar | 3 | N |
| b dime | 3 | N |
| b nickel | 3 | N |
| b quarter | 3 | N |
| b coin | 4 | N, V |
| b rand | 4* | N |
| b guinea | 5 | N |
| b shilling | 5 | N |
| b token | 6* | N |

| Minicluster | Grade Level | Part of Speech |
|---|---|---|
| **28c.3. Ticket** | | |
| b ticket | 3 | N |
| b check | 3 | N |
| receipt (receive) | 6 | N |
| **28c.4. Postage** | | |
| b postage | 4* | N |

## 28d Money Related Actions

| Minicluster | Grade Level | Part of Speech |
|---|---|---|
| **28d.1. Earn** | | |
| b earn | 2 | V |
| b pay | 2 | N, V |
| b spend | 3 | V |
| b afford | 4 | V |
| b owe | 4 | V |
| b bet | 4 | N, V |
| b invest | 5* | V |
| repay (pay) | 5* | V |

---

### Key

**Basic words**

    Basic words are preceded by *b*.
    All other words are followed by the basic word in parentheses.

**Grade levels**

| | |
|---|---|
| K-6 | The grade level at which a word is introduced. |
| * | Indicates a word does not appear frequently in student reading material, but when it does appear it is at the level indicated. |
| – | Words or phrases for which a grade level could not be determined. |

Content specific words are indicated by the content area in which they are used:

| | |
|---|---|
| SS | Social Studies |
| EN | English |
| MA | Math |
| SC | Science |

**Part of Speech**

| | |
|---|---|
| N | Noun |
| V | Verb |
| A | Adjective |
| AV | Adverb |
| AV (+ly) | Adverb when suffix -ly is added |
| PRO | Pronoun |
| PREP | Preposition |
| INT | Interjection |
| DET | Determiner |
| AX | Auxiliary verb |
| RM | Relationship marker |

## 28d.2. **Sell**

| | Grade Level | Part of Speech |
|---|---|---|
| b sell | 2 | V |
| b buy | 2 | V |
| b purchase | 5 | N, V |

## 28d.3. **Sale**

| | | |
|---|---|---|
| b sale | 3 | N |
| b bargain | 4 | N |
| b auction | 6* | N |

## 28e Money Related Characteristics

| Minicluster | Grade Level | Part of Speech |
|---|---|---|
| 28e.1. **Expensive** | | |
| b free | 3 | A, AV (+ly) |
| costly (cost) | 3 | A |
| expensive (expense) | 4 | A, AV (+ly) |
| b cheap | 4 | A, AV (+ly) |
| inexpensive (expense) | 6* | A, AV (+ly) |
| 28e.2. **Poor** | | |
| b poor | 2 | A, AV (+ly) |
| b broke | 3 | A |
| b rich | 3 | A, AV (+ly) |

## 28f Places Where Money Is Kept

| Minicluster | Grade Level | Part of Speech |
|---|---|---|
| 28f.1. **Bank** | | |
| b bank | 2 | N, V |
| b safe | 2 | N |
| b purse | 4 | N |
| b vault | 5 | N |
| b wallet | 5* | N |
| b mint | 6* | N |

# Supercluster 29
## Soil/Metal/Rock

### 29a Metals

| Minicluster | Grade Level | Part of Speech |
|---|---|---|
| 29a.1. **Iron** | | |
| b iron | 2 | N |
| b gold | 2 | N |
| b silver | 2 | N |
| b lead | 3 | N |
| b copper | 3 | N |
| b steel | 4 | N |
| b brass | 4 | N |
| b aluminum | 4* | N |
| b bronze | 5* | N |
| 29a.2. **Metal** | | |
| b metal | 3 | N |
| b alloy | 5* | N |
| 29a.3. **Beryl** | | |
| b beryl | SC | N |
| b carbon | SC | N |
| b flint | SC | N |
| b zinc | SC | N |
| b uranium | SC | N |
| b sulfur | SC | N |
| b mercury | SC | N |
| b tungsten | SC | N |
| b cobalt | SC | N |
| b silicon | SC | N |
| b phosphorus | SC | N |
| b asphalt | SC | N |
| 29a.4. **Graphite** | | |
| b beryllium | SC | N |
| b manganese | SC | N |
| b potassium | SC | N |
| b radium | SC | N |
| b thorium | SC | N |
| b barium | SC | N |
| b graphite | SC | N |
| b feldspar | SC | N |
| b bauxite | SC | N |
| b hornblende | SC | N |
| b mica | SC | N |
| b calcium | SC | N |
| b pitchblende | SC | N |

## 29a.5. Obsidian

| | | |
|---|---|---|
| b obsidian | SC | N |
| b pumice | SC | N |
| b coke | SC | N |
| b gneiss | SC | N |
| b shale | SC | N |
| b magma | SC | N |
| b anthracite | SC | N |
| b carbonate | SC | N |

## 29b Jewels/Rock

| Minicluster | Grade Level | Part of Speech |
|---|---|---|
| **29b.1. Diamond** | | |
| b diamond | 3 | N |
| b coral | 3 | N |
| b jewel | 4 | N |
| b crystal | 4 | N |
| b gem | 4* | N |
| b jade | 5 | N |
| b emerald | 5* | N |
| b quartz | 5* | N |
| b ruby | 6 | N |
| b turquoise | 6* | N |
| b amethyst | SC | N |
| **29b.2. Stone** | | |
| b rock | 2 | N |
| b stone | 2 | N, V |
| b marble | 4 | N |
| b granite | 5 | N |
| b coal | 5 | N |
| b charcoal | 5 | N |
| b slate | 5* | N |
| b limestone | 5* | N |
| b cobblestone | 6 | N |
| b lava | 6 | N |
| b gravel | 6 | N |

## 29c Characteristics of Rocks

| Minicluster | Grade Level | Part of Speech |
|---|---|---|
| **29c.1. Sedimentary** | | |
| b crude | 6 | A |
| sedimentary (sediment) | SC | A |
| b bituminous | SC | A |

## 29d Actions of Metals

| Minicluster | Grade Level | Part of Speech |
|---|---|---|
| **29d.1. Rust** | | |
| b rust | 4 | N, V |
| b tarnish | 6 | V |

## 29e Soil Types

| Minicluster | Grade Level | Part of Speech |
|---|---|---|
| **29e.1. Dirt** | | |
| b ground | 2 | N |
| b dirt | 3 | N |
| b soil | 4 | N, V |
| b clay | 4 | N |
| b sod | 5 | N |
| b peat | 5* | N |
| b turf | 6 | N |
| b clod | 6 | N |
| b ore | 6 | N |
| **29e.2. Sand** | | |
| b sand | 2 | N |
| b dust | 3 | N, V |
| b pebble | 4 | N |
| b sawdust | 5* | N |
| b powder | 6 | N |

## 29f Actions Done to Soil/Crops

| Minicluster | Grade Level | Part of Speech |
|---|---|---|
| **29f.1. Plow** | | |
| b till | 3 | V |
| b plow | 3 | N, V |
| b sow | 3* | V |
| b harvest | 4 | N, V |
| b tend | 4 | V |
| b irrigate | 4* | V |
| b grub | 5 | V |
| b plant | 5 | N, V |
| b thresh | 5* | V |
| b cultivate | 6 | V |
| b fertilize | 6* | V |
| **29f.1.1 _____** | | |
| irrigation (irrigate) | 4* | N |
| cultivation (cultivate) | SS | N |

# Supercluster 30
## Rooms/Furnishings/ Parts of Dwellings

### 30a Rooms

| Minicluster | Grade Level | Part of Speech |
|---|---|---|
| **30a.1. Bedroom** | | |
| b room | 2 | N |
| b kitchen | 2 | N |
| b garage | 2 | N |
| b cellar | 2 | N |
| b bedroom | 3 | N |
| b balcony | 3 | N |
| b bathroom | 3* | N |
| b attic | 3* | N |
| b porch | 4 | N |
| b closet | 4 | N |
| nursery (nurse) | 4* | N |
| b den | 5 | N |
| b loft | 5 | N |
| b chamber | 5* | N |
| b parlor | 6 | N |
| **30a.2. Hall** | | |
| b hall | 2 | N |
| b doorway | 3 | N |
| entrance (enter) | 4 | N |
| b aisle | 5 | N |
| b corridor | 5 | N |
| b hallway | 6 | N |

### 30b Parts of a Home

| Minicluster | Grade Level | Part of Speech |
|---|---|---|
| **30b.1. Chimney** | | |
| b chimney | 3 | N |
| b smokestack | 4* | N |
| b flue | 5* | N |
| b fireplace | 6 | N |
| b hearth | 6 | N |
| **30b.2. Wall** | | |
| b wall | 2 | N |
| b floor | 2 | N |
| b ceiling | 3 | N |
| **30b.3. Roof** | | |
| b roof | 4* | N, V |
| b spire | 5* | N |
| b steeple | 5* | N |
| b belfry | 6 | N |
| b dome | 6 | N |
| **30b.4. Window** | | |
| b window | 1 | N |
| b pane | 2* | N |
| b sill | 3 | N |
| shutter (shut) | 4* | N |
| b vent | 5 | N |
| b lattice | MA | N |
| **30b.5. Stairs** | | |
| b stair(s) | 3 | N |
| railing (rail) | 3 | N |
| b stairway | 4* | N |
| b banister | 6* | N |

### 30c Fences/Ledges

| Minicluster | Grade Level | Part of Speech |
|---|---|---|
| **30c.1. Ledge** | | |
| b ledge | 4 | N |
| b gutter | 5 | N |
| b curb | 6 | N, V |
| b sewer | SS | N |
| **30c.2. Fence** | | |
| b fence | 2 | N, V |
| b gate | 2 | N |
| b screen | 3 | N, V |
| b mailbox | 3* | N |
| b hedge | 5* | N, V |
| b barbed wire | SS | N |

### 30d Furniture

| Minicluster | Grade Level | Part of Speech |
|---|---|---|
| **30d.1. Furniture** | | |
| furniture (furnish) | 4 | N |
| furnishing (furnish) | 5* | N |

## 30d.2. Table

| | Word | Grade Level | Part of Speech |
|---|---|---|---|
| b | table | 1 | N |
| b | desk | 3 | N |
| b | counter | 6 | N |
| b | tabletop | 6* | N |

## 30d.3. Chair

| | Word | Grade Level | Part of Speech |
|---|---|---|---|
| b | chair | 2 | N |
| b | seat | 2 | N, V |
| b | bench | 3 | N, V |
| b | stool | 3 | N |
| b | couch | 6 | N |
| b | sofa | 6 | N |
| | rocker (rock) | 6* | N |

## 30d.4. Cupboard

| | Word | Grade Level | Part of Speech |
|---|---|---|---|
| b | drawer | 3 | N |
| b | shelf | 3* | N, V |
| b | rack | 4 | N, V |
| b | cupboard | 4 | N |
| b | hutch | 4 | N |
| b | bookcase | 4* | N |
| b | bureau | 5 | N |
| b | bunker | 5 | N |
| b | cabinet | 5* | N |

## 30d.5. Bed

| | Word | Grade Level | Part of Speech |
|---|---|---|---|
| b | bed | 1 | N |
| b | crib | 4 | N |
| b | mattress | 4 | N |
| b | cot | 4 | N |
| b | mat | 5 | N |
| b | cradle | 5 | N, V |
| b | hammock | 6 | N |

# 30e Decorations

| Minicluster | Grade Level | Part of Speech |
|---|---|---|

## 30e.1. Decoration

| | Word | Grade Level | Part of Speech |
|---|---|---|---|
| | decoration (decor) | 4 | N |
| b | accessory | 5 | N |

### 30e.1.1 _____

| | Word | Grade Level | Part of Speech |
|---|---|---|---|
| | decorate (decor) | 4 | V |

## 30e.2. Carpet

| | Word | Grade Level | Part of Speech |
|---|---|---|---|
| b | curtain | 3 | N |
| b | rug | 3 | N |
| b | carpet | 4 | N |
| b | canopy | 6 | N |

## 30e.3. Ornament

| | Word | Grade Level | Part of Speech |
|---|---|---|---|
| b | flag | 3 | N, V |
| b | ornament | 4 | N |
| b | emblem | 6 | N |

## 30e.4. Vase

| | Word | Grade Level | Part of Speech |
|---|---|---|---|
| b | vase | 6 | N |
| | pottery (pot) | 6 | N |
| b | tapestry | 6* | N |

## 30e.5. Domestic

| | Word | Grade Level | Part of Speech |
|---|---|---|---|
| b | homemade | 4* | A |
| b | domestic | 6* | A, AV (+ly) |
| b | homespun | SS | A |

---

**Key**

Basic words
> Basic words are preceded by *b*.
> All other words are followed by the basic word in parentheses.

Grade levels
> K-6    The grade level at which a word is introduced.
> \*    Indicates a word does not appear frequently in student reading material, but when it does appear it is at the level indicated.
> –    Words or phrases for which a grade level could not be determined.

Content specific words are indicated by the content area in which they are used:

| | |
|---|---|
| SS | Social Studies |
| EN | English |
| MA | Math |
| SC | Science |

Part of Speech

| | |
|---|---|
| N | Noun |
| V | Verb |
| A | Adjective |
| AV | Adverb |
| AV (+ly) | Adverb when suffix -ly is added |
| PRO | Pronoun |
| PREP | Preposition |
| INT | Interjection |
| DET | Determiner |
| AX | Auxiliary verb |
| RM | Relationship marker |

## 30f Linens

| Minicluster | Grade Level | Part of Speech |
|---|---|---|
| 30f.1. **Blanket** | | |
| b cover | 2 | N, V |
| b pillow | 3 | N |
| b sheet | 3 | N |
| b blanket | 3 | N |
| b napkin | 4* | N |
| b quilt | 4* | N, V |
| b tablecloth | 4* | N |
| b towel | 5 | N |
| b bedspread | 5* | N |
| b cushion | 6 | N |

# Supercluster 31
## Attitudinals

### 31a Attitudinals (Truth)

| Minicluster | Grade Level | Part of Speech |
|---|---|---|
| 31a.1. **Truly** | | |
| surely (sure) | 2 | AV |
| flatly (flat) | 2 | AV |
| clearly (clear) | 2 | AV |
| really (real) | 2 | AV |
| seriously (serious) | 3 | AV |
| truly (true) | 3 | AV |
| certainly (certain) | 3 | AV |
| plainly (plain) | 3 | AV |
| simply (simple) | 4 | AV |
| frankly (frank) | 4 | AV |
| honestly (honest) | 4 | AV |
| actually (actual) | 4 | AV |
| strictly (strict) | 5 | AV |
| obviously (obvious) | 5 | AV |
| definitely (define) | 6 | AV |
| essentially (essential) | 6 | AV |
| bluntly (blunt) | 6 | AV |
| evidently (evident) | 6 | AV |
| apparently (apparent) | 6 | AV |
| literally (literal) | 6* | AV |
| undoubtedly (doubt) | 6* | AV |
| truthfully (true) | 6* | AV |
| admittedly (admit) | 6* | AV |
| undeniably (deny) | 6* | AV |
| unquestionably (question) | 6* | AV |
| basically (base) | 6* | AV |
| fundamentally (fundamental) | 6* | AV |
| candidly (candid) | 6* | AV |

### 31b Attitudinals (Lack of Truth/ Doubt)

| Minicluster | Grade Level | Part of Speech |
|---|---|---|
| 31b.1. **Maybe/Doubtless** | | |
| b maybe | 1 | AV |
| b perhaps | 3 | AV |
| probably (probable) | 3 | AV |
| possibly (possible) | 4 | AV |
| ideally (idea) | 5 | AV |
| technically (technical) | 6 | AV |
| arguably (argue) | 6* | AV |
| allegedly (allege) | 6* | AV |
| conceivably (conceive) | 6 | AV |
| doubtless (doubt) | 6* | AV |
| presumably (presume) | 6* | AV |
| reportedly (report) | 6* | AV |
| supposedly (suppose) | 6* | AV |
| seemingly (seem) | 6* | AV |
| superficially (superficial) | 6* | AV |
| theoretically (theory) | 6* | AV |

## 31c Attitudinals (Expected or Unexpected)

| Minicluster | Grade Level | Part of Speech |
|---|---|---|
| 31c.1. **Oddly/ Appropriately** | | |
| strangely (strange) | 2 | AV |
| curiously (curious) | 3 | AV |
| unexpectedly (expect) | 4 | AV |
| appropriately (appropriate) | 5 | AV |
| remarkably (remark) | 6* | AV |
| amazingly (amaze) | 6* | AV |
| astonishingly (astonish) | 6* | AV |
| incredibly (credible) | 6* | AV |
| ironically (ironic) | 6* | AV |
| oddly (odd) | 6* | AV |
| inevitably (evitable) | 6* | AV |
| naturally (nature) | 6* | AV |
| predictably (predict) | 6* | AV |
| typically (type) | 6* | AV |
| understandably (understand) | 6* | AV |
| b not unnaturally | – | AV |

## 31d Attitudinals (Fortunate/ Unfortunate)

| Minicluster | Grade Level | Part of Speech |
|---|---|---|
| 31d.1. **Luckily** | | |
| happily (happy) | 1 | AV |
| sadly (sad) | 2 | AV |
| unhappily (happy) | 2 | AV |
| luckily (luck) | 2 | AV |
| thankfully (thank) | 3 | AV |
| fortunately (fortune) | 4 | AV |
| unfortunately (fortune) | 6 | AV |
| unluckily (luck) | 6* | AV |
| tragically (tragic) | 6* | AV |

## 31e Attitudinals (Satisfaction/ Dissatisfaction)

| Minicluster | Grade Level | Part of Speech |
|---|---|---|
| 31e.1. **Delightfully/ Regretably** | | |
| delightfully (delight) | 5* | AV |
| annoyingly (annoy) | 6* | AV |
| disappointingly (disappoint) | 6* | AV |
| disturbingly (disturb) | 6* | AV |
| refreshingly (refresh) | 6* | AV |
| regrettably (regret) | 6* | AV |

## 31f Attitudinals (Correctness/ Incorrectness)

| Minicluster | Grade Level | Part of Speech |
|---|---|---|
| 31f.1. **Rightly/Wrongly** | | |
| rightly (right) | 1 | AV |
| wrongly (wrong) | 2 | AV |
| correctly (correct) | 4 | AV |
| incorrectly (correct) | 4* | AV |
| unjustly (just) | 6* | AV |
| justly (just) | 6* | AV |

## 31g Attitutinals (Wisdom/Lack of Wisdom)

| Minicluster | Grade Level | Part of Speech |
|---|---|---|
| **31g.1. Wisely/Unwisely** | | |
| cleverly (clever) | 2 | AV |
| wisely (wise) | 2 | AV |
| foolishly (fool) | 3 | AV |
| shrewdly (shrewd) | 5 | AV |
| prudently (prude) | 6* | AV |
| reasonably (reason) | 6* | AV |
| unreasonably (reason) | 6* | AV |
| artfully (art) | 6* | AV |
| sensibly (sense) | 6* | AV |
| unwisely (wise) | 6* | AV |
| cunningly (cunning) | 6 | AV |

## 31h Other Attitudinals

| Minicluster | Grade Level | Part of Speech |
|---|---|---|
| **31h.1. Please** | | |
| b please | 1 | AV |
| hopefully (hope) | 4 | AV |
| preferably (prefer) | 6* | AV |

# Supercluster 32
## Shapes/Dimensions

### 32a Shapes (General Names)

| Minicluster | Grade Level | Part of Speech |
|---|---|---|
| **32a.1. Shape** | | |
| b shape | 2 | N, V |
| b form | 3 | N, V |
| b figure | 3 | N |
| b pattern | 4 | N, V |
| b silhouette | 6 | N |
| b outline | 6* | N, V |
| **32a.1.1** _____ | | |
| formation (form) | 6 | N |
| **32a.2. Skyline** | | |
| b skyline | 5* | N |
| **32a.3. Frame** | | |
| b frame | 3 | N, V |
| b framework | 4 | N |

### 32b Circular or Curved Shapes

| Minicluster | Grade Level | Part of Speech |
|---|---|---|
| **32b.1. Circle** | | |
| b circle | 3 | N, V |
| b cone | 3 | N |
| b sphere | 4* | N |
| b disk | 6 | N |
| b cylinder | 6 | N |
| b oval | 6* | N |
| **32b.2. Curve** | | |
| b bend | 3 | N, V |
| b curl | 3 | N, V |
| b twist | 4 | N, V |
| b curve | 4 | N, V |
| b loop | 4 | N, V |
| spiral (spire) | 4* | N, A |
| arc (arch) | 5 | N, A |
| circuit (circle) | 6 | N |
| curvature (curve) | SC | N |

### 32b.3. **Round**

| Minicluster | | Grade Level | Part of Speech |
|---|---|---|---|
| b | round | 2 | A |
| | circular (circle) | 6 | A |
| | spherical (sphere) | SC | A, AV (+ly) |
| b | convex | SC | A |
| b | concave | SC | A |

## 32c Rectangular or Square Shapes

| Minicluster | | Grade Level | Part of Speech |
|---|---|---|---|
| **32c.1.** | **Square** | | |
| b | square | 3 | N, A |
| | rectangle (angle) | 3* | N |
| | triangle (angle) | 5 | N |
| b | pentagon | 5* | N |
| b | hexagon | MA | N |
| b | trapezoid | MA | N |
| b | octagon | MA | N |
| b | parallelogram | MA | N |
| b | polygon | MA | N |
| **32c.1.1** _____ | | | |
| | rectangular (angle) | 4* | A, AV (+ly) |
| | triangular (angle) | 5* | A, AV (+ly) |
| | quadrilateral (lateral) | MA | A |
| | equilateral (lateral) | MA | A |
| **32c.2.** | **Cube** | | |
| b | block | 2 | N |
| b | cube | 3* | N |
| b | prism | 4* | N |
| b | pyramid | 4* | N |
| **32c.2.1** _____ | | | |
| | cubic (cube) | 6 | A |

## 32d Straightness/Crookedness

| Minicluster | | Grade Level | Part of Speech |
|---|---|---|---|
| **32d.1.** | **Strip** | | |
| b | line | 2 | N, V |
| b | cross | 2 | N, V |
| b | strip | 3 | N |
| b | stripe | 4 | N, V |
| b | zigzag | 5 | N |
| b | crisscross | 6 | N, V |
| **32d.2.** | **Straight** | | |
| b | straight | 2 | A |
| | bent (bend) | 3 | A |
| | crooked (crook) | 4 | A, AV (+ly) |
| | linear (line) | MA | A, AV (+ly) |

---

### Key

**Basic words**

Basic words are preceded by *b*.
All other words are followed by the basic word in parentheses.

**Grade levels**

K-6   The grade level at which a word is introduced.

\*   Indicates a word does not appear frequently in student reading material, but when it does appear it is at the level indicated.

–   Words or phrases for which a grade level could not be determined.

Content specific words are indicated by the content area in which they are used:

SS   Social Studies
EN   English
MA   Math
SC   Science

**Part of Speech**

| | |
|---|---|
| N | Noun |
| V | Verb |
| A | Adjective |
| AV | Adverb |
| AV (+ly) | Adverb when suffix -ly is added |
| PRO | Pronoun |
| PREP | Preposition |
| INT | Interjection |
| DET | Determiner |
| AX | Auxiliary verb |
| RM | Relationship marker |

## 32e Sharpness/Bluntness

| Minicluster | Grade Level | Part of Speech |
|---|---|---|
| **32e.1. Sharp/Blunt** | | |
| b sharp | 3 | A |
| b dull | 4 | A |
| b blunt | 6 | A |
| **32e.2. Sharpen** | | |
| flatten (flat) | 4* | V |
| sharpen (sharp) | 5* | V |
| b taper | 6* | V |

## 32f Dimension

| Minicluster | Grade Level | Part of Speech |
|---|---|---|
| **32f.1. Length** | | |
| b long | 1 | A |
| b wide | 2 | A |
| b tall | 2 | A |
| b short | 2 | A |
| **32f.1.1** _____ | | |
| length (long) | 3 | N |
| height (high) | 4 | N |
| b volume | 5 | N |
| width (wide) | 6 | N |
| **32f.2. Thick** | | |
| b deep | 2 | A, AV (+ly) |
| b thick | 3 | A |
| b thin | 3 | A, V, AV (+ly) |
| b narrow | 3 | A, V, AV (+ly) |
| b shallow | 4 | A, AV (+ly) |
| b dense | 5 | A, AV (+ly) |
| **32f.2.1** _____ | | |
| thickness (thick) | 3 | N |
| depth (deep) | 5 | N |
| density (dense) | 6 | N |

## 32f.3. Widen

| | Grade Level | Part of Speech |
|---|---|---|
| straighten (straight) | 3 | V |
| widen (wide) | 4* | V |
| thicken (thick) | 5* | V |
| deepen (deep) | 5* | V |
| lengthen (long) | 5* | V |

## 32g Fullness/Emptiness

| Minicluster | Grade Level | Part of Speech |
|---|---|---|
| **32g.1. Full/Empty** | | |
| b full | 2 | A |
| b empty | 2 | A, V |
| b hollow | 4 | A, AV (+ly) |
| b vacant | 4 | A |
| swollen (swell) | 5 | A |
| **32g.1.1** _____ | | |
| b fill | 2 | V |

## 32h Inclination

| Minicluster | Grade Level | Part of Speech |
|---|---|---|
| **32h.1. Flat** | | |
| b flat | 2 | A, AV (+ly) |
| b steep | 3 | A |
| b level | 4 | A |
| b incline | 5 | A |
| b erect | 6 | A |
| **32h.1.1** _____ | | |
| b lean | 3 | V, A |

# Supercluster 33
## Destructive and Helpful Actions

### 33a Destructive Actions (General)

| Minicluster | Grade Level | Part of Speech |
|---|---|---|
| **33a.1. Accident** | | |
| b accident | 3 | N |
| b crash | 3 | N, V |
| collision (collide) | 6* | N |
| mishap (happen) | 6* | N |
| **33a.1.1** _____ | | |
| accidental (accident) | 5* | A, AV (+ly) |
| **33a.2. Dent** | | |
| b dent | 3 | N, V |
| b mar | 5 | N, V |
| b nick | 6 | N, V |
| **33a.3. Break** | | |
| b break | 2 | N, V |
| b destroy | 4 | V |
| b ruin | 4 | N, V |
| b shatter | 5 | V |
| b damage | 6 | V |
| b crush | 6 | V |
| **33a.4. Wreck** | | |
| b wreck | 4 | N, V |
| b smash | 5 | V |
| b clash | 5* | N, V |
| b collide | 6 | V |
| **33a.4.1** _____ | | |
| wreckage (wreck) | 5* | N |

### 33b Actions Destructive to Humans

| Minicluster | Grade Level | Part of Speech |
|---|---|---|
| **33b.1. Hurt** | | |
| b hurt | 2 | N, V |
| b injure | 5 | V |
| b abuse | 6 | V |
| **33b.2. Kill** | | |
| b kill | 2 | V |
| b shoot | 3 | V |
| b harm | 3 | N, V |
| b attack | 3 | N, V |
| b slay | 5 | V |
| b murder | 5* | N, V |
| b slaughter | 5* | N, V |
| b massacre | 6 | N, V |
| **33b.2.1** _____ | | |
| attacker | 5* | N |
| **33b.3. Strain** | | |
| b strain | 4 | N, V |
| b stun | 5 | V |
| b afflict | 6* | V |
| **33b.4. Dead** | | |
| deadly (die) | 3 | A, AV (+ly) |
| fatal (fate) | 5 | A, AV (+ly) |
| poisonous (poison) | 5 | A |
| **33b.5. Punish** | | |
| b punish | 3 | V |
| b badger | 3* | V |
| b torment | 6 | N, V |
| b torture | 6* | N, V |

### 33c Fighting

| Minicluster | Grade Level | Part of Speech |
|---|---|---|
| **33c.1. Fight** | | |
| b fight | 1 | N, V |
| scuffle (scuff) | 5 | N, V |
| b rumble | 5 | N, V |
| b fray | 5 | N |
| disturbance (disturb) | 6 | N |
| b combat | 6 | N |
| b conflict | 6* | N, V |

## 33c.2. War

| | Grade Level | Part of Speech |
|---|---|---|
| b war | 3 | N, V |
| revolution (revolt) | 4 | N |
| b battle | 4 | N, V |
| destruction (destroy) | 6 | N |
| b riot | 6 | N, V |
| b warfare | 6* | N |
| b bloodshed | SS | N |

## 33c.3. Invasion

| | | |
|---|---|---|
| invasion (invade) | 6 | N |
| b siege | 6 | N |

## 33c.4. Peace

| | | |
|---|---|---|
| b peace | 4 | N |

## 33d Actions Helpful to Humans

| Minicluster | Grade Level | Part of Speech |
|---|---|---|
| **33d.1. Help** | | |
| b help | K | N, V |
| b assist | 5* | V |
| b benefit | 6 | N, V |
| b contribute | 6 | V |
| **33d.2. Relieve** | | |
| relieve (relief) | 5 | V |
| b refresh | 6* | V |
| **33d.3. Nourish** | | |
| b foster | 5 | V |
| b promote | 5* | V |
| b nourish | 6 | V |
| enable (able) | 6 | V |
| **33d.4. Improve** | | |
| b improve | 4 | V |
| enrich (rich) | 5* | V |
| **33d.5. Guide** | | |
| b guide | 4 | N, V |
| b escort | 6 | N, V |
| **33d.6. Heal** | | |
| b heal | 4 | V |
| b aid | 4 | N, V |
| b cure | 4 | N, V |
| b recover | 4 | V |
| b revive | 6 | V |

## 33d.7. Protect

| | | |
|---|---|---|
| b save | 2 | N, V |
| b protect | 3 | V |
| b rescue | 4 | N, V |
| b defend | 4 | V |

## 33d.8. Miracle

| | | |
|---|---|---|
| b miracle | 5 | N |

# Supercluster 34
## Sports/Recreation

### 34a Sports/Recreation

| Minicluster | Grade Level | Part of Speech |
|---|---|---|
| **34a.1. Sport** | | |
| b hobby | 4 | N |
| b sport | 4 | N |
| recreation (recreate) | 5* | N |
| **34a.2. Game** | | |
| b game | 1 | N |
| b contest | 3 | N |
| b match | 3 | N |
| championship (champion) | 4 | N |
| b derby | 6 | N |
| b tournament | 6 | N |
| competition (compete) | 6 | N |
| b bout | 6* | N |
| **34a.2.1 _____** | | |
| b compete | 6 | V |

### 34b Specific Sports

| Minicluster | Grade Level | Part of Speech |
|---|---|---|
| **34b.1. Football** | | |
| b football | 3 | N |
| b baseball | 3 | N |
| b basketball | 3* | N |
| b hockey | 4* | N |
| b polo | 5* | N |
| b soccer | 5* | N |
| b softball | 5* | N |

## 34b.2. Tennis

| | | | |
|---|---|---|---|
| b | golf | 4* | N, V |
| b | tennis | 5 | N |
| b | croquet | 6 | N |

## 34b.3. Racing

| | | |
|---|---|---|
| racing (race) | 1 | N |
| skating (skate) | 2 | N |
| bicycling (bicycle) | 3 | N |
| swimming (swim) | 3 | N |
| b skiing (ski) | 5 | N |

## 34b.3.1 _____

| | | | |
|---|---|---|---|
| b | race | 1 | N, V |
| b | swim | 2 | V |
| b | skate | 2 | V |
| b | bicycle | 3 | N, V |
| b | ski | 5 | N, V |

## 34b.4. Boxing

| | | |
|---|---|---|
| boxing (box) | 1 | N |
| fencing (fence) | 2 | N |
| wrestling (wrestle) | 5 | N |
| jousting (joust) | SS | N |

## 34b.4.1 _____

| | | | |
|---|---|---|---|
| b | box | 1 | V |
| b | fence | 2 | V |
| b | joust | SS | V |

## 34c Equipment Used in Sports

| Minicluster | Grade Level | Part of Speech |
|---|---|---|

### 34c.1. Base

| | | | |
|---|---|---|---|
| b | net | 3 | N |
| b | base | 4 | N |
| b | bound(s) | 5 | N |
| b | hurdle | 6 | N, V |
| b | target | 6 | N |

### 34c.2. Ball

| | | | |
|---|---|---|---|
| b | ball | K | N |
| b | bat | 4 | N, V |
| b | putter | 4 | N |
| b | racket | 4 | N |
| b | javelin | 6* | N |

### 34c.3. Swing

| | | | |
|---|---|---|---|
| b | swing | 3 | N, V |
| b | trapeze | 3* | N |

## 34c.4. Touchdown

| | | | |
|---|---|---|---|
| b | out | 3 | N |
| b | touchdown | 3 | N |
| b | inning | 4 | N |
| b | goal | 5 | N |
| b | tackle | 5 | N, V |
| | homer (home) | 6 | N |
| b | bunt | 6 | N, V |

## 34c.5. Offense

| | | |
|---|---|---|
| defense (defend) | 5 | N |
| offense (offend) | 6 | N |
| b teamwork | 6* | N |

---

## Key

Basic words

Basic words are preceded by *b*.
All other words are followed by the basic word in parentheses.

Grade levels

K-6   The grade level at which a word is introduced.

\*   Indicates a word does not appear frequently in student reading material, but when it does appear it is at the level indicated.

–   Words or phrases for which a grade level could not be determined.

Content specific words are indicated by the content area in which they are used:

| | |
|---|---|
| SS | Social Studies |
| EN | English |
| MA | Math |
| SC | Science |

Part of Speech

| | |
|---|---|
| N | Noun |
| V | Verb |
| A | Adjective |
| AV | Adverb |
| AV (+ly) | Adverb when suffix -ly is added |
| PRO | Pronoun |
| PREP | Preposition |
| INT | Interjection |
| DET | Determiner |
| AX | Auxiliary verb |
| RM | Relationship marker |

## 34d Exercising

| Minicluster | Grade Level | Part of Speech |
|---|---|---|
| **34d.1. Jogging** | | |
| b exercise | 4 | N, V |
| jogging (jog) | 5 | N |
| sprinting (sprint) | 6 | N |
| **34d.1.1** _____ | | |
| b sprint | 6 | N, V |
| b jog | 6 | N, V |
| **34d.2. Somersault** | | |
| b somersault | 5 | N, V |
| b cartwheel | 5* | N, V |
| **34d.3. Play** | | |
| b play | K | N, V |

## 34e Magic

| Minicluster | Grade Level | Part of Speech |
|---|---|---|
| **34e.1. Stunt** | | |
| b magic | 2 | N |
| b trick | 2 | N, V |
| b stunt | 5 | N |
| b gimmick | 6* | N |
| **34e.1.1** _____ | | |
| magical (magic) | 6 | A, AV (+ly) |

## 34f Board Games

| Minicluster | Grade Level | Part of Speech |
|---|---|---|
| **34f.1. Checkers** | | |
| b cards | 2 | N |
| b checkers | 5* | N |
| b chess | 6 | N |

# Supercluster 35
# Language

## 35a Language and Language Conventions

| Minicluster | Grade Level | Part of Speech |
|---|---|---|
| **35a.1. Grammar** | | |
| b language | 3 | N |
| b grammar | 5* | N |
| **35a.2. Diction** | | |
| pronunciation (pronounce) | 4 | N |
| b accent | 5 | N, V |
| b emphasis | 5* | N |
| b dialect | 6 | N |
| punctuation (punctuate) | 6 | N |
| b diction | 6* | N |
| **35a.3. Parenthesis** | | |
| b comma | 3* | N |
| b period | 4 | N |
| b parenthesis | 4* | N |
| b colon | 5* | N |
| b apostrophe | EN | N |
| capitalization (capital) | EN | N |

## 35b Words/Sentence

| Minicluster | Grade Level | Part of Speech |
|---|---|---|
| **35b.1. Paragraphs** | | |
| b word | K | N, V |
| b sentence | 4 | N |
| b paragraph | 4 | N |
| b chapter | 6 | N |
| b phrase | 6 | N, V |
| **35b.2. Consonant** | | |
| b vowel | 4 | N |
| b prefix | 4 | N |
| b consonant | 4* | N |
| b suffix | 4* | N |
| b syllable | 5 | N |
| abbreviation (abbreviate) | 5* | N |
| b affix | EN | N |

## 35b.3. **Interrogative**

| | | | |
|---|---|---|---|
| | interrogative (interrogate) | EN | A |
| | exclamatory (claim) | EN | A |
| b | superlative | EN | A |

## 35b.4. **Noun**

| | | | |
|---|---|---|---|
| b | noun | 4* | N |
| b | verb | 4* | N |
| | pronoun (noun) | 5* | N |
| b | synonym | 5* | N |
| b | adjective | 5* | N |
| | modifier (modify) | EN | N |
| b | conjunction | EN | N |
| b | antonym | EN | N |
| b | preposition | EN | N |
| b | predicate | EN | N, V |

## 35c Letters/Alphabet

| Minicluster | Grade Level | Part of Speech |
|---|---|---|
| **35c.1. Letter** | | |
| b letter | 1 | N, V |
| b alphabet | 4 | N |
| b alpha | 5* | N |
| b beta | 5* | N |
| b italics | 6 | N |
| b cuneiform | SS | N |
| **35c.1.1** _____ | | |
| alphabetically (alphabet) | 4* | AV |
| **35c.1.2** _____ | | |
| alphabetic (alphabet) | EN | A |
| **35c.2. Code** | | |
| b code | 4 | N, V |
| b symbol | 4 | N |
| notation (note) | MA | N |

# Supercluster 36
## Ownership/Possession

### 36a Losing/Giving Up

| Minicluster | Grade Level | Part of Speech |
|---|---|---|
| **36a.1. Lose** | | |
| b lose | 3 | V |
| b abandon | 5 | V |
| misplace (place) | 6 | V |
| **36a.2. Discard** | | |
| displace (place) | 4* | V |
| b dismiss | 5 | V |
| b dispose | 6 | V |
| b discard | 6 | V |
| **36a.3. Trade** | | |
| b trade | 3 | N, V |
| b share | 3 | N, V |
| b borrow | 3 | V |
| exchange (change) | 4 | N, V |
| lend (loan) | 5 | V |
| b loan | 5 | N, V |
| b swap | 5* | V |

### 36b Freedom/Lack of Freedom

| Minicluster | Grade Level | Part of Speech |
|---|---|---|
| **36b.1. Free** | | |
| b free | 3 | A, V, AV (+ly) |
| b escape | 3 | V |
| b flee | 3 | V |
| b release | 5 | N, V |
| b liberate | 6 | V |
| **36b.2. Surrender** | | |
| b surrender | 6 | V |
| b sacrifice | 6 | V |
| b concede | 6* | V |
| **36b.3. Freedom** | | |
| freedom (free) | 4 | N |
| independence (depend) | 5 | N |

179

## 36c Possession/Ownership

| Minicluster | Grade Level | Part of Speech |
|---|---|---|
| **36c.1. Possession** | | |
| possession (possess) | 4 | N |
| ownership (own) | 5* | N |
| **36c.2. Have** | | |
| b have | K | V |
| b own | 1 | V, A |
| b possess | 6 | V |
| b occupy | 6 | V |
| **36c.3. Belong** | | |
| b belong | 2 | A |

## 36d Winning/Losing

| Minicluster | Grade Level | Part of Speech |
|---|---|---|
| **36d.1. Win** | | |
| b win | 2 | N, V |
| b lose | 3 | V |
| b conquer | 5 | V |
| b defeat | 5 | N, V |
| b outnumber | 5* | V |
| **36d.2. Prevail** | | |
| b prevail | 6 | V |
| b overcome | 6 | V |
| b overtake | 6* | V |
| b overthrow | SS | V |
| b overrun | SS | V |
| **36d.2.1** _____ | | |
| b repel | SC | V |
| **36d.3. Triumph** | | |
| b triumph | 5 | N, V |
| conquest (conquer) | 6* | N |
| **36d.3.1** _____ | | |
| triumphant (triumph) | 5 | A, AV (+ly) |
| **36d.4. Loss** | | |
| loss (lose) | 4 | N |
| failure (fail) | 6 | N |

| Minicluster | Grade Level | Part of Speech |
|---|---|---|
| **36d.5. Winner** | | |
| winner (win) | 4* | N |
| loser (lose) | 6* | N |

## 36e Taking/Receiving Actions

| Minicluster | Grade Level | Part of Speech |
|---|---|---|
| **36e.1. Obtain** | | |
| b get | K | V |
| b receive | 4 | V |
| b acquire | 6 | V |
| b obtain | 6 | V |
| b achieve | 6 | V |
| b extract | 6 | V |
| b inherit | 6* | V |
| regain (gain) | SS | V |
| **36e.2. Attract** | | |
| b attract | 5 | V |
| **36e.3. Arrest** | | |
| b arrest | 4 | N, V |
| b capture | 4 | V |
| b invade | 6 | V |
| **36e.4. Seize** | | |
| b seize | 3 | V |
| b steal | 3 | V |
| b rob | 3 | V |

## 36f Finding/Keeping

| Minicluster | Grade Level | Part of Speech |
|---|---|---|
| **36f.1. Locate** | | |
| b find | 1 | N, V |
| b locate | 4 | V |
| **36f.2. Keep** | | |
| b hide | 2 | V |
| b keep | 2 | V |
| b tuck | 4 | N, V |
| b retain | 6* | V |

# Supercluster 37
## Disease/Health

### 37a Disease

| Minicluster | Grade Level | Part of Speech |
|---|---|---|
| **37a.1. Illness** | | |
| b disease | 4 | N |
| sickness (sick) | 5 | N |
| ailment (ail) | 6 | N |
| illness (ill) | 6 | N |
| injury (injure) | 6 | N |
| b handicap | 6 | N |
| **37a.1.1** _____ | | |
| b ill | 3 | A |
| b sick | 3 | A |
| stricken (strike) | 5 | A |
| **37a.2. Epidemic** | | |
| b epidemic | 6 | N |
| b famine | 6 | N |
| b plague | 6* | N |
| starvation (starve) | 6* | N |
| **37a.3. Well** | | |
| b well | 2 | A |
| healthful (health) | 5* | A |
| b hale | 5* | A |
| **37a.3.1** _____ | | |
| b health | 4 | N |

### 37b Specific Diseases/Ailments

| Minicluster | Grade Level | Part of Speech |
|---|---|---|
| **37b.1. Cancer** | | |
| b cancer | 5* | N |
| b polio | 6 | N |
| b diphtheria | 6 | N |
| b tuberculosis | 6* | N |
| b malaria | 6* | N |
| b scurvy | SC | N |
| b rickets | SC | N |
| b beriberi | SC | N |
| **37b.2. Infection** | | |
| b cold | 1 | N |
| b mumps | 3 | N |
| b fever | 5 | N |
| infection (infect) | 6 | N |
| b influenza | 6* | N |
| b virus | SC | N |
| **37b.3. Blind** | | |
| b blind | 4 | N, A |
| b lame | 4 | N, A |
| b deaf | 4 | N, A |
| **37b.3.1** _____ | | |
| blindness (blind) | 5* | N |

## Key
Basic words
   Basic words are preceded by *b*.
   All other words are followed by the basic word in parentheses.

Grade levels
   K-6   The grade level at which a word is introduced.
   *     Indicates a word does not appear frequently in student reading material, but when it does appear it is at the level indicated.
   –     Words or phrases for which a grade level could not be determined.
   Content specific words are indicated by the content area in which they are used:
   SS      Social Studies
   EN      English
   MA      Math
   SC      Science

Part of Speech
   N            Noun
   V            Verb
   A            Adjective
   AV           Adverb
   AV (+ly)     Adverb when suffix -ly is added
   PRO          Pronoun
   PREP         Preposition
   INT          Interjection
   DET          Determiner
   AX           Auxiliary verb
   RM           Relationship marker

## 37c Symptoms of Diseases

| Minicluster | Grade Level | Part of Speech |
|---|---|---|
| **37c.1. Pain** | | |
| b ache | 4 | N, V |
| b pain | 4 | N, V |
| b pang | 6 | N |
| b headache | 6 | N |
| exhaustion (exhaust) | 6 | N |
| weariness (weary) | 6 | N |
| b fatigue | 6 | N |
| **37c.1.1** _____ | | |
| painful (pain) | 4 | A, AV (+ly) |
| exhausted (exhaust) | 5 | A |
| **37c.2. Sore** | | |
| b dizzy | 4 | A |
| b sore | 4 | A |
| allergic (allergy) | 6* | A |

## 37d Specific Types of Germs/Genes

| Minicluster | Grade Level | Part of Speech |
|---|---|---|
| **37d.1. Germ** | | |
| b germ | 3* | N |
| b bacteria | 5* | N |
| b microbe | 6* | N |
| b organism | 6* | N |
| b enzyme | SC | N |
| b gene | SC | N |
| **37d.1.1** _____ | | |
| genetic (gene) | SC | A, AV (+ly) |

## 37e Actions Related to Injury/Disease

| Minicluster | Grade Level | Part of Speech |
|---|---|---|
| **37e.1. Wound** | | |
| b burn | 2 | N, V |
| b wound | 3 | N, V |
| b sunburn | 3* | N, V |
| b gash | 6 | N, V |
| **37e.2. Cripple** | | |
| b cripple | 6 | N, V |
| paralyze (paralysis) | 6 | V |

## 37f Medicine

| Minicluster | Grade Level | Part of Speech |
|---|---|---|
| **37f.1. Treatment** | | |
| treatment (treat) | 5 | N |
| operation (operate) | 5 | N |
| b remedy | 6 | N, V |
| b transfusion | 6 | N |
| b surgery | 6* | N |
| vaccination (vaccine) | SC | N |
| **37f.1.1** _____ | | |
| b operate | 4* | V |
| transplant (plant) | 5* | N, V |
| **37f.2. Medicine** | | |
| b medicine | 2 | N |
| b drug | 3 | N, V |
| b poison | 4 | N, V |
| b iodine | 5* | N |
| b pill | 6 | N |
| b dose | 6 | N |
| b vitamin | 6* | N |
| b pencillin | 6* | N |
| b antibiotics | SC | N |
| b vaccine | SC | N |
| tranquilizer (tranquil) | SC | N |
| b aspirin | SC | N |
| prescription (prescribe) | SC | N |
| b limewater | SC | N |

## 37f.3. **Bandage**

| | | Grade Level | Part of Speech |
|---|---|---|---|
| b | bandage | 4 | N, V |
| b | sling | 4 | N |
| b | cast | 4 | N |
| b | splint | 6* | N, V |
| b | Band-Aid | SC | N |

# Supercluster 38
# Light

## 38a Light/Lightness

| Minicluster | | Grade Level | Part of Speech |
|---|---|---|---|
| **38a.1. Daylight** | | | |
| b | lamplight | 3* | N |
| b | sunshine | 4 | N |
| b | daylight | 4 | N |
| b | sunlight | 4 | N |
| b | moonlight | 4* | N |
| b | starlight | 5* | N |
| b | candlelight | 6 | N |
| **38a.2. Gleam** | | | |
| b | gleam | 5 | N, V |
| b | glimmer | 6 | N |
| b | glint | 6 | N |
| **38a.3. Light** | | | |
| b | light | 1 | N |
| | lightness (light) | 5* | N |
| | brightness (bright) | 5* | N |
| **38a.4. Brightness** | | | |
| b | bright | 2 | A, AV (+ly) |
| b | clear | 2 | A |
| | shiny (shine) | 3 | A |
| b | vivid | 5 | A, AV (+ly) |
| | radiant (ray) | 5 | A, AV (+ly) |
| b | brilliant | 5 | A, AV (+ly) |
| b | luminous | 6 | A, AV (+ly) |

## 38b Actions of Light

| Minicluster | | Grade Level | Part of Speech |
|---|---|---|---|
| **38b.1. Shine** | | | |
| b | shine | 3 | V |
| | sparkle (spark) | 3 | N, V |
| b | flash | 3 | N, V |
| b | glow | 4 | N, V |
| b | glitter | 4 | N, V |
| b | glisten | 4 | N, V |
| b | twinkle | 4 | N, V |
| b | shimmer | 5 | N, V |
| | dazzle (daze) | 5 | V |
| | radiate (ray) | 5* | V |
| **38b.2. Illuminate** | | | |
| | brighten (bright) | 6 | V |
| | lighten (light) | 6 | V |
| | illuminate (illumine) | 6 | V |
| b | reflect | 6 | V |

## 38c Darkness

| Minicluster | | Grade Level | Part of Speech |
|---|---|---|---|
| **38c.1. Darkness** | | | |
| | darkness (dark) | 3 | N |
| b | shade | 3 | N, V |
| b | shadow | 3 | N |
| b | gloom | 4 | N |
| **38c.1.1** _____ | | | |
| b | dark | 1 | N, A |
| | shady (shade) | 4* | A |
| **38c.2. Darken** | | | |
| b | blot | 4* | N, V |
| b | blur | 5 | N, V |
| | darken (dark) | 5* | V |
| | blacken (black) | 6 | V |

## 38d Producers of Light

| Minicluster | | Grade Level | Part of Speech |
|---|---|---|---|
| **38d.1. Torch** | | | |
| b | flare | 4 | N, V |
| b | torch | 4 | N, V |

183

### 38d.2. **Candle**
| | | |
|---|---|---|
| b candle | 2 | N |
| b wick | 5* | N |

### 38d.3. **Lamp**
| | | |
|---|---|---|
| b light | 1 | N, V |
| b lamp | 3 | N |
| b lantern | 4 | N |

### 38d.4. **Bulb**
| | | |
|---|---|---|
| b bulb | 4 | N |
| b lightbulb | 6* | N |
| b filament | SC | N |

### 38d.5. **Beam**
| | | |
|---|---|---|
| b beam | 3 | N, V |
| b ray | 5 | N |
| b laser | 5* | N |

## 38e Clarity

| Minicluster | Grade Level | Part of Speech |
|---|---|---|
| **38e.1. Clarity** | | |
| b focus | 6 | N, V |
| clarity (clear) | 6* | N |
| **38e.2. Dim** | | |
| b dim | 3 | V, A, AV (+ly) |
| b pale | 3 | V, A, AV (+ly) |
| b dull | 4 | V, A, AV (+ly) |
| b faint | 4 | A, AV (+ly) |
| fuzzy (fuzz) | 5 | A |
| murky (murk) | 5* | A |
| b vague | 6 | A, AV (+ly) |
| b transparent | 6 | A |
| b opaque | 6* | A |

# Supercluster 39
# Causality

## 39a Causality

| Minicluster | Grade Level | Part of Speech |
|---|---|---|
| **39a.1. Result** | | |
| b result | 4 | N |
| b effect | 4 | N, V |
| conclusion (conclude) | 5 | N |
| b outcome | 5* | N |
| b impact | 6 | N |
| b consequence | 6 | N |
| **39a.2. Cause** | | |
| b cause | 3 | N, V |
| b reason | 3 | N |
| b purpose | 4 | N |
| intent (intend) | 5 | N |
| b motive | 6 | N |
| b impetus | 6* | N |
| b stimulus | SC | N |
| **39a.3. Stimulate** | | |
| stimulate (stimulus) | 5* | V |
| b spearhead | 6* | V |
| b initiate | 6* | V |
| **39a.4. Affect** | | |
| b change | 3 | N, V |
| b affect | 5 | N |
| b influence | 5 | N, V |

## 39b Causality (Relationship Markers)

| Minicluster | Grade Level | Part of Speech |
|---|---|---|
| **39b.1. Reason** | | |
| b to | K | RM |
| b for | K | RM |
| b so | K | RM |
| b from | K | RM |
| b by | 1 | RM |
| because (cause) | 2 | RM |
| b since | 3 | RM |
| b because of | – | RM |
| b on account of | – | RM |
| b in that | – | RM |
| b so that | – | RM |
| b for the fact that | – | RM |
| **39b.2. Result** | | |
| b therefore | 4 | RM |
| b thus | 4 | RM |
| accordingly (according) | 4 | RM |
| b hence | 6* | RM |
| consequently (consequence) | 6* | RM |
| b whereupon | 6* | RM |
| b now that | – | RM |
| b as a consequence | – | RM |
| b for all that | – | RM |
| b as a result | – | RM |
| b too *(adj.)* to | – | RM |
| **39b.3. Inference** | | |
| b then | K | RM |
| b else | 2 | RM |
| b in that case | – | RM |
| **39b.4. Condition** | | |
| b if | 1 | RM |
| b now that | – | RM |
| b if only | – | RM |
| b where...there | – | RM |
| b when...then | – | RM |
| b if...then | – | RM |
| b until...then | – | RM |

# Supercluster 40
## Weather

### 40a Weather/Nature (General)

| Minicluster | Grade Level | Part of Speech |
|---|---|---|
| **40a.1. Weather** | | |
| b weather | 3 | N |
| b climate | 5 | N |
| **40a.2. Nature** | | |
| b nature | 4 | N |
| environment (environ) | 6 | N |
| **40a.3. Atmosphere** | | |
| b air | 2 | N |
| b atmosphere | 5 | N |
| atmospheric (atmosphere) | SC | A, AV (+ly) |

---

### Key

Basic words
  Basic words are preceded by *b*.
  All other words are followed by the basic word in parentheses.

Grade levels
  K-6  The grade level at which a word is introduced.
  *    Indicates a word does not appear frequently in student reading material, but when it does appear it is at the level indicated.
  –    Words or phrases for which a grade level could not be determined.
  Content specific words are indicated by the content area in which they are used:
  SS    Social Studies
  EN    English
  MA    Math
  SC    Science

Part of Speech
  N          Noun
  V          Verb
  A          Adjective
  AV         Adverb
  AV (+ly)   Adverb when suffix -ly is added
  PRO        Pronoun
  PREP       Preposition
  INT        Interjection
  DET        Determiner
  AX         Auxiliary verb
  RM         Relationship marker

## 40b Storms

| Minicluster | Grade Level | Part of Speech |
|---|---|---|
| **40b.1. Storm** | | |
| b blizzard | 3 | N |
| b storm | 3 | N, V |
| b snowstorm | 3 | N |
| **40b.2. Rainstorm** | | |
| b scud | 4* | N |
| b downpour | 4* | N |
| b torrent | 6 | N |
| b rainstorm | 6 | N |
| b monsoon | SS | N |
| **40b.3. Tornado** | | |
| b wind | 2 | N |
| b breeze | 4 | N, V |
| b gust | 5 | N, V |
| b gale | 5 | N |
| b hurricane | 5* | N |
| twister (twist) | 5* | N |
| b cyclone | 5* | N |
| b chinook | 5* | N |
| b tornado | 6 | N |
| **40b.4. Thunder** | | |
| b thunder | 3 | N, V |
| lightning (light) | 3 | N |
| b thunderstorm | 4* | N |
| b thunderbolt | 6 | N |
| b thunderhead | SC | N |

## 40c Clouds

| Minicluster | Grade Level | Part of Speech |
|---|---|---|
| **40c.1. Cirrus** | | |
| b cloud | 3 | N, V |
| b cirrus | SC | N |
| b cirrostratus | SC | N |
| b cirrocumulus | SC | N |
| b cumulus | SC | N |
| b cumulonimbus | SC | N |

## 40d Natural Catastrophes

| Minicluster | Grade Level | Part of Speech |
|---|---|---|
| **40d.1. Flood** | | |
| b drought | 3* | N |
| b flood | 4 | N, V |
| b earthquake | 4 | N |
| b landslide | 5* | N |
| b avalanche | 6 | N |
| **40d.2. Disaster** | | |
| b disaster | 5 | N |
| tragedy (tragic) | 5 | N |
| b emergency | 5 | N |
| b doom | 5 | N, V |
| b downfall | 5 | N |
| b crisis | 6 | N |
| b ordeal | 6 | N |
| **40d.2.1 _____** | | |
| disastrous (disaster) | 6* | N |

## 40e Characteristics of Weather

| Minicluster | Grade Level | Part of Speech |
|---|---|---|
| **40e.1. Foggy** | | |
| foggy (fog) | 3 | A |
| icy (ice) | 4 | A |
| sunny (sun) | 4 | A |
| b sultry | 6 | A |
| wintry (winter) | 6* | A |
| b muggy | SC | A |

# Supercluster 41
## Cleanliness/Uncleanliness

### 41a Filth/Uncleanliness

| Minicluster | Grade Level | Part of Speech |
|---|---|---|
| **41a.1. Trash** | | |
| b trash | 4 | N |
| b garbage | 4 | N |
| b litter | 4 | N,V |
| pollution (pollute) | 4* | N |
| sewage (sewer) | 4* | N |
| b grit | 5 | N |
| b junk | 5 | N,V |
| b grime | 5* | N |
| b rubbish | 5* | N |
| b filth | 6 | N |
| b clutter | 6 | N,V |
| impurity (pure) | SC | N |
| **41a.1.1 _____** | | |
| b pollute | 5* | V |
| b infect | 5* | V |
| b contaminate | 6* | V |
| **41a.2. Smear** | | |
| b smear | 4 | N,V |
| b streak | 4 | N,V |
| b stain | 5 | N,V |
| darken (dark) | 5* | V |
| b smudge | 6 | N,V |
| blacken (black) | 6* | V |
| **41a.3. Dirty** | | |
| dirty (dirt) | 2 | A |
| b dreary | 5 | A, AV (+ly) |
| b bleak | 5* | A, AV (+ly) |
| filthy (filth) | 6 | A |
| b dingy | 6 | A |
| b dismal | 6 | A, AV (+ly) |
| muddy (mud) | 6 | A |

### 41b Cleanliness

| Minicluster | Grade Level | Part of Speech |
|---|---|---|
| **41b.1 Wash** | | |
| b wash | 2 | N, V |
| b clean | 2 | V, A |
| b wipe | 3 | N, V |
| b sweep | 3 | V |
| b scrub | 3 | V |
| bathe (bath) | 4 | V |
| b scour | 4 | V |
| b polish | 4 | N, V |
| b wax | 4 | N, V |
| b whitewash | 5* | N, V |
| **41b.2 Cleanliness** | | |
| sanitation (sanitary) | 6 | N |
| cleanliness (clean) | 6 | N |
| b hygiene | 6 | N |
| **41b.3. Purify** | | |
| purify (pure) | 5* | V |
| b pasteurize | 5* | V |
| sterilize (sterile) | SC | V |

### 41c Tools for Cleaning

| Minicluster | Grade Level | Part of Speech |
|---|---|---|
| **41c.1. Broom** | | |
| cleaner (clean) | 3* | N |
| b broom | 3 | N |
| b brush | 3 | N, V |
| b mop | 4 | N, V |
| b vacuum | 5 | N, V |
| **41c.2. Soap** | | |
| b soap | 4 | N, V |
| b lather | 5 | N, V |
| b lotion | SC | N |
| **41c.3. Toothpaste** | | |
| b toothbrush | 6 | N |
| b toothpaste | 6 | N |
| b toothpick | 6* | N |
| b floss | 6* | N, V |

# Supercluster 42
## Popularity/Knownness

### 42a Popularity/Familiarity

| Minicluster | Grade Level | Part of Speech |
|---|---|---|
| **42a.1. Familiar** | | |
| b familiar | 3 | A |
| b usual | 3 | A, AV (+ly) |
| famous (fame) | 3 | A |
| b public | 5 | A, AV (+ly) |
| b popular | 5 | A, AV (+ly) |
| b prominent | 6 | A, AV (+ly) |
| accustomed (accustom) | 6 | A |
| legendary (legend) | 6* | A, AV (+ly) |
| universal (universe) | 6* | A, AV (+ly) |
| **42a.2. Common** | | |
| b common | 3 | A, AV (+ly) |
| b ordinary | 4 | A, AV (+ly) |
| b regular | 4 | A, AV (+ly) |
| b obvious | 5 | A, AV (+ly) |
| b normal | 5 | A, AV (+ly) |
| typical (type) | 5 | A, AV (+ly) |
| b widespread | 5* | A |
| traditional (tradition) | 5* | A, AV (+ly) |
| b standard | 6 | A |
| customary (custom) | 6 | A, AV (+ly) |
| b evident | 6 | A, AV (+ly) |
| congruent (congruous) | MA | A, AV (+ly) |

### 42a.3. Fame

| | Grade Level | Part of Speech |
|---|---|---|
| b appeal | 4 | N, V |
| b fame | 4 | N |
| attraction (attract) | 5* | N |

### 42b Lack of Popularity/Familiarity

| Minicluster | Grade Level | Part of Speech |
|---|---|---|
| **42b.1. Secrecy** | | |
| secrecy (secret) | 6 | N |
| privacy (private) | 6 | N |
| solitude (sole) | 6* | N |
| loneliness (lone) | 6* | N |
| **42b.2. Unknown** | | |
| b secret | 3 | N, A, AV (+ly) |
| unknown (know) | 4 | A |
| b private | 4 | A, AV (+ly) |
| unfamiliar (familiar) | 4* | A, AV (+ly) |
| undiscovered (discover) | SC | A |

### 42c Likelihood

| Minicluster | Grade Level | Part of Speech |
|---|---|---|
| **42c.1. Likely** | | |
| b likely | 2 | A |
| b sure | 2 | A, AV (+ly) |
| b certain | 3 | A, AV (+ly) |
| b accurate | 5 | A, AV (+ly) |
| b absolute | 5 | A, AV (+ly) |
| definite (define) | 6 | A, AV (+ly) |
| b probable | 6 | A, AV (+ly) |

| 42c.2. **Doubtful** | | |
|---|---|---|
| doubtful (doubt) | 4 | A, AV (+ly) |
| unlikely (likely) | 4 | A |
| mysterious (mystery) | 4 | A, AV (+ly) |
| indefinite (define) | 4* | A, AV (+ly) |
| uncertain (certain) | 5* | A, AV (+ly) |
| b random | SC | A, AV (+ly) |

| 42c.3. **Chance** | | |
|---|---|---|
| b chance | 2 | N, V |
| b venture | 5 | N, V |

| 42c.4. **Gamble** | | |
|---|---|---|
| b bet | 4 | N, V |
| b bid | 4 | N, V |
| b gamble | 6 | N, V |

# Supercluster 43
## Physical Traits of People

### 43a Physical Traits

| Minicluster | Grade Level | Part of Speech |
|---|---|---|
| 43a.1. **Athletic** | | |
| b rugged | 5 | A, AV (+ly) |
| athletic (athlete) | 5 | A, AV (+ly) |
| muscular (muscle) | SC | A, AV (+ly) |
| 43a.2. **Strong** | | |
| b strong | 2 | A, AV (+ly) |
| powerful (power) | 3* | A, AV (+ly) |
| b sturdy | 4 | A, AV (+ly) |

| 43a.3. **Strength** | | |
|---|---|---|
| b might | 2 | N |
| b beauty | 3 | N |
| b health | 4 | N |
| strength (strong) | 4 | N |
| b vigor | 4* | N |
| agility (agile) | 6* | N |

| 43a.4. **Clumsy** | | |
|---|---|---|
| b awkward | 4 | A, AV (+ly) |
| b clumsy | 4 | A, AV (+ly) |
| graceful (grace) | 6 | A, AV (+ly) |

**Key**

Basic words

Basic words are preceded by *b*.
All other words are followed by the basic word in parentheses.

Grade levels

K-6  The grade level at which a word is introduced.

\*   Indicates a word does not appear frequently in student reading material, but when it does appear it is at the level indicated.

–   Words or phrases for which a grade level could not be determined.

Content specific words are indicated by the content area in which they are used:

| SS | Social Studies |
|---|---|
| EN | English |
| MA | Math |
| SC | Science |

Part of Speech

| N | Noun |
|---|---|
| V | Verb |
| A | Adjective |
| AV | Adverb |
| AV (+ly) | Adverb when suffix -ly is added |
| PRO | Pronoun |
| PREP | Preposition |
| INT | Interjection |
| DET | Determiner |
| AX | Auxiliary verb |
| RM | Relationship marker |

## 43a.5. Weak

| | | | |
|---|---|---|---|
| b | weak | 3 | A, AV (+ly) |
| b | gaunt | 6 | A |
| b | scrawny | 6 | A |
| b | puny | 6 | A |
| b | frail | 6 | A, AV (+ly) |
| b | feeble | 6 | A, AV (+ly) |

### 43a.5.1 _____

| | | |
|---|---|---|
| weakness (weak) | 6* | N |

## 43b Neatness

| Minicluster | Grade Level | Part of Speech |
|---|---|---|

### 43b.1. Messy

| | | |
|---|---|---|
| messy (mess) | 5 | A |
| sloppy (slop) | 6 | A, AV (+ly) |

### 43b.2. Neat

| | | | |
|---|---|---|---|
| b | neat | 3 | A |
| b | tidy | 5 | A |

## 43c Attractiveness

| Minicluster | Grade Level | Part of Speech |
|---|---|---|

### 43c.1. Lovely

| | | | |
|---|---|---|---|
| b | pretty | 2 | A |
| b | lovely | 2 | A |
| | beautiful (beauty) | 2 | A, AV (+ly) |
| b | cute | 3 | A, AV (+ly) |
| b | handsome | 3 | A, AV (+ly) |
| | attractive (attract) | 5* | A, AV (+ly) |

### 43c.2. Elegant

| | | | |
|---|---|---|---|
| b | elegant | 4 | A, AV (+ly) |
| b | gorgeous | 6 | A, AV (+ly) |
| | majestic (majesty) | 6 | A, AV (+ly) |
| b | formal | 5* | A, AV (+ly) |
| | classic (class) | 6* | A, AV (+ly) |
| | adorable (adore) | 6* | A, AV (+ly) |

### 43c.3. Ugly

| | | | |
|---|---|---|---|
| b | homely | K | A |
| b | ugly | 2 | A |
| | unattractive (attract) | 6 | A, AV (+ly) |

## 43d Size as a Physical Trait

| Minicluster | Grade Level | Part of Speech |
|---|---|---|

### 43d.1. Slender

| | | | |
|---|---|---|---|
| b | slender | 4 | A |
| b | slim | 4 | A |
| b | skinny | 4 | A |
| b | slight | 4 | A |
| | lanky (lank) | 6 | A |

### 43d.1.1 _____

| | | | |
|---|---|---|---|
| b | dainty | 6 | A, AV (+ly) |

### 43d.2. Fat

| | | | |
|---|---|---|---|
| b | fat | 1 | A |
| b | husky | 2 | A |
| b | plump | 5 | A |
| b | stout | 6 | A |

# Supercluster 44
## Touching/Grabbing Actions

### 44a Feeling/Striking Actions

| Minicluster | Grade Level | Part of Speech |
|---|---|---|
| 44a.1. **Feel** | | |
| b feel | 2 | N, V |
| b stroke | 4 | N, V |
| b grope | 5 | V |
| 44a.1.1 _____ | | |
| b contact | 5 | N, V |
| 44a.1.2 _____ | | |
| b tickle | 4 | V |
| 44a.2. **Nudge** | | |
| b pat | 2 | N, V |
| b tap | 3 | N, V |
| b nudge | 4 | N, V |
| b butt | 5 | V |
| b jab | 5 | N, V |
| b rap | 5 | V |
| b dab | 5* | N, V |
| b prod | 6 | V |
| 44a.3. **Strike** | | |
| b knock | 2 | N, V |
| b beat | 3 | V |
| b strike | 3 | V |
| b pound | 3 | V |
| b slap | 3 | N, V |
| b smack | 4 | N, V |
| b hit | 4 | N, V |
| b punch | 4 | N, V |
| b lash | 4 | V |
| b whack | 4 | N, V |
| b spank | 4 | N, V |
| b thrash | 5 | V |
| b wallop | 6 | N, V |

### 44b Grabbing/Holding Actions

| Minicluster | Grade Level | Part of Speech |
|---|---|---|
| 44b.1. **Grab** | | |
| b hold | 1 | N, V |
| b catch | 1 | N, V |
| b squeeze | 3 | N, V |
| b grab | 3 | N, V |
| b grip | 4 | N, V |
| b clutch | 4 | V |
| b clasp | 5 | N, V |
| b wring | 5 | V |
| b clench | 6 | V |
| 44b.2. **Pick** | | |
| b pick | 1 | V |
| b pinch | 4 | N, V |
| b pluck | 6 | V |
| b nip | 6 | N, V |
| 44b.3. **Hug** | | |
| b hug | 3 | N, V |
| b wrap | 3 | V |
| b cling | 4 | V |
| b nuzzle | 4 | V |
| b embrace | 6 | N, V |
| snuggle (snug) | 6 | V |

### 44c Specific Actions Done with the Hands

| Minicluster | Grade Level | Part of Speech |
|---|---|---|
| 44c.1. **Wave** | | |
| b point | 2 | N, V |
| b wave | 2 | N, V |
| b clap | 3 | V |
| b shrug | 4 | N, V |
| b salute | 4 | N, V |

# Supercluster 45
## Pronouns

### 45a Pronouns

| Minicluster | Grade Level | Part of Speech |
|---|---|---|
| 45a.1. **I** | | |
| b you | K | PRO |
| b I | K | PRO |
| b he | K | PRO |
| b it | K | PRO |
| b me | K | PRO |
| b we | K | PR O |
| b she | K | PRO |
| b they | K | PRO |
| b them | K | PRO |

### 45b Possessive Pronouns

| Minicluster | Grade Level | Part of Speech |
|---|---|---|
| 45b.1. **My** | | |
| b my | K | PRO |
| its (it) | K | PRO |
| your (you) | K | PRO |
| yours (you) | K | PRO |
| b her | 1 | PRO |
| hers (her) | 1 | PRO |
| b his | 1 | PRO |
| b our | 1 | PRO |
| ours (our) | 1 | PRO |
| their (they) | 1 | PRO |
| theirs (they) | 1 | PRO |
| b mine | 1 | PRO |

### 45c Relative Pronouns

| Minicluster | Grade Level | Part of Speech |
|---|---|---|
| 45c.1. **Who** | | |
| b who | K | PRO |
| b that | K | PRO |
| b which | 1 | PRO |
| whom (who) | 4 | PRO |

### 45d Interrogative Pronouns

| Minicluster | Grade Level | Part of Speech |
|---|---|---|
| 45d.1. **What** | | |
| b what | K | PRO |
| b where | 1 | PRO |
| b when | 1 | PRO |
| b why | 1 | PRO |
| b how | 1 | PRO |
| whose (who) | 3 | PRO |
| b whatever | 4 | PRO |
| b wherever | 4 | PRO |
| b whenever | 4 | PRO |
| b whichever | 4* | PRO |
| b whomever | 6* | PRO |

### 45e Indefinite Pronouns

| Minicluster | Grade Level | Part of Speech |
|---|---|---|
| 45e.1. **Someone** | | |
| b no one | K | PRO |
| b something | K | PRO |
| b some | K | PRO |
| b nothing | 1 | PRO |
| b everyone | 2 | PRO |
| b everything | 2 | PRO |
| b someone | 2 | PRO |
| b anyone | 2 | PRO |
| b anything | 2 | PRO |
| b enough | 2 | PRO |
| b each | 2 | PRO |
| b everybody | 3 | PRO |
| b somebody | 3 | PRO |
| b either | 3 | PRO |
| neither (either) | 3 | PRO |
| b anybody | 4 | PRO |
| b nobody | 4 | PRO |

# Supercluster 46
## Contractions

### 46a Contractions (Not)

| Minicluster | Grade Level | Part of Speech |
|---|---|---|
| 46a.1. **Can't** | | |
| can't (can not) | 1 | V |
| won't (will not) | 1 | V |
| don't (do not) | 1 | V |
| couldn't (could not) | 2 | V |
| cannot (can not) | 2 | V |
| wasn't (was not) | 4 | V |
| wouldn't (would not) | 4 | V |
| aren't (are not) | 4 | V |
| shouldn't (should not) | 4 | V |
| weren't (were not) | 4 | V |
| hasn't (has not) | 4 | V |
| hadn't (had not) | 4 | V |
| doesn't (does not) | 4 | V |
| haven't (have not) | 4 | V |
| ain't (are not) | 5 | V |
| mustn't (must not) | 6 | V |
| isn't (is not) | 6 | V |

### 46b Contractions (Have)

| Minicluster | Grade Level | Part of Speech |
|---|---|---|
| 46b.1. **I've** | | |
| I've (I have) | 2 | V |
| you've (you have) | 3 | V |
| they've (they have) | 4 | V |
| we've (we have) | 4 | V |

### 46c Contractions (Will)

| Minicluster | Grade Level | Part of Speech |
|---|---|---|
| 46c.1. **I'll** | | |
| I'll (I will) | 1 | V |
| we'll (we will) | 2 | V |
| you'll (you will) | 2 | V |
| they'll (they will) | 3 | V |
| she'll (she will) | 4 | V |
| he'll (he will) | 4 | V |

### 46d Contractions (Is)

| Minicluster | Grade Level | Part of Speech |
|---|---|---|
| 46d.1. **It's** | | |
| how's (how is) | 1 | V |
| it's (it is) | 2 | V |
| that's (that is) | 2 | V |
| he's (he is) | 4 | V |
| she's (she is) | 4 | V |
| there's (there is) | 4 | V |
| what's (what is) | 4 | V |
| where's (where is) | 4 | V |
| here's (here is) | 4 | V |
| b tis | 4 | V |

---

**Key**

Basic words
    Basic words are preceded by *b*.
    All other words are followed by the basic word in parentheses.

Grade levels
    K-6    The grade level at which a word is introduced.
    *      Indicates a word does not appear frequently in student reading material, but when it does appear it is at the level indicated.
    –      Words or phrases for which a grade level could not be determined.

Content specific words are indicated by the content area in which they are used:
    SS     Social Studies
    EN     English
    MA     Math
    SC     Science

Part of Speech
    N         Noun
    V         Verb
    A         Adjective
    AV        Adverb
    AV (+ly)  Adverb when suffix -ly is added
    PRO       Pronoun
    PREP      Preposition
    INT       Interjection
    DET       Determiner
    AX        Auxiliary verb
    RM        Relationship marker

### 46e Contractions (Had)

| Minicluster | Grade Level | Part of Speech |
|---|---|---|
| **46e.1.  I'd** | | |
| I'd (I had) | 2 | V |
| they'd (they had) | 4 | V |
| we'd (we had) | 4 | V |
| you'd (you had) | 4 | V |
| she'd (she had) | 4 | V |
| he'd (he had) | 4 | V |

### 46f Contractions (Are)

| Minicluster | Grade Level | Part of Speech |
|---|---|---|
| **46f.1.  You're** | | |
| I'm (I am) | 2 | V |
| you're (you are) | 3 | V |
| they're (they are) | 4 | V |

# Supercluster 47
## Entertainment/The Arts

### 47a Plays/Movies

| Minicluster | Grade Level | Part of Speech |
|---|---|---|
| **47a.1.  Performance** | | |
| b  act | 2 | N, V |
| b  program | 4 | N |
| performance (perform) | 5 | N |
| rehearsal (rehearse) | 6 | N |
| **47a.1.1** _____ | | |
| b  perform | 5 | V |
| **47a.2.  Show** | | |
| b  show | K | N, V |
| b  cartoon | 3* | N |
| b  movie | 4 | N |
| b  scene | 4 | N |
| **47a.3.  Climax** | | |
| b  plot | 4 | N, V |
| setting (set) | 4 | N |
| b  climax | 6 | N, V |

| Minicluster | Grade Level | Part of Speech |
|---|---|---|
| **47a.4.  Stage** | | |
| b  stage | 4 | N, V |
| scenery (scene) | 4* | N |
| b  theater | 5 | N |

### 47b Music/Dance

| Minicluster | Grade Level | Part of Speech |
|---|---|---|
| **47b.1.  Music** | | |
| b  music | 3 | N |
| **47b.1.1** _____ | | |
| musical (music) | 5 | N, A, AV (+ly) |
| **47b.2.  Concert** | | |
| b  concert | 4 | N |
| b  opera | 5* | N |
| b  symphony | 6* | N |
| **47b.3.  Dance** | | |
| b  dance | 2 | N, V |
| b  ballet | 2 | N |
| **47b.4.  Solo** | | |
| b  solo | 4* | N |
| duet (duo) | 6* | N |
| **47b.5.  Conduct** | | |
| b  conduct | 6 | V |
| **47b.5.1.** _____ | | |
| conductor (conduct) | 5 | N |

### 47c Instruments

| Minicluster | Grade Level | Part of Speech |
|---|---|---|
| **47c.1.  Piano** | | |
| b  piano | 3 | N |
| b  drum | 3 | N, V |
| b  fife | 3* | N |
| b  organ | 4 | N |
| b  trumpet | 5 | N, V |
| b  tom-tom | 5 | N |
| b  recorder | 5* | N |
| b  clarinet | 6 | N |
| b  accordion | 6 | N |

## 47c.2. **Violin**

| | | Grade Level | Part of Speech |
|---|---|---|---|
| b | harp | 1* | N |
| b | violin | 4 | N |
| b | fiddle | 5 | N, V |

## 47d Art

| Minicluster | Grade Level | Part of Speech |
|---|---|---|
| 47d.1. **Art** | | |
| b art | 4 | N |
| 47d.1.1 _____ | | |
| artistic (art) | 6 | A, AV (+ly) |
| 47d.2. **Painting** | | |
| painting (paint) | K | N |
| b picture | 1 | N, V |
| b statue | 3 | N |
| b photo | 4 | N |
| portrait (portray) | 5* | N |
| sculpture (sculpt) | 5* | N, V |
| b snapshot | 5* | N |
| b photograph | 6 | N, V |
| b mosaic | 6* | N |
| b mural | 6* | N |
| 47d.2.1 _____ | | |
| photography (photograph) | - | N |

# Supercluster 48
## Actions Involving the Legs

### 48a Running/Walking Actions

| Minicluster | Grade Level | Part of Speech |
|---|---|---|
| 48a.1. **Run** | | |
| b run | K | N, V |
| b dance | 2 | N, V |
| b trot | 2 | N, V |
| b skip | 4 | N, V |
| b lope | 4 | V |
| b jog | 5 | N, V |
| scamper (scamp) | 5 | V |
| b romp | 5* | N, V |
| b prance | 6 | V |
| b ramble | 6 | V |
| 48a.2. **Walk** | | |
| b walk | 1 | N, V |
| b march | 3 | N, V |
| b tiptoe | 3 | V |
| b waddle | 4 | N, V |
| b strut | 4 | N, V |
| b swagger | 4 | N, V |
| b stride | 4 | N, V |
| b trudge | 4 | V |
| b plod | 4 | V |
| b stroll | 5 | N, V |
| b hike | 5 | N, V |
| b saunter | 5 | V |
| b tread | 6 | V |
| 48a.3. **Limp** | | |
| b limp | 4 | N, V |
| b shuffle | 4 | N, V |
| b stumble | 4 | V |
| b stagger | 5 | N, V |
| b hobble | 6 | V |

### 48b Lurking/Creeping

| Minicluster | Grade Level | Part of Speech |
|---|---|---|
| 48b.1. **Creep** | | |
| b crawl | 2 | N, V |
| b creep | 4 | V |

## 48b.2. **Prowl**

| | Grade Level | Part of Speech |
|---|---|---|
| b sneak | 4 | V |
| b prowl | 4 | V |
| b lurk | 5 | V |
| b slither | 6 | V |

## 48c Kicking

| Minicluster | Grade Level | Part of Speech |
|---|---|---|
| **48c.1. Kick** | | |
| b stamp | 2 | V |
| b kick | 3 | N, V |
| b tramp | 4 | V |
| b stomp | 5 | N, V |
| trample (tramp) | 6 | V |

## 48d Jumping

| Minicluster | Grade Level | Part of Speech |
|---|---|---|
| **48d.1. Jump** | | |
| b jump | K | N, V |
| b hop | 1 | N, V |
| b spring | 2 | N, V |
| b pounce | 5 | V |
| b leap | 5 | N, V |

## 48e Standing/Stationary Actions

| Minicluster | Grade Level | Part of Speech |
|---|---|---|
| **48e.1. Stand** | | |
| b stand | 2 | N, V |
| b straddle | 5 | V |
| b curtsy | 6 | V |

# Supercluster 49
## Mathematics

### 49a Branches of Mathematics

| Minicluster | Grade Level | Part of Speech |
|---|---|---|
| **49a.1. Arithmetic** | | |
| b arithmetic | 3 | N |
| b mathematics | 5 | N |
| b math | 5* | N |
| b geometry | 5* | N |
| b algebra | 5* | N |

### 49b Mathematical Quantities

| Minicluster | Grade Level | Part of Speech |
|---|---|---|
| **49b.1. Maximum** | | |
| b maximum | 6* | N, A |
| b minimum | 6* | N, A |
| **49b.2. Total** | | |
| b total | 4 | N, V, A, AV (+ly) |
| b fraction | 4* | N |
| b sum | 5 | N, V |
| b average | 5 | N, V, A |
| b percent | 5* | N |
| proportion (portion) | 6 | N, V |
| percentage (percent) | 6* | N |
| b mulitple | 6* | N, A |
| b ratio | MA | N |
| b median | MA | N |

### 49c Equations/Formulas

| Minicluster | Grade Level | Part of Speech |
|---|---|---|
| **49c.1. Equation** | | |
| equation (equal) | 5* | N |
| b formula | 5* | N |

49c.2. **Denominator**

| | | |
|---|---|---|
| b denominator | MA | N |
| numerator (number) | MA | N |
| remainder (remain) | MA | N |
| b exponent | MA | N |
| b pi | MA | N |
| addend (add) | MA | N |
| divisor (divide) | MA | N |
| b quotient | MA | N |

## 49d Mathematical Operation

| Minicluster | Grade Level | Part of Speech |
|---|---|---|
| **49d.1. Addition** | | |
| addition (add) | 5 | N |
| multiplication (multiple) | 5* | N |
| division (divide) | 6 | N |
| subtraction (subtract) | 6 | N |
| 49d.1.1 _____ | | |
| divisible (divide) | 5* | A |
| 49d.1.2 _____ | | |
| b add | 2 | V |
| b count | 2 | N, V |
| b divide | 3 | V |
| b plus | 3* | V |
| b subtract | 5 | V |
| multiply (multiple) | 6 | V |
| b minus | 6 | V |
| b tally | 6 | V |
| **49d.2. Per** | | |
| b per | 6 | PREP |

# Supercluster 50
## Auxiliary/Helping Verbs

### 50a Auxiliary Verbs

| Minicluster | Grade Level | Part of Speech |
|---|---|---|
| **50a.1. Are** | | |
| b are | K | AX |
| b is | K | AX |
| b am | 1 | AX |
| b be | 1 | AX |
| b was | 1 | AX |
| b were | 1 | AX |
| been (be) | 2 | AX |
| being (be) | 4 | AX |

---

**Key**

Basic words

  Basic words are preceded by *b*.
  All other words are followed by the basic word in parentheses.

Grade levels

  K-6   The grade level at which a word is introduced.

  *       Indicates a word does not appear frequently in student reading material, but when it does appear it is at the level indicated.

  –       Words or phrases for which a grade level could not be determined.

Content specific words are indicated by the content area in which they are used:

  SS     Social Studies
  EN     English
  MA     Math
  SC     Science

Part of Speech

  N            Noun
  V            Verb
  A            Adjective
  AV          Adverb
  AV (+ly)   Adverb when suffix -ly is added
  PRO         Pronoun
  PREP       Preposition
  INT         Interjection
  DET         Determiner
  AX           Auxiliary verb
  RM           Relationship marker

## 50b Primary Auxiliaries

| Minicluster | Grade Level | Part of Speech |
|---|---|---|
| 50b.1. **Do** | | |
| b do | K | AX |
| did (do) | K | AX |
| doing (do) | K | AX |
| does (do) | 1 | AX |
| done (do) | 2 | AX |
| 50b.2. **Have** | | |
| b have | K | AX |
| has (have) | K | AX |
| had (have) | K | AX |

## 50c Modals

| Minicluster | Grade Level | Part of Speech |
|---|---|---|
| 50c.1. **Should** | | |
| b will | K | AX |
| b can | K | AX |
| b may | K | AX |
| b should | 1 | AX |
| b could | 1 | AX |
| b would | 1 | AX |
| b must | 1 | AX |
| b might | 1 | AX |
| b shall | 2 | AX |
| b used to | – | AX |
| b ought to | – | AX |

## 50d Semiauxiliaries

| Minicluster | Grade Level | Part of Speech |
|---|---|---|
| 50d.1. **Have to** | | |
| b is about to | – | AX |
| b is apt to | – | AX |
| b is bound to | – | AX |
| b is going to | – | AX |
| b is liable to | – | AX |
| b is sure to | – | AX |
| b had better | – | AX |
| b had best | – | AX |
| b have to | – | AX |
| b get to | – | AX |
| b is certain to | – | AX |
| b seems to | – | AX |

## 50e Linking Verbs

| Minicluster | Grade Level | Part of Speech |
|---|---|---|
| 50e.1. **Appear** | | |
| b stay | 1 | V |
| b seem | 2 | V |
| b appear | 3 | V |
| b become | 3 | V |
| b remain | 4 | V |

# Supercluster 51
# Events

## 51a Dates/Events (General)

| Minicluster | Grade Level | Part of Speech |
|---|---|---|
| 51a.1. **Event** | | |
| b event | 4 | N |
| happening (happen) | 4 | N |
| b affair | 4 | N |
| b process | 5 | N |
| b incident | 5 | N |
| b occasion | 5 | N |
| b experience | 5 | N, V |
| development (develop) | 5* | N |
| b instance | 6 | N |
| occurrence (occur) | 6 | N |
| 51a.2. **Endeavor** | | |
| b project | 5 | N |
| b feat | 6 | N |
| b endeavor | 6* | N |
| 51a.3. **Situation** | | |
| b situation | 4 | N |
| b circumstance | 6 | N |
| b context | 6 | N |
| environment (environ) | 6 | N |

## 51b Festive/Recreational Events

| Minicluster | Grade Level | Part of Speech |
|---|---|---|
| **51b.1. Vacation** | | |
| b vacation | 3 | N, V |
| b holiday | 4 | N |
| b pastime | 5 | N |
| b leisure | 6* | N |
| **51b.2. Celebration** | | |
| b party | 1 | N |
| b birthday | 1 | N |
| festival (festive) | 4 | N |
| celebration (celebrate) | 5 | N |
| graduation (graduate) | 6 | N |
| b prom | 6 | N |
| b ceremony | 6 | N |
| b bazaar | 6 | N |
| inauguration (inaugurate) | SS | N |
| **51b.3. Parade** | | |
| b parade | 2 | N, V |
| b pageant | 5 | N |
| b caravan | 6 | N |
| procession (proceed) | 6 | N |
| **51b.4. Fair** | | |
| b fair | 2 | N |
| b circus | 2 | N |
| b rodeo | 4 | N |
| b carnival | 6 | N |
| **51b.5. Amusement** | | |
| amusement (amuse) | 4* | N |
| entertainment (entertain) | 6 | N |

## 51c Political Events

| Minicluster | Grade Level | Part of Speech |
|---|---|---|
| **51c.1. Election** | | |
| election (elect) | 5* | N |
| b campaign | 6 | N, V |

| | Grade Level | Part of Speech |
|---|---|---|
| **51c.2. Vote** | | |
| b vote | 5 | N, V |
| b elect | 5 | V |
| reelect (elect) | SS | V |
| **51c.2.1** _____ | | |
| voter (vote) | 5* | V |

# Supercluster 52
## Temperature/Fire

### 52a Temperature

| Minicluster | Grade Level | Part of Speech |
|---|---|---|
| **52a.1. Temperature** | | |
| b temperature | 4 | N |
| b Fahrenheit | SC | N |
| b centigrade | SC | N |
| **52a.2. Coldness** | | |
| b cold | 1 | N, A, AV (+ly) |
| b cool | 3 | V, A, AV (+ly) |
| b arctic | 5 | A |
| b frigid | 6 | A, AV (+ly) |
| **52a.2.1** _____ | | |
| b chill | 3 | N, V |
| **52a.3. Heat** | | |
| b warm | 2 | V, A, AV (+ly) |
| b hot | 2 | A, AV (+ly) |
| b temperate | 5* | A, AV (+ly) |
| b lukewarm | 6 | A |
| b tepid | 6 | A |
| **52a.3.1** _____ | | |
| b heat | 2 | N, V |
| warmth (warm) | 4 | N |

## 52a.4. **Parch**

| | Grade Level | Part of Speech |
|---|---|---|
| b parch | 6 | V |
| b swelter | 6* | V |

## 52b Insulation

| Minicluster | Grade Level | Part of Speech |
|---|---|---|
| **52b.1. Insulation** | | |
| insulator (insulate) | SC | N |
| insulation (insulate) | SC | N |
| **52b.1.1** _____ | | |
| b insulate | 6 | N |
| **52b.1.2** _____ | | |
| b fireproof | SS | V, A |

## 52c Fire

| Minicluster | Grade Level | Part of Speech |
|---|---|---|
| **52c.1. Fire** | | |
| b fire | 1 | N |
| b campfire | 3* | N |
| b blaze | 4 | N, V |
| b combustion | SC | N |
| inferno (infernal) | SC | N |
| **52c.2. Flame** | | |
| b flame | 3 | N |
| b spark | 3 | N |
| **52c.3. Burn** | | |
| b burn | 2 | N, V |
| b singe | 3 | V |
| b scorch | 5 | V |
| b spark | 5 | N, V |
| b sizzle | 6 | V |
| **52c.4. Flicker** | | |
| flicker (flick) | 4 | N, V |
| b smolder | 6 | V |

## 52d Products of Fire

| Minicluster | Grade Level | Part of Speech |
|---|---|---|
| **52d.1. Ash** | | |
| b ash | 4 | N |
| b cinder | 4 | N |
| b ember | 6 | N |
| **52d.2. Smoke** | | |
| b smoke | 2 | N, V |
| b soot | 4* | N |
| **52d.2.1** _____ | | |
| smoky (smoke) | 6 | A |

## 52e Fire Producers

| Minicluster | Grade Level | Part of Speech |
|---|---|---|
| **52e.1. Burner** | | |
| burner (burn) | SC | N |
| extinguisher (extinguish) | SC | N |
| **52e.2. Firewood** | | |
| b firewood | 4* | N |

# Supercluster 53
## Images/Perceptions

### 53a Visual Images/Perception

| Minicluster | Grade Level | Part of Speech |
|---|---|---|
| **53a.1. Image** | | |
| b image | 5 | N |
| reflection (reflect) | 6 | N |
| representation (represent) | 6* | N |
| portrayal (portray) | 6* | N |

## 53a.2. Scene

| | | Grade Level | Part of Speech |
|---|---|---|---|
| | sight (see) | 2 | N, V |
| b | view | 4 | N, V |
| b | scene | 4 | N |
| b | vision | 5 | N |

### 53a.2.1 _____

| | | | |
|---|---|---|---|
| | visual (vision) | 6* | A, AV (+ly) |

### 53a.3. Recognition

| | | | |
|---|---|---|---|
| | recognition (recognize) | 5* | N |

### 53a.4. Blindfold

| | | | |
|---|---|---|---|
| b | blindfold | 5* | N, V |

### 53a.5. Observer

| | | | |
|---|---|---|---|
| | observer (observe) | 6* | N |

### 53a.6. Portray

| | | | |
|---|---|---|---|
| b | represent | 4 | V |
| b | display | 5 | N, V |
| b | portray | 6 | V |

## 53b Looking/Perceiving Actions

| Minicluster | Grade Level | Part of Speech |
|---|---|---|

### 53b.1. Look

| | | | |
|---|---|---|---|
| b | look | K | N, V |
| b | see | K | V |
| b | spot | 2 | N, V |
| b | watch | 2 | V |
| | behold (hold) | 3 | V |

### 53b.2. Appear

| | | | |
|---|---|---|---|
| b | appear | 3 | V |
| | reappear (appear) | 4* | V |

### 53b.3. Glance

| | | | |
|---|---|---|---|
| b | wink | 3 | N, V |
| b | blink | 3 | N, V |
| b | peek | 3 | N, V |
| b | glance | 4 | N, V |
| b | glimpse | 4 | N, V |
| b | squint | 4 | V |

### 53b.4. Gaze

| | | | |
|---|---|---|---|
| b | stare | 2 | N, V |
| b | gaze | 3 | N, V |
| b | peer | 3 | V |
| b | glare | 4 | N, V |
| b | gape | 4 | V |
| b | glower | 6 | V |

### 53b.5. Observe/Ignore

| | | | |
|---|---|---|---|
| b | notice | 3 | N, V |
| b | recognize | 3 | V |
| b | observe | 4 | V |
| b | attend | 4 | V |
| b | ignore | 5 | V |
| b | distract | 6 | V |
| | review (view) | 6 | V |
| b | perceive | 6 | V |

### 53b.6. Aim

| | | | |
|---|---|---|---|
| b | aim | 3 | N, V |

### 53b.7. Spy

| | | | |
|---|---|---|---|
| b | spy | 3 | N, V |

---

## Key

**Basic words**
Basic words are preceded by *b*.
All other words are followed by the basic word in parentheses.

**Grade levels**
| K-6 | The grade level at which a word is introduced. |
|---|---|
| * | Indicates a word does not appear frequently in student reading material, but when it does appear it is at the level indicated. |
| – | Words or phrases for which a grade level could not be determined. |

Content specific words are indicated by the content area in which they are used:
| SS | Social Studies |
|---|---|
| EN | English |
| MA | Math |
| SC | Science |

**Part of Speech**
| N | Noun |
|---|---|
| V | Verb |
| A | Adjective |
| AV | Adverb |
| AV (+ly) | Adverb when suffix -ly is added |
| PRO | Pronoun |
| PREP | Preposition |
| INT | Interjection |
| DET | Determiner |
| AX | Auxiliary verb |
| RM | Relationship marker |

# Supercluster 54
## Life/Survival

### 54a Life, Birth, Death

| Minicluster | Grade Level | Part of Speech |
|---|---|---|
| **54a.1. Existence** | | |
| b life | 2 | N |
| b birth | 3* | N |
| death (dead) | 4 | N |
| reproduction (produce) | 5* | N |
| existence (exist) | 6 | N |
| **54a.2. Live** | | |
| live (life) | 1 | V |
| b exist | 4* | V |
| b inhabit | 5 | V |
| b dwell | 6* | V |
| **54a.2.1** _____ | | |
| alive (life) | 3 | A |
| **54a.3. Die** | | |
| b die | 3 | V |
| b perish | 5* | V |
| **54a.3.1** _____ | | |
| b dead | 3 | A |
| nonliving (life) | SC | A |
| **54a.4. Funeral** | | |
| b wake | 3 | N |
| b funeral | 6* | N |
| b burial | 6* | N |
| b cremation | 6* | N |
| **54a.5. Reproduce** | | |
| b hatch | 3 | V |
| b bare | 3 | V |
| b breed | 5 | V |
| reproduce (produce) | SC | V |
| germinate (germ) | SC | V |
| b spawn | SC | V |

### 54b Survival/Growth

| Minicluster | Grade Level | Part of Speech |
|---|---|---|
| **54b.1. Endurance** | | |
| endurance (endure) | 5 | N |
| survival (survive) | 6* | N |
| tolerance (tolerate) | 6*. | N |
| **54b.2. Survive** | | |
| b survive | 5 | V |
| b endure | 6 | V |
| b tolerate | 6* | V |
| **54b.3. Flourish** | | |
| b thrive | 5 | V |
| b flourish | 6 | V |
| b prosper | 6 | V |
| **54b.4. Grow** | | |
| b grow | 2 | V |
| b bloom | 4 | V |
| b mature | 5* | V |
| b evolve | 6* | V |

# Supercluster 55
## Conformity/Complexity

### 55a Conformity to a Norm

| Minicluster | Grade Level | Part of Speech |
|---|---|---|
| **55a.1. Special** | | |
| b special | 3 | A, AV (+ly) |
| original (origin) | 4 | A, AV (+ly) |
| b scarce | 4 | A, AV (+ly) |
| distinctive (distinct) | 5* | A, AV (+ly) |
| b unique | 6 | A, AV (+ly) |
| b distinct | 6 | A, AV (+ly) |
| uncommon (common) | 6* | A, AV (+ly) |
| b rare | 6* | A, AV (+ly) |
| **55a.2. Strange** | | |
| b strange | 2 | A, AV (+ly) |
| b queer | 2 | A, AV (+ly) |
| b peculiar | 4 | A, AV (+ly) |
| b odd | 4 | A, AV (+ly) |
| b severe | 5 | A, AV (+ly) |
| b weird | 5 | A, AV (+ly) |

### 55b Complexity/Order

| Minicluster | Grade Level | Part of Speech |
|---|---|---|
| **55b.1. Complex** | | |
| b fancy | 3 | A |
| b complex | 4* | A, AV (+ly) |
| b elaborate | 6 | A, AV (+ly) |
| **55b.2. Order** | | |
| b order | 3 | N, V |
| disorder (order) | 4* | N |
| disarray (array) | 6* | N |
| **55b.3. Steady** | | |
| b steady | 3 | A, AV (+ly) |
| b balance(d) | 4 | A |
| b uniform | 4 | A, AV (+ly) |
| unbroken (break) | 4* | A |
| b neutral | 5* | A, AV (+ly) |
| unchanged (change) | 5* | A |
| **55b.4. Bare** | | |
| b bare | 3 | A |
| b blank | 6 | A |
| **55b.5. Incomplete** | | |
| unfinished (finish) | 4* | A |
| incomplete (complete) | 5* | A, AV (+ly) |
| **55b.6. Pure** | | |
| b pure | 3 | A, AV (+ly) |
| b plain | 3 | A, AV (+ly) |
| b simple | 4 | A, AV (+ly) |

# Supercluster 56
## Difficulty/Danger

### 56a Difficulty/Ease

| Minicluster | Grade Level | Part of Speech |
|---|---|---|
| **56a.1. Ease** | | |
| difficulty (difficult) | 3 | N |
| b ease | 4 | N, V |
| convenience (convenient) | 6 | N |
| **56a1.1** _____ | | |
| simplify (simple) | 5* | V |

## 56a.2. Comfortable

| | Grade Level | Part of Speech |
|---|---|---|
| easy (ease) | 2 | A, AV (+ly) |
| comfortable (comfort) | 3 | A, AV (+ly) |
| b convenient | 4 | A, AV (+ly) |

## 56a.3. Difficult

| | Grade Level | Part of Speech |
|---|---|---|
| b difficult | 3 | A, AV (+ly) |
| impossible (possible) | 3 | A, AV (+ly) |
| tiresome (tire) | 4* | A |
| troublesome | 5* | A |
| uneasy (ease) | 5* | A, AV (+ly) |

## 56b Danger/Safety

| Minicluster | Grade Level | Part of Speech |
|---|---|---|
| **56b.1. Safety** | | |
| safety (safe) | 3 | N |
| prevention (prevent) | 6 | N |
| **56b.2. Danger** | | |
| b trouble | 2 | N, V |
| b danger | 3 | N |
| b risk | 5 | N, V |
| b peril | 6* | N |
| **56b.2.1 _____** | | |
| endanger (danger) | 6* | V |
| **56b.3. Harmful** | | |
| dangerous (danger) | 3 | A, AV (+ly) |
| harmful (harm) | 4* | A, AV (+ly) |
| hazardous (hazard) | 5* | A, AV (+ly) |
| unsafe (safe) | 5* | A, AV (+ly) |
| b grave | 6 | A, AV (+ly) |
| treacherous (treachery) | 6 | A, AV (+ly) |
| perilous (peril) | 6 | A, AV (+ly) |

## 56b.4. Harmless

| | Grade Level | Part of Speech |
|---|---|---|
| b safe | 2 | A, AV (+ly) |
| harmless (harm) | 4* | A, AV (+ly) |

# Supercluster 57
## Texture/Durability

### 57a Texture

| Minicluster | Grade Level | Part of Speech |
|---|---|---|
| **57a.1. Texture** | | |
| b texture | SC | N |
| **57a.2. Hard/Soft** | | |
| b hard | 1 | A |
| b soft | 2 | A, AV (+ly) |
| b smooth | 3 | A, AV (+ly) |
| b stiff | 3 | A, AV (+ly) |
| b solid | 4 | A, AV (+ly) |
| b tough | 4 | A |
| b brittle | 5 | A, AV (+ly) |
| b rigid | 5 | A, AV (+ly) |
| **57a.3. Rough** | | |
| b crisp | 3 | A, AV (+ly) |
| b rough | 4 | A, AV (+ly) |
| stony (stone) | 4* | A |
| prickly (prick) | 5 | A |
| b coarse | 6 | A |
| porous (pore) | SC | A |
| **57a.4. Choppy** | | |
| bumpy (bump) | 2 | A |
| choppy (chop) | 6 | A |
| **57a.5. Furry** | | |
| furry (fur) | 4 | A |
| shaggy (shag) | 6 | A |
| spongy (sponge) | 6* | A |

### 57a.6. **Harden**

| | Grade Level | Part of Speech |
|---|---|---|
| harden (hard) | 4 | V |
| soften (soft) | 5* | V |
| stiffen (stiff) | 6 | V |

## 57b Durability

| Minicluster | Grade Level | Part of Speech |
|---|---|---|
| **57b.1. Durability** | | |
| durability (durable) | 6* | N |
| **57b.2. Strong** | | |
| b strong | 2 | A, AV (+ly) |
| b formidable | 6 | A, AV (+ly) |
| **57b.3. Weak** | | |
| b weak | 3 | A, AV (+ly) |
| b flimsy | 5 | A, AV (+ly) |
| b shabby | 6 | A, AV (+ly) |
| **57b.4. Delicate** | | |
| b delicate | 5 | A, AV (+ly) |
| b fragile | 6 | A, AV (+ly) |
| b frail | 6 | A, AV (+ly) |

# Supercluster 58
# Color

## 58a Color

| Minicluster | Grade Level | Part of Speech |
|---|---|---|
| **58a.1. Red** | | |
| b green | K | N, A |
| b red | K | N, A |
| b blue | K | N, A |
| b yellow | K | N, A |

| | Grade Level | Part of Speech |
|---|---|---|
| b white | 1 | N, A |
| b black | 1 | N, A |
| b brown | 1 | N, A |
| b pink | 2 | N, A |
| b gray | 2 | N, A |
| b silver | 2 | N, A |
| b gold | 2 | N, A |
| b purple | 3 | N, A |
| b orange | 3 | N, A |
| golden (gold) | 3 | N, A |
| b tan | 4 | N, A |
| b indigo | 6 | N, A |
| b crimson | 6 | N, A |
| b amber | 6 | N, A |

---

**Key**

Basic words
    Basic words are preceded by *b.*
    All other words are followed by the basic word in parentheses.

Grade levels
  K-6  The grade level at which a word is introduced.
  *    Indicates a word does not appear frequently in student reading material, but when it does appear it is at the level indicated.
  –    Words or phrases for which a grade level could not be determined.
  Content specific words are indicated by the content area in which they are used:
  SS    Social Studies
  EN    English
  MA    Math
  SC    Science

Part of Speech
  N      Noun
  V      Verb
  A      Adjective
  AV    Adverb
  AV (+ly)  Adverb when suffix -ly is added
  PRO  Pronoun
  PREP  Preposition
  INT    Interjection
  DET   Determiner
  AX    Auxiliary verb
  RM   Relationship marker

58a.2. **Blonde**

| | | |
|---|---|---|
| b blonde | 5* | N, A |
| b brunette | 5* | N, A |

58a.3. **Color**

| | | |
|---|---|---|
| b color | 1 | N, V |
| b hue | 4* | N |
| b tint | 6 | N, V |

58a.3.1 _____

| | | |
|---|---|---|
| b colorful (color) | 4* | A, AV (+ly) |
| b colorless (color) | 5* | A, AV (+ly) |

## 58b Paint

| Minicluster | Grade Level | Part of Speech |
|---|---|---|
| 58b.1. **Paint** | | |
| b paint | K | N, V |
| b dye | 5 | N, V |
| b lacquer | 6* | N |
| b enamel | 6* | N |

# Supercluster 59
## Chemicals

### 59a Chemicals

| Minicluster | Grade Level | Part of Speech |
|---|---|---|
| 59a.1. **Chemical** | | |
| b compound | 4 | N, V |
| chemical (chemistry) | 4* | N |
| 59a.2. **Oxygen** | | |
| b helium | SC | N |
| b oxygen | SC | N |
| b dioxide | SC | N |
| b nitrogen | SC | N |
| b hydrogen | SC | N |
| b neon | SC | N |
| b cellulose | SC | N |
| b nitrate | SC | N |
| b phosphate | SC | N |

59a.3. **Boron**

| | | |
|---|---|---|
| b sodium | SC | N |
| b oxide | SC | N |
| b chlorine | SC | N |
| b krypton | SC | N |
| b boron | SC | N |
| b ammonia | SC | N |
| b bromine | SC | N |
| b sulfate | SC | N |
| b carbohydrate | SC | N |

59a.3.1 _____

| | | |
|---|---|---|
| chlorinate (chlorine) | SC | V |

## 59b Acids

| Minicluster | Grade Level | Part of Speech |
|---|---|---|
| 59a.1. **Acid** | | |
| b acid | 5* | N |
| 58a.1.1 _____ | | |
| sulfuric (sulfur) | SC | A |
| hydrochloric (chlorine) | SC | A |

# Supercluster 60
## Facial Expressions/Actions

### 60a Facial Expression

| Minicluster | Grade Level | Part of Speech |
|---|---|---|
| 60a.1. **Smile** | | |
| b smile | 2 | N, V |
| b grin | 3 | N, V |
| b frown | 3 | N, V |
| b scowl | 4 | N, V |
| b sneer | 4 | N, V |
| 60a.2. **Nod** | | |
| b nod | 3 | N, V |

## 60b Actions Associated with the Nose

| Minicluster | Grade Level | Part of Speech |
|---|---|---|
| **60b.1. Smell** | | |
| b smell | 2 | N, V |
| b sniff | 3 | N, V |
| b sneeze | 3 | N, V |
| b snort | 4 | N, V |
| b snore | 6 | N, V |

## 60c Actions Associated with the Mouth

| Minicluster | Grade Level | Part of Speech |
|---|---|---|
| **60c.1. Lick** | | |
| b lick | 2 | N, V |
| b kiss | 3 | N, V |
| b suck | 4 | V |
| b choke | 4 | V |
| b spit | 5 | V |

## 60d Breathing

| Minicluster | Grade Level | Part of Speech |
|---|---|---|
| **60d.1. Puff** | | |
| b blow | 2 | V |
| b puff | 3 | N, V |
| breathe (breath) | 4 | V |
| b exhale | SC | V |
| b inhale | SC | V |
| **60d.1.1** _____ | | |
| b breath | 3 | N |

# Supercluster 61
## Electricity/Particles of Matter

### 61a Electricity

| Minicluster | Grade Level | Part of Speech |
|---|---|---|
| **61a.1. Electricity** | | |
| electricity (electric) | 3 | N |
| **61a.1.1** _____ | | |
| b electric | 3 | A |
| electrical (electric) | 4* | A, AV (+ly) |
| b electronic | 5* | A, AV (+ly) |
| hydroelectric (electric) | SC | A, AV (+ly) |
| electromagnetic (magnet) | SC | A, AV (+ly) |
| **61a.2. Radiation** | | |
| radiation (ray) | 6* | N |
| **61a.2.1** _____ | | |
| b radioactive | 6* | A |

### 61b Molecules/Atoms

| Minicluster | Grade Level | Part of Speech |
|---|---|---|
| **61b.1. Molecule** | | |
| b molecule | 6* | N |
| **61b.1.1** _____ | | |
| molecular (molecule) | SC | A, AV (+ly) |
| **61b.2. Atom** | | |
| b ion | 5* | N |
| b atom | 6 | N |
| b electron | 6* | N |
| b neutron | SC | N |
| b proton | SC | N |
| b nucleus | SC | N |
| nuclei (nucleus) | SC | N |
| b isotope | SC | N |
| b photon | SC | N |
| **61b.2.1** _____ | | |
| atomic (atom) | 6* | A, AV (+ly) |

# Appendix B
# Alphabetized Words

## A

| | | | | | | | |
|---|---|---|---|---|---|---|---|
| a | 3i.1 | ache | 37c.1 | advice | 10g.1 |
| abacus | 3c.1 | achieve | 36e.1 | advice | 12g.1 |
| abandon | 36a.1 | acid | 59b.1 | advise | 10e.3 |
| abbot | 1w.1 | acknowledge | 10d.4 | adviser | 1i.2 |
| abbreviation | 35b.2 | acorn | 6j.4 | aerial | 11d.1.1 |
| ability | 5r.1 | acquaintance | 9e.1 | affair | 51a.1 |
| a bit | 3j.6 | acquire | 36e.1 | affect | 39a.4 |
| able | 12k.4 | acre | 20a.1 | affection | 5o.2 |
| aboard | 14i.1.2 | acreage | 20a.1 | affectionate | 13a.6 |
| abolish | 2f.2 | acrobat | 1d.4 | affix | 35b.2 |
| abound | 3g.7 | act | 47a.1 | afflict | 33b.3 |
| about | 2x.6 | action | 2a.1 | afford | 28d.1 |
| above | 14i.2 | active | 13b.6 | afloat | 16h.1 |
| abreast | 14k.2.1 | activity | 2a.1 | afraid | 5b.3 |
| abroad | 14k.1.2 | actor | 1h.1 | Africa | 18b.3 |
| abrupt | 7j.5 | actress | 1h.1 | after | 7g.5 |
| absence | 14L.1 | actual | 26a.3 | afternoon | 7c.1 |
| absent | 14L.1.1 | actually | 27b.3 | after that | 7h.2 |
| absolute | 42c.1 | actually | 31a.1 | afterwards | 7h.2 |
| absolute(ly) | 3k.1 | ad | 15f.2 | again | 7k.4 |
| absorb | 16b.7 | adapt | 22f.5 | age | 7d.1 |
| abundance | 3g.5 | add | 49d.1.2 | agility | 43a.3 |
| abundant | 3g.4 | addend | 49c.2 | ago | 7g.1 |
| absurd | 26d.5 | addition | 49d.1 | agony | 5b.1 |
| abuse | 33b.1 | additional | 3g.6 | a great deal | 3k.2 |
| abusive | 5f.1.1 | address | 3d.1 | agree | 10g.4 |
| academy | 21f.1 | adept | 12k.4 | agreement | 27a.2 |
| accent | 35a.2 | adjective | 35b.4 | agriculture | 1L.1 |
| accept | 5o.3 | adjoin | 2v.2 | ah | 10k.1 |
| acceptable | 26a.4 | adjust | 22f.5 | aha | 10k.1 |
| accessory | 30e.1 | administrator | 1b.3 | ahead | 14f.2.1 |
| accident | 33a.1 | admiration | 5o.2 | ahead of | 14f.2.2 |
| accidental | 33a.1.1 | admire | 5o.1 | aid | 8e.1 |
| accompany | 2v.6 | admit | 10h.2 | aid | 33d.6 |
| accomplish | 22f.2.1 | admittedly | 31a.1 | ailment | 37a.1 |
| accomplishment | 22f.2 | adobe | 22d.1 | aim | 53b.6 |
| accordingly | 39b.2 | adolescence | 7f.3 | aimless | 13c.2 |
| accordion | 47c.1 | adorable | 43c.2 | ain't | 46a.1 |
| account | 28a.1 | adore | 5o.1 | air | 40a.3 |
| accountant | 1s.1 | advance | 2g.8 | aircraft | 11d.1 |
| accurate | 42c.1 | adventure | 2g.3 | airfield | 11h.10 |
| accuse | 10b.8 | adventurous | 13b.6 | air force | 25d.1 |
| accustomed | 42a.1 | advertisement | 15f.2 | airline | 11d.1 |

| | | | | | |
|---|---|---|---|---|---|
| aquarium | 4m.1 | Asia | 18b.3 | at the same time | 7i.4 |
| aquarium | 16i.4 | aside | 14k.2.1 | at this point | 7i.1 |
| aqueduct | 11h.9.1 | ask | 10f.2 | attic | 30a.1 |
| arc | 32b.2 | asleep | 12e.2 | attitude | 5r.2 |
| arch | 23g.1 | aspect | 5r.3 | attorney | 1y.1 |
| archeologist | 1k.1 | aspen | 24b.1 | attract | 36e.2 |
| archeology | 1L.2 | asphalt | 29a.3 | attraction | 42a.3 |
| architect | 1g.1 | aspirin | 37f.2 | attractive | 43c.1 |
| architecture | 1L.2 | assemble | 25a.5 | attribute | 5r.1 |
| archive | 21f.2 | assembly | 25e.3 | auction | 28d.3 |
| arctic | 52a.2 | assign | 2v.4 | audience | 25e.3 |
| are | 50a.1 | assignment | 12c.3 | auditorium | 21g.1 |
| area | 20a.2 | assist | 33d.1 | August | 7e.1 |
| arena | 21g.1 | assistant | 1b.1 | aunt | 9n.9 |
| aren't | 46a.1 | association | 25e.1 | auricle | 23c.3 |
| arguably | 31b.1 | assortment | 25a.1 | Australia | 18b.3 |
| argue | 10b.1 | assume | 12d.4 | author | 1e.2 |
| argument | 10b.5 | assure | 10d.2 | authority | 10g.6 |
| arise | 2o.2 | aster | 24d.3 | auto | 11a.1 |
| arithmetic | 49a.1 | astern | 14f.1.1 | autobiography | 15c.2 |
| Arizona | 18c.1 | astonish | 5j.2 | autograph | 15a.2 |
| Arkansas | 18c.1 | astonishingly | 31c.1 | automatic | 7j.5 |
| arm | 23f.1 | astonishment | 5j.1 | automatically | 7j.5.1 |
| armor | 17h.1 | astronaut | 1k.1 | automobile | 11a.1 |
| arms | 8n.1 | astronomer | 1k.1 | autumn | 7d.2 |
| army | 25d.1 | astronomy | 1L.2 | available | 14L.2 |
| around | 2x.6 | astound | 5j.2 | avalanche | 40d.1 |
| arouse | 5e.4 | as well | 27b.2 | avenue | 11h.1 |
| arrange | 25a.5 | as well as | 27b.1 | average | 49b.2 |
| arrangement | 25a.1 | as yet | 7h.2 | avoid | 2f.3 |
| arrest | 36e.3 | at | 7i.2 | aw | 10k.1 |
| arrival | 2g.1 | at | 14g.1 | await | 2b.3 |
| arrive | 2g.7 | at any rate | 27d.4 | awake | 12e.1 |
| arrow | 8n.5 | at first | 7g.2 | awaken | 12e.5 |
| arrowhead | 8f.3 | athlete | 1d.2 | award | 28a.2 |
| art | 47d.1 | athletic | 43a.1 | aware | 12k.2 |
| artery | 23i.2 | atlas | 15c.4 | away | 14k.1.1 |
| artfully | 31g.1 | at least | 3j.3 | awe | 5j.1 |
| article | 15c.5 | atmosphere | 40a.3 | awful | 26d.2 |
| artist | 1g.1 | atmospheric | 40a.3 | awhile | 7k.6 |
| artistic | 47d.1.1 | atom | 61b.2 | awkward | 43a.4 |
| as | 7i.3 | atomic | 67b.2.1 | awl | 8e.5 |
| as a consequence | 39b.2 | atop | 14i.1.1 | axe | 8f.1 |
| as a result | 39b.2 | attack | 33b.2 | axis | 14a.2 |
| asbestos | 22d.1 | attacker | 33b.2.1 | axle | 11f.1 |
| ascend | 2o.2 | attend | 53b.5 | ay | 10k.1 |
| ascent | 2o.2.1 | attendance | 25e.3 | aye | 10k.2 |
| as good as | 3j.7 | attendant | 1b.1 | | |
| ash | 52d.1 | attention | 12f.1 | | |
| ashore | 16h.1 | attentive | 13a.6 | | |

# B

| | |
|---|---|
| babe | 9d.1 |
| baboon | 4g.1 |
| baby | 9d.1 |
| babysitter | 1cc.1 |
| bachelor | 9c.2 |
| back | 14f.1 |
| backbone | 23j.1 |
| background | 14f.1 |
| backward | 14f.1.1 |
| backwards | 14f.1.1 |
| backyard | 20g.1 |
| bacon | 6e.1 |
| bacteria | 37d.1 |
| bad | 26d.2 |
| badge | 17g.3 |
| badger | 33b.5 |
| badly | 3k.2 |
| baffle | 12g.5 |
| bag | 22a.7 |
| baggage | 22a.10 |
| bail | 28b.1 |
| bait | 10e.1 |
| bake | 6k.1 |
| baker | 1n.2 |
| bakery | 21d.2 |
| balanced | 55b.3 |
| balcony | 30a.1 |
| bale | 25a.4 |
| ball | 34c.2 |
| ballad | 15d.2 |
| ballet | 47b.3 |
| balloon | 11d.2 |
| balsa | 24b.1 |
| balsam | 24c.2 |
| bamboo | 24e.4 |
| ban | 2f.2 |
| banana | 6i.5 |
| band | 25b.2 |
| bandage | 37f.3 |
| Band-Aid | 37f.3 |
| bandit | 9g.5 |
| banister | 30b.5 |
| bank | 28f.1 |
| banker | 1s.1 |
| banquet | 6a.2 |
| bar | 22d.3 |
| barb | 8f.3 |
| barbecue | 6k.1 |
| barbed wire | 30c.2 |

| | |
|---|---|
| barbershop | 21d.1 |
| bare | 54a.5 |
| bare | 55b.4 |
| bareback | 4o.5 |
| barefoot | 17j.3 |
| barely | 3j.6 |
| bargain | 28d.3 |
| barge | 11e.5 |
| barium | 29a.4 |
| bark | 19d.1 |
| bark | 24c.1 |
| barker | 1h.2 |
| barley | 6j.3 |
| barn | 21k.1 |
| barnacle | 4i.3 |
| barnyard | 20g.1 |
| baron | 1c.3 |
| barrel | 22a.6 |
| barren | 20b.5 |
| barrow | 11b.2 |
| base | 34c.1 |
| baseball | 34b.1 |
| baseman | 1d.3 |
| basic | 26c.1 |
| basically | 31a.1 |
| basin | 22a.9 |
| bask | 2b.5 |
| basket | 22a.7 |
| basketball | 34b.1 |
| bass | 4h.2 |
| bat | 34c.2 |
| bath | 22a.9 |
| bathe | 41b.1 |
| bathroom | 30a.1 |
| bathtub | 22a.9 |
| baton | 8j.5 |
| batter | 1d.3 |
| batter | 6g.1 |
| battle | 33c.2 |
| battlefield | 20f.1 |
| battleground | 20f.1 |
| battleship | 11e.3 |
| bauxite | 29a.4 |
| bawl | 19c.5 |
| bay | 16f.3 |
| bazaar | 51b.2 |
| be | 50a.1 |
| beach | 16g.2 |
| bead | 17g.5 |
| beagle | 4b.3 |

| | |
|---|---|
| beak | 4L.4 |
| beam | 38d.5 |
| bean | 6j.1 |
| beanstalk | 24e.2 |
| bear | 2i.1 |
| bear | 4e.7 |
| beard | 23b.3 |
| bearded | 23b.3.1 |
| bearing | 5r.2 |
| beast | 4a.1 |
| beat | 44a.3 |
| beater | 8m.7 |
| beautiful | 43c.1 |
| beauty | 43a.3 |
| beaver | 4f.3 |
| becalm | 5L.3 |
| because | 39b.1 |
| because of | 39b.1 |
| beckon | 10f.2 |
| become | 50e.1 |
| bed | 30d.5 |
| bedroom | 30a.1 |
| bedspread | 30f.1 |
| bedtime | 7a.1 |
| bee | 4k.1 |
| beech | 24b.1 |
| beef | 6e.1 |
| beehive | 4m.2 |
| been | 50a.1 |
| beer | 6h.2 |
| beet | 6j.1 |
| beetle | 4k.2 |
| before | 7h.3 |
| beforehand | 7g.2 |
| before now | 7g.2 |
| before that | 7g.2 |
| beggar | 9h.2 |
| begin | 2c.1 |
| beginnner | 2c.1.2 |
| beginning | 2c.1.1 |
| behavior | 5r.2 |
| behind | 14f.1.2 |
| behold | 53b.1 |
| being | 9a.1 |
| being | 50a.1 |
| belch | 19c.2 |
| belfry | 30b.3 |
| belief | 5n.1 |
| belief | 12L.1 |
| believe | 5o.3 |

| | | | | | | |
|---|---|---|---|---|---|---|---|
| bell | 19b.2 | birth | 54a.1 | blue | 58a.1 |
| bellow | 19c.3 | birthday | 51b.2 | blueberry | 6i.3 |
| belly | 23a.2 | birthmark | 23b.4 | bluebird | 4j.1 |
| belong | 36c.3 | birthplace | 18a.1 | blueprint | 15e.1 |
| beloved | 26c.3 | biscuit | 6d.3 | bluff | 20d.2 |
| below | 14j.1 | bishop | 1w.1 | blunder | 26a.2 |
| belt | 17g.1 | bison | 4e.3 | blunt | 32e.1 |
| bench | 30d.3 | bit | 3f.1 | bluntly | 31a.1 |
| bend | 32b.2 | bite | 6m.1 | blur | 38c.2 |
| beneath | 14j.1 | bitter | 6L.2 | blurt | 19c.3 |
| benefit | 33d.1 | bitterness | 5e.2 | board | 22c.2 |
| bent | 32d.2 | bitterness | 6L.2.1 | boast | 10c.4 |
| beriberi | 37b.1 | bituminous | 29c.1 | boat | 11e.1 |
| beryl | 29a.3 | black | 58a.1 | boathouse | 21k.1 |
| beryllium | 29a.4 | blackboard | 15g.3 | boatload | 3e.5 |
| beside | 14k.2.1 | blacken | 41a.2 | body | 23a.1 |
| besides | 27d.4 | blacken | 38c.2 | bog | 16f.1 |
| besides | 27b.2 | blacksmith | 1n.1 | boil | 6k.1 |
| best | 26c.2 | blade | 8f.3 | boil | 16b.5 |
| bestow | 2i.7 | blame | 10b.8 | boiler | 8d.2 |
| bet | 28d.1 | blank | 55b.4 | bold | 13n.3 |
| bet | 42c.4 | blanket | 30f.1 | bolt | 8h.5 |
| beta | 35c.1 | blare | 19c.3 | bomb | 8n.2 |
| betray | 10b.3 | blast | 2s.4 | bond | 2v.1 |
| better | 26c.4 | blast off | 2o.2 | bone | 23j.1 |
| between | 14k.4 | blaze | 52c.1 | bonnet | 17d.1 |
| beware | 10b.6 | bleak | 20b.5 | bonny | 5k.2 |
| bewilder | 12g.5 | bleak | 41a.3 | book | 15c.1 |
| beyond | 14k.1.3 | bleat | 19d.1 | bookcase | 30d.4 |
| Bible | 15c.4 | bleed | 23i.3 | booklet | 15c.1 |
| bicep | 23f.1 | blend | 6k.2 | bookstore | 21d.1 |
| bicycle | 11a.4 | blessing | 10d.6.1 | boomerang | 8n.5 |
| bicycle | 34b.3.1 | blight | 28b.3 | boost | 2o.1 |
| bicycling | 34b.3 | blimp | 11d.2 | boot | 17e.1 |
| bid | 10f.2 | blind | 37b.3 | booth | 21e.1 |
| bid | 42c.4 | blindfold | 53a.4 | border | 14b.1 |
| big | 3a.3 | blindness | 37b.3.1 | boron | 59a.3 |
| bike | 11a.4 | blink | 53b.3 | borrow | 36a.3 |
| bill | 4L.4 | bliss | 10d.6 | boss | 1b.2 |
| billboard | 15f.2 | blizzard | 40b.1 | botanist | 1k.1 |
| billion | 3h.3 | block | 32c.2 | both | 3g.9 |
| billow | 2s.3 | blonde | 58a.2 | bother | 5i.1 |
| bin | 22a.6 | blood | 23i.1 | bottle | 22a.8 |
| bind | 22g.1 | bloodshed | 33c.2 | bottom | 14i.3.1 |
| binoculars | 8k.1 | bloom | 54b.4 | bough | 24c.1 |
| biography | 15c.2 | blossom | 24d.1 | boulevard | 11h.1 |
| biologist | 1k.1 | blot | 38c.2 | bounce | 2n.1 |
| biology | 1L.2 | blouse | 17c.1 | boundary | 14b.1 |
| birch | 24b.1 | blow | 60d.1 | bounds | 34c.1 |
| bird | 4j.1 | blubber | 23b.1 | bout | 34a.2 |

214

| | | | |
|---|---|---|---|
| chalk | 15g.2 | chill | 52a.2.1 |
| chalkboard | 15g.3 | chime | 19b.2 |
| chamber | 30a.1 | chimney | 30b.1 |
| champion | 9k.1 | chimpanzee | 4g.1 |
| championship | 34a.2 | chin | 23c.2 |
| chance | 42c.3 | china | 18b.4 |
| change | 27c.3 | chinaware | 8m.6 |
| change | 39a.4 | chinook | 40b.3 |
| channel | 16i.4 | chipmunk | 4f.3 |
| chant | 19c.3 | chips | 6d.4 |
| chapel | 21i.1 | chirp | 19d.1 |
| chapter | 35b.1 | chisel | 8e.7 |
| character | 9a.1 | chivalrous | 13a.8 |
| characteristic | 5r.3 | chlorinate | 59a.3.1 |
| charcoal | 29b.2 | chlorine | 59a.3 |
| charge | 7j.3 | chlorophyll | 24c.2 |
| chariot | 11a.6 | chocolate | 6c.4 |
| charity | 13a.1 | choice | 12j.1.1 |
| charm | 10d.2 | choke | 60c.1 |
| chart | 15e.1 | choose | 12j.1 |
| charter | 15h.2 | chop | 8g.1 |
| chase | 2h.2 | choppy | 57a.4 |
| chasm | 20c.4 | chopsticks | 8m.1 |
| chat | 10a.2 | chore | 1a.3 |
| chatter | 19c.6 | chorus | 25b.2 |
| cheap | 28e.1 | chow | 6a.1 |
| check | 28c.3 | chrysanthemum | 24d.3 |
| checkers | 34f.1 | chuckle | 19c.4 |
| cheek | 23c.2 | chug | 19e.2 |
| cheep | 19d.1 | chum | 9e.1 |
| cheer | 19c.1 | chunk | 3f.5 |
| cheerful | 5k.2 | church | 21i.1 |
| cheese | 6f.1 | churn | 6k.2 |
| chef | 1aa.1 | chute | 11h.7 |
| chemical | 59a.1 | cicada | 4k.1 |
| chemist | 1k.1 | cider | 6h.1 |
| chemistry | 1L.2 | cigar | 6o.1 |
| cherish | 5o.1 | cigarette | 6o.1 |
| cherry | 6i.3 | Cincinnati | 18d.1 |
| chess | 34f.1 | cinder | 52d.1 |
| chest | 23a.2 | cinnamon | 6g.2 |
| chestnut | 6j.4 | circle | 32b.1 |
| chew | 6m.1 | circuit | 32b.2 |
| Cheyenne | 18d.1 | circular | 32b.3 |
| Chicago | 18d.1 | circulate | 23i.3 |
| chick | 4d.1 | circulation | 2x.1 |
| chicken | 4j.3 | circulation | 23k.1.1 |
| chief | 1c.4 | circulatory | 23k.1 |
| child | 9d.2 | circumference | 3d.2 |
| childhood | 7f.3 | circumstance | 51a.3 |

| | | | |
|---|---|---|---|
| circus | 51b.4 |
| cirrocumulus | 40c.1 |
| cirrostratus | 40c.1 |
| cirrus | 40c.1 |
| citizen | 9i.3 |
| citrus | 24b.1 |
| city | 18a.3 |
| civic | 9o.3.1 |
| civil | 13a.8 |
| civilization | 25c.5 |
| civilize | 5L.3 |
| clad | 17j.3 |
| claim | 10c.4 |
| clam | 4i.3 |
| clamber | 2o.2 |
| clamp | 8h.2 |
| clang | 19e.2 |
| clank | 19e.1 |
| clap | 44c.1 |
| clarinet | 47c.1 |
| clarity | 38e.1 |
| clash | 33a.4 |
| clasp | 44b.1 |
| class | 25b.4 |
| classic | 43c.2 |
| classification | 25a.1 |
| classify | 25a.5 |
| classmate | 9e.1 |
| classroom | 21f.1 |
| clatter | 19a.3 |
| claw | 4L.5 |
| clay | 29e.1 |
| clean | 41b.1 |
| cleaner | 41c.1 |
| cleanliness | 41b.2 |
| clear | 38a.4 |
| clearing | 20a.2 |
| clearly | 31a.1 |
| clench | 44b.1 |
| cleft | 20c.3 |
| clerk | 1y.1 |
| Cleveland | 18d.1 |
| clever | 12k.4 |
| cleverly | 31g.1 |
| click | 19e.1 |
| cliff | 20d.1 |
| climate | 40a.1 |
| climax | 47a.3 |
| cling | 44b.3 |
| clinic | 21h.1 |

| | | | |
|---|---|---|---|
| clink | 19e.2 | coffee | 6h.1 | common | 7k.1 |
| clipper | 8e.5 | coin | 28c.2 | common | 42a.2 |
| cloak | 17f.2 | coke | 29a.5 | commonwealth | 25c.1 |
| clock | 7b.1 | cold | 37b.2 | commotion | 19a.3 |
| clockwise | 2k.7 | cold | 52a.2 | communicate | 10a.2 |
| clod | 29e.1 | collapse | 2p.1 | communist | 9o.1 |
| clog | 2f.5 | collar | 4n.1 | community | 25c.5 |
| clop | 19e.1 | collar | 17b.3 | compact | 3a.2 |
| close | 2u.1 | collect | 25a.5 | comparative | 27a.3 |
| close | 14k.2. | collection | 25a.1 | comparison | 27c.1 |
| closeness | 14k.2 | collective | 25a.1.2 | compartment | 22a.2 |
| closet | 30a.1 | collector | 25a.1.1 | compass | 3c.1 |
| closure | 2r.1 | college | 21f.1 | compete | 34a.2.1 |
| cloth | 17k.1 | collide | 33a.4 | competition | 34a.2 |
| clothes | 17a.1 | collie | 4b.3 | complain | 10b.2 |
| clothespin | 8h.2 | collision | 33a.1 | complaint | 10b.5 |
| clothing | 17a.1 | cologne | 17g.6 | complete | 2e.1 |
| cloud | 16d.3 | colon | 35a.3 | complete(ly) | 3k.1 |
| cloud | 40c.1 | colonial | 7f.5 | completion | 2e.1.1 |
| clover | 24e.4 | colonist | 9i.1 | complex | 55b.1 |
| cloves | 6g.2 | colony | 18a.3 | complexion | 23b.1 |
| clown | 1h.2 | color | 15i.3 | compose | 12d.1 |
| club | 25b.4 | color | 58a.3 | composer | 1g.2 |
| cluck | 19d.1 | Colorado | 18c.1 | composite | 25a.2 |
| clue | 12d.5 | colorful | 58a.3.1 | composition | 15b.1 |
| clump | 25a.4 | colorless | 58a.3.1 | compound | 25a.2 |
| clumsy | 43a.4 | colossus | 3a.3.1 | compound | 59a.1 |
| cluster | 25a.4 | colt | 4d.1 | comprehend | 12d.2 |
| clutch | 44b.1 | Columbus | 18d.1 | compress | 2r.2 |
| clutter | 41a.1 | comb | 17g.4 | compression | 2r.1 |
| coach | 1d.5 | combat | 33c.1 | compressor | 8b.2 |
| coach | 12g.2 | combination | 25a.2 | compulsive | 13b.7 |
| coal | 29b.2 | combine | 2v.2 | compute | 12d.1 |
| coarse | 57a.3 | combustion | 52c.1 | computer | 8L.2 |
| coast | 16g.2 | come | 2g.7 | comrade | 9e.1 |
| coastal | 20b.3 | comedy | 15b.2 | concave | 32b.3 |
| coat | 17f.1 | comfort | 5L.1 | concede | 36b.2 |
| coax | 10e.2 | comfortable | 5L.5 | conceit | 13b.2 |
| cob | 24e.2 | comfortable | 56a.2 | conceivably | 31b.1 |
| cobalt | 29a.3 | comet | 20h.5 | concentration | 12f.1 |
| cobbler | 1n.1 | comic | 1h.2 | concern | 5d.2 |
| cobblestone | 29b.2 | comma | 35a.3 | concert | 47b.2 |
| cock | 4j.3 | command | 10g.2 | conclude | 12d.2 |
| cockpit | 11f.4 | commandment | 15h.1 | conclusion | 39a.1 |
| cockroach | 4k.2 | comment | 10a.1 | concord | 27a.2 |
| cocoa | 6c.4 | commerce | 28c.1 | concrete | 22d.1 |
| coconut | 6i.5 | commercial | 15f.2 | concurrently | 7i.4 |
| cocoon | 4m.2 | commission | 25e.1 | condemn | 10b.8 |
| cod | 4h.2 | commit | 2d.1 | condensation | 16d.2 |
| code | 35c.2 | committee | 25e.1 | condense | 2r.2 |

| | | | | | |
|---|---|---|---|---|---|
| conduct | 47b.5 | contemplation | 12a.1 | cornerstone | 22d.1.1 |
| conductor | 1g.2 | contemporaneously | 7i.4 | cornfield | 20f.1 |
| conductor | 47b.5.1 | content | 5L.5 | corps | 25d.2 |
| cone | 32b.1 | contentment | 5L.1 | corral | 4m.1 |
| confederacy | 25c.1 | contest | 34a.2 | correct | 10b.6 |
| confederate | 9o.1 | contestant | 1d.2 | correct | 26a.3 |
| conference | 25e.2 | context | 51a.3 | correctly | 31f.1 |
| confess | 10h.1 | continent | 18b.2 | correspond | 10a.2 |
| confide | 10h.1 | continental | 18b.2.1 | correspondence | 15f.1 |
| confidence | 13e.1.1 | continual | 7k.1 | corridor | 30a.2 |
| confident | 13e.1 | continue | 7k.7 | cosmetics | 17g.7 |
| conflict | 33c.1 | continuous | 7k.1 | cost | 28b.2 |
| confront | 10b.6 | contract | 15h.2 | costly | 28e.1 |
| confuse | 12g.5 | contraction | 2r.1 | costume | 17a.1 |
| confusion | 5n.3 | contractor | 1p.1 | cot | 30d.5 |
| congregation | 25e.3 | contraption | 8a.2 | cottage | 21b.1 |
| congress | 25c.3 | contrariwise | 27d.2 | cotton | 17k.3 |
| congressman | 1c.1 | contrastingly | 27d.2 | cottonwood | 24b.1 |
| congresswoman | 1c.1 | contribute | 33d.1 | couch | 30d.3 |
| congratulate | 10d.4 | contribution | 28a.4 | cougar | 4b.1 |
| congratulations | 10d.3 | control | 10g.5 | cough | 19c.2 |
| congruent | 42a.2 | convenience | 56a.1 | could | 50c.1 |
| conjunction | 35b.4 | convenient | 56a.2 | couldn't | 46a.1 |
| connect | 2v.2 | convent | 21i.1 | council | 25e.1 |
| Connecticut | 18c.1 | convention | 25e.2 | councilor | 1c.1 |
| connection | 2v.1 | conversation | 10a.3 | counselor | 1i.2 |
| conquer | 36d.1 | converse | 10a.2 | counselor | 1y.1 |
| conquest | 36d.3 | conversely | 27d.2 | count | 49d.1.2 |
| conscience | 12a.1 | convert | 10e.1 | countdown | 3d.3 |
| conscious | 12e.1 | convex | 32b.3 | counter | 30d.2 |
| consent | 10g.4 | convey | 10c.2 | counterclockwise | 2x.7 |
| consequence | 39a.1 | conveyor | 11b.3 | countless | 3g.4 |
| consequently | 39b.2 | convince | 10e.1 | country | 18b.1 |
| consider | 12a.3 | cook | 6k.1 | country | 25c.2 |
| consideration | 13a.2 | cookbook | 15c.3 | countryman | 9i.4 |
| console | 5L.4 | cookie | 6c.2 | couple | 3g.9 |
| consonant | 35b.2 | cool | 52a.2 | courage | 13n.2 |
| constant | 7k.1 | coop | 4m.1 | courageous | 13n.4 |
| constellation | 20h.4 | cooperate | 10g.4 | course | 11h.8 |
| constitution | 15h.2 | copilot | 1v.1 | court | 21g.2 |
| constitutional | 15h.2.1 | copper | 29a.1 | courteous | 13a.8 |
| construct | 22f.3 | copra | 6i.5 | courtesy | 13a.2 |
| construction | 21a.1 | copy | 15i.2 | courtyard | 20g.1 |
| construction | 22f.1 | copy | 27a.6 | cousin | 9n.9 |
| consul | 1c.1 | coral | 29b.1 | cove | 16f.3 |
| consult | 10f.2 | cord | 8h.4 | cover | 22b.1 |
| consume | 6m.2 | cork | 22b.1 | cover | 30f.1 |
| contact | 44a.1.1 | corkscrew | 8m.4 | cow | 4e.3 |
| container | 22a.1 | corn | 6j.3 | cowboy | 1f.3 |
| contaminate | 41a.1.1 | corner | 14b.1 | cower | 5c.1 |

| | | | | | | | |
|---|---|---|---|---|---|---|---|
| cowgirl | 1f.3 | critical | 26c.1 | curiosity | 12f.1 |
| cowhand | 1f.3 | criticism | 10b.5 | curiously | 31c.1 |
| coyote | 4b.2 | criticize | 12j.2 | curl | 32b.2 |
| cozy | 5L.5 | critter | 4a.1 | current | 7g.4 |
| crab | 4i.2 | croak | 19d.1 | current | 16f.4 |
| crack | 20c.3 | crocodile | 4c.3 | curry | 6g.2 |
| cracker | 6d.4 | crooked | 32d.2 | curse | 10b.4 |
| crackle | 19e.2 | crop | 6b.2 | curtain | 30e.2 |
| cradle | 30d.5 | croquet | 34b.2 | curtsy | 48e.1 |
| craft | 1a.2 | cross | 32d.1 | curvature | 32b.2 |
| craftsman | 1a.1 | crossroad | 11h.2 | curve | 32b.2 |
| crag | 20d.2 | crouch | 2q.1 | cushion | 30f.1 |
| cram | 2r.3 | crow | 4j.1 | custard | 6c.3 |
| cramp | 2r.3 | crowbar | 8e.3 | custodian | 1r.1 |
| cranberry | 6i.3 | crowd | 25b.1 | custom | 12L.1 |
| crane | 4j.4 | crown | 17d.1 | customary | 7k.1 |
| crank | 8j.2 | crude | 29c.1 | customary | 42a.2 |
| crash | 33a.1 | cruel | 5f.1.1 | customer | 1m.1 |
| crate | 22a.3 | cruelty | 5f.1 | cut | 8g.4 |
| crater | 20c.4 | cruise | 11g.1 | cute | 43c.1 |
| crave | 5q.1 | crumb | 3f.5 | cutter | 1f.5 |
| crawl | 48b.1 | crumble | 2r.4 | cycle | 7d.1 |
| crayfish | 4i.2 | crumple | 2r.4 | cyclone | 40b.3 |
| crayon | 15g.2 | crunch | 19e.1 | cylinder | 32b.1 |
| crazy | 13o.1 | crush | 33a.3 | czar | 1c.3 |
| creak | 19e.1 | crystal | 29b.1 |
| cream | 6f.1 | cry | 19c.5 |
| crease | 20c.3 | cub | 4d.1 |
| create | 12d.1 | cube | 32c.2 | **D** |
| creative | 12k.5 | cubic | 32c.2.1 | dab | 44a.2 |
| creature | 4a.1 | cuckoo | 4j.2 | dad | 9n.3 |
| credit | 28a.6 | cucumber | 6j.1 | daddy | 9n.3 |
| creek | 16f.1 | cuff | 17b.3 | daffodil | 24d.3 |
| creep | 48b.1 | culminate | 2e.1 | dagger | 8f.2 |
| cremation | 54a.4 | cult | 25c.6 | daily | 7k.5 |
| crest | 20d.2 | cultivate | 29f.1 | dainty | 43d.1.1 |
| crevasse | 20c.4 | cultivation | 29f.1.1 | dairy | 21L.1 |
| crevice | 20c.4 | culture | 25c.5 | daisy | 24d.3 |
| crew | 25b.5 | cumulonimbus | 40c.1 | dale | 20e.1 |
| crib | 30d.5 | cumulus | 40c.1 | Dallas | 18d.1 |
| cricket | 4k.2 | cuneiform | 35c.1 | dam | 16i.4 |
| crime | 26a.2 | cunning | 12k.1.1 | damage | 33a.3 |
| criminal | 9g.5 | cunningly | 31g.1 | dame | 9b.1 |
| crimson | 58a.1 | cup | 8m.5 | damp | 16b.8 |
| crinkle | 2r.4 | cupboard | 30d.4 | dance | 47b.3 |
| cripple | 37e.2 | cupcake | 6c.2 | dance | 48a.1 |
| crisis | 40d.2 | cupful | 3e.5 | dancer | 1h.1 |
| crisp | 57a.3 | curb | 30c.1 | dandelion | 24d.3 |
| crisscross | 32d.1 | cure | 33d.6 | dandy | 26c.4 |
| critic | 1e.2 | curious | 13p.1 | danger | 56b.2 |

| | | | | | | |
|---|---|---|---|---|---|
| dangerous | 56b.3 | deerskin | 4L.1 | derrick | 11b.3 |
| dangle | 2b.2 | defeat | 36d.1 | descend | 2p.1 |
| dare | 10b.10 | defend | 33d.7 | descendant | 9n.2 |
| dark | 38c.1.1 | defendant | 1y.1 | descent | 2p.1.1 |
| darken | 38c.2 | defense | 34c.5 | describe | 10c.1 |
| darken | 41a.2 | defensive | 5m.2 | deserve | 5q.1 |
| darkness | 38c.1 | define | 12i.2 | design | 12d.1 |
| darling | 9e.2 | definite | 42c.1 | design | 17i.1 |
| darn | 17i.2 | definitely | 31a.1 | designer | 1g.1 |
| dart | 8n.5 | definition | 12i.1 | desirable | 26c.3 |
| dash | 7j.3 | degree | 3e.4 | desire | 5q.1 |
| data | 3h.2 | Delaware | 18c.1 | desk | 30d.2 |
| date | 7a.1.1 | delay | 2b.4 | Des Moines | 18d.1 |
| daughter | 9n.6 | delegate | 1c.1 | desolate | 20b.5 |
| dawn | 7c.1 | deliberate | 12a.3 | despair | 5h.1 |
| day | 7c.1 | delicacy | 6b.1 | desperate | 5b.3 |
| daydream | 12e.3 | delicate | 57b.4 | desperation | 5b.1 |
| daylight | 38a.1 | delicious | 6L.2 | despise | 5e.3 |
| daytime | 7a.1 | delight | 5k.1 | despite | 27d.4 |
| daze | 12e.3 | delightful | 26c.4 | dessert | 6a.3 |
| dazzle | 38b.1 | delightfully | 31e.1 | destination | 2g.1.1 |
| deacon | 1w.1 | deliver | 2i.7 | destroy | 33a.3 |
| dead | 54a.3.1 | delta | 16f.2 | destroyer | 11e.3 |
| deadly | 33b.4 | demand | 10g.2 | destruction | 33c.2 |
| deaf | 37b.3 | democracy | 25c.1 | destructive | 5f.2 |
| deafening | 19a.5 | democratic | 9o.3 | detail | 25d.2 |
| dear | 26c.6 | demon | 9f.4 | detect | 12g.3 |
| death | 54a.1 | demonstrate | 10c.1 | detective | 1j.1 |
| debate | 10b.5 | demonstration | 10a.1 | determination | 13b.2 |
| debt | 28b.2 | den | 30a.1 | determine | 12d.2 |
| decade | 7d.3 | denominator | 49c.2 | detour | 11h.1 |
| decay | 6k.3 | denounce | 10b.8 | Detroit | 18d.1 |
| deceive | 10b.3 | dense | 32f.2 | develop | 22f.4 |
| December | 7e.1 | density | 32f.2.1 | develop | 27c.3 |
| decide | 12j.1 | dent | 33a.2 | developed | 20b.4 |
| decimal | 3h.2 | dentist | 1u.1 | development | 22f.4.1 |
| decimeter | 3e.1 | Denver | 18d.1 | development | 51a.1 |
| decision | 12j.1.1 | deny | 10g.7 | device | 8e.1 |
| deck | 11f.3 | depart | 2g.4 | devil | 9f.4 |
| declaration | 10a.1 | department | 3f.6 | devote | 5o.3 |
| declare | 10c.4 | departure | 2g.1 | devotion | 13n.1 |
| decline | 10g.7 | dependability | 13b.1 | devour | 6m.2 |
| decorate | 30e.1.1 | dependable | 13b.5 | dew | 16d.1 |
| decoration | 30e.1 | dependent | 13d.2 | dewdrop | 16d.1 |
| decrease | 3g.7 | deposit | 2i.7 | diagonal | 14c.1 |
| dedicate | 10d.6 | depot | 21j.1 | diagram | 15e.1 |
| deep | 32f.2 | depress | 5i.1 | dial | 8i.1 |
| deepen | 32f.3 | depth | 32f.2.1 | dialect | 35a.2 |
| deeply | 3k.2 | derby | 34a.2 | dialogue | 10a.3 |
| deer | 4e.1 | derive | 12d.1 | diameter | 3d.2 |

| | | | | | | |
|---|---|---|---|---|---|---|---|
| diamond | 29b.1 | disagreeable | 5g.1 | disturb | 5i.1 |
| diaphragm | 23h.1 | disappear | 2g.5 | disturbance | 33c.1 |
| diary | 15f.1 | disappoint | 10b.3 | disturbingly | 31e.1 |
| dictation | 1c.4 | disappointingly | 31e.1 | ditch | 20c.2 |
| dictator | 1c.4 | disappointment | 5h.1 | dive | 16b.6 |
| diction | 35a.2 | disarray | 55b.2 | diver | 1d.4 |
| dictionary | 15c.4 | disaster | 40d.2 | divide | 49d.1.2 |
| did | 50b.1 | disastrous | 40d.2.1 | dividend | 28a.6 |
| die | 54a.3 | disbelief | 5j.1 | divine | 13j.1 |
| diesel | 8b.3 | discard | 36a.2 | divisible | 49d.1.1 |
| diet | 6b.4 | discontent | 5d.3 | division | 49d.1 |
| differ | 27c.2.1 | discharge | 2s.4 | divisor | 49c.2 |
| difference | 27c.1 | disconnect | 2w.1 | dizzy | 37c.2 |
| different | 27c.2 | discount | 10b.1 | do | 2d.1 |
| difficult | 56a.3 | discourage | 10e.1 | do | 50b.1 |
| difficulty | 56a.1 | discover | 12g.3 | dock | 16i.3 |
| diffusion | 2s.1 | discoverer | 1k.2 | doctor | 1u.1 |
| dig | 8g.5 | discovery | 12d.5 | document | 15g.1 |
| digest | 23i.3 | discuss | 10a.2 | doe | 4e.1 |
| digestion | 23k.1.1 | discussion | 10a.3 | does | 50b.1 |
| digestive | 23k.1 | disdain | 5e.1 | doesn't | 46a.1 |
| digger | 1f.2 | disease | 37a.1 | dog | 4b.3 |
| digit | 3h.2 | disgrace | 10b.9 | doggie | 4b.3 |
| dignify | 5o.3 | disguise | 10b.3 | doghouse | 4m.1 |
| dignitary | 1c.1 | disgust | 5e.1 | dogsled | 11c.1 |
| dike | 16i.4 | dish | 8m.6 | doing | 50b.1 |
| diligent | 13b.7 | dishonest | 13m.1 | dollar | 28c.2 |
| dilute | 16b.7 | dishwasher | 1aa.1 | dolphin | 4h.1 |
| dim | 38e.2 | disk | 32b.1 | dolt | 9g.2 |
| dime | 28c.2 | dislike | 5e.1 | dome | 30b.3 |
| diminish | 2r.2 | disloyalty | 13n.1.1 | domestic | 30e.5 |
| dine | 6m.2 | dismal | 41a.3 | dominate | 10g.5 |
| dingo | 4b.2 | dismay | 5h.1 | dominant | 13e.1 |
| dingy | 41a.3 | dismiss | 36a.2 | dominion | 18a.6 |
| dinner | 6a.1 | disobey | 10b.1 | don | 17i.1 |
| dinnertime | 7a.1 | disorder | 55b.2 | done | 50b.1 |
| dinosaur | 4c.2 | dispatch | 2i.4 | donkey | 4e.2 |
| dioxide | 59a.2 | displace | 36a.2 | don't | 46a.1 |
| dip | 2p.3 | display | 53a.6 | doodle | 15i.1 |
| diphtheria | 37b.1 | displease | 5e.4 | doom | 40d.2 |
| dipper | 8m.3 | dispose | 36a.2 | doorbell | 19b.2 |
| direct | 10g.5 | dissatisfied | 5d.3 | doorknob | 8i.1 |
| direction | 10g.1 | dissolve | 16b.5 | doorway | 30a.2 |
| direction | 12g.1 | distance | 14a.1 | dose | 37f.2 |
| direction | 14a.1 | distant | 14k.1 | dot | 3f.1 |
| director | 1b.2 | distinct | 55a.1 | double | 3g.9 |
| directory | 25a.1 | distinctive | 55a.1 | doubt | 5n.3 |
| dirigible | 11d.2 | distract | 53b.5 | doubtful | 42c.2 |
| dirt | 29e.1 | distress | 5h.1 | doubtless | 31b.1 |
| dirty | 41a.3 | distribute | 2i.7 | dough | 6g.1 |
| disagree | 10b.1 | district | 20a.3 | doughnut | 6c.2 |

| | | | | | |
|---|---|---|---|---|---|
| embankment | 20d.2 | enlarge | 2s.2 | eternal | 7k.1 |
| embarrass | 10b.9 | enlighten | 12g.2 | eternity | 7f.2 |
| embarrassment | 5d.1 | enlist | 10e.1 | euphemism | 15a.1 |
| ember | 52d.1 | enliven | 5j.3 | evaporate | 16b.5 |
| emblem | 30e.3 | enormous | 3a.3 | evaporation | 16d.2 |
| embrace | 44b.3 | enough | 3j.4 | eve | 7c.2 |
| embroider | 17i.3 | enough | 45e.1 | evening | 7c.2 |
| embroidery | 17i.3.1 | enrage | 5e.4 | event | 51a.1 |
| embryo | 9d.1 | enrich | 33d.4 | eventual | 7h.2.1 |
| emerald | 29b.1 | enter | 14h.4 | eventually | 7h.1 |
| emergency | 40d.2 | entertain | 5k.3 | evergreen | 24b.1 |
| emotion | 5a.1 | entertainer | 1h.3 | every | 3i.1 |
| empathize | 5L.4 | entertainment | 51b.5 | everybody | 45e.1 |
| empathy | 5L.2 | enthrall | 5j.3 | everyday | 7f.1 |
| emperor | 1c.4 | enthusiasm | 13b.2 | everyone | 45e.1 |
| emphasis | 35a.2 | enthusiastic | 13b.6 | everything | 45e.1 |
| emphasize | 10c.5 | entire | 3g.3 | everywhere | 14d.1 |
| empire | 18a.6 | entire(ly) | 3k.1 | evidence | 12d.5 |
| employ | 1dd.2 | entitle | 15a.1.1 | evident | 42a.2 |
| employee | 1a.1 | entrance | 30a.2 | evidently | 31a.1 |
| employer | 1b.2 | entrust | 5o.3 | evil | 26d.2 |
| employment | 1a.2 | envelope | 15f.1 | evolve | 54b.4 |
| empress | 1c.4 | environment | 40h.2 | exact | 27a.3 |
| empty | 32g.1 | environment | 51a.3 | exactly | 3j.2 |
| enable | 33d.3 | envy | 5m.1 | exaggerate | 10b.3 |
| enamel | 58b.1 | enzyme | 37d.1 | exaggeration | 10b.11 |
| enchant | 5j.3 | epidemic | 37a.2 | examination | 10f.3 |
| encircle | 2x.5 | equal | 27a.3 | examination | 12c.1 |
| enclose | 2x.5 | equality | 27a.1 | examine | 12c.2 |
| encompass | 2x.5 | equally | 27b.2 | exasperate | 5i.1 |
| encounter | 2v.6 | equation | 49c.1 | excavate | 8g.5 |
| encourage | 10d.2 | equilateral | 32c.1.1 | exceedingly | 3k.1 |
| encyclopedia | 15c.4 | equip | 8a.1.1 | excellent | 26c.5 |
| end | 2e.1 | equipment | 8a.1 | except for | 27d.4 |
| end | 14f.1 | equivalent | 27a.3 | exceptional | 26c.5 |
| endanger | 56b.2.1 | eraser | 15g.2 | exceptionally | 3k.1 |
| endeavor | 51a.2 | erect | 32h.1 | exchange | 36a.3 |
| endless | 7k.1 | error | 26a.2 | excite | 5j.3 |
| endpoint | 14f.1 | erupt | 2s.4 | excitement | 5j.1 |
| endurance | 54b.1 | escalator | 11b.3 | exclaim | 10c.4 |
| endure | 54b.2 | escape | 36b.1 | exclamation | 10a.1 |
| enemy | 9g.3 | escort | 33d.5 | exclamatory | 35b.3 |
| energetic | 13b.6 | especially | 3j.3 | exclusively | 3j.2 |
| enforce | 10g.5.1 | essential | 26c.1 | excrete | 16b.1 |
| engine | 8b.1 | essentially | 31a.1 | excursion | 2g.2 |
| engineer | 1k.1 | establish | 22f.3 | excuse | 10g.3 |
| engrave | 15i.3 | establishment | 21a.2 | exercize | 34d.1 |
| enjoy | 5o.1 | estate | 21b.2 | exhale | 60d.1 |
| enjoyable | 5k.2 | estimate | 12d.4 | exhausted | 37c.1.1 |
| enjoyment | 5k.1 | etch | 15i.3 | exhaustion | 37c.1 |

| | | | | | | |
|---|---|---|---|---|---|---|
| genetic | 37d.1.1 | glimmer | 38a.2 | grade | 3e.4 |
| genius | 9L.1 | glimpse | 53b.3 | graduation | 51b.2 |
| gentle | 13a.3 | glint | 38a.2 | grain | 6j.3 |
| gentleman | 9c.2 | glisten | 38b.1 | gram | 3e.3 |
| gentlemen | 9c.2 | glitter | 38b.1 | grammar | 35a.1 |
| geographer | 1k.1 | gloat | 5e.3 | grand | 3a.3 |
| geographic | 20b.1 | global | 20h.1.1 | grandchildren | 9n.8 |
| geographical | 20b.1 | globe | 20h.1 | grandfather | 9n.8 |
| geography | 1L.2 | gloom | 38c.1 | grandma | 9n.8 |
| geological | 1L.2.1 | glorious | 13j.1 | grandmother | 9n.8 |
| geologist | 1k.1 | glory | 13n.6 | grandpa | 9n.8 |
| geology | 1L.2 | gloves | 17e.2 | grandparent | 9n.8 |
| geometry | 49a.1 | glow | 38b.1 | grandson | 9n.8 |
| Georgia | 18c.1 | glower | 53b.4 | granite | 29b.2 |
| geranium | 24d.3 | glue | 22g.1 | granny | 9n.8 |
| germ | 37d.1 | gnat | 4k.1 | grant | 28a.5 |
| Germany | 18b.4 | gnaw | 6m.1 | grape | 6i.2 |
| germinate | 54a.5 | gneiss | 29a.5 | grapefruit | 6i.4 |
| get | 2i.3 | go | 2g.8 | grapevine | 24e.2 |
| get | 36e.1 | goal | 34c.4 | graph | 15e.1 |
| get to | 50d.1 | goat | 4e.4 | graphite | 29a.4 |
| geyser | 16f.1 | goatskin | 4L.1 | grass | 24e.4 |
| ghost | 9f.2 | gobble | 19d.1 | grasshopper | 4k.1 |
| ghostly | 26d.2 | goblin | 9f.4 | grassland | 20e.1 |
| giant | 3a.3 | god | 9f.3 | grate | 8g.3 |
| giant | 9j.1 | goggles | 17d.2 | grateful | 13a.4 |
| giddy | 5k.2 | gold | 29a.1 | gratitude | 5o.2 |
| gift | 28a.4 | gold | 58a.1 | grave | 56b.3 |
| giggle | 19c.4 | golden | 58a.1 | gravel | 29b.2 |
| gill | 4L.7 | goldfish | 4h.3 | gray | 58a.1 |
| gimmick | 34e.1 | goldsmith | 1n.1 | graze | 4o.2 |
| gin | 6h.2 | golf | 34b.1 | grease | 8c.1 |
| ginger | 6g.2 | gondola | 11e.7 | greasy | 6L.4 |
| gingerbread | 6c.2 | gong | 19b.2 | great | 3a.3 |
| giraffe | 4e.7 | good | 26c.4 | greatly | 3k.2 |
| girl | 9b.2 | goodby | 10k.3 | greatness | 26c.6.1 |
| girlfriend | 9e.2 | good-bye | 10k.3 | greed | 5m.1 |
| give | 2i.6 | goodness | 13a.1 | greedy | 5q.2 |
| glacier | 16a.4 | goose | 4j.7 | green | 58a.1 |
| glad | 5k.2 | gorge | 6m.2 | greenery | 24a.2 |
| glance | 53b.3 | gorgeous | 43c.2 | greenhouse | 21k.1.1 |
| gland | 23j.3 | gorilla | 4g.1 | Greenland | 18b.3 |
| glare | 53b.4 | gossip | 9g.1 | greet | 10d.5 |
| glass | 8m.5 | govern | 10g.5 | greeting | 10d.1 |
| glasses | 17d.2 | government | 25c.3 | greyhound | 4b.3 |
| gleam | 38a.2 | governor | 1c.1 | grid | 25a.3 |
| glee | 5k.1 | gown | 17c.3 | griddle | 8d.1 |
| gleeful | 5k.2 | grab | 44b.1 | grieve | 5h.3 |
| glen | 20e.1 | grace | 13b.2 | grill | 6k.1 |
| glide | 11g.1 | graceful | 43a.4 | grim | 26d.4 |
| glider | 11d.2 | gracious | 13a.8 | grime | 41a.1 |

228

| | | | | | | |
|---|---|---|---|---|---|---|
| housework | 1a.3 | | | imprison | 2x.5 |
| Houston | 18d.1 | **I** | | improve | 33d.4 |
| how | 45d.1 | I | 45a.1 | impulse | 5a.1 |
| howdy | 10k.3 | ice | 16a.4 | impurity | 41a.1 |
| however | 27d.4 | iceberg | 16a.4 | in | 14h.1.1 |
| howl | 19d.1 | icebox | 8d.3 | inactive | 13c.1 |
| how's | 46d.1 | icicle | 16a.4 | in addition | 27b.2 |
| hub | 11f.1 | icy | 40e.1 | in all respects | 3k.1 |
| huckleberry | 24d.4 | I'd | 46e.1 | in any case | 27d.4 |
| huddle | 25b.5 | Idaho | 18c.1 | in any event | 27d.4 |
| hue | 58a.3 | ideal | 12L.1 | inauguration | 51b.2 |
| hug | 44b.3 | ideally | 31b.1 | incessant | 7k.1 |
| huge | 3a.3 | identical | 27a.3 | inch | 3e.1 |
| hulk | 11e.1 | idle | 13c.1 | incident | 51a.1 |
| hull | 11f.3 | idol | 9k.1 | incline | 32h.1 |
| hum | 19c.6 | if | 39b.4 | include | 2v.4 |
| human | 9a.1 | if only | 39b.4 | income | 28a.3 |
| humiliation | 5d.1 | if...then | 39b.4 | incoming | 14h.1.2 |
| hummingbird | 4j.2 | igloo | 21b.3 | in comparison | 27d.2 |
| humor | 5k.3 | ignorance | 12k.1 | incomplete | 55b.5 |
| humor | 13i.1.1 | ignorant | 12k.1.2 | incorrect | 26a.5 |
| humorous | 13i.1 | ignore | 53b.5 | incorrectly | 31f.1 |
| hump | 20d.1 | ill | 37a.1.1 | increase | 3g.7 |
| humus | 24a.2 | I'll | 46c.1 | incredible | 26c.5 |
| hundred | 3h.3 | Illinois | 18c.1 | incredibly | 31c.1 |
| hunger | 6n.1 | illness | 37a.1 | indeed | 27b.3 |
| hungry | 6n.1.1 | illuminate | 38b.2 | indefinite | 7k.2 |
| hunt | 4o.4 | illusion | 12e.3 | indefinite | 42c.2 |
| hunter | 1f.1 | illustrate | 15i.3 | indent | 15i.2 |
| hurdle | 34c.1 | illustration | 15e.1 | independence | 36b.3 |
| hurrah | 10k.1 | I'm | 46f.1 | independent | 13d.1 |
| hurricane | 40b.3 | image | 53a.1 | index | 15c.6 |
| hurry | 7j.3 | imagination | 12a.1 | Indiana | 18c.1 |
| hurt | 33b.1 | imaginative | 12k.5 | Indianapolis | 18d.1 |
| hurtle | 7j.3 | imitate | 27a.6 | indicate | 10c.2 |
| husband | 9n.7 | imitation | 27a.5 | indication | 12d.5 |
| hush | 19a.2 | immediate | 7j.5 | indicator | 12d.5 |
| husky | 43d.2 | immediately | 7i.1 | indignant | 5e.5 |
| hustle | 7j.3 | immense | 3a.3 | indignation | 5e.2 |
| hut | 21k.1 | immigrant | 9i.3.1 | indigo | 58a.1 |
| hutch | 30d.4 | impact | 39a.1 | individual | 9a.1 |
| hydrant | 16c.1 | impartial | 13n.7 | indoors | 14h.1.1 |
| hydrochloric | 59a.1.1 | impatient | 13f.1 | industrious | 13b.7 |
| hydroelectric | 61a.1.1 | imperial | 1c.4.1 | industry | 1L.1 |
| hydrogen | 59a.2 | impetus | 39a.2 | inequality | 27c.1 |
| hyena | 4b.2 | imply | 10e.3 | inertia | 2b.1 |
| hygiene | 41b.2 | import | 2i.8 | inevitably | 31c.1 |
| hymn | 15d.2 | important | 26c.1 | inexpensive | 28e.1 |
| | | impossible | 56a.3 | infant | 9d.1 |
| | | impression | 5a.1 | infect | 41a.1.1 |
| | | impressive | 26d.4 | | |

| infection | 37b.2 | instant | 7c.3 | invent | 12d.1 |
| inferno | 52c.1 | instant | 7j.5 | invention | 12d.5 |
| infinite | 3g.4 | instance | 51a.1 | inventor | 1k.2 |
| infirmary | 21h.1 | instinct | 12L.2 | invert | 2x.3 |
| inflate | 2s.2 | institute | 25e.1 | invertebrate | 4a.2 |
| influence | 10e.1 | instruct | 12g.2 | invest | 28d.1 |
| influence | 39a.4 | instruction | 10g.1 | investigate | 12c.2 |
| influenza | 37b.2 | instruction | 12g.1 | investigation | 12c.1 |
| informal | 17j.2 | instructor | 1i.1 | invite | 10d.5 |
| information | 12d.5 | insulate | 52b.1.1 | involve | 2v.4 |
| infrequent | 7k.2 | insulation | 52b.1 | inward | 14h.1.1 |
| ingredient | 6g.3 | insulator | 52b.1 | iodine | 37f.2 |
| inhabit | 54a.2 | insult | 10b.9 | ion | 61b.2 |
| inhabitant | 9i.2 | insurance | 28a.8 | Iowa | 18c.1 |
| inhale | 60d.1 | intelligence | 12k.1 | Iran | 18b.4 |
| inherit | 36e.1 | intelligent | 12k.1.1 | iron | 29a.1 |
| inheritance | 28a.5 | intense | 3k.2 | ironically | 31c.1 |
| initial | 7g.3 | intensity | 19a.6 | irregular | 7k.2 |
| initial | 2c.1.3 | intent | 39a.2 | irrigate | 29f.1 |
| initially | 7g.2 | interest | 12f.1 | irrigation | 29f.1.1 |
| initiate | 39a.3 | interim | 7d.1 | irritable | 5g.1 |
| initiation | 2c.1.1 | interior | 14h.1 | irritate | 5e.4 |
| inject | 14h.4 | internal | 14h.1.2 | is | 50a.1 |
| injure | 33b.1 | international | 25c.2.1 | is about to | 50d.1 |
| injury | 37a.1 | interpret | 12i.2 | is apt to | 50d.1 |
| ink | 15g.2 | interpretation | 10j.1 | is bound to | 50d.1 |
| inland | 14h.1.1 | interrogative | 35b.3 | is certain to | 50d.1 |
| inland | 16h.1 | interrupt | 2b.4 | is going to | 50d.1 |
| inlet | 16f.3 | interruption | 2b.4.1 | island | 16g.1 |
| inmate | 1t.1 | intersect | 2v.5 | isle | 16g.1 |
| inn | 21b.4 | intersection | 11h.2 | is liable to | 50d.1 |
| inning | 34c.4 | interval | 7d.1 | isn't | 46a.1 |
| innocence | 26a.6 | interview | 10f.2 | isolate | 5p.2 |
| innocent | 26a.6.1 | intestine | 23h.1 | isotope | 61b.2 |
| in part | 3j.5 | in that | 39b.1 | Israel | 18b.4 |
| in particular | 3j.2 | in that case | 39b.3 | issue | 15c.6 |
| inquire | 10f.2 | in the beginning | 7g.2 | is sure to | 50d.1 |
| inscribe | 15i.3 | in the end | 7h.2 | it | 45a.1 |
| inscription | 15a.2 | in the interim | 7i.4 | italicize | 15i.4 |
| insect | 4k.1 | in the least | 3j.6 | italics | 35c.1 |
| insert | 14h.4 | in the least bit | 3j.6 | Italy | 18b.4 |
| inside | 14h.1.1 | in the meantime | 7i.4 | item | 3f.3 |
| insignificant | 26d.1 | in the slightest | 3j.6 | its | 45b.1 |
| insist | 10g.2 | intrigue | 12f.1 | it's | 46d.1 |
| in some respects | 3j.5 | introduce | 2c.1 | I've | 46b.1 |
| inspect | 12c.2 | introduction | 2c.1.1 | ivory | 4L.6 |
| inspection | 12c.1 | introductory | 2c.1.3 | | |
| inspector | 1j.1 | invade | 36e.3 | | |
| inspire | 10d.2 | invaluable | 26c.5 | | |
| install | 22f.4 | invariable | 7k.1 | | |
| installation | 21a.2 | invasion | 33c.3 | | |

231

| | | | | | | | |
|---|---|---|---|---|---|---|---|
| Lansing | 18d.1 | legislative | 25c.4 | limbs | 23a.2 |
| lantern | 38d.3 | legislature | 25c.3 | lime | 6i.4 |
| lap | 23a.2 | leisure | 51b.1 | limerick | 15d.1 |
| large | 3a.3 | lemon | 6i.4 | limestone | 29b.2 |
| largely | 3j.3 | lemonade | 6h.1 | limewater | 6h.1 |
| lark | 4j.1 | lend | 36a.3 | limit | 14b.1 |
| laser | 38d.5 | length | 32f.1.1 | limp | 48a.3 |
| lash | 44a.3 | lengthen | 32f.3 | line | 32d.1 |
| lass | 9b.2 | lenient | 13a.3 | linear | 32d.2 |
| lasso | 8h.4 | lens | 8k.2 | linen | 17k.3 |
| latch | 8i.1 | leopard | 4b.1 | liner | 11e.2 |
| late | 7h.2.1 | less | 3g.10 | linger | 2b.3 |
| lately | 7g.1 | lesson | 12c.3 | lining | 17b.2 |
| later | 7h.2 | let | 10g.3 | link | 2v.2 |
| lather | 41c.2 | letter | 15f.1 | lion | 4b.1 |
| latitude | 3d.1 | letter | 35c.1 | lioness | 4b.1 |
| latter | 7h.2 | lettuce | 6j.2 | lip | 23d.1 |
| lattice | 30b.4 | level | 32h.1 | liquid | 16a.1 |
| laugh | 19c.4 | lever | 8e.3 | liquor | 6h.2 |
| laughter | 19c.1 | lever | 8j.1 | list | 25a.1 |
| launch | 11g.1 | liar | 9g.1 | listen | 19a.4 |
| lava | 29b.2 | liberate | 36b.1 | literal | 27a.3 |
| lavender | 24d.3 | liberator | 1c.4 | literally | 31a.1 |
| law | 1L.1 | librarian | 1i.1 | literature | 15b.1 |
| law | 15h.1 | library | 21f.2 | litter | 41a.1 |
| lawful | 15h.1.1 | lichen | 24e.1 | little | 3a.2 |
| lawless | 15h.1.1 | lick | 60c.1 | little | 3g.10 |
| lawnmower | 8e.5 | licorice | 6c.4 | live | 54a.2 |
| lawyer | 1y.1 | lid | 22b.1 | livelihood | 1a.2 |
| lay | 2p.2 | lie | 2q.2 | lively | 13b.6 |
| lazy | 13c.1 | lie | 10b.11 | liver | 23h.1 |
| lead | 29a.1 | life | 54a.1 | livery | 4m.1 |
| leader | 1b.3 | lifeguard | 1d.4 | lizard | 4c.3 |
| leadership | 10g.6 | lifetime | 7a.1 | llama | 4e.4 |
| leaf | 24c.1 | lift | 2o.1 | load | 2o.1 |
| league | 25e.1 | ligament | 23j.2 | loaf | 6d.3 |
| leak | 16b.3 | light | 38a.3 | loan | 36a.3 |
| lean | 2k.3 | light | 38d.3 | loaves | 6d.3 |
| lean | 32h.1.1 | light bulb | 38d.4 | lobster | 4i.2 |
| leap | 48d.1 | lighten | 38b.2 | local | 14k.2.1 |
| learn | 12g.3 | lighthouse | 16i.2 | locate | 36f.1 |
| leash | 4n.1 | lightness | 38a.3 | location | 14a.1 |
| leather | 17k.3 | lightning | 40b.4 | location | 20a.2 |
| leave | 2g.4 | like | 5o.1 | lock | 8h.5 |
| lecture | 10a.3 | like | 27a.3 | locket | 17g.5 |
| ledge | 30c.1 | likely | 42c.1 | locomotive | 11a.5 |
| left | 14e.2 | likeness | 27a.1 | locust | 24b.1 |
| leg | 23g.2 | likewise | 27b.2 | lodge | 21b.4 |
| legal | 26a.3 | lilac | 24d.3 | loft | 30a.1 |
| legendary | 42a.1 | lily | 24d.3 | log | 22c.2 |
| legion | 25d.2 | limb | 24c.1 | logger | 1f.5 |

| | | | | | | |
|---|---|---|---|---|---|---|
| logical | 12k.3 | lump | 23b.4 | man | 9c.2 |
| lollipop | 6c.3 | lunar | 20h.3.1 | manage | 10g.5 |
| lone | 3g.12 | lunch | 6a.1 | manager | 1b.2 |
| loneliness | 42b.1 | lung | 23h.1 | mane | 4L.2 |
| lonely | 5i.4 | lungfish | 4i.1 | maneuver | 12h.1 |
| long | 7k.1 | lurch | 2n.1 | manganese | 29a.4 |
| long | 32f.1 | lurk | 48b.2 | mankind | 9a.1.1 |
| longevity | 7k.3 | lust | 5m.1 | manner | 5r.2 |
| longhorn | 4e.3 | | | manor | 21b.2 |
| longitude | 3d.1 | | | mansion | 21b.2 |
| look | 53b.1 | | | mantis | 4k.1 |
| loop | 32b.2 | **M** | | mantle | 17f.2 |
| loosen | 2w.2 | ma | 9n.5 | manual | 15c.1 |
| lope | 48a.1 | ma'am | 9b.1 | manufacture | 22f.3 |
| lord | 1c.4 | macaroni | 6d.1 | manufacturer | 1p.1 |
| Los Angeles | 18d.1 | machine | 8a.1 | manuscript | 15g.1 |
| lose | 36a.1 | machinery | 8a.1 | many | 3g.8 |
| lose | 36d.1 | madame | 9b.1 | maple | 24b.1 |
| loser | 1d.1 | magazine | 15c.5 | mar | 33a.2 |
| loser | 36d.5 | magic | 34e.1 | marble | 29b.2 |
| loss | 28b.2 | magical | 34e.1.1 | March | 7e.1 |
| loss | 36d.4 | magician | 1h.2 | march | 48a.2 |
| lot | 3g.2 | magma | 29a.5 | mare | 4e.2 |
| lot | 20a.1 | magnificent | 26c.5 | margarine | 6f.1 |
| lotion | 41c.2 | magnify | 2s.2 | margin | 14b.1 |
| loud | 19a.5 | mahogany | 24b.1 | marigold | 24d.3 |
| loudspeaker | 19b.1 | maid | 1z.1 | marines | 25d.1 |
| Louisiana | 18c.1 | maiden | 9b.2 | market | 21d.2 |
| Louisville | 18d.1 | mail | 2i.4 | maroon | 5p.2 |
| lounge | 2b.5 | mailbox | 30c.2 | marriage | 2v.3 |
| love | 5o.1 | mailman | 1bb.1 | marrow | 23j.3 |
| lovely | 43c.1 | main | 26c.2 | marry | 2v.2 |
| lover | 9e.2 | Maine | 18c.1 | Mars | 20h.3 |
| low | 14i.4 | mainland | 16g.2 | marsh | 16f.1 |
| lower | 2p.2 | mainly | 3j.3 | marshmallow | 6c.3 |
| lowland | 20d.1.1 | maintain | 22f.5 | marvel | 5j.2 |
| loyal | 13n.7 | maintenance | 22f.5.1 | marvelous | 26c.5 |
| loyalty | 13n.1 | maize | 6j.3 | Maryland | 18c.1 |
| lubricate | 11g.1 | majestic | 43c.2 | mason | 1x.1 |
| lubrication | 8c.1 | majesty | 1c.2 | mass | 25b.1 |
| luck | 13g.1.1 | major | 26c.2 | Massachusetts | 18c.1 |
| luckily | 31d.1 | majority | 3g.5 | massacre | 33b.2 |
| lucky | 13g.1 | make | 22f.3 | massive | 3a.3 |
| luggage | 22a.10 | malaria | 37b.1 | mast | 11f.3 |
| lukewarm | 52a.3 | male | 9c.2 | master | 1c.2 |
| lull | 19a.2 | mallard | 4j.7 | mat | 30d.5 |
| lullaby | 15d.2 | malt | 6j.3 | match | 27a.4 |
| lumber | 22c.1 | mama | 9n.5 | match | 34a.2 |
| lumberjack | 1f.5 | mamma | 9n.5 | mate | 9e.2 |
| lumberman | 1f.5 | mammal | 4a.2 | material | 17k.1 |
| luminous | 38a.4 | mammoth | 3a.3 | material | 22e.1 |

| | | | | | | |
|---|---|---|---|---|---|---|
| math | 49a.1 | merchandise | 6b.2 | millionaire | 9m.1 |
| mathematics | 49a.1 | merchant | 1m.2 | millionth | 3h.1 |
| mathematician | 1k.1 | merciless | 5f.1.1 | Milwaukee | 18d.1 |
| mattress | 30d.5 | mercury | 29a.3 | mimic | 27a.6 |
| mature | 54b.4 | Mercury | 20h.3 | mince | 8g.3 |
| maximum | 49b.1 | mercy | 13a.1 | mind | 23c.1 |
| May | 7e.1 | mere | 3j.5 | mine | 45b.1 |
| may | 50c.1 | merge | 2v.2 | miner | 1f.2 |
| maybe | 10k.2 | meridian | 3d.2 | mingle | 2v.6 |
| maybe | 31b.1 | mermaid | 9f.1 | miniature | 3a.2 |
| mayor | 1c.1 | merry | 5k.2 | minimum | 49b.1 |
| me | 45a.1 | mesa | 20e.1 | minister | 1w.1 |
| mead | 6h.2 | message | 15f.1 | mink | 4f.2 |
| meadow | 20e.1 | messenger | 1bb.1 | Minnesota | 18c.1 |
| meal | 6a.1 | messy | 43b.1 | minnow | 4h.3 |
| mealtime | 7a.1 | metal | 29a.2 | minor | 9d.2 |
| mean | 5f.1.1 | meteor | 20h.5 | mint | 28f.1 |
| meaning | 12i.1 | meteorologist | 1k.1 | minus | 49d.1.2 |
| meanness | 5f.1 | method | 12h.1 | minute | 7c.3 |
| meanwhile | 7i.4 | metric | 3e.4 | miracle | 33d.8 |
| measure | 3b.1 | metropolitan | 20b.4 | miraculous | 13j.1 |
| measurement | 3b.1 | Mexico | 18b.4 | mirror | 11f.2 |
| meat | 6b.3 | Miami | 18d.1 | mischief | 13m.1.1 |
| mechanic | 1x.1 | mica | 29a.4 | mischievous | 13m.1 |
| mechanical | 8a.1.2 | Michigan | 18c.1 | miser | 9m.1 |
| mechanism | 8a.1 | microbe | 37d.1 | miserable | 5i.3 |
| medal | 28a.7 | microscope | 8k.1 | mishap | 33a.1 |
| median | 49b.2 | microscopic | 3a.2 | misjudge | 12j.2 |
| medicine | 1L.2 | mid | 14f.3.1 | misplace | 36a.1 |
| medicine | 37f.2 | midday | 7c.1 | miss | 5q.1 |
| medieval | 7f.5 | middle | 14f.3 | missile | 8n.2 |
| medium | 3g.9.1 | midget | 9j.1 | mission | 21i.1 |
| medula | 23c.3 | midnight | 7c.2 | missionary | 1w.1 |
| meek | 13L.1 | midst | 14f.3 | Mississippi | 18c.1 |
| meet | 2v.6 | midstream | 16h.1 | Missouri | 18c.1 |
| mellow | 5L.5 | midway | 14f.3 | misspell | 15i.2 |
| melody | 15d.2 | midwest | 14e.1 | mist | 16d.3 |
| melon | 6i.1 | might | 43a.3 | mistake | 26a.2 |
| melt | 16b.5 | might | 50c.1 | mister | 9c.2 |
| member | 3f.3 | migrate | 2g.6 | mistress | 9b.1 |
| membership | 25e.4 | migration | 2g.2 | mite | 4k.1 |
| membrane | 23b.1 | mild | 13L.1 | mitt | 17e.2 |
| memorable | 26c.3 | mild | 3j.5 | mittens | 17e.2 |
| memorial | 21m.1 | mile | 3e.1 | mix | 6g.1 |
| memorize | 12a.2 | military | 1L.1 | mixture | 25a.2 |
| memory | 12a.1 | milk | 6h.1 | moan | 19c.5 |
| Memphis | 18d.1 | milkman | 1n.2 | moat | 16i.4 |
| mend | 17i.2 | mill | 21e.2 | mob | 25b.1 |
| mention | 10c.2 | millennium | 7d.3 | mobile | 2a.1.1 |
| menu | 15c.3 | miller | 1n.3 | moccasin | 17e.1 |
| meow | 19d.1 | million | 3h.3 | mockingbird | 4j.2 |

# P

| | | | | | | | |
|---|---|---|---|---|---|---|---|
| pa | 9n.3 | parlor | 30a.1 | peach | 6i.1 |
| pack | 22g.1 | parrot | 4j.1 | peak | 20d.1 |
| package | 22a.5 | parsley | 6g.2 | peal | 19a.3 |
| packet | 22a.1 | part | 3f.3 | peanut | 6j.4 |
| paddle | 11f.3.1 | partial | 3g.13 | pear | 6i.1 |
| paddy | 20f.1 | participate | 10g.4 | peas | 6j.1 |
| pageant | 51b.3 | particle | 3f.1 | peasant | 9m.1 |
| pail | 22a.8 | particularly | 3j.2 | peat | 29e.1 |
| pain | 37c.1 | partly | 3j.5 | pebble | 29e.2 |
| painful | 37c.1.1 | partner | 9e.1 | pecan | 6j.4 |
| paint | 15i.3 | partnership | 25e.4 | peck | 8g.1 |
| paint | 58b.1 | partridge | 4j.6 | peculiar | 55a.2 |
| painter | 1g.1 | party | 51b.2 | pedal | 8j.2 |
| painting | 47d.2 | pass | 2j.1 | peddler | 1m.2 |
| pair | 3g.9 | pass | 11h.3 | peek | 53b.3 |
| pal | 9e.1 | passage | 11h.3 | peel | 8g.3 |
| pale | 38e.2 | passageway | 11h.3 | peep | 19d.1 |
| palm | 23f.2 | passenger | 9h.3 | peer | 53b.4 |
| pan | 8m.2 | passenger | 11g.2 | peg | 8h.1 |
| pancake | 6d.3 | passion | 5j.1 | pellet | 8n.2 |
| pane | 30b.4 | passive | 13c.1 | pelt | 4L.1 |
| panel | 22c.2 | past | 7f.2 | pen | 15g.2 |
| pang | 37c.1 | past | 14k.1.3 | pencil | 15g.2 |
| panic | 5b.1 | pasteurize | 41b.3 | penicillin | 37f.2 |
| pantheon | 21i.1 | pastime | 51b.1 | penmanship | 15i.6 |
| panther | 4b.1 | pastry | 6c.2 | peninsula | 16g.1 |
| pants | 17c.2 | pasture | 20f.1 | Pennsylvania | 18c.1 |
| papa | 9n.3 | pat | 44a.2 | penny | 28c.2 |
| paper | 15g.3 | patch | 17i.2 | pentagon | 32c.1 |
| paperboy | 1cc.1 | path | 11h.8 | people | 9a.1.1 |
| papoose | 9d.1 | pathway | 11h.8 | Peoria | 18d.1 |
| parade | 51b.3 | patience | 13a.1 | pepper | 6g.2 |
| paradise | 18a.2 | patient | 1u.1 | per | 49d.2 |
| paraffin | 37f.2 | patient | 13f.1 | perceive | 53b.5 |
| paragraph | 35b.1 | patio | 20g.1 | percent | 49b.2 |
| parakeet | 4j.1 | patriot | 9i.4 | percentage | 49b.2 |
| parallel | 27a.3 | patriotic | 13n.5 | perch | 4h.2 |
| parallelogram | 32c.1 | patrol | 25d.2 | perfect | 26c.2 |
| paralyze | 37e.2 | patron | 1m.1 | perfectly | 3k.1 |
| parasol | 17g.2 | pattern | 32a.1 | perform | 47a.1.1 |
| parcel | 22a.5 | pauper | 9m.1 | performance | 47a.1 |
| parch | 52a.4 | pause | 2b.3 | performer | 1h.3 |
| parchment | 15g.3 | pave | 22d.1.2 | perfume | 17g.6 |
| pardon | 5o.3 | pavement | 22d.1 | perhaps | 31b.1 |
| pare | 8g.3 | paw | 4L.5 | peril | 56b.2 |
| parent | 9n.4 | pay | 28d.1 | perilous | 56b.3 |
| parenthesis | 35a.3 | payment | 28a.4 | perimeter | 14b.1 |
| park | 20g.1 | peace | 33c.4 | period | 7d.1 |
| parliament | 25c.3 | peaceful | 5L.5 | period | 35a.3 |
| | | peacetime | 7a.1 | periodic | 7k.2 |

| | | | | | | |
|---|---|---|---|---|---|
| periscope | 8k.1 | pierce | 8g.1 | plank | 22c.2 |
| perish | 54a.3 | pig | 4e.5 | plant | 24a.1 |
| perishable | 6k.3 | pigeon | 4j.1 | plant | 29f.1 |
| permanent | 7k.1 | pigtail | 23b.3 | plantation | 21L.1 |
| permit | 10g.3 | pike | 4h.2 | platform | 8j.4 |
| perpendicular | 14c.1 | pile | 25a.4 | platoon | 25d.2 |
| perplex | 12g.5 | pilgrim | 9i.1 | platter | 8m.6 |
| persist | 7k.7 | pill | 37f.2 | platypus | 4j.7 |
| person | 9a.1 | pillow | 30f.1 | play | 5k.4 |
| personality | 5r.2 | pilot | 1v.1 | play | 34d.3 |
| perspiration | 23i.1 | pin | 8h.3 | player | 1d.2 |
| persuade | 10e.1 | pin | 17g.3 | playful | 13b.6 |
| pest | 9g.2 | pinch | 44b.2 | playground | 20g.1 |
| pet | 4a.1 | pinch | 3e.5 | playmate | 9e.1 |
| petal | 24d.1 | pine | 24b.1 | plaza | 20g.1 |
| petrify | 5b.2 | pineapple | 6i.5 | plea | 10i.1 |
| petroleum | 8c.1 | ping | 19e.1 | plead | 10e.2 |
| petticoat | 17c.3 | pink | 58a.1 | pleasant | 13a.5 |
| petunia | 24d.3 | pinpoint | 14a.2 | please | 5k.3 |
| phantom | 9f.4 | pint | 3e.5 | please | 31h.1 |
| phase | 7d.1 | pinto | 4e.2 | pleasure | 5k.1 |
| pheasant | 4j.6 | pioneer | 9i.1 | pledge | 10i.1 |
| Philadelphia | 18d.1 | pipe | 6o.1 | plenty | 3g.5 |
| philosophy | 12L.1 | pipe | 22d.2 | pliers | 8e.2 |
| Phoenix | 18d.1 | pipeline | 22d.2 | plod | 48a.2 |
| phone | 19b.1 | pirate | 9g.5 | plop | 19e.2 |
| phonograph | 8d.4 | pistil | 24d.2 | plot | 20a.1 |
| phony | 13m.1 | pistol | 8n.3 | plot | 47a.3 |
| phosphate | 59a.2 | piston | 8b.2 | plover | 4j.2 |
| phosphorus | 29a.3 | pit | 20c.2 | plow | 29f.1 |
| photo | 47d.2 | pitch | 2j.1 | pluck | 44b.2 |
| photograph | 47d.2 | pitch | 19a.6 | plug | 22b.1 |
| photographer | 1g.1 | pitchblende | 29a.4 | plum | 6i.2 |
| photography | 47d.2.1 | pitcher | 22a.8 | plumber | 1x.1 |
| photon | 61b.2 | pith | 24c.2 | plume | 4L.3 |
| phrase | 35b.1 | pitiful | 26d.1 | plummet | 2p.1 |
| physics | 1L.2 | Pittsburgh | 18d.1 | plump | 43d.2 |
| physical | 23a.1.1 | pity | 5L.2 | plunge | 2p.1 |
| physician | 1u.1 | pivot | 2x.4 | plunk | 19e.2 |
| pi | 49c.2 | place | 2i.6 | plural | 3g.14 |
| piano | 47c.1 | place | 14a.2 | plus | 49d.1.2 |
| pick | 12j.1 | place | 20a.2 | Pluto | 20h.3 |
| pick | 44b.2 | plague | 37a.2 | plywood | 22c.1 |
| picker | 1f.4 | plaid | 17k.3 | pocket | 17b.3 |
| pickle | 6j.1 | plain | 55b.6 | pod | 24d.1 |
| pickup | 11a.2 | plainly | 31a.1 | pod | 25b.3 |
| picnic | 6a.2 | plan | 12b.2 | poem | 15d.1 |
| picture | 47d.2 | plane | 11d.1 | poet | 1e.2 |
| piece | 3f.3 | planet | 20h.3 | poetic | 15d.1.1 |
| pier | 16i.3 | planetarium | 21f.3 | poetry | 15d.1 |

| | | | | | |
|---|---|---|---|---|---|
| point | 14a.2 | pose | 17i.1.1 | present | 10c.4 |
| point | 44c.1 | position | 14a.1 | present | 14L.1.1 |
| pointer | 8j.5 | possess | 36c.2 | presently | 7i.1 |
| poise | 13b.2 | possibly | 31b.1 | preserve | 22f.5 |
| poison | 37f.2 | possession | 36c.1 | president | 1c.4 |
| poisonous | 33b.4 | possessive | 5m.2 | presidential | 1c.4.1 |
| polar | 20b.2 | post | 22d.3 | press | 15g.2 |
| pole | 22d.3 | postage | 28c.4 | pressure | 2t.1 |
| police | 25d.1 | postcard | 15f.1 | presumably | 31b.1 |
| policeman | 1j.1 | poster | 15f.2 | pretend | 12e.6 |
| policewoman | 1j.1 | postmaster | 1bb.1 | pretty | 43c.1 |
| policy | 15h.2 | pot | 8m.2 | prevail | 36d.2 |
| polio | 37b.1 | potassium | 29a.4 | prevent | 2f.2 |
| polish | 41b.1 | potato | 6j.1 | prevention | 56b.1 |
| polite | 13a.8 | potter | 1g.1 | preview | 15i.5 |
| political | 25c.4 | pottery | 30e.4 | previous | 7g.3 |
| politician | 1c.1 | pouch | 4L.7 | price | 28b.2 |
| politics | 1L.1 | poultry | 6e.1 | prick | 8g.1 |
| polo | 34b.1 | pounce | 48d.1 | prickly | 57a.3 |
| pollen | 24d.2 | pound | 3e.3 | pride | 13e.1.1 |
| pollinate | 24e.3 | pound | 44a.3 | priest | 1w.1 |
| pollination | 24e.3.1 | pour | 16b.4 | primary | 26c.1 |
| pollute | 41a.1.1 | poverty | 28b.3 | primate | 4a.2 |
| pollution | 41a.1 | powder | 29e.2 | primer | 15c.1 |
| polygon | 32c.1 | power | 13n.6 | primitive | 7f.5 |
| pond | 16f.1 | powerful | 43a.2 | prince | 1c.3 |
| ponder | 12a.3 | practically | 3j.7 | princess | 1c.3 |
| pony | 4e.2 | praise | 10d.3 | principal | 1i.1 |
| poodle | 4b.3 | prance | 48a.1 | principle | 12d.5 |
| pooh | 10k.1 | pray | 10d.6 | printer | 1q.1 |
| pool | 16i.4 | prayer | 10d.6.1 | prior to | 7g.5 |
| poor | 28e.2 | preach | 10d.6 | prism | 32c.2 |
| pop | 6h.1 | precious | 26c.6 | prison | 21c.2 |
| popcorn | 6j.3 | precipice | 20d.2 | prisoner | 1t.1 |
| pope | 1w.1 | precisely | 3j.2 | privacy | 42b.1 |
| poplar | 24b.1 | predicate | 35b.4 | private | 42b.2 |
| poppy | 24d.3 | predict | 12d.3 | prize | 28a.7 |
| popular | 42a.1 | predictably | 31c.1 | probable | 42c.1 |
| porcelain | 22d.1 | prediction | 10b.7 | probably | 31b.1 |
| porch | 30a.1 | prediction | 12d.3.1 | probe | 12c.2 |
| porcupine | 4f.3 | prefer | 5o.1 | proceed | 2g.8 |
| pork | 6e.1 | preferably | 31h.1 | procedure | 12h.1 |
| porous | 57a.3 | prefix | 35b.2 | process | 12h.1 |
| porpoise | 4h.1 | prehistoric | 7f.5 | process | 51a.1 |
| porridge | 6d.2 | premises | 20a.2 | procession | 51b.3 |
| porter | 1v.1 | prepare | 22f.4 | proclaim | 10c.4 |
| portion | 3f.3 | preposition | 35b.4 | proclamation | 10a.1 |
| Portland | 18d.1 | prescription | 37f.2 | prod | 44a.2 |
| portrait | 47d.2 | presence | 14L.1 | produce | 22f.3 |
| portray | 53a.6 | present | 2i.7 | producer | 1b.4 |
| portrayal | 53a.1 | present | 7f.2 | production | 1a.3 |

241

| | | | |
|---|---|---|---|
| rainfall | 16a.2 | reason | 39a.2 |
| rainstorm | 40b.2 | reasonably | 31g.1 |
| raise | 2o.1 | rebel | 10b.1 |
| raisin | 6i.2 | rebuild | 22f.5 |
| rake | 8e.6 | recall | 12a.4 |
| ram | 4e.4 | recede | 2g.4 |
| ramble | 48a.1 | receipt | 28c.3 |
| ramp | 11h.7 | receive | 36e.1 |
| ranch | 21L.1 | receiver | 19b.1 |
| rancher | 1f.3 | recent | 7g.4 |
| rand | 28c.2 | receptionist | 1o.2 |
| random | 42c.2 | recipe | 15c.3 |
| range | 20d.1 | recite | 15d.2.1 |
| ranger | 1f.3 | reckless | 13o.1 |
| rank | 3b.1 | reckon | 12a.3 |
| rap | 44a.2 | recognition | 53a.3 |
| rapid | 7j.4 | recognize | 53b.5 |
| rare | 7k.2 | recommend | 10e.3 |
| rare | 55a.1 | record | 10j.1.1 |
| rascal | 9g.2 | recorder | 47c.1 |
| rasp | 8e.7 | recording | 10j.1 |
| raspberry | 6i.3 | recover | 33d.6 |
| rat | 4f.2 | recreation | 34a.1 |
| rate | 3b.1 | rectangle | 32c.1 |
| rather | 3j.4 | rectangular | 32c.1.1 |
| ratify | 12j.3 | red | 58a.1 |
| ratio | 49b.2 | reduce | 2r.2 |
| ration | 3f.3 | redwood | 24b.1 |
| rattle | 19e.1 | reed | 24e.4 |
| rattlesnake | 4c.1 | reef | 16f.2 |
| raven | 4j.2 | reelect | 51c.2 |
| ravenous | 6n.1.1 | referee | 1d.5 |
| ravine | 20c.1 | refinery | 21e.2 |
| raw | 6L.4 | reflect | 38b.2 |
| ray | 38d.5 | reflection | 53a.1 |
| rayon | 17k.3 | reform | 27c.3 |
| razor | 8f.2 | reformatory | 21c.2 |
| razor | 17g.4 | refrigerator | 8d.3 |
| react | 2d.3 | refresh | 33d.2 |
| reaction | 2d.3.1 | refreshingly | 31e.1 |
| reactor | 21f.3 | refreshment | 6a.3 |
| read | 15i.5 | refuel | 11g.1 |
| ready | 7g.4.1 | refuge | 21c.1 |
| realistic | 26a.1.1 | refuse | 10g.7 |
| reality | 26a.1 | regain | 36e.1 |
| realize | 12g.3 | regard | 5o.1 |
| really | 31a.1 | regardless of | 27d.4 |
| reaper | 11b.1 | regiment | 25d.2 |
| reappear | 53b.2 | region | 20a.3 |
| rear | 14f.1 | regret | 5h.3 |
| rearrange | 22f.5 | regretably | 31e.1 |

| | | | |
|---|---|---|---|
| regular | 7k.1 | | |
| regular | 42a.2 | | |
| regulate | 10g.5 | | |
| regulation | 15h.1 | | |
| rehearsal | 47a.1 | | |
| rein | 4n.1 | | |
| reindeer | 4e.1 | | |
| reject | 10g.7 | | |
| rejoice | 5j.3 | | |
| relate | 10c.2 | | |
| related | 27a.3 | | |
| relative | 9n.2 | | |
| relax | 2b.5 | | |
| relay | 2i.4 | | |
| release | 36b.1 | | |
| relent | 7k.7 | | |
| reliable | 13b.5 | | |
| reliability | 13b.1 | | |
| relief | 5L.1 | | |
| relieve | 33d.2 | | |
| religion | 1L.1 | | |
| religious | 13j.1 | | |
| reluctant | 13L.1 | | |
| remain | 2b.3 | | |
| remain | 50e.1 | | |
| remainder | 49c.2 | | |
| remark | 10a.1 | | |
| remarkable | 26c.5 | | |
| remarkably | 31c.1 | | |
| remedy | 37f.1 | | |
| remember | 12a.4 | | |
| remind | 10b.6 | | |
| remote | 14k.1 | | |
| remove | 2i.5 | | |
| rename | 15a.1.1 | | |
| Reno | 18d.1 | | |
| repair | 22f.5 | | |
| repairman | 1x.1 | | |
| repay | 28d.1 | | |
| repeal | 12j.3 | | |
| repeat | 7k.7.1 | | |
| repel | 36d.2.1 | | |
| replace | 22f.5 | | |
| replace | 27a.6 | | |
| replacement | 27a.5 | | |
| reply | 10f.1 | | |
| report | 15f.1 | | |
| reporter | 1e.2 | | |
| reportedly | 31b.1 | | |
| represent | 12i.2 | | |
| represent | 53a.6 | | |

| | | | | | | | |
|---|---|---|---|---|---|---|---|
| representation | 53a.1 | Rhode Island | 18c.1 | rod | 22d.3 |
| reproduce | 54a.5 | rhyme | 15d.1 | rodent | 4f.3 |
| reproduction | 54a.1 | rib | 23j.1 | rodeo | 51b.4 |
| reproductive | 23k.1 | ribbon | 17g.1 | role | 1a.2 |
| reptile | 4c.1 | rice | 6j.3 | roller | 8j.3 |
| republic | 25c.1 | rich | 28e.2 | romp | 48a.1 |
| republican | 9o.3 | Richmond | 18d.1 | roof | 30b.3 |
| require | 10g.2 | rickets | 37b.1 | room | 30a.1 |
| rescue | 33d.7 | rid | 2i.5 | rooster | 4j.3 |
| research | 12c.2 | ride | 11g.1 | root | 24e.2 |
| researcher | 1k.2 | rider | 11g.2 | rope | 8h.4 |
| resemblance | 27a.1 | ridge | 14b.1 | rose | 24d.3 |
| resemble | 27a.4 | ridge | 20d.2 | rot | 6k.3 |
| resent | 5e.3 | ridicule | 10b.9 | rotate | 2x.2 |
| reservoir | 16i.4 | ridiculous | 26d.5 | rotation | 2x.1 |
| resident | 9i.2 | rifle | 8n.3 | rotor | 11f.4 |
| resign | 1dd.3 | rift | 20c.3 | rotten | 6L.4 |
| resin | 24c.2 | right | 14e.2 | rough | 57a.3 |
| resist | 2f.4 | right | 26a.3 | roughly | 3j.1 |
| resolution | 10a.1 | rightful | 26a.3 | round | 32b.3 |
| resolve | 12d.1 | rightly | 31f.1 | roundworm | 4k.2 |
| resort | 18a.3 | rigid | 57a.2 | route | 11h.3 |
| respect | 5o.1 | rim | 14b.1 | rove | 2g.6 |
| respectful | 13a.8 | ring | 17g.5 | rover | 9h.2 |
| respiratory | 23k.1 | ring | 19e.1 | row | 11g.1 |
| respond | 10f.1 | rink | 21g.2 | rowboat | 11e.7 |
| responsible | 13b.5 | riot | 33c.2 | rubber | 24c.2 |
| responsibility | 13b.3 | rip | 17i.4 | rubbish | 41a.1 |
| rest | 2b.5 | ripe | 6L.3 | ruby | 29b.1 |
| restless | 13c.2 | ripen | 6k.3 | rudder | 11f.3.1 |
| restore | 22f.5 | ripple | 16b.1 | rude | 5g.1 |
| restaurant | 21d.3 | rise | 2o.2 | ruffle | 17b.3 |
| result | 39a.1 | risk | 56b.2 | rug | 30e.2 |
| retain | 36f.2 | rival | 9g.3 | rugged | 43a.1 |
| retina | 23e.2 | river | 16f.1 | ruin | 33a.3 |
| retire | 1dd.3 | riverside | 16g.2 | rule | 15h.1 |
| retort | 10f.1 | rivet | 8h.1 | ruler | 3c.1 |
| retreat | 21c.1 | road | 11h.1 | rumble | 33c.1 |
| return | 2i.2 | roadside | 11h.1.1 | rumor | 10b.11 |
| revenge | 5e.1 | roadway | 11h.1 | run | 48a.1 |
| revenue | 28c.1 | roam | 2g.6 | runaway | 9h.2 |
| revere | 5o.1 | roar | 19c.1 | runner | 1d.4 |
| reverse | 2x.3 | roast | 6k.1 | runt | 9j.1 |
| review | 53b.5 | rob | 36e.4 | runway | 11h.10 |
| revive | 33d.6 | robber | 9g.5 | rural | 20b.4 |
| revolt | 10b.1 | robe | 17c.3 | rush | 7j.3 |
| revolution | 33c.2 | robin | 4j.1 | rust | 29d.1 |
| revolve | 2x.2 | robot | 8L.2 | rustle | 19e.1 |
| revolver | 8n.3 | rock | 29b.2 | rustler | 9g.5 |
| reward | 28a.5 | rocker | 30d.3 | rut | 20c.3 |
| rewrite | 15i.2 | rocket | 11d.3 | rye | 6j.3 |

# S

| | | | | | | | |
|---|---|---|---|---|---|---|---|
| sac | 4L.7 | saucer | 8m.6 | scramble | 2s.5 |
| sack | 22a.7 | saunter | 48a.2 | scrap | 3f.5 |
| sacred | 13j.1 | sausage | 6e.1 | scrapbook | 15g.1 |
| sacrifice | 36b.2 | save | 33d.7 | scrape | 8g.2 |
| sad | 5h.2 | savings | 28a.1 | scraper | 8e.7 |
| saddle | 4n.1 | savior | 9k.1 | scratch | 8g.2 |
| sadly | 31d.1 | saw | 8e.5 | scrawny | 43a.5 |
| sadness | 5h.1 | sawdust | 29e.2 | screech | 19c.3 |
| safari | 2g.2 | sawmill | 21e.2 | screen | 30c.2 |
| safe | 28f.1 | say | 10c.2 | screw | 8h.1 |
| safe | 56b.4 | scale | 3c.1 | screwdriver | 8e.2 |
| safety | 56b.1 | scallop | 4i.3 | scribble | 15i.1 |
| sag | 2p.3 | scalp | 23b.1 | scribe | 1q.1 |
| sage | 9L.1 | scamper | 48a.1 | script | 15b.2 |
| sail | 11g.1 | scan | 15i.5 | scripture | 15c.4 |
| sailboat | 11e.6 | scant | 3g.13 | scroll | 15g.3 |
| saint | 9f.3 | scar | 23b.4 | scrub | 41b.1 |
| salad | 6d.6 | scarce | 55a.1 | scud | 40b.2 |
| salary | 28a.3 | scarcely | 3j.6 | scuff | 8g.2 |
| sale | 28d.3 | scarcity | 3g.11 | scuffle | 33c.1 |
| salesman | 1m.2 | scare | 5b.2 | sculptor | 1g.1 |
| saliva | 23i.1 | scarf | 17g.1 | sculpture | 47d.2 |
| salivary | 23k.1 | scatter | 2s.5 | scum | 16e.2 |
| salmon | 4h.2 | scene | 47a.2 | scurry | 7j.3 |
| salt | 6g.2 | scene | 53a.2 | scurvy | 37b.1 |
| Salt Lake City | 18d.1 | scenery | 47a.4 | scuttle | 11g.1 |
| salute | 44c.1 | scent | 17L.1 | scythe | 8e.5 |
| same | 27a.3 | scheme | 12b.2 | sea | 16f.3 |
| sample | 3f.4 | scholar | 9L.1 | seacoast | 16g.2 |
| San Antonio | 18d.1 | scholarship | 28a.5 | seafaring | 11e.9 |
| sand | 29e.2 | school | 21f.1 | seafood | 6b.3 |
| sandal | 17e.1 | schoolhouse | 21f.1 | seagoing | 11e.9 |
| sandpaper | 8e.7 | schoolroom | 21f.1 | seal | 4h.1 |
| sandwich | 6d.5 | schoolyard | 20g.1 | seam | 17b.2 |
| San Francisco | 18d.1 | schooner | 11e.6 | seaman | 1v.1 |
| sanitation | 41b.2 | science | 1L.2 | seaport | 16i.1 |
| Santa Fe | 18d.1 | scientific | 1L.2.1 | search | 12c.2 |
| sap | 24c.2 | scientist | 1k.1 | seashore | 16g.2 |
| sardine | 4h.2 | scissors | 8e.5 | season | 7d.1 |
| sash | 17g.1 | scoff | 10b.9 | seat | 30d.3 |
| satellite | 20h.5 | scold | 10b.9 | seatbelt | 11f.2 |
| satin | 17k.3 | scoop | 8g.5 | Seattle | 18d.1 |
| satisfactory | 26a.4 | scooter | 11a.4 | seaway | 11h.9 |
| satisfy | 5L.3 | scorch | 52c.3 | seaweed | 24e.1 |
| saturate | 16b.7 | scorn | 5e.2 | second | 3h.1 |
| Saturday | 7e.2 | scornful | 5g.1 | second | 7c.3 |
| Saturn | 20h.3 | scour | 41b.1 | secondary | 3h.1.1 |
| satyr | 4c.2 | scout | 1f.3 | secrecy | 42b.1 |
| saucepan | 8m.2 | scow | 11e.5 | secret | 42b.2 |
| | | scowl | 60a.1 | secretary | 1o.2 |

| | | | | | | | |
|---|---|---|---|---|---|---|---|
| section | 3f.3 | setting | 47a.3 | shepherd | 1f.3 |
| sedan | 11a.2 | settle | 2b.5 | sheriff | 1j.1 |
| sediment | 16e.1 | settlement | 18a.3 | she's | 46d.1 |
| sedimentary | 29c.1 | settler | 9i.1 | shield | 17h.1 |
| see | 53b.1 | seven | 3h.3 | shift | 2m.1 |
| seed | 6j.4 | seventeen | 3h.3 | shilling | 28c.2 |
| seed | 24d.2 | seventeenth | 3h.1 | shimmer | 38b.1 |
| seek | 5q.1 | seventh | 3h.1 | shine | 38b.1 |
| seem | 50e.1 | seventy | 3h.3 | shingle | 22c.2 |
| seemingly | 31b.1 | several | 3g.5 | shiny | 38a.4 |
| seems to | 50d.1 | severe | 55a.2 | ship | 2i.4 |
| seep | 16b.1 | sew | 17i.2 | ship | 11e.1 |
| seethe | 5e.3 | sewage | 41a.1 | shipbuilding | 11e.8 |
| segment | 3f.3 | sewer | 30c.1 | shipload | 22a.5.1 |
| seismograph | 3c.1 | shabby | 57b.3 | shipment | 22a.5.1 |
| seize | 36e.4 | shack | 21k.1 | shipwreck | 11e.8 |
| seldom | 7k.6 | shade | 38c.1 | shipyard | 16i.1 |
| select | 12j.1 | shadow | 38c.1 | shirt | 17c.1 |
| selection | 12j.1.1 | shady | 38c.1.1 | shiver | 2L.1 |
| self | 9a.1 | shaft | 20c.2 | shoal | 16f.2 |
| selfish | 5q.2 | shaggy | 57a.5 | shock | 5b.1 |
| sell | 28d.2 | shake | 2L.1 | shoe | 17e.1 |
| seller | 1m.2 | shale | 29a.5 | shoemaker | 1n.1 |
| seminary | 21i.1 | shall | 50c.1 | shoot | 33b.2 |
| senator | 1c.1 | shallow | 32f.2 | shop | 21e.1 |
| send | 2i.4 | sham | 10b.11 | shopper | 1m.1 |
| senior | 9d.3 | shame | 5d.1 | shore | 16g.2 |
| señor | 9c.2 | shape | 22f.4 | short | 32f.1 |
| sensation | 5a.1 | shape | 32a.1 | shortage | 3g.11 |
| sensible | 12k.3 | share | 36a.3 | shorten | 2r.2 |
| sensibly | 31g.1 | sharecropper | 1f.4 | shortly | 7h.2 |
| sensitive | 13a.3 | shark | 4h.1 | shorts | 17c.2 |
| sensory | 23k.1 | sharp | 32e.1 | shortstop | 1d.3 |
| sentence | 35b.1 | sharpen | 32e.2 | shotgun | 8n.3 |
| sentry | 1t.2 | shatter | 33a.3 | should | 50c.1 |
| separate | 2w.1 | shave | 8g.2 | shoulders | 23a.2 |
| separate | 27c.2 | shawl | 17f.2 | shouldn't | 46a.1 |
| September | 7e.1 | she | 45a.1 | shout | 19c.3 |
| sequence | 3b.1 | sheath | 17h.1 | shovel | 8e.6 |
| sequoia | 24b.1 | shed | 21k.1 | show | 10c.1 |
| serf | 1f.4 | she'd | 46e.1 | show | 47a.2 |
| series | 25a.1 | sheep | 4e.4 | shred | 8g.3 |
| serious | 5i.2 | sheer | 17j.1 | shrewd | 12k.1.1 |
| seriously | 31a.1 | sheet | 30f.1 | shrewdly | 31g.1 |
| serpent | 4c.1 | sheik | 1c.3 | shriek | 19c.3 |
| servant | 1z.1 | shelf | 30d.4 | shrill | 19a.5 |
| serve | 6k.2 | shell | 4i.3 | shrimp | 4i.2 |
| service | 13b.3 | she'll | 46c.1 | shrine | 21i.1 |
| session | 25e.2 | shellfish | 4i.2 | shrink | 2r.2 |
| set | 2i.6 | shelter | 21a.1 | shrivel | 2r.2 |

| | | | |
|---|---|---|---|
| smile | 60a.1 | sofa | 30d.3 |
| smog | 16d.3 | so far | 7h.2 |
| smoke | 52d.2 | soft | 57a.2 |
| smokestack | 30b.1 | soften | 57a.6 |
| smokey | 52d.2.1. | softball | 34b.1 |
| smolder | 52c.4 | soggy | 16b.8 |
| smooth | 57a.2 | soil | 29e.1 |
| smother | 2f.5 | solar | 20h.3.1 |
| smudge | 41a.2 | solemn | 5i.2 |
| snack | 6a.3 | solid | 57a.2 |
| snail | 4i.4 | solitude | 42b.1 |
| snake | 4c.1 | solo | 47b.4 |
| snap | 2n.1 | soloist | 1g.2 |
| snapper | 4h.2 | solve | 12d.1 |
| snapshot | 47d.2 | somber | 5i.2 |
| snare | 4o.4 | some | 45e.1 |
| snarl | 19d.1 | somebody | 45e.1 |
| sneak | 48b.2 | someday | 7f.1 |
| sneer | 60a.1 | someone | 45e.1 |
| sneeze | 60b.1 | somersault | 34d.2 |
| snicker | 19c.4 | something | 45e.1 |
| sniff | 60b.1 | sometimes | 7k.6 |
| snip | 8g.3 | somewhat | 3j.5 |
| snooze | 12e.4 | somewhere | 14d.1 |
| snore | 19c.2 | son | 9n.6 |
| snore | 60b.1 | song | 15d.2 |
| snort | 19d.1 | songbird | 4j.2 |
| snout | 4L.4 | sonnet | 15d.1 |
| snow | 16a.3 | soon | 7h.1 |
| snowball | 16a.3.1 | soot | 52d.2 |
| snowfall | 16a.3 | soothe | 5L.4 |
| snowflake | 16a.3 | soothe | 10d.2 |
| snowman | 16a.3.1 | sore | 37c.2 |
| snowplow | 11c.1 | sorority | 25b.4 |
| snowstorm | 40b.1 | sorrow | 5h.1 |
| snug | 5L.5 | sorrowful | 5h.2 |
| snuggle | 44b.3 | sorry | 5h.2 |
| so | 3k.2 | sort of | 3j.4 |
| so | 39b.1 | so that | 39b.1 |
| soak | 16b.7 | soul | 9f.2 |
| soap | 41c.2 | sound | 19a.1 |
| soar | 4o.1 | soup | 6h.3 |
| sob | 19c.5 | sour | 6L.2 |
| sober | 5i.2 | sourdough | 6g.1 |
| soccer | 34b.1 | south | 14e.1 |
| socialist | 9o.1 | South America | 18b.3 |
| society | 25c.5 | South Carolina | 18c.1 |
| sock | 17e.1 | South Dakota | 18c.1 |
| sod | 29e.1 | southeast | 14e.1 |
| soda | 6h.1 | southeastern | 14e.1.1 |
| sodium | 59a.3 | southern | 14e.1.1 |

| | | | |
|---|---|---|---|
| southward | 14e.1.1 | sow | 29f.1 |
| southwest | 14e.1 | sow | 4e.5 |
| southwestern | 14e.1.1 | soybean | 6j.3 |
| | | space | 20h.2 |
| | | spacecraft | 11d.3 |
| | | spade | 8e.6 |
| | | spaghetti | 6d.1 |
| | | Spain | 18b.4 |
| | | span | 11h.5 |
| | | spaniel | 4b.3 |
| | | spank | 44a.3 |
| | | spare | 26d.1 |
| | | spark | 52c.2 |
| | | sparkle | 38b.1 |
| | | sparrow | 4j.1 |
| | | sparse | 3g.13 |
| | | spatter | 16b.2 |
| | | spawn | 54a.5 |
| | | speak | 10a.2 |
| | | speaker | 1e.2 |
| | | spear | 8f.2 |
| | | spearhead | 39a.3 |
| | | special | 55a.1 |
| | | specialist | 9L.1 |
| | | specifically | 3j.2 |
| | | specimen | 3f.4 |
| | | speck | 3f.1 |
| | | speckle | 3f.1 |
| | | spectacles | 17d.2 |
| | | spectacular | 26c.5 |
| | | spectator | 9h.3 |
| | | speed | 7j.1 |
| | | speedy | 7j.4 |
| | | speedometer | 3c.1 |
| | | spell | 15i.2 |
| | | spend | 28d.1 |
| | | sphere | 32b.1 |
| | | spherical | 32b.3 |
| | | spice | 6g.2 |
| | | spider | 4k.2 |
| | | spike | 8h.1 |
| | | spill | 16b.3 |
| | | spin | 2x.2 |
| | | spinach | 6j.1 |
| | | spinal | 23j.1.1 |
| | | spindle | 8j.3 |
| | | spine | 23j.1 |
| | | spinster | 9b.1 |

| | | | |
|---|---|---|---|
| spiral | 32b.2 | squid | 4i.5 | stay | 50e.1 |
| spire | 30b.3 | squint | 53b.3 | steadfast | 13h.1 |
| spirit | 9f.2 | squire | 1c.3 | steady | 55b.3 |
| spiritual | 13j.1 | squirrel | 4f.3 | steak | 6e.1 |
| spit | 60c.1 | squirt | 16b.2 | steal | 36e.4 |
| spite | 5e.1 | stab | 8g.4 | steamboat | 11e.4 |
| splash | 16b.2 | stable | 4m.1 | steamer | 11e.4 |
| splint | 37f.3 | stack | 25a.4 | steamship | 11e.4 |
| splinter | 3f.1 | stadium | 21g.1 | steed | 4e.2 |
| split | 2w.1 | staff | 22d.3 | steel | 29a.1 |
| spoil | 6k.3 | stag | 4e.2 | steep | 32h.1 |
| Spokane | 18d.1 | stage | 47a.4 | steeple | 30b.3 |
| sponge | 4i.1 | stagecoach | 11a.3 | steer | 4e.3 |
| spongy | 57a.5 | stagger | 48a.3 | stereo | 8d.4 |
| sponsor | 1b.4 | stain | 41a.2 | sterilize | 41b.3 |
| spool | 8j.3 | stairs | 30b.5 | stern | 13h.1 |
| spoon | 8m.1 | stairway | 30b.5 | steward | 1v.1 |
| spoonful | 3e.5 | stale | 6L.4 | stewardess | 1v.1 |
| spore | 24d.2 | stalk | 24e.2 | stick | 2v.7 |
| sport | 34a.1 | stall | 4m.1 | stick | 22c.2 |
| sportscaster | 1e.1 | stallion | 4e.2 | stiff | 57a.2 |
| sportsman | 1f.1 | stamen | 24d.2 | stiffen | 57a.6 |
| spot | 14a.2 | stammer | 19c.6 | stifle | 2f.5 |
| spot | 53b.1 | stamp | 48c.1 | still | 27d.4 |
| spouse | 9n.7 | stampede | 4o.3 | stillness | 2b.1 |
| spout | 16c.2 | stand | 48e.1 | stilt | 22d.4 |
| sprawl | 2q.2 | standard | 42a.2 | stimulate | 39a.3 |
| spray | 16b.2 | standstill | 2b.1 | stimulus | 39a.2 |
| spring | 7d.2 | stanza | 15d.1 | sting | 4o.1 |
| spring | 48d.1 | star | 9k.1 | stir | 16b.4 |
| Springfield | 18d.1 | star | 20h.4 | stirrup | 4n.1 |
| springtime | 7a.1 | starch | 6g.1 | stitch | 17i.2 |
| sprinkle | 16b.1 | stare | 53b.4 | St. Louis | 18d.1 |
| sprinkler | 16c.1 | starfish | 4i.1 | stockade | 21c.2 |
| sprint | 34d.1.1 | starlight | 38a.1 | stocking | 17e.1 |
| sprinting | 34d.1 | starling | 4j.2 | stockman | 1f.3 |
| sprout | 24d.2 | start | 2c.1 | stockyard | 4m.1 |
| spruce | 24b.1 | starter | 8b.2 | stomach | 23h.1 |
| spur | 17e.1.1 | startle | 5b.2 | stomp | 48c.1 |
| spurt | 16b.2 | starvation | 37a.2 | stone | 29b.2 |
| sputter | 2L.2 | starve | 6n.2 | stony | 57a.3 |
| spy | 53b.7 | state | 10c.2 | stool | 30d.3 |
| squadron | 25d.2 | state | 18a.6 | stoop | 2q.1 |
| square | 32c.1 | statement | 10a.1 | stop | 2f.1 |
| squash | 6j.2 | statesman | 1c.1 | stopper | 22b.1 |
| squat | 2q.1 | static | 2b.1.1 | store | 21d.2 |
| squaw | 9b.1 | station | 21j.1 | storehouse | 21k.1 |
| squawk | 19d.1 | stationary | 2b.1.1 | storeroom | 21k.1 |
| squeak | 19e.1 | statue | 47d.2 | storm | 40b.1 |
| squeal | 19c.3 | staunch | 13h.1 | story | 15b.2 |
| squeeze | 44b.1 | stay | 2b.3 | storyteller | 9g.1 |

| | | | | | | |
|---|---|---|---|---|---|
| stout | 43d.2 | sub | 11e.3 | sunny | 40e.1 |
| stove | 8d.1 | subheading | 15a.2 | sunrise | 7c.1 |
| straddle | 48e.1 | subject | 12b.1 | sunset | 7c.2 |
| straight | 32d.2 | submarine | 11e.3 | sunshine | 38a.1 |
| straighten | 32f.3 | submit | 10g.4 | super | 26c.2 |
| strain | 33b.3 | subsequent to | 7g.5 | superb | 26c.2 |
| strand | 16g.2 | subsequently | 7h.2 | superficially | 31b.1 |
| strange | 55a.2 | subset | 3f.3 | superintendent | 1b.3 |
| strangely | 31c.1 | substance | 22e.1 | superior | 26c.2 |
| stranger | 9h.1 | substitute | 27a.5 | superlative | 35b.3 |
| strap | 8h.4 | subtract | 49d.1.2 | supermarket | 21d.2 |
| straw | 24e.4 | subtraction | 49d.1 | superstition | 12L.1 |
| strawberry | 6i.3 | suburb | 18a.5 | supervise | 10g.5 |
| stray | 2g.6 | subway | 11a.3 | supervision | 10g.5.1 |
| streak | 41a.2 | succeed | 26b.1.1 | supervisor | 1b.3 |
| stream | 16f.1 | success | 13g.1.1 | supper | 6a.1 |
| street | 11h.1 | success | 26b.1 | supplies | 6b.2 |
| streetcar | 11a.5 | successful | 13g.1 | support | 2k.2 |
| strength | 43a.3 | such | 3k.2 | support | 5o.3 |
| strengthen | 22f.5 | suck | 60c.1 | support | 10g.3 |
| stress | 10c.5 | sudden | 7j.5 | support | 10d.3 |
| stricken | 37a.1.1 | suffer | 5h.3 | suppose | 12a.3 |
| strict | 13h.1 | sufficiently | 3j.4 | supposedly | 31b.1 |
| strictly | 31a.5 | suffix | 35b.2 | supreme | 26c.2 |
| stride | 48a.2 | sugar | 6g.2 | sure | 3k.2 |
| strike | 44a.3 | suggest | 10e.3 | sure | 13e.1 |
| string | 8h.4 | suggestion | 10g.1 | sure | 42c.1 |
| strip | 32d.1 | suggestion | 12g.1 | surely | 31a.1 |
| stripe | 32d.1 | suit | 17a.1 | surf | 16f.4 |
| stroke | 44a.1 | suitable | 26a.4 | surface | 20a.2 |
| stroll | 48a.2 | suitcase | 22a.10 | surge | 16b.2 |
| strong | 43a.2 | sulfate | 59a.3 | surgeon | 1u.1 |
| strong | 57b.2 | sulfide | 59a.3 | surgery | 37f.1 |
| stronghold | 21c.1 | sulfur | 29a.3 | surprise | 5j.2 |
| structure | 21a.1 | sulfuric | 59a.1.1 | surrender | 36b.2 |
| struggle | 1dd.1 | sullen | 5i.2 | surround | 2x.5 |
| strut | 48a.2 | sultan | 1c.3 | survey | 12a.3 |
| stubborn | 13h.1 | sultry | 40e.1 | surveyor | 1k.2 |
| stubby | 3a.2 | sum | 49b.2 | survival | 54b.1 |
| student | 1i.1 | summarize | 25a.5 | survive | 54b.2 |
| studio | 21e.1 | summary | 15c.6 | suspect | 10f.4 |
| stuffs | 6b.2 | summer | 7d.2 | suspect | 12j.2 |
| stumble | 48a.3 | summertime | 7a.1 | suspend | 2b.2 |
| stump | 24c.1 | summon | 10f.2 | suspense | 5d.2 |
| stun | 33b.3 | sun | 20h.3 | suspension | 2b.2.1 |
| stunt | 34e.1 | sunburn | 37e.1 | suspicion | 5n.3 |
| stupid | 12k.1.2 | Sunday | 7e.2 | suspicious | 13p.1 |
| stupidity | 12k.1 | sundial | 7b.1 | swagger | 48a.2 |
| sturdy | 43a.2 | sundown | 7c.2 | swallow | 6m.1 |
| stutter | 19c.6 | sunflower | 24d.3 | swamp | 16f.1 |
| style | 17a.2 | sunlight | 38a.1 | swan | 4j.4 |

| | | | | | | |
|---|---|---|---|---|---|---|
| swap | 36a.3 | tail | 4L.5 | teaspoon | 8m.1 |
| swarm | 4o.1 | tail | 11f.4 | teaspoonful | 3e.5 |
| sway | 2x.4 | tailor | 1n.3 | technically | 31b.1 |
| swear | 10b.4 | take | 2i.1 | technician | 1x.1 |
| sweat | 23i.1 | tale | 15b.2 | technique | 12h.1 |
| sweater | 17c.1 | talent | 5r.1 | teeth | 23d.1 |
| sweep | 41b.1 | talk | 10a.2 | telecast | 10c.3 |
| sweet | 6L.2 | talkative | 10a.4 | telegram | 15f.1 |
| sweetness | 6L.2.1 | tall | 32f.1 | telegraph | 15f.1 |
| sweets | 6c.4 | tally | 49d.1.2 | telegrapher | 1bb.1 |
| swell | 2s.2 | tame | 5L.3 | telephone | 19b.1 |
| swelter | 52a.4 | Tampa | 18d.1 | telescope | 8k.1 |
| swerve | 2x.4 | tan | 58a.1 | teletype | 8L.2 |
| swift | 7j.4 | tangerine | 6i.4 | television | 8d.4 |
| swim | 16b.6 | tank | 22a.9 | tell | 10c.1 |
| swim | 34b.3.1 | tanker | 11e.2 | teller | 1s.1 |
| swimmer | 1d.4 | tanner | 1f.1 | temper | 5e.1 |
| swimming | 34b.3 | tannery | 21e.2 | temperate | 52a.3 |
| swing | 34c.3 | tap | 44a.2 | temperature | 52a.1 |
| swirl | 2x.4 | tape | 22g.1 | temple | 21i.1 |
| swish | 19e.1 | taper | 32e.2 | temporary | 7k.2 |
| switch | 8j.1 | tapestry | 30e.4 | tempt | 10e.1 |
| swollen | 32g.1 | target | 34c.1 | ten | 3h.3 |
| swoop | 4o.1 | tariff | 28b.1 | tenant | 9i.2 |
| sword | 8f.2 | tarnish | 29d.1 | tend | 29f.1 |
| swordfish | 4h.1 | tarpaulin | 22b.2 | tender | 13a.3 |
| syllable | 35b.2 | tart | 6c.2 | tendon | 23j.2 |
| symbol | 35c.2 | task | 1a.3 | Tennessee | 18c.1 |
| symbolize | 12i.2 | tassel | 17g.1 | tennis | 34b.2 |
| sympathetic | 13a.3 | taste | 6L.1 | tense | 5d.3 |
| sympathize | 5L.4 | taste | 6m.1 | tension | 5d.2 |
| sympathy | 5L.2 | tasty | 6L.2 | tent | 21b.3 |
| symphony | 47b.2 | tatter | 17i.4 | tenth | 3h.1 |
| synonym | 35b.4 | tavern | 21d.3 | tepee | 21b.3 |
| syrup | 6c.1 | tax | 28b.1 | tepid | 52a.3 |
| system | 25a.1 | taxation | 28b.1 | term | 7d.1 |
| | | taxi | 11a.3 | terminal | 8L.2 |
| | | taxicab | 11a.3 | terminal | 21j.1 |
| | | tea | 6.h1 | termite | 4k.2 |
| **T** | | teach | 12g.2 | terrace | 20g.1 |
| | | teacher | 1i.1 | terrain | 20a.3 |
| table | 30d.2 | teak | 24b.1 | terrible | 26d.2 |
| tablecloth | 30f.1 | teakettle | 8m.2 | terribly | 3k.2 |
| tablespoon | 8m.1 | teakwood | 22c.1 | terrier | 4b.3 |
| tablespoonful | 3e.5 | team | 25b.5 | terrific | 26c.5 |
| tablet | 15g.3 | teammate | 9e.1 | terrify | 5b.2 |
| tabletop | 30d.2 | teamwork | 34c.5 | territory | 20a.3 |
| tack | 8h.3 | teapot | 8m.2 | terror | 5b.1 |
| tackle | 34c.4 | tear | 17i.4 | terry | 17k.3 |
| tactful | 13a.8 | tear | 23i.1 | test | 10f.3 |
| tadpole | 4d.1 | tease | 10b.9 | testament | 15c.4 |
| tag | 15a.2 | | | | |

| | | | | | | | |
|---|---|---|---|---|---|---|---|
| top | 14i.3 | tranquilizer | 37f.2 | trillion | 3h.3 | | |
| Topeka | 18d.1 | transfer | 2i.4 | trimmer | 8e.5 | | |
| topic | 12b.1 | transform | 27c.3 | trio | 25b.2 | | |
| topple | 2p.1 | transfusion | 37f.1 | trip | 2g.2 | | |
| torch | 38d.1 | transistor | 8L.1 | tripod | 8j.4 | | |
| torment | 33b.5 | translate | 10j.1.2 | triumph | 36d.3 | | |
| tornado | 40b.3 | translation | 10j.1 | triumphant | 36d.3.1 | | |
| torpedo | 8n.2 | transmission | 8b.2 | troop | 25d.2 | | |
| torrent | 40b.2 | transmit | 10c.3 | trooper | 1j.1 | | |
| torso | 23a.1 | transmitter | 8L.1 | trophy | 28a.7 | | |
| tortilla | 6d.3 | transparent | 38e.2 | tropical | 20b.2 | | |
| tortoise | 4c.3 | transplant | 2i.4 | tropics | 20e.1 | | |
| torture | 33b.5 | transplant | 37f.1.1 | trot | 48a.1 | | |
| to some extent | 3j.5 | transport | 11g.3 | trouble | 56b.2 | | |
| toss | 2j.1 | transportation | 11g.3.1 | troublesome | 56a.3 | | |
| tot | 9d.1 | trap | 4o.4 | trough | 22a.9 | | |
| total | 49b.2 | trapeze | 34c.3 | trousers | 17c.2 | | |
| totally | 3k.1 | trapezoid | 32c.1 | trout | 4h.2 | | |
| tote | 2i.1 | trapper | 1f.1 | truce | 10d.1 | | |
| totem | 21m.1 | trash | 41a.1 | truck | 11a.2 | | |
| touchdown | 34c.4 | travel | 2g.2 | trudge | 48a.2 | | |
| tough | 57a.2 | tray | 8m.6 | true | 26a.3 | | |
| toupee | 23b.3 | treacherous | 56b.3 | truly | 31a.1 | | |
| tour | 2g.2 | tread | 48a.2 | trumpet | 47c.1 | | |
| tourist | 9h.1 | treason | 13n.1.1 | trunk | 11f.2 | | |
| tournament | 34a.2 | treasure | 28a.2 | trunk | 23a.1 | | |
| tow | 2k.1 | treat | 6a.3 | trust | 5n.1 | | |
| towel | 30f.1 | treatment | 37f.1 | trustworthiness | 13b.1 | | |
| tower | 21a.1 | treaty | 15h.2 | trustworthy | 13b.5 | | |
| town | 18a.3 | tree | 24a.1 | truth | 26a.1 | | |
| townspeople | 9i.2 | treeless | 20b.5 | truthfully | 31a.1 | | |
| trace | 15i.1 | treetop | 24c.1 | tub | 22a.9 | | |
| track | 2h.2 | tremble | 2L.1 | tube | 22d.2 | | |
| track | 11h.6 | tremendous | 26c.5 | tuberculosis | 37b.1 | | |
| tract | 20a.1 | trench | 20c.2 | tuck | 36f.2 | | |
| tractor | 11b.1 | Trenton | 18d.1 | Tuesday | 7e.2 | | |
| trade | 36a.3 | trial | 1y.1.1 | tuft | 23b.3 | | |
| trader | 1m.2 | triangle | 32c.1 | tug | 11e.5 | | |
| tradition | 12L.1 | triangular | 32c.1.1 | tugboat | 11e.5 | | |
| traditional | 42a.2 | tribal | 25c.6.1 | tulip | 24d.3 | | |
| tragedy | 40d.2 | tribe | 25c.6 | tumble | 2p.1 | | |
| tragic | 26d.4 | tribesman | 9i.2 | tumor | 23b.4 | | |
| tragically | 31d.1 | tribune | 1c.1 | tuna | 4h.2 | | |
| trail | 11h.8 | tributary | 16f.1 | tune | 15d.2 | | |
| trailer | 11a.6 | tribute | 28a.4 | tungsten | 29a.3 | | |
| train | 11a.5 | trick | 12g.4 | tunic | 17c.1 | | |
| trainer | 1d.5 | trick | 34e.1 | tunnel | 11h.5 | | |
| trait | 5r.3 | trickle | 16b.1 | turbine | 8b.3 | | |
| traitor | 9i.4 | tricky | 13m.1 | turf | 29e.1 | | |
| tramp | 48c.1 | tricycle | 11a.4 | turkey | 4j.3 | | |
| trample | 48c.1 | trigger | 8j.1 | turn | 2x.4 | | |

| | | | | | | |
|---|---|---|---|---|---|---|
| useless | 26d.1 | verdict | 12j.1.1 | voter | 51c.2.1 |
| usher | 1z.1 | Vermont | 18c.1 | vow | 10i.1 |
| usual | 7k.1 | verse | 15d.1 | vowel | 35b.2 |
| usual | 42a.1 | version | 3f.2 | voyage | 2g.2 |
| Utah | 18c.1 | vertebrae | 23j.1 | vulture | 4j.5 |
| utensil | 8e.1 | vertex | 3d.2 | | |
| utter | 10a.2 | vertical | 14c.1 | | |
| utter(ly) | 3k.1 | very | 3k.2 | | |
| | | vessel | 11e.1 | | |
| | | vessel | 23i.2 | **W** | |
| | | veteran | 9d.3 | | |
| **V** | | veterinarian | 1k.1 | wad | 25a.4 |
| | | vibrate | 2L.2 | waddle | 48a.2 |
| vacant | 32g.1 | vibration | 2L.2.1 | wade | 16b.6 |
| vacation | 51b.1 | vice president | 1c.4 | wage | 28a.3 |
| vacationer | 9h.1 | vicious | 5f.1.1 | wagon | 11a.6 |
| vaccination | 37f.1 | victim | 9g.5 | wail | 19c.5 |
| vaccine | 37f.2 | view | 53a.2 | wait | 2b.3 |
| vacuum | 41c.1 | vigor | 43a.3 | waiter | 1aa.1 |
| vagabond | 9h.2 | vigorous | 13b.6 | waitress | 1aa.1 |
| vague | 38e.2 | village | 18a.3 | wake | 12e.5 |
| vain | 13e.1 | villager | 9i.2 | wake | 54a.4 |
| valentine | 15f.1 | villain | 9g.5 | waken | 12e.5 |
| valley | 20c.1 | vine | 24e.2 | walk | 48a.2 |
| valuable | 26c.6 | vinegar | 6g.2 | wall | 30b.2 |
| value | 5o.1 | vineyard | 20f.1 | wallet | 28f.1 |
| valve | 16c.2 | violent | 5f.2 | wallop | 44a.3 |
| van | 11a.2 | violin | 47c.2 | walnut | 6j.4 |
| vanilla | 6c.4 | violinist | 1g.2 | walrus | 4h.1 |
| vanish | 2g.5 | virgin | 9b.1 | wand | 8j.5 |
| vapor | 17L.2 | Virginia | 18c.1 | wander | 2g.6 |
| variation | 27c.1 | virtually | 3j.7 | wanderer | 9h.2 |
| variety | 3g.2 | virtue | 26a.1 | want | 5q.1 |
| various | 3g.2.1 | virus | 37b.2 | war | 33c.2 |
| vary | 27c.3 | vision | 12e.3 | ward | 9n.4 |
| vase | 30e.4 | vision | 53a.2 | ward | 21h.1 |
| vast | 3a.3 | visit | 2g.7 | warden | 1t.1 |
| vat | 22a.9 | visitor | 9h.1 | warehouse | 21k.1 |
| vault | 28f.1 | visor | 17d.2 | warfare | 33c.2 |
| vegetables | 6b.3 | visual | 53a.2.1 | warlike | 5f.2 |
| vegetation | 24a.2 | visualize | 12a.2 | warm | 52a.3 |
| vehicle | 11a.1 | vitamin | 37f.2 | warmth | 52a.3.1 |
| vein | 23i.2 | vivid | 38a.4 | warn | 10b.6 |
| velocity | 7j.1 | vocal | 10a.4 | warning | 10b.7 |
| velvet | 17k.3 | voice | 23d.2 | warship | 11e.3 |
| vendor | 1m.2 | voiceless | 19a.5 | wart | 23b.4 |
| vent | 30b.4 | volcanic | 20b.3.1 | was | 50a.1 |
| ventricle | 23i.2 | volt | 3e.2 | wash | 41b.1 |
| venture | 42c.3 | volume | 15c.6 | Washington | 18c.1 |
| Venus | 20h.3 | volume | 32f.1.1 | Washington, DC | 18d.1 |
| verb | 35b.4 | vote | 51c.2 | wasn't | 46a.1 |
| verbose | 10a.4 | | | wasp | 4k.1 |
| | | | | wasteful | 13o.1 |

| | | | |
|---|---|---|---|
| watch | 7b.1 | West Virginia | 18c.1 |
| watch | 53b.1 | westward | 14e.1.1 |
| watchful | 13p.1 | wet | 16b.8 |
| watchman | 1t.2 | we've | 46b.1 |
| water | 16a.1 | whack | 44a.3 |
| waterfall | 16f.1 | whale | 4h.1 |
| watermelon | 6i.1 | wharf | 16i.3 |
| watershed | 16f.2 | what | 45d.1 |
| waterway | 11h.9 | whatever | 45d.1 |
| watt | 3e.2 | what's | 46d.1 |
| wave | 44c.1 | wheat | 6j.3 |
| waver | 2L.2 | wheel | 11f.1 |
| wax | 41b.1 | wheelbarrow | 11b.2 |
| way | 11h.3 | wheeze | 19c.2 |
| wayfarer | 9h.2 | when | 7i.3 |
| we | 45a.1 | when | 45d.1 |
| weak | 57b.3 | whenever | 45d.1 |
| weak | 43a.5 | when...then | 39b.4 |
| weakness | 43a.5.1 | where | 14d.1 |
| wealth | 28a.2 | where | 45d.1 |
| weapon | 8n.1 | whereas | 27d.2 |
| wear | 17i.1 | where's | 46d.1 |
| weariness | 37c.1 | where...there | 39b.4 |
| weary | 12e.2 | whereupon | 39b.2 |
| weasel | 4e.8 | wherever | 45d.1 |
| weather | 40a.1 | which | 45c.1 |
| weatherman | 1e.1 | whichever | 45d.1 |
| weave | 17i.3 | while | 7i.3 |
| weaver | 1n.3 | whilst | 7i.3 |
| web | 25a.3 | whimper | 19c.5 |
| wed | 2v.2 | whine | 19c.5 |
| we'd | 46e.1 | whinny | 19d.1 |
| wedding | 2v.3 | whip | 8n.6 |
| wedge | 8e.3 | whir | 19e.1 |
| Wednesday | 7e.2 | whirl | 2x.2 |
| wee | 3a.2 | whisk | 2i.3.1 |
| week | 7d.3 | whisker | 4L.2 |
| weekend | 7d.3 | whisper | 19c.6 |
| weekly | 7k.5 | whistle | 19c.3 |
| weigh | 3b.1 | white | 58a.1 |
| weight | 3b.1.1 | whitewash | 41b.1 |
| weird | 55a.2 | whittle | 8g.2 |
| welcome | 10d.5 | who | 45c.1 |
| well | 3k.2 | whole | 3g.3 |
| well | 37a.3 | whom | 45c.1 |
| we'll | 46c.1 | whomever | 45d.1 |
| were | 50a.1 | whoop | 19c.3 |
| weren't | 46a.1 | whose | 45d.1 |
| west | 14e.1 | why | 45d.1 |
| western | 14e.1.1 | Wichita | 18d.1 |
| westernmost | 14e.1.1 | wick | 38d.2 |

| | | | |
|---|---|---|---|
| wicked | 5f.1.1 | | |
| wide | 32f.1 | | |
| widely | 3k.1 | | |
| widen | 32f.3 | | |
| widespread | 42a.2 | | |
| widow | 9b.1 | | |
| width | 32f.1.1 | | |
| wig | 23b.3 | | |
| wiggle | 2L.2 | | |
| wigwam | 21b.3 | | |
| wife | 9n.7 | | |
| wild | 13o.1 | | |
| wildcat | 4b.1 | | |
| wilderness | 20e.1 | | |
| will | 50c.1 | | |
| willing | 13a.7 | | |
| win | 36d.1 | | |
| wince | 5c.1 | | |
| wind | 40b.3 | | |
| windmill | 21e.3 | | |
| window | 30b.4 | | |
| windpipe | 23d.2 | | |
| windshield | 11f.2 | | |
| wine | 6h.2 | | |
| wing | 11f.4 | | |
| wingspan | 11f.4.1 | | |
| wink | 53b.3 | | |
| winner | 1d.1 | | |
| winner | 36d.5 | | |
| winter | 7d.2 | | |
| wintertime | 7a.1 | | |
| wintry | 40e.1 | | |
| wipe | 41b.1 | | |
| wire | 22d.2 | | |
| wireless | 8L.1 | | |
| Wisconsin | 18c.1 | | |
| wisdom | 12k.1 | | |
| wise | 12k.1.1 | | |
| wisely | 31g.1 | | |
| wish | 5q.1 | | |
| wisp | 3f.5 | | |
| wistful | 5h.2 | | |
| wit | 12k.1 | | |
| witch | 9f.5 | | |
| with | 14k.2.1 | | |
| with | 27b.1 | | |
| withdraw | 2g.4 | | |
| wither | 2r.2 | | |
| without | 27d.1 | | |
| witness | 1y.1 | | |
| witty | 13i.1 | | |

| | | | |
|---|---|---|---|
| wizard | 9f.5 | writing | 15b.1 |
| woe | 5h.1 | wrong | 26a.5 |
| wolf | 4b.2 | wrongly | 31f.1 |
| woman | 9b.1 | wry | 13i.1 |
| wonder | 12a.3 | Wyoming | 18c.1 |
| wonderful | 26c.5 | | |
| wonderland | 18a.2 | | |
| won't | 46a.1 | | |
| wood | 22c.1 | | |
| woodchuck | 4f.3 | | |
| woodcutter | 1f.5 | | |
| woodland | 20e.1 | | |
| woodpecker | 4j.1 | | |
| woodsman | 1f.5 | | |
| wool | 17k.3 | | |
| woolen | 17k.3.1 | | |
| word | 35b.1 | | |
| work | 1dd.1 | | |
| worker | 1a.1 | | |
| workman | 1a.1 | | |
| workmen | 1a.1 | | |
| workshop | 21e.1 | | |
| world | 20h.1 | | |
| worm | 4k.2 | | |
| worn | 7f.4 | | |
| worry | 5d.2 | | |
| worship | 10d.6 | | |
| worth | 28a.2 | | |
| worthless | 26d.1 | | |
| worthwhile | 26c.4 | | |
| would | 50c.1 | | |
| wouldn't | 46a.1 | | |
| wound | 37e.1 | | |
| wow | 10k.1 | | |
| wrap | 22g.1 | | |
| wrap | 44b.3 | | |
| wrapper | 22b.1 | | |
| wrath | 5e.1 | | |
| wreck | 33a.4 | | |
| wreckage | 33a.4.1 | | |
| wren | 4j.1 | | |
| wrench | 8e.2 | | |
| wrestler | 1d.4 | | |
| wrestling | 34b.4 | | |
| wretched | 5i.3 | | |
| wring | 44b.1 | | |
| wrinkle | 17i.4 | | |
| wrist | 23f.1 | | |
| wristwatch | 7b.1 | | |
| write | 15i.2 | | |
| writer | 1e.2 | | |

**Y**

| | |
|---|---|
| yacht | 11e.6 |
| yak | 4e.7 |
| yam | 6j.1 |
| yank | 2k.1 |
| yap | 19d.1 |
| yard | 3e.1 |
| yard | 20g.1 |
| yardstick | 3c.1 |
| yarn | 17k.2 |
| yawn | 19c.2 |
| year | 7d.3 |
| yearling | 4d.1 |
| yearn | 5q.1 |
| yeast | 6g.1 |
| yell | 19c.3 |
| yellow | 58a.1 |
| yelp | 19d.1 |
| yes | 10k.2 |
| yesterday | 7f.1 |
| yet | 27d.1 |
| yield | 10g.4 |
| yoke | 4n.1 |
| yolk | 6f.1 |
| you | 45a.1 |
| you'd | 46e.1 |
| you'll | 46c.1 |
| youngster | 9d.2 |
| your | 45b.1 |
| you're | 46f.1 |
| yours | 45b.1 |
| youth | 9d.2 |
| you've | 46b.1 |
| yowl | 19d.1 |

**Z**

| | |
|---|---|
| zebra | 4e.7 |
| zigzag | 32d.1 |
| zinc | 29a.3 |
| zip | 17i.1 |
| zipper | 17b.1 |

| | |
|---|---|
| zone | 20a.3 |
| zoo | 4m.1 |
| zoom | 19e.2 |

# Appendix C
# Commonly Confused Terms

**Affect, effect**  *Affect* is a verb meaning "to influence." *Bad weather affects my mood. Effect* is either a verb or a noun. When used as a verb, it means "to bring about." *He effected a change through his persistence.* When used as a noun, it means "result." *The effect of the storm was felt for days.*

**Ain't**  *Ain't* is nonstandard and is unacceptable in writing unless used in dialogue. However, it is becoming more widely accepted in informal spoken language.

**All, all of**  In many cases the *of* in *all of* can be dropped. However, this is not true when a pronoun follows immediately: *all the dignitaries, all of them.*

**Alot, a lot**  Although pronounced as one word, *a lot* is written as two words.

**Already, all ready**  *Already* is an adverb meaning something has occurred prior to a stated time. *He has gone already. All ready* is a phrase expressing the state of being prepared. *He was all ready.*

**Alter, altar**  *Alter* is a verb meaning "to change something." *They altered their plans. Altar* is a noun meaning "a table used for worship." *The altar was covered with flowers.*

**All right, alright**  *All right* is correct. *Alright* is unacceptable.

**Amidst, amongst**  These are acceptable but infrequently used substitutes for *amid* and *among.*

**Amount, number**  *Amount* should be used with mass nouns (nouns that cannot be counted). *The amount of cash she had was amazing. Number* should be used with count nouns (nouns that can be counted). *The number of people I saw was amazing.*

**Anyplace, anywhere**  In spoken language, these can be used interchangeably. In written language, *anywhere* is preferred because it is more formal.

**Assent, ascent**  *Assent* is a verb meaning "to approve." *Ascent* is a noun signifying the act of climbing. *Will your parents assent to your ascent of the mountain?*

**Awful, awfully**  *Awful* is commonly used colloquially to mean "very bad" (*an awful person*). *Awfully* is an intensifier used before adjectives (*awfully pretty, awfully nice*). Both are informal.

**Awhile, a while**  These forms can be used interchangeably. *He waited a while. He waited awhile.*

**Bath, bathe**  Commonly confused spelling. *Bath* is a noun. *Bathe* is a verb.

**Being as, being that**  Both phrases are nonstandard forms for *since* or *because.* It is better to avoid them in formal writing.

**Beside, besides**  Both are prepositions but with different meanings. *Beside* means "at the side of." *He stood beside his mother. Besides* means "in addition to." *Who else besides Joni is coming?*

**Between, among**  *Between* is used to express a relationship between two things. *It was between Mary and Bill to decide the winner. Among* is used when there are more than two elements. *He was very popular among members of the team.* However, *between* can also be used to express interrelationships between several elements when they are considered individually rather than as a group. *He traveled frequently between Boston, New York, and Chicago.*

**Breathe, breath, breadth**  *Breathe* is a verb meaning "to take in air." *Breathe deeply. Breath* is a noun meaning "an exhalation of air." *She stopped to catch her breath. Breadth* is a noun meaning "distance" or "width." *What is the breadth of the room?*

**Burned, burnt**  Both forms are acceptable alternatives for the past tense and past participle of *burn.*

**Can, may**  Technically, there is a difference in meaning between these two verbs. *Can* means "ability to do something." *May* means "permission to do something." However, it is becoming acceptable to use *can* for both meanings.

**Cannot, can not**  These are interchangeable. Both are acceptable in written language.

**Cite, site**  *Cite* is a verb meaning "to refer to" or "quote." *Cite the source of your information. Site* is a noun meaning "a place or location." *This is the site of our new house.*

**Continual, continuous**  Although the distinction gradually is being lost, these two adjectives have different meanings. *Continual* refers to a series of events. *His back pain has been continual for two years. It happens to him about twice a month. Continuous* refers to an event that occurs without interruption. *His back pain has been continuous for three hours. The pain has not stopped during that time.*

**Credible, creditable, credulous**  *Credible* means "believable." *His story was credible. Creditable* means "worthy of credit." *His efforts were creditable. Credulous* means "gullible." *You have to be extremely credulous to believe a story like that.*

**Desert, dessert**  A *desert* is a large expanse of dry land. *Dessert* is something sweet eaten after the main course of a meal.

**Discreet, discrete**  *Discreet* means "cautious." *Be discreet in what you say. Discrete* means "separate" or "distinct." *Reading and writing are discrete skills.*

**Dissent, descent**  *Dissent* is a verb meaning "to differ in opinion." *The senator for Texas dissented from his colleagues. Descent* is a noun meaning "the act of coming down from a high place." *The descent of Everest is treacherous.*

**Disinterested, uninterested**  Although some dictionaries consider these words interchangeable, they are not properly synonyms. *Disinterested* means "impartial." *We need a disinterested judge to make the debate fair. Uninterested* means "having no interest." *I am uninterested in sports.*

**Divulge, disclose** Both words mean "to make known what was intended to be confidential." *Divulge* refers to sharing knowledge with a select group. *She divulged the secret of her friends.* *Disclose* usually refers to a general sharing of information. *The Senator disclosed new information to the reporters.*

**Each and every** This phrase is redundant. *Each* or *every* should be used; not both.

**Eminent, imminent** *Eminent* means "distinguished." *He is an eminent guest.* *Imminent* means "about to happen." *The disaster was imminent.*

**Ever so often, every so often** Although very close in pronunciation, these phrases have different meanings. *Ever so often* means "very often." *We go to the movies ever so often, almost twice a week.* *Every so often* means "now and then." *We go to the movies every so often, usually only two or three times a year.*

**Farther, further** Once these two words had different meanings. Now they mean basically the same thing—distant—with *farther* the more commonly used form.

**Fewer, less** *Fewer* is used with count nouns. *He made fewer errors than I did.* *Less* is used with abstract and mass nouns. *I was less excited than he was.*

**Former, latter** Both are formal ways of referring to things already mentioned. *Former* refers to the first of two elements mentioned previously; *latter* refers to the second.

**Formerly, formally** *Formerly* is an adverb meaning "previously." *She was formerly a police officer.* *Formally* is an adverb meaning "in a formal fashion." *He dressed formally for the dance.*

**Good, well** These words can be used interchangeably when used as adjectives meaning "in a sound state of health." *I feel good. I feel well.* However, when *well* is used as an adverb, *good* cannot be used as its substitute. *He performed well.*

**Had better, had best, you'd better** All acceptable but awkward substitues for *should* or *ought.*

**Had ought, hadn't ought** These phrases are nonstandard and should be avoided.

**Half a, half an, a half, a half a** The first three are acceptable and can be used interchangeably. The fourth is not standard.

**Hanged, hung** The principal parts of *hang* are *hang, hung, hung. He hung the picture on the wall.* However, when referring to the death penalty, the principal parts are *hang, hanged, hanged. The murderer was hanged for his crimes.*

**Have got to** This phrase is used as a substitute for *must, should,* and *ought to.* Although acceptable in spoken language, it should be avoided in writing.

**Hardly, barely, scarcely** All three mean "not quite" and generally can be used interchangeably. Because all three have negative connotations, it is not correct

to use another negative with them. For example, *hardly didn't know* and *scarcely never listens* are nonstandard.

**If, whether**   The two conjunctions are used interchangeably after verbs such as *ask, doubt, know, remember, see,* and *wonder.* However, if an alternative is stated, *whether* is acceptable. *He didn't know whether to leave or stay.*

**Imply, infer**   *Imply* means "to state indirectly, hint, or intimate." *What are you implying by your remarks? Infer* means "to draw a conclusion or make a deduction based on facts." *What do you infer from his remarks?*

**Inability, disability**   *Inability* means "lack of ability." *His inability to speak before crowds hurt his campaign. Disability* means "a permanent lack of ability, usually due to a handicap." *Her disability was caused by an automobile accident.*

**In regards to, with regards to**   Both are nonstandard. Correct forms are *in regard to* and *with regard to.*

**Irregardless**   Nonstandard form of *regardless.*

**Its, it's**   *Its* is the possessive form of *it. The car lost its wheel. It's* is the contraction for *it is. It's cold outside.*

**Kind of, sort of**   Colloquial substitutes for *rather* or *somewhat.*

**Lay, lie**   *Lay* means "to place." *Did you lay the book on the table? Lie* means "to recline." The past tense of *lie* is *lay,* which often causes confusion. *This morning I lay down for a nap.*

**Lead, led**   *Lead* used as a verb means "to conduct." *He will lead the horse to water.* Although spelled the same, *lead* is pronounced differently when used as a noun. *Pencils have lead in them. Led* is the past tense of the verb *lead. He led the horse to water.*

**Leave, let**   When the meaning is "allow to remain," these two words can be used interchangeably. *Leave me alone. Let me alone.*

**Lend, loan**   Both are acceptable as verbs in spoken language. *Will you lend/ loan me the money?* However, many writers and speakers prefer the use of *lend* as a verb and *loan* as a noun. *The bank will lend me money after I apply for a loan.*

**Liable, likely, apt**   All three can mean *probable* and are considered interchangeable.

**Lighted, lit**   Both are acceptable past tense forms of *to light. He lighted the candle. He lit the candle.*

**Like, as**   In the past, *like* was considered a conjunction and *as* a preposition. That distinction is fading; *like* is now acceptable as a conjunction.

**Lose, loose**   *Lose* is a verb meaning "to be unable to find something." *Did you lose your purse? Loose* is an adjective meaning "unfastened." *Some of the screws are loose.*

**Maybe, may be**   *Maybe* is an adverb meaning "perhaps." *Maybe he will come. May be* is a verb phrase meaning "possibly will be." *He may be coming.*

**Mighty** It is acceptable to use *mighty* in spoken language to mean "very" — *mighty nice.* However, the usage is considered informal and usually is avoided in writing.

**Miner, minor** *Miner* is a noun meaning "one who works in a mine." *Minor* is an adjective meaning "of less importance" or "under legal age."

**Moral, morale** *Moral* is an adjective meaning "ethical." *He is a moral person. Morale* is a noun meaning "mental and emotional state." *His morale is always good.*

**Muchly** *Much* can be used either as an adjective or an adverb. The *ly* is unnecessary.

**Must** At one time *must* functioned as an auxiliary verb. *He must help us.* Now it is often used as a noun. *Visiting Disneyland is a must.*

**Nowhere, nowheres, no place** *Nowhere* is the most formal of the three. *Nowheres* is nonstandard and should be avoided. *No place* is used frequently in speech.

**Of** In speech, the verb *have* is sometimes replaced with *of* — *might of, would of.* In writing, this is nonstandard and should be avoided.

**OK, okay** These are variations of an acceptable spoken expression.

**Pair, pare** *Pair* is a noun meaning "two related objects." *These socks are a pair. Pare* is a verb meaning "to cut down or dimenish." *I pare the apples.*

**Percent, percentage** *Percent* usually is written as one word. *The interest rate is ten percent. Percentage* often is used as a substitute for *percent* to mean "fraction" or "portion." *A large percentage of people like music.*

**Personal, personnel** *Personal* is an adjective meaning "private." *This is a personal conversation. Personnel* is a noun meaning "employees." *I took the assignment because I like the personnel working on it.*

**Practical, practicable** *Practical* means "useful." *A hammer is a practical tool. Practicable* means "feasible." *His plan was practicable.*

**Pretty** As an adverb meaning "moderately," *pretty* is overused in speech and should be used sparingly in writing. *I was pretty happy.*

**Proved, proven** Both are acceptable past participial forms of *prove.*

**Provided, providing** These words are used interchangeably as subordinating conjunctions.

**Quite, quiet** *Quite* is an intensifier meaning "rather." *His home is quite nice. Quiet* is an adjective meaning "calm." *This is a quiet night.*

**Real, really** *Real* is an adjective. *Really* is an adverb.

**Reason is because** This is nonstandard and inappropriate in formal situations.

**Rise, raise** The principal parts of *rise* are *rise, rose, risen. Rise* is used when a person or thing elevates under its own power. *He rose from the chair to get a drink of water.* The principal parts of *raise are raise, raised, raised. Raise* is used when someone or something is increasing the elevation of someone or something else. *They raised me up from the chair because I was unable to walk.*

**Shall, will**   Previously, *shall* was the only auxiliary verb that could be used with the pronoun *I* to express future tense. *I shall be there.* Now the auxiliary verb *will* has replaced *shall* almost totally.

**Sit, set**   The principal parts of *sit* are *sit, sat, sat.* The principal parts of *set* are *set, set, set. Sit* is transitive; *set* is intransitive. *He set his cup on the table and then sat down to drink.*

**Sure, surely**   *Sure* is an adjective. *I am sure I'm right. Surely* is an adverb. *That is surely a mistake.* In informal situations, *sure* is sometimes used as an adverb— *He sure can play the piano.* However, this use should be avoided in writing.

**Than, then**   *Than* is a conjunction used in comparative statements. *He is taller than I am. Then* is an adverb designating time. *It happened then.* In speech, *then* often is substituted for *than* because of the similarity of sound. This is not acceptable in writing.

**That, which, whom**   When used as a relative pronoun, *that* may refer to persons, animals, or things. *Which* may refer to animals and things, but not persons. *Who* (*whom*) may refer to persons only. When choosing between *that* and *which, that* should be used to introduce restrictive clauses. *Bring me the book that you read. Which* is used to introduce nonrestrictive clauses. *The book, which I had read before, was on the shelf.*

**Their, there, they're, there's**   *Their* is the possessive pronoun form of *they.* It is *their house. There* is an adverb indicating place. *He lives there. They're* is the contracted form of *they are. They're friends of mine. There's* is the contracted form of *there is. There's gold in those hills.*

**Though, although**   Both are acceptable forms when used as subordinating conjunctions and often are used interchangeably.

**Thusly**   *Thus* is an adverb. The *ly* is unnecessary.

**Type, type of**   *Type* is colloquial for *type of* and should not be used in formal situations.

**Whether, weather**   *Whether* is a conjunction. (See *if, whether.*) *Weather* is a noun meaning "the state of the atmosphere." *Because the weather looked forbidding, he wasn't sure whether to go sailing.*

**Whose, who's**   *Whose* is the possessive form of *who. Whose scarf is laying on the floor? Who's* is the contraction for *who is. Who's responsible for this mistake?*

**Your, you're**   *Your* is the possessive form of *you. This is your first day on the job. You're* is the contraction for *you are. You're a fine swimmer.*

0593